THE NIV APPLICATION COMMENTARY SERIES

THE NIV APPLICATION COMMENTARY

From biblical text . . . to contemporary life

DOUGLAS J. MOO

ZONDERVAN®

ZONDERVAN.com/
AUTHORTRACKER
follow your favorite authors

 **ZONDERVAN®**

The NIV Application Commentary: 2 Peter and Jude
Copyright © 1996 by Douglas J. Moo

Requests for information should be addressed to:

Zondervan, *Grand Rapids, Michigan* 49530

Library of Congress Cataloging-in-Publication Data

Moo, Douglas J.
    2 Peter, and Jude / Douglas J. Moo.
       p.   cm.—(NIV application commentary)
    Includes bibliographical references and indexes.
    ISBN-10: 0-310-20104-7 (hardcover)
    ISBN-13: 978-0-310-20104-5
    1. Bible. N.T. Peter, 2nd—Commentaries.   2. Bible. N.T. Jude—Commentaries. I.
Title.   II. Series.
BS 2795.3.M66 1966
227'.93077—cd20   96-35833

This edition printed on acid-free paper.

Printed in the United States of America

10 11 12 13 14 15 • 22 21 20 19 18 17 16 15

Table of Contents

The NIV Application Commentary Series

When complete, the NIV Application Commentary
will include the following volumes:

To see which titles are available,
visit our web site at http://www.zondervan.com

NIV Application Commentary
Series Introduction

THE NIV APPLICATION COMMENTARY SERIES is unique. Most commentaries help us make the journey from the twentieth century back to the first century. They enable us to cross the barriers of time, culture, language, and geography that separate us from the biblical world. Yet they only offer a one-way ticket to the past and assume that we can somehow make the return journey on our own. Once they have explained the *original meaning* of a book or passage, these commentaries give us little or no help in exploring its *contemporary significance*. The information they offer is valuable, but the job is only half done.

Recently, a few commentaries have included some contemporary application as *one* of their goals. Yet that application is often sketchy or moralistic, and some volumes sound more like printed sermons than commentaries.

The primary goal of the NIV Application Commentary Series is to help you with the difficult but vital task of bringing an ancient message into a modern context. The series not only focuses on application as a finished product but also helps you think through the *process* of moving from the original meaning of a passage to its contemporary significance. These are commentaries, not popular expositions. They are works of reference, not devotional literature.

The format of the series is designed to achieve the goals of the series. Each passage is treated in three sections: *Original Meaning, Bridging Contexts,* and *Contemporary Significance.*

THIS SECTION HELPS you understand the meaning of the biblical text in its first-century context. All of the elements of traditional exegesis—in concise form—are discussed here. These include the historical, literary, and cultural context of the passage. The authors discuss matters related to grammar and syntax, and the meaning of biblical words. They also seek to explore the main ideas of the passage and how the biblical author develops those ideas.[1]

---

1. Please note that when the authors discuss words in the original biblical languages, this series uses the general rather than the scholarly method of transliteration.

After reading this section, you will understand the problems, questions, and concerns of the *original audience* and how the biblical author addressed those issues. This understanding is foundational to any legitimate application of the text today.

THIS SECTION BUILDS a bridge between the world of the Bible and the world of today, between the original context and the contemporary context, by focusing on both the timely and timeless aspects of the text.

God's Word is *timely*. The authors of Scripture spoke to specific situations, problems, and questions. Paul warned the Galatians about the consequences of circumcision and the dangers of trying to be justified by law (Gal. 5:2–5). The author of Hebrews tried to convince his readers that Christ is superior to Moses, the Aaronic priests, and the Old Testament sacrifices. John urged his readers to "test the spirits" of those who taught a form of incipient Gnosticism (1 John 4:1–6). In each of these cases, the timely nature of Scripture enables us to hear God's Word in situations that were *concrete* rather than abstract.

Yet the timely nature of Scripture also creates problems. Our situations, difficulties, and questions are not always directly related to those faced by the people in the Bible. Therefore, God's word to them does not always seem relevant to us. For example, when was the last time someone urged you to be circumcised, claiming that it was a necessary part of justification? How many people today care whether Christ is superior to the Aaronic priests? And how can a "test" designed to expose incipient Gnosticism be of any value in a modern culture?

Fortunately, Scripture is not only timely but *timeless*. Just as God spoke to the original audience, so he still speaks to us through the pages of Scripture. Because we share a common humanity with the people of the Bible, we discover a *universal dimension* in the problems they faced and the solutions God gave them. The timeless nature of Scripture enables it to speak with power in every time and in every culture.

Those who fail to recognize that Scripture is both timely and timeless run into a host of problems. For example, those who are intimidated by timely books such as Hebrews or Galatians might avoid reading them because they seem meaningless today. At the other extreme, those who are convinced of the timeless nature of Scripture, but who fail to discern its timely element, may "wax eloquent" about the Melchizedekian priesthood to a sleeping congregation.

The purpose of this section, therefore, is to help you discern what is timeless in the timely pages of the New Testament—and what is not. For example, if Paul's primary concern is not circumcision (as he tells us in Gal. 5:6), what *is* he concerned about? If discussions about the Aaronic priesthood or Melchizedek seem irrelevant today, what is of abiding value in these passages? If people try to "test the spirits" today with a test designed for a specific first-century heresy, what other biblical test might be more appropriate?

Yet this section does not merely uncover that which is timeless in a passage but also helps you to see *how* it is uncovered. The author of the commentary seeks to take what is implicit in the text and make it explicit, to take a process that normally is intuitive and explain it in a logical, orderly fashion. How do we know that circumcision is not Paul's primary concern? What clues in the text or its context help us realize that Paul's real concern is at a deeper level?

Of course, those passages in which the historical distance between us and the original readers is greatest require a longer treatment. Conversely, those passages in which the historical distance is smaller or seemingly nonexistent require less attention.

One final clarification. Because this section prepares the way for discussing the contemporary significance of the passage, there is not always a sharp distinction or a clear break between this section and the one that follows. Yet when both sections are read together, you should have a strong sense of moving from the world of the Bible to the world of today.

THIS SECTION ALLOWS the biblical message to speak with as much power today as it did when it was first written. How can you apply what you learned about Jerusalem, Ephesus, or Corinth to our present-day needs in Chicago, Los Angeles, or London? How can you take a message originally spoken in Greek and Aramaic and communicate it clearly in our own language? How can you take the eternal truths originally spoken in a different time and culture and apply them to the similar-yet-different needs of our culture?

In order to achieve these goals, this section gives you help in several key areas.

First, it helps you identify contemporary situations, problems, or questions that are truly comparable to those faced by the original audience. Because contemporary situations are seldom identical to those faced in the first century, you must seek situations that are analogous if your applications are to be relevant.

Second, this section explores a variety of contexts in which the passage might be applied today. You will look at personal applications, but you will also be encouraged to think beyond private concerns to the society and culture at large.

Third, this section will alert you to any problems or difficulties you might encounter in seeking to apply the passage. And if there are several legitimate ways to apply a passage (areas in which Christians disagree), the author will bring these to your attention and help you think through the issues involved.

In seeking to achieve these goals, the contributors to this series attempt to avoid two extremes. They avoid making such specific applications that the commentary might quickly become dated. They also avoid discussing the significance of the passage in such a general way that it fails to engage contemporary life and culture.

Above all, contributors to this series have made a diligent effort not to sound moralistic or preachy. The NIV Application Commentary Series does not seek to provide ready-made sermon materials but rather tools, ideas, and insights that will help you communicate God's Word with power. If we help you to achieve that goal, then we have fulfilled the purpose for this series.

—The Editors

General Editor's Preface

"THE LETTERS OF 2 PETER AND JUDE warn us about any tendency to treat sin lightly, to suppose that an immoral lifestyle can be pursued without penalty." Thus Douglas Moo, in this excellent commentary, sums up the relevance of these two short letters for twenty-first century Christians.

An important message—and one we need to hear today. On the one hand, it is sad that we must be warned that doing bad things means bad things will happen to us. Time was, it seems, when parents considered it their sacred duty to instill this lesson in their children. No more. On the other hand, since cultural and familial structures no longer emphasize this important truth, at least as clearly as they once did, we are fortunate to have these two biblical letters to remind us.

It might be relevant, however, to take a look at the reason why the "sin-leads-to-judgment" message is so muted in our culture today. Our overloaded court system is filled with people attempting to avoid (and often succeeding) the consequences of their "sins." Our whole public educational system is predicated on the invalid assumption that all values are temporary, conditioned solely by historical and cultural factors, an assumption that makes sin more a matter of bad judgment than of wrongdoing. Even churches pull their punches when it comes to sin. How long has it been since you heard a good sermon on the topic?

How have we come to this pretty pass? I think there is probably a good explanation. It can be traced, in part at least, to our current generation's rejection of authority. This rejection is not a knee-jerk attempt at self-promotion or an immature adolescent testing of parental authority writ large; it is rather a response to a century-long, worldwide misuse of authority by those in charge. The "stars" of our century—Hitler, Stalin, Amin, Pol Pot, Saddam Hussein, etc.—broke a centuries-old connection between truth and authority and made authority the only thing that mattered. "Might makes right" was their watchword, and they were ruthless in its execution.

It didn't take genius to see that something was wrong, that our political leaders and nations were drunk on power but short on truth. Yet instead of restoring the biblical balance between and authority, the 1960s generation decided to maintain the separation, with one important difference. Instead of emphasizing authority at the expense of truth, they cut truth free from authority. Instead of one authoritative truth, we each have our own truth—

value systems that are "true for me" but not necessarily true for you. This "I'm okay, you're okay" attitude makes it almost impossible to talk about universal values, because the minute you talk about values that apply to everyone, you are talking again about authority.

The ironic result, of course, is that in such an authority vacuum, the very worst sorts of leaders rush to fill it. The best among us attempt to live out the anti-authority ideal, adopting some sort of pragmatism or tolerant personalism, while the worst of us work the levers of power in the same old totalitarian ways. They may do this behind the scenes, "despising authority" in public and "blaspheming in matters they do not understand" (2 Peter 2:10, 12). But their goal is to replace biblical truth and authority with their own.

The Bible teaches that truth and authority go together. Truth, by its universal, singular nature, has its own authority. It so happens that biblical authority is authority woven out of strands of grace-filled love, giving the resulting cloth a rich, soft texture that wears like iron against the false teachings of the world.

The message of 2 Peter and Jude is that there are true teachings and false teachings. We must resist with all our might the false teachers, without adopting the selfish, antibiblical methodologies they use. We cannot resort to a false dogmatism that contradicts the gospel message of love. We must restore the twin towers of truth and authority, the message of the gospel of Jesus Christ.

—Terry C. Muck

Abbreviations

AB	Anchor Bible
ASV	American Standard Version
BAGD	Bauer, Arndt, Gingrich, and Danker, *A Greek-English Lexicon of the New Testament and Other Early Christian Literature*
BBR	*Bulletin for Biblical Research*
CBC	Cambridge Bible Commentary
CBQ	*Catholic Biblical Quarterly*
EBC	*Expositor's Bible Commentary*
HNTC	Harper New Testament Commentary
HUT	Hermeneutisches Untersuchungen zur Theologie
ICC	International Critical Commentary
ISBE	*International Standard Bible Encyclopedia*
JB	Jerusalem Bible
KJV	King James Version
LBP	Living Bible Paraphrased
LCL	Loeb Classical Library
LXX	Septuagint (Greek translation of the Old Testament)
MeyerK	Meyer Kommentar
NASB	New American Standard Bible
NEB	New English Bible
NIBC	New International Bible Commentary
NICNT	New International Commentary on the New Testament
NIGTC	New International Greek Testament Commentary
NIV	New International Version
NJB	New Jerusalem Bible
NRSV	New Revised Standard Version
NTD	Das Neue Testament Deutsch
REB	Revised English Bible
RSV	Revised Standard Version
SBLDS	Society of Biblical Literature Dissertation Series
TDNT	*Theological Dictionary of the New Testament*
TEV	Today's English Version
TNTC	Tyndale New Testament Commentary
TrinJ	*Trinity Journal*

Abbreviations

TS	*Theological Studies*
WBC	Word Biblical Commentary
WTJ	*Westminster Theological Journal*
WUNT	Wissenschaftliche Untersuchungen zum Neuen Testament

Introduction to
2 Peter and Jude

MOST OF US DON'T LIKE to focus on the negative. And maybe that's why 2 Peter and Jude would probably come toward the last of most people's list of "favorite books in the New Testament." Both these letters—though Jude more than 2 Peter—have a lot of negative things to say. Jude and Peter do not tell us much about the wonderful blessings that God has given his people; but they say a great deal about the dangerous and damnable practices and teachings of certain false teachers. But, even if it might not be our first choice, we all understand that the negative is sometimes needed. When I used to play basketball (mature years and a back injury have forced me to hang up my sneakers), I loved to hear fans cheering my occasional dunks. I didn't much like hearing my coaches scolding me for failing to box out my man. Yet the scolding was just as important as the cheering in helping me become a better basketball player.

So in the Christian life: We need to hear the negative now and then that we might be warned about dangers and steer clear of them. Peter (in his second letter) and Jude found themselves in situations where the negative was needed. As Jude makes clear (v. 3), he was hoping to write an uplifting, positive letter about "the salvation we share." But the need of the hour forced him to write a very different kind of letter. Thus Jude, and Peter also, wrote about false teachers. Pulling no punches, they labeled these teachers for what they were: deviant, selfish, greedy, sarcastic, skeptical, destructive. Given the option (which we will probably soon have) of choosing on our cable service the kind of sermon we would like to hear on Sunday morning, not many of us would probably choose "Denunciation of False Teachers." But it might be the message we most need to hear. We are inundated by allegedly "Christian" teaching of all kinds; and the pluralistic mindset of our age encourages us to be tolerant of this wide range of teaching. Too easily lost in this atmosphere of easy-going tolerance is a concern for *truth*. This was the concern that motivated Jude and Peter to write as they did. They knew that some things were true and others were false. They believed the Lord when he claimed, "The truth will set you free" (John 8:32). And so they used all their energy to plead with their readers to stick to the truth and to reject falsehood—knowing that the decision their readers would make meant, literally, heaven or hell.

False Teaching Then and Now

ONE MIGHT WONDER why this volume of the NIV Application Commentary includes 2 Peter and Jude rather than 1 and 2 Peter. For it would seem natural to group together books apparently written by the same author. The reason for this is simple: 2 Peter and Jude closely resemble each other. Each was written in response to false teaching; the false teaching they oppose appears to be almost the same; and they denounce the false teachers in similar terms. The following chart sets forth a few of the more striking parallels:

Jude		2 Peter
4	the false teachers' "condemnation" from the past	2:3
4	[they] "deny" the "Sovereign [and] Lord"	2:1
6	angels confined for judgment—"gloomy" (2 Peter) and "darkness" (Jude) translate the same Greek word (*zophos*)	2:4
7	Sodom and Gomorrah as examples of judgment of gross evil	2:6
8	[they] "reject [Jude]/despise [2 Peter] authority"	2:10
	[they] "slander celestial beings"	
9	angels do not bring "slanderous accusation[s]"	2:11
12	[the false teachers are] "blemishes"	2:13
12	Jude: "clouds without rain, blown along by the wind"	2:17
	Peter: "springs without water and mists driven by a storm"	
18	"scoffers" following "their own evil [Peter]/ungodly [Jude] desires"	3:3

These parallels, while not lengthy, are nevertheless striking; many involve words and expressions not found elsewhere in the Bible and, as can be seen, they occur in the same order in both letters. And there are numerous other minor agreements that we have not included above.

How are we to explain this startling similarity? A few interpreters think that the parallels between the letters reveal no more than that Peter and Jude were using a common early Christian oral tradition as they wrote.[1] But most scholars are convinced that the parallels point more naturally to some kind of *literary* relationship. One way of understanding this relationship is to think that the same author has had a hand in writing both letters. One attractive hypothesis, for instance, has it that Jude was the scribe (or amanuensis) that

---

1. See, e.g., Carroll D. Osburn, "Discourse Analysis and Jewish Apocalyptic in the Epistle of Jude," 311 (Note: all works without bibliographical data are listed in the Annotated Bibliography).

Peter used when writing his letter. Jude then added his own note to Peter's warnings.[2] But most scholars think that Peter and Jude borrowed material when they wrote their letters. This could have happened in three different ways: (1) Peter could have borrowed from the letter of Jude; (2) Jude could have used the letter of 2 Peter; or (3) both Peter and Jude could have used another document that we no longer have.

Most scholars favor the first option. They argue that it makes perfect sense to think that Peter would have wanted to expand on Jude, whereas it is hard to imagine why there would have been a need for Jude if 2 Peter already existed. But this argument is far from convincing. Surely one can imagine a situation in which a writer would have wanted to extract certain points from another letter that had particular relevance to a situation. Those who favor the primacy of Jude also claim that a detailed comparison of the two letters shows that Peter is the one who has borrowed from Jude.[3] But this is a subjective evaluation. Moreover, many scholars, already convinced of the direction of borrowing, look at the evidence from only one direction, explaining how Peter "redacted" Jude. They often fail to consider the evidence from the other direction. The other arguments usually mounted in favor of the dependence of 2 Peter on Jude are no more compelling.[4]

Few contemporary scholars argue for the primacy of 2 Peter. Those who did so in the past often appealed to Peter's apostolic status as a key point. They thought that it would be unlikely for an apostle of Peter's rank to borrow from an nonapostle. But I think this objection rests on an inappropriate view of apostles—important and authoritative figures though they were, they certainly did not develop their ideas independently of early Christian teaching and tradition. Scholars favoring 2 Peter's primacy also appeal to a comparison of the details of the texts; with as much success as those who argued the opposite view.

Sensing a stalemate on this issue and finding evidence that could point either direction, a few scholars have suggested that both Jude and 2 Peter

---

2. J. A. T. Robinson, *Redating the New Testament* (London: SCM, 1976), 193–99; R. Riesner, "Der Zweite Petrus-Brief und die Eschatologie," in *Zukunftserwartung in Biblischer Sicht: Beiträge zur Eschatologie*, ed. Gerhard Maier (Giessen: Brunnen, 1984), 130–31.

3. See the detailed comparisons in Duane F. Watson, *Invention, Arrangement, and Style: Rhetorical Criticism of Jude and 2 Peter*, 163–87.

4. Other reasons for thinking that 2 Peter borrowed from Jude are: (1) Peter's failure to include the references to noncanonical books found in Jude suggest that it was written later, when the church has a stronger "canon consciousness"; (2) Jude's tight structure makes it likely that it was freely composed rather than based on another document; and (3) the false teaching combated in 2 Peter is probably later than that combated in Jude. For these arguments, see esp. Werner Georg Kümmel, *Introduction to the New Testament* (rev. ed.; London: SCM, 1975), 430–31; Bauckham, *Jude, 2 Peter*, 141–43.

borrowed independently from a common source.[5] But without any positive evidence to support it, this theory suffers a death-blow from the principle of "Occam's Razor": Simpler theories should be preferred to more complicated ones.

My own conclusion is that none of the three usual theories has enough positive evidence in its favor to accept as even a working hypothesis. Nevertheless, if I were forced to the wall, I would probably opt for the theory that has Jude borrowing from Peter.[6] My reason for doing so roots in the striking similarity between two texts in these letters:

> First of all, you must understand that in the last days scoffers will come, scoffing and following their own evil desires. (2 Peter 3:3)

> But, dear friends, remember what the apostles of our Lord Jesus Christ foretold. They said to you, "In the last times there will be scoffers who will follow their own ungodly desires." (Jude 17–18)

The text from Jude reads very much like a quotation of 2 Peter 3:3. If this were the case, then the situation would have been something like this: Peter, having written a letter castigating false teachers in a specific community, shared its contents with Jude. Jude then borrowed freely those portions of 2 Peter that were relevant to a similar false teaching that he was dealing with in his community. But I am the first to admit that the identification is by no means certain.[7] And so I want to reassert again my skepticism about each of the theories. That being the case, I will not use any of the literary scenarios as a basis for explaining the text. Where relevant and helpful in interpretation, I will note parallels between Jude and 2 Peter. But I will make no assumptions about who has "redacted" whom.

However we explain them, the similarities between 2 Peter and Jude suggest that they are fighting the same kind of false teaching. Since both writers are more interested in condemning the false teaching than they are in describing it, we do not have a lot of explicit information about just what the teaching is. Both make clear that these people are trying to convince others of their false views (see 2 Peter 2:1–3; Jude 19). But the only clear reference

---

5. Michael Green (*The Second Epistle General of Peter and the General Epistle of Jude*, 50–55) provides a solid defense of this option.

6. For this view, see especially Theodor Zahn, *Introduction to the New Testament* (Grand Rapids: Kregel, 1953; reprint), 2.238–55; Bigg, *The Epistles of St. Peter and St. Jude*, 216–24. See also Donald Guthrie, *New Testament Introduction* (Downers Grove: InterVarsity, 1990), 924.

7. Two of the problems with the identification are: (1) Jude refers to "apostles" (plural); and (2) the scoffers in 2 Peter are questioning the return of Christ, an issue not clearly present in Jude. But Jude may be using the Peter text as a convenient summary of apostolic teaching generally; and Jude may also be referring to people who mocked the idea of future judgment.

to a doctrinal error comes in Peter's warning about "scoffers," who are questioning whether the Lord Jesus really will return to judge the world (2 Peter 3:3–4). What Peter and Jude concentrate on, then, is not what these people are *teaching* but the way they are *living*. They are obviously concerned that these false "behaviorists" will draw other Christians into their own sinful and destructive lifestyles.

What does this lifestyle look like? In a word, these false teachers are libertines. They assume that the grace of God revealed in Christ gives them the "liberty" to do just about anything they want to do (2 Peter 2:19–20; Jude 4). They have no use for any kind of authority (especially spiritual authorities, like angels; cf. 2 Peter 2:10–11; Jude 8–9). And so they engage in all manner of "sins of the flesh": illicit sex, perhaps including homosexuality, excess drinking and eating, greed for money (2 Peter 2:13–16, 18–20; Jude 16, 19). What is especially shocking is that both Peter and Jude make clear that these profligates are claiming to be Christians (2 Peter 2:1, 21–22; Jude 4).[8] They are, in effect at least, "denying the Lord" and are therefore destined for the condemnation reserved for those who rebel against the Lord.

I have drawn this brief profile of the false teachers from both letters; and, indeed, as we have seen, Jude and Peter describe them in similar terms. But there is one major difference: Only Peter mentions their scepticism about the return of Christ. This may mean that we are wrong to lump the false teachers of Jude and 2 Peter together.[9] But the similarities between the two descriptions greatly outweigh this single clear difference. Furthermore, Jude's brief reference to "scoffers" (v. 18) may suggest that he, too, is aware of the false teachers' mockery of the idea of the Lord's return. We certainly should not make the mistake of reading what Jude says into Peter or vice versa. And Jude and Peter may very well be dealing with different specific outbreaks of the false teaching. But that the false teaching they combat is pretty much the same is clear.

Can we identify more precisely what this false teaching was? Many have tried, but without much success. The most popular suggestion is that Jude and Peter are condemning gnostics. Gnostics had a hard time believing that the spiritual and the material worlds could interact. They therefore denied that Jesus could have been both divine and human. More to the point, they often were not greatly concerned about sins "of the flesh"—for what a person did with one's flesh had little, if anything, to do with his or her spiritual existence. Peter and Jude's description of the false teachers' immorality certainly fits

---

8. This is also the implication of Jude 5–6, where Jude argues that the false teachers will share the fate of the Old Testament people of God who rebelled after being delivered at the Exodus and "the angels who did not keep their positions of authority" (Jude 6).

9. See esp. Bauckham, *Jude, 2 Peter*, 154–57.

the gnostics.[10] But the descriptions are so vague that they also fit almost any group who combined skepticism about future judgment with an immoral lifestyle. And neither Peter nor Jude makes any mention of what was the most characteristic doctrine of the gnostics: their dualism. Moreover, full-fledged Gnosticism did not come into being until the second century—much too late for either Peter or Jude (see below on authorship and date).[11]

What Peter and Jude are dealing with, then, is an outbreak of false teaching that saw in the free forgiveness of the gospel a golden opportunity to indulge their own selfish and sinful desires (see 2 Peter 2:19; Jude 4). We find similar outbreaks in the church at Corinth (1 Corinthians) at about the same time or a bit earlier, and a bit later in some of the churches in Asia Minor.[12]

Since we know so little about the heresy combatted in these letters, we cannot match it with an exact counterpart in our own day. But this certainly does not mean that Peter and Jude have nothing to say to us today—far from it! For the saying that "there is nothing new under the sun" applies to false teaching as much as it does to anything else. Perversions of Christian truth tend to fall into a few quite recognizable patterns. And the pattern we can discern in Jude and 2 Peter is one easily recognized in the church today.

Some church-goers may not even understand the truth about Christ's return in glory, attributing any such ideas to the "lunatic fringe." Many more of us do confess that the Lord is coming again and that we will stand before him to answer for our behavior in this life. But how easily we put the truth of future judgment so far into the realm of theory that it has little to do with how we actually live. We may even sport a bumper sticker that proclaims the return of Christ, but we move through the days, months, and years without really coming to grips with that truth. And certain trends within the church also deflect our interest in the time of judgment to come. The tendency today, reflecting certain counseling approaches, is to help Christians "feel good" about themselves. The result can be an imbalance in our perception of two key Christian truths: that God graciously forgives our sins through his Son and that God will call Christians to account for their behavior. Like the people whom Jude condemns, we can end up, in practice, "chang[ing] the grace of our God into a license for immorality" (Jude 4). "God will forgive; that's his business," was the pagan Voltaire's way of excusing his sin.

---

10. Among those who make the identification are Kümmel, *Introduction to the New Testament*, 426, 432; Ernst Käsemann, "An Apologia for Primitive Christian Eschatology," in *Essays on New Testament Themes* (London: SCM, 1964), 171–72.

11. It is for this reason that a few scholars think that Peter and Jude might be combating "incipient gnosticism" (cf. Kelly, *The Epistles of Peter and of Jude*, 227–31). This is possible.

12. See the references to the "Nicolaitans" at the church of Ephesus and Pergamum (Rev. 2:6, 15) and the followers of the teaching of Balaam in the church at Pergamum (2:14–15).

The letters of 2 Peter and Jude warn us about any tendency to treat sin lightly, to suppose that an immoral lifestyle can be pursued without any penalty. Perhaps we think that the problems in our day are not as serious as those with which Jude and Peter had to deal. But when we hear all too regularly of pastors sleeping with women in their churches and of believers lying and cheating on tax forms, we must wonder if things are all that much better today. The condemnation that Peter and Jude pronounce on the false teachers of their day warns us about the danger of even beginning to follow that road. And they teach us the way to avoid this destructive path: by "remembering" (taking to heart, internalizing) the message of Christ and his apostles.

Now that we have a general idea about the problems that both Peter and Jude are fighting, we have learned what is most important to our transfer of the meaning of these letters to our day. But the more we know about each of these letters and their situations, the more we will be able to apply them accurately and pointedly. So we now want to look at a few more specifics about each of these letters.

Peter and His Letter

WHEN WE TURN to the book of the Bible we call 2 Peter, we find an immediate claim about that book: that it was written by "Simon Peter, a servant and apostle of Jesus Christ" (1:1). Few readers of the New Testament would fail to recognize this name. Simon was one of the first apostles called by Jesus to follow him (Mark 1:16–18 and parallels; cf. John 1:40–42). Along with James and John, he seems to have been part of the "inner circle" of apostles (see Mark 5:37 and parallels; 9:2 and parallels). It was Simon who was led by God to recognize that Jesus was the promised Messiah, the Son of God; and, as a result, Jesus himself designated Simon "Peter" (meaning rock) (Matt. 16:13–18; cf. John 1:42).

Simon Peter comes both to typify the apostles and to stand out as their leader. His denials of Jesus before the cross and resurrection revealed the unavoidable weakness of Jesus' followers before the coming of the Spirit; and his bold proclamation of Christ in Jerusalem after Pentecost put him in the front rank of early Christian leaders (see Acts 2–5). Persecution eventually forces Peter to flee Jerusalem (12:17), although he returns for the Apostolic Council a few years later (ch. 15). Subsequent references to Peter in the New Testament are few, though he seems to have spent some time in Corinth (see 1 Cor. 1:12; 9:5[13]).

---

13. The "Cephas" in these verses is a transliteration of the Aramaic word for "rock" and is thus equivalent to "Peter" (Gk. *petros*).

Then, about A.D. 60, Peter seems to have been in Rome; and from here he wrote a letter to Christians in northern Asia Minor—our canonical 1 Peter.[14] We have only later legends to go by in reconstructing the last years of the apostle. But, in addition to 1 Peter, we have evidence that Peter ministered for a time in Rome.[15] He cannot, however, as Irenaeus (end of the second century) claims,[16] have been a co-founder of the church in Rome along with Paul. For Paul makes clear in his letter to the Roman Christians that he had not founded the church; and his claim not to be "building on someone else's foundation" (Rom. 15:20) makes it unlikely that Peter had been heavily involved in the church there. Early and, it seems, generally reliable tradition has it that Peter perished, with Paul, in the persecution of the Emperor Nero in Rome (A.D. 64–65).[17] But the tradition that Peter was crucified head downward is late and unreliable.[18]

This is undoubtedly the Simon Peter whose name we find in 2 Peter 1:1— a supposition confirmed by the author's personal reminiscence of the Lord's prediction of his death (1:13–14; see John 21:20–23) and the Transfiguration (2 Peter 1:16–18). Why is it, then, that a quick survey of recent commentaries reveals that more than half of them do not think that the apostle Peter wrote this letter? Scholars cite six main reasons. (1) The letter is filled with language and concepts drawn from the Hellenistic world. (2) The false teaching combatted in the letter is second-century Gnosticism. (3) The letter's assumption that the letters of Paul were part of Scripture (cf. 3:15–16) was not possible in the lifetime of the apostles. (4) References to apostolic tradition (cf. 3:2, 16) betray a late date, when there was a fixed ecclesiastical authority (what some scholars have labeled "early Catholicism"). (5) The early church expressed a lot of doubts about whether 2 Peter should be accepted into the canon. (6) The letter takes the form of a "testament," in which a person would write in the name of a great hero of the faith after that hero's death.[19]

Scholars who are convinced by these arguments that Peter could not have written the letter therefore conclude that it is *pseudonymous*—literally, "a falsely named" book. Many books of this sort were written by Jews in the

---

14. Peter sends greetings from "she who is in Babylon" (1 Peter 5:13), probably a reference to the church in Rome.

15. See Eusebius, *The History of the Church* 2.25.8

16. Irenaeus, *Against the Heretics* 3.1.1.

17. See *1 Clement* 5–6; cf. Tacitus, *Ann.* 15.44.

18. This tradition is found in the apocryphal book, *The Acts of Peter*. On Peter's life and death, see R. P. Martin, "Peter," in *The International Standard Bible Encyclopedia*, ed. G. W. Bromiley (4 vols.; Grand Rapids: Eerdmans, 1979–88), 3.802–7.

19. For these points, see especially Kümmel, *Introduction*, 430–33; Mayor, *The Epistle of St. Jude and the Second Epistle of St. Peter*, cxv-cxlv; Bauckham, *Jude, 2 Peter*, 158–62; Käsemann, "Apologia," 169–77.

centuries just before and just after Christ—books claiming to be written by Adam or Enoch or Moses or Abraham. Someone in the early church, these scholars think, continued this tradition, writing a letter in the name of the apostle Peter after the latter's death. This author would not have been out to deceive anyone; he would have seen himself adopting a popular literary device that people would have immediately recognized for what it was—just as we have no problem understanding exactly what is going on when our pastor dresses up in a Middle Eastern costume for a sermon and pretends to speak to us as Elijah.[20]

Viewed in this light, it is possible to believe at the same time that Peter did not write 2 Peter and that the Bible is without any error. And we have therefore seen in recent years a few evangelical scholars beginning to express openness to the idea that 2 Peter, along with some other New Testament letters, may be pseudonymous.

But we think this is an unfortunate move. The acceptance of 2 Peter as both pseudonymous and inerrant requires us to believe that the claim in 1:1 would not have been understood in its day as a claim to authorship—which is unlikely. We have many examples of certain kinds of books being written in someone else's name—apocalypses especially. And we have evidence that some people, even in the early church, wrote *letters* in other people's names (cf. 2 Thess. 2:2). But what we also find is that such books and letters were always regarded with suspicion. L. R. Donelson concludes after a thorough study: "No one ever seems to have accepted a document as religiously and philosophically prescriptive which was known to be forged. I do not know of a single example."[21]

The very fact that 2 Peter was accepted as a canonical book, then, presumes that the early Christians who made this decision were positive that Peter wrote it.[22] Those who did not think that Peter wrote it barred it from

---

20. In a recent monograph David Meade has suggested a different perspective on this issue. He claims that references to people like Peter at the beginning of many books were not intended to be a claim to authorship, but were only a claim that the book carried on the tradition associated with that name (David G. Meade, *Pseudonymity and Canon: An Investigation Into the Relationship of Authorship and Authority in Jewish and Earliest Christian Tradition*, WUNT 39 [Tübingen: Mohr, 1986]). But it is manifestly the case that, at least with respect to letters (both biblical and nonbiblical), the name in the salutation was intended as a claim to authorship.

21. L. R. Donelson, *Pseudepigraphy and Ethical Argument in the Pastoral Epistles*, HUT 22 (Tübingen: Mohr-Siebeck, 1986), 11. We have good reason to think that the early Christians also condemned *any* kind of book that was pseudonymous; Green notes the strong reaction against *The Gospel of Peter* and *The Acts of Paul and Thecla* (see *The Second Epistle General of Peter and the General Epistle of Jude*, 32).

22. The connection between authorship and canonicity is the burden of the article by Stanley E. Porter, "Pauline Authorship and the Pastoral Epistles: Implications for Canon," *BBR* 5 (1995): 105–23.

the canon for this reason. In other words, we have to choose between (1) viewing 2 Peter as a forgery, intended perhaps to claim an authority that the author did not really have—and therefore omit it from the canon; and (2) viewing 2 Peter as an authentic letter of the apostle Peter. The "have-your-cake-and-eat-it-too" theory of a canonical pseudepigraphon does not seem to be an alternative.

As a matter of fact, however, we do not think the reasons scholars put forward for thinking that the apostle Peter could not have written this letter are at all convincing. Let me deal briefly with each of the objections we listed above.

(1) The Greek of 2 Peter has an undeniable literary and even philosophical flavor, quite different from the Greek of 1 Peter. But (a) there is nothing in the letter that Peter, after many years of ministry in the Greek world, could not have written; (b) Peter may have deliberately chosen to write in this style because of the needs of his readers; and (c) the more commonplace Greek of 1 Peter may be the result of the help of an amanuensis (Silvanus?—see 1 Peter 5:12).

(2) Nothing the false teachers were propagating is unknown in the first century church.

(3) Other New Testament texts suggest that the words of the Lord and certain New Testament books were being regarded as scriptural from an early period.

(4) While some Christians expressed doubts about 2 Peter, many others accepted the book from the beginning. People probably had doubts because the book was not widely used and because there were so many Petrine forgeries about.

(5) Nothing in 2 Peter suggests any kind of ecclesiastical organization or hierarchy; and "early Catholicism" itself is a dubious concept.

(6) Resemblances between 2 Peter and the "testament" form are undeniable. But the use of this form within a letter renders comparison with other "testaments" dubious.[23] We should accept the plain meaning of the letter's opening words and accept it as an authentic letter of the apostle Peter.

If the apostle Peter wrote 2 Peter, the letter must have been written before about A.D. 65, when reliable early tradition records Peter's death as a martyr at the time of the emperor Nero's persecution of Christians in Rome. And it was probably written shortly before his death. Peter himself suggests this when, referring to the Lord's prophecy about his death in John 21:18–19, he says the time of his departure from this life is near (2 Peter 1:13–14). Peter

---

23. For a thorough rehearsal of these arguments, see Guthrie, *Introduction,* 805–42; Bigg, *The Epistles of St. Peter and St. Jude,* 199–247.

probably borrows in his letter from the ancient Jewish "testament," in which a spiritual leader used the nearness of his death to add special force to his warnings and admonitions.[24] We should picture Peter, then, writing probably from Rome,[25] and perhaps with Nero's persecution already underway. The apostle senses that the time for the fulfillment of the Lord's prophecy about his martyrdom had come and thus writes a final note of advice and caution before his end.

We do not know much else about the circumstances of this letter. Peter addresses it "to those who through the righteousness of our God and Savior Jesus Christ have received a faith as precious as ours" (2 Peter 1:1). This vague identification has led Christians in the past to denote 2 Peter as a "catholic" (in its original meaning of "universal") or "general" letter—that is, a letter written to the Christian church at large. But 2 Peter gives every indication of being written to a specific group of Christians, who are being bothered by certain false teachers and who have received at least one of Paul's letters (3:15). We would know rather specifically where these Christians lived if 3:1, where Peter refers to his letter as "my second letter to you," means that this second letter was written to the same people as was 1 Peter. For 1 Peter is addressed specifically to Christians living in several provinces in northern Asia Minor (modern Turkey).[26] But we cannot be certain of this; Peter may just as well be referring to a letter we no longer have.[27]

The most we can say, then, is that the Christians Peter writes to probably lived in Asia Minor, Macedonia, or Greece, since these are the regions in which Paul ministered and to which he addressed his letters. For this same reason, we can also surmise that at least most of the Christians Peter addresses in the letter were Gentiles. The opening verses of the letter might also point to a Gentile audience. Peter says that these Christians have "received a faith as precious as ours" (2 Peter 1:1), where the "ours" probably refers to Jewish Christians. And Peter's warning about escaping "the corruption in the world caused by evil desires" (1:4) fits Christians from a Gentile background better than Jewish Christians. To be sure, some scholars have argued for a Jewish audience because of the many allusions in chapter 2 to Old Testament and

---

24. The best biblical example of such a "testament" is Jacob's address of his sons in Gen. 49:1–28. Several Jewish books during the intertestamental period used the same form, most notably *The Testaments of the Twelve Patriarchs*.

25. Peter wrote his first letter from Rome (= "Babylon" in 1 Peter 5:12) shortly before this; and we know that he was martyred in Rome.

26. See, e.g., Bigg, *The Epistles of St. Peter and St. Jude*, 288–89. Scholars who think 2 Peter is pseudonymous also usually think the reference is to 1 Peter, the unknown author thereby lending a further note of authenticity to his production (see, e.g., Neyrey, *2 Peter, Jude*, 229).

27. See, e.g., Green, *The Second Epistle General of Peter and the General Epistle of Jude*, 123–24.

Jewish traditions.[28] But we know that Gentile converts to Christianity early became acquainted with the Old Testament; and each of the allusions Peter makes would have made good sense to those who had this kind of knowledge.

The language of the letter points in the same direction. Many scholars find it difficult to believe that Peter, the Galilean fisherman, could have used some of the philosophical and religious terminology that we find in 2 Peter. But we should see this as evidence that Peter has adapted his message to his audience. By using "religious" language that his readers would have been familiar with, he "contextualizes" the gospel to meet their needs.

Outline of 2 Peter

I. **The Letter Opening** (1:1–15)
   A. Salutation and Greeting (1:1–2)
   B. "Strive" to Grow in Knowledge of Christ (1:3–11)
   C. The Weight of Peter's Words as One Near Death (1:12–15)

II. **The Body of the Letter** (1:16–3:13)
   A. Christ Will Certainly Return, as Promised (1:16–21)
     1. Peter Himself Saw Christ's Final Glory (1:16–18)
     2. The Prophecies Are Utterly Reliable (1:19–21)
   B. Growth in Christ Requires That We Recognize and Resist False Christians (2:1–22)
     1. Peter Warns About the Coming of False Christians (2:1–3)
     2. Peter Reminds His Readers That False Believers Will Be Condemned But True Believers Saved (2:4–10a)
     3. Peter Details the Sins of the False Christians (2:10b–16)
     4. Peter Warns His Readers by Showing How the False Christians Will Suffer for Turning from the Truth (2:17–22)
   C. We Must Hold Fast to the Promise of Christ's Return (3:1–13)
     1. The False Christians Deny the Return of Christ (3:1–7)
     2. Christ Will Certainly Return and Bring an End to This World (3:8–10)
     3. Peter Encourages Godly Living in Light of the End of the World (3:11–13)

III. **The Letter Closing: Strive to Grow in Knowledge of Christ** (3:14–18)

---

28. E.g., Zahn, *Introduction*, 2.194–209.

Jude and His Letter

CHRISTIANS AND NON-CHRISTIANS alike know who the apostle Peter was (however much their understanding of him may be distorted and incomplete). But few Christians have heard of Jude apart from the name of the biblical book that they may know is buried somewhere toward the end of their Bible. This ignorance is not surprising. For the name "Jude" occurs in most English versions (e.g., NIV; NASB; NRSV) only in Jude 1 in the New Testament. In fact, however, the Greek word behind our English Jude (*Ioudas*) occurs forty-three other times—usually translated "Judah" (to refer to the Old Testament patriarch or to the territory that takes its name from him) or "Judas." The latter name usually denotes Judas Iscariot, Jesus' betrayer, but there are references also to four other men named Judas: "Judas the Galilean," an infamous revolutionary (Acts 5:37); "Judas son of James," one of the Twelve (Luke 6:16; Acts 1:13); "Judas, also called Barsabbas," an early Christian prophet (Acts 15:22, 27, 32); and a brother of Jesus named "Judas" (Mark 6:3).

Any of the last three men could have written this letter. But Jude further characterizes himself in the opening of his letter as "a servant of Jesus Christ and a brother of James" (v. 1). Now almost any Christian could claim to be a "servant of Jesus Christ," but the James Jude mentions is almost certainly the man who became a prominent leader in the early church (see Acts 15:13–21; 21:18; Gal. 2:9) and who wrote the letter we now have in the New Testament. And this James was a "brother of the Lord" (Gal. 1:19; see also Mark 6:3/Matt. 13:55; John 7:5).[29]

But if Jude was then himself a brother of the Lord Jesus, why does he not mention this when he identifies himself? An early Christian theologian, Clement of Alexandria, thought that Jude may have deliberately avoided the title given to him by believers, "brother of the Lord," in favor of a title that focused on a point of greater significance for his ministry and for his right to address other Christians: "servant of the Lord."[30] This is probably on the right track. Like James in his own letter, Jude sees no point in claiming a physical relationship to Jesus that brought him no spiritual benefit and that did not give to him any special authority.[31]

---

29. At least three other men named James appear in the New Testament: (1) James, the son of Zebedee, one of the Twelve (Mark 1:19, etc.); (2) James, the son of Alphaeus, another member of the Twelve (Mark 3:18 and parallels); and (3) James, the father of Judas (Luke 6:16). See, for discussion, Douglas J. Moo, *The Letter of James*, TNTC (Grand Rapids: Eerdmans, 1985), 19–20.

30. See Bigg, *The Epistles of St. Peter and St. Jude*, 318; see also the discussion in Bauckham, *Jude, 2 Peter*, 23–24.

31. Many scholars (e.g., Kelly, *The Epistles of Peter and of Jude*, 233–34) think that Jude is pseudonymous, that is, that it was written by someone in the name of Jude. They argue that

While we can be rather sure that the letter of Jude was written by a brother of Jesus with that name, we can be sure of almost nothing else about this letter. We can assume that the letter was written sometime between about A.D. 40 (to allow time for the false teaching to develop) and A.D. 80 (when even a younger brother of Jesus would have been at least seventy years old). But where to place it within this time period is not easy to decide. Many scholars date the letter on the basis of a specific identification of the false teachers. But, as we have seen, we cannot be sure about who these false teachers were. Others date Jude by reference to its relationship to 2 Peter. This is a more fruitful approach. To be sure, we have concluded that we cannot pin down the literary relationship between the two letters. But the degree of similarity between the two does suggest that they were dealing with similar false teaching, and probably at about the same time. Second Peter, as we have seen, was written toward the end of Peter's life, in the middle 60s. We should probably date Jude at about the same time.

To whom was Jude writing? The evidence points to a "Jewish-Christian community in a Gentile society."[32] Jude's quotations from Jewish noncanonical books suggests that his audience was Jewish in background. But the libertine lifestyle of the false teachers is more associated with Gentiles than with Jews. Probably, then, these false teachers are either themselves Gentiles or have been influenced by Gentiles. Where was this Jewish Christian community located? We simply cannot know. Paul's reference to the "Lord's brothers" in 1 Corinthians 9:5 suggests that Jude may well have traveled extensively in the eastern Mediterranean world; and there are many locales that fit the circumstances of the letter.

---

the historical setting of the letter makes it impossible to put it early enough for a brother of the Lord to have written it. But this objection, as we will see, is unfounded. And the idea that ancient authors would have written letters in the name of someone else has serious difficulties (see the discussion above, in the section on the author of 2 Peter).

Some Christians in the early church had problems with the idea that Jesus may have had brothers—particularly as the doctrine of the perpetual virginity of Mary developed. The church father Jerome and others therefore suggested that James, Jude, and the others were not *brothers* of Jesus but *cousins* (this came to be known as the "Hieronymian" view). Still others thought that Jesus' brothers may have been sons of Joseph and a wife before Mary (the "Epiphanian" view). But (1) the Greek word translated "brother" almost always means just that; and (2) no doctrinal problem exists with the notion that Joseph and Mary had other children after Jesus. The simplest explanation, therefore, is the "Helvidian": James, Jude, and the others had the same "human" parents as Jesus: Joseph and Mary.

32. Bauckham, *Jude, 2 Peter,* 16.

Outline of Jude

I. Introduction (1–2)

II. Occasion and Theme: Contending for the Faith (3–4)

III. Description and Condemnation of the False Teachers (5–16)

    A. The False Teachers Are Destined for Condemnation (Three Scriptural Examples) (5–10)

    B. The False Teachers Living Ungodly Lives (Three Scriptural Examples) (11–13)

    C. The False Teachers Are Destined for Condemnation (Illustration from Tradition) (14–16)

IV. Closing Appeal: Holding Fast to the Faith (17–23)

V. Concluding Doxology (24–25)

Annotated Bibliography

Technical Commentaries

Balz, Horst, and Wolfgang Schrage. *Die "katholischen"Briefe: Die Briefe des Jakobus, Petrus, Johannes, und Judas. NTD. 12th ed.* Göttingen: Vandenhoeck & Ruprecht, 1973. Brief, technical discussion, assuming that 2 Peter is pseudonymous.

Bauckham, Richard. *Jude, 2 Peter.* WBC. Waco, Tex.: Word, 1983. The most important conservative commentary on these letters in decades; arguably the best technical commentary now available. Rich in references to extrabiblical materials and marred only by its assumption of pseudonymity for 2 Peter.

Bigg, Charles. *A Critical and Exegetical Commentary on the Epistles of St. Peter and St. Jude.* ICC. New York: Scribners, 1903. Classic treatment, oriented to historical and grammatical issues.

Huther, J. E. *Critical and Exegetical Handbook to the General Epistles of James, Peter, John, and Jude.* New York: Funk and Wagnalls, 1887. Focus on the Greek text.

Mayor, Joseph B. *The Epistle of St. Jude and the Second Epistle of St. Peter: Greek Text with Introduction, Notes and Comments.* Grand Rapids: Baker, 1979 (= 1907). Lengthy treatment, focusing especially on historical and linguistic matters.

Neyrey, Jerome H. *2 Peter, Jude: A New Translation with Introduction and Commentary.* AB. New York: Doubleday, 1993. The most recent English-language technical commentary, incorporating social-critical and literary approaches.

Paulsen, Henning. *Der zweite Petrusbrief und der Judasbrief.* Meyer Kommentar. Göttingen: Vandenhoeck & Ruprecht, 1992. Straightforward interpretation.

Other Commentaries and Expositions

Blum, Edwin A. "2 Peter." In *The Expositor's Bible Commentary, vol. 12,* ed. by Frank E. Gaebelein. Grand Rapids: Zondervan, 1981. Solid exposition.

Calvin, John. *The Epistle of Paul the Apostle to the Hebrews and the First and Second Epistles of St. Peter.* Grand Rapids: Eerdmans, 1963. Fine literary and theological insight from the prince of Reformation commentators.

Green, Michael. *The Second Epistle General of Peter and the General Epistle of Jude.* TNTC. Grand Rapids: Eerdmans, 1968. Pungently written, clear and practical exposition. Excellent defense of the Petrine authorship of 2 Peter.

Hillyer, Norman. *1 and 2 Peter, Jude.* NIBC. Peabody, Mass.: Hendrickson, 1992. Useful mid-level exposition.

Kelly, J. N. D. *A Commentary on the Epistles of Peter and of Jude.* HNTC. San Francisco: Harper & Row, 1969. Careful treatment of the text.

Lloyd-Jones, D. M. *Expository Sermons on 2 Peter.* London: Banner of Truth, 1983. Theological and practical application of the text or of points from within the text.

Important Monographs and Articles

Bauckham, Richard J. *Jude and the Relatives of Jesus in the Early Church.* Edinburgh: T. & T. Clark, 1990. The most thorough exploration of Jude's background and place in church history now available.

Charles, Daryl. *Literary Strategy in the Epistle of Jude.* London: Associated University Presses, 1993. A rare monograph on Jude, focusing on its structure, but including treatment of many more issues.

Green, E. M. B. *2 Peter Reconsidered.* London: Tyndale, 1961. Oustanding defense of the Petrine authorship of 2 Peter.

Osburn, Carroll D. "Discourse Analysis and Jewish Apocalyptic in the Epistle of Jude," in *Linguistics and New Testament Interpretation: Essays on Discourse Analysis,* ed. David Alan Black (Nashville: Broadman, 1992), 287–319.

Watson, Duane F. *Invention, Arrangement, and Style: Rhetorical Criticism of Jude and 2 Peter.* SBLDS 104. Atlanta: Scholars, 1988. Interesting insight into the arguments of the letters against the Greco-Roman background.

2 Peter 1:1–2

🔥

S IMON PETER, A servant and apostle of Jesus Christ, To those who through the righteousness of our God and Savior Jesus Christ have received a faith as precious as ours: ²Grace and peace be yours in abundance through the knowledge of God and of Jesus our Lord.

 SECOND PETER OPENS with those elements that we would expect to find at the beginning of a letter and which, in fact, are typical of the openings of New Testament letters: (1) an identification of the writer of the letter; (2) an identification of the recipients of the letter; and (3) an introductory greeting.

The author of the letter, we learn first, is "Simon Peter, a servant and apostle of Jesus Christ." Double names like "Simon Peter" were common in the ancient Near East. Many people used both the name they were given in their native language and a Greek name, since Greek was so widely spoken. Thus "Simon," one of the most common Jewish names at that time, comes from the Hebrew, while "Peter" comes from the Greek. This double name is frequently used in the New Testament. But only here and in Acts 15:14 is the name "Simon" spelled the way it is here (*Symeon* in place of the usual *Simon*; note the RSV, NRSV, REB, and NJB spelling "Simeon"). This form of the name is a fairly exact transliteration of the Hebrew, and since it is so rare, we would not expect someone writing in Peter's name to use it. But it makes perfectly good sense for Peter himself to spell it this way, since it would have been the form natural to him from birth.[1]

In calling himself a "servant . . . of Jesus Christ," Peter is, of course, conveying his sense of humility in relationship to his Lord. The word translated "servant" is not the Greek *diakonos*, the "household servant," but *doulos*, which can also be translated "slave." It is not Peter, in himself, who possesses any particular authority; his authority stems entirely from the master whom he serves. But the title "servant" also carries with it a sense of honor. Great figures in Israel's past had similarly been called "servants" of God—especially Moses (e.g., Josh. 14:7; 2 Kings 18:12) and David (e.g., Ps. 18:1; Ezek. 34:23). Naming himself a "servant," therefore, also conveys to his audience that Peter

---

1. See, e.g., Bigg, *The Epistles of St. Peter and St. Jude*, 248-49.

is claiming to stand in the line of these significant figures in Israel's religious history.

Peter's right to speak authoritatively to these Christians is emphasized even more clearly in the second title, "apostle." This word (Greek *apostolos*) can mean simply "messenger" and is so used occasionally in the New Testament (e.g., 2 Cor. 8:23; Phil. 2:25). But the word more often has a technical sense, denoting those men chosen specially by the Lord to be his authoritative representatives. They form, as Paul puts it, along with the prophets, "the foundation" of the church (Eph. 2:20). They were commissioned not only to proclaim the good news but also to develop and guarantee the truth of the gospel message. Peter, of course, was one of the most famous of the apostles. He, along with James and John, formed a kind of "inner circle" among the Twelve (see Mark 5:37; 9:2; 14:33). Peter was the outstanding spokesperson for the Christian message in the early days of the church, as Luke makes clear in Acts 2–12. Being an apostle gave Peter the right to tell these Christians—and us!—what they should believe and how they should live.

If Peter's description of himself sets up the letter by establishing his right to address them, his description of his readers also anticipates some of the points he is going to make in the letter. First, these Christians, who are Gentiles, have "received a faith as precious as ours." Peter may be comparing the faith of these Christians to that of himself and other apostles.[2] Certainly in 1:16–18, when Peter describes the Transfiguration, he distinguishes between apostles ("we") and these other Christians ("you"). But the emphasis here is not on revelation (as it is in vv. 16–21), but on faith. And this makes it more likely that Peter wants to assure these Gentile Christians that they have a status in the new covenant community of believers fully equal to that of himself and other Jewish Christians.[3] By breaking through all ethnic barriers, the gospel message has enabled Gentiles, who were at one time "foreigners to the covenants of the promise" (Eph. 2:12), to believe in Jesus Christ and so be saved from their sins. Gentile Christians are no second-class citizens in the kingdom of heaven.

Such an assurance was probably important for these Gentile Christians to hear so that they could take confidence in their full status as God's children and not allow the false teachers to sow doubt in their minds on this point. The word "faith," then, we are suggesting, has here its usual active

---

2. Ibid., 249.

3. See, for instance, Mayor, *The Epistle of St. Jude and the Second Epistle of St. Peter*, 81. Those who think that 2 Peter is pseudonymous often argue that the author is comparing the faith of the original first-generation Christians and that of a later generation (see Kelly, *The Epistles of Peter and of Jude*, 296–97).

sense: the act of believing.[4] To be sure, speaking of faith in this sense as something that is "received" is unusual; and many commentators therefore think that Peter is referring to faith in its passive sense: that which Christians believe, i.e., Christian truth or doctrine.[5] But the word translated "receive" (*lanchano*) suggests the idea of an appointment or distribution by lot. Faith is itself a gift from God, distributed alike to both Jews and Gentiles.

Peter further describes these Christians to whom he writes as those who have obtained this faith "through the righteousness of our God and Savior Jesus Christ." "Righteousness" (*dikaiosyne*) has a broad range of meaning in the Bible. One of its meanings is "justice" or "fairness," and some commentators think that this meaning fits very well here: It is through the "fairness" of God that Gentile Christians are able to share equally with Jews in the benefits of Christ's work.[6] But "righteousness" normally refers to the act by which God puts sinners in a right relationship to him. And this seems to be the more likely meaning here.[7] What is unusual about this phrase, however, is that this is the only place in the New Testament where we read of "the righteousness of . . . Jesus Christ." Everywhere else the righteousness is attributed to God. But this reference to Christ is in keeping with the whole tenor of the letter, which consistently puts Christ at the same level as God.

The very wording at the end of this phrase makes this point even clearer. By translating "our God and Savior Jesus Christ," the NIV makes clear that both the titles "God" and "Savior" apply to Jesus Christ. (Contrast the KJV rendering "of God and our Savior Jesus Christ," or the NRSV margin, "of our God and the Savior Jesus Christ".) The NIV translation is almost certainly correct.[8] Here, therefore, we have one of the few verses in the New Testament where Jesus is explicitly called "God." This does not, of course, mean that for Peter Jesus Christ has taken the place of the Old Testament God he has worshiped since childhood. It means, rather, that he has now come to understand that Jesus, along with the Father, is God. Nor is it likely that in saying this Peter is giving up monotheism and conceiving of Jesus as another God alongside the Father. While it would be a gross anachronism to attribute to the

---

4. Along with, e.g., Green, *The Second Epistle General of Peter and the General Epistle of Jude*, 60; Bauckham, *Jude, 2 Peter*, 168.

5. See Kelly, *The Epistles of Peter and of Jude*, 296.

6. Green, *The Second Epistle General of Peter and the General Epistle of Jude*, 60; Kelly, *The Epistles of Peter and of Jude*, 297; Bauckham, *Jude, 2 Peter*, 168.

7. See Calvin, *Hebrews and 1 and 2 Peter*, 327–28; Mayor, *The Epistle of St. Jude and the Second Epistle of St. Peter*, 81.

8. See especially Murray J. Harris, *Jesus as God: The New Testament Use of Theos in Reference to Jesus* (Grand Rapids: Baker, 1992). The book offers convincing exegetical evidence that the New Testament authors call Jesus "God."

apostle at this point a fully worked-out Trinitarian understanding of God, what he says here, along with other similar verses in the New Testament, provides the building blocks for the later elaboration of that central Christian doctrine.

Verse 2, which follows generally the typical New Testament "greeting" form, continues to sound notes that will be heard throughout 2 Peter. "Grace" and "peace" appear frequently in these New Testament salutations. But only here in a New Testament letter opening do we find a prayer that "knowledge" might be "yours in abundance." "Knowledge" is a key idea in the letter. Significantly, Peter both opens and closes the letter with a reference to the knowledge of God and or Christ (see also 3:18). He refers to this knowledge again in 1:3 and 8 as the foundation for his readers' Christian experience. In a similar vein, he claims that the false teachers' fate will be all the more serious because they had come to know Christ but had then turned away from that knowledge (2:20–21). In its biblical context, "knowledge" involves relationship (see "Contemporary Significance" section). And it was just this relationship with Christ that is the ultimate issue in 2 Peter. Peter's central purpose in this letter is to encourage Christians to make this "knowledge of God and of Jesus our Lord" productive and fruitful (see 1:8).

WE CANNOT APPLY the biblical message until we understand it. But we cannot understand it until we take into account the original setting of that message. In this section, we want to bring up two matters that will help us accurately to translate into our own day and age the message of 2 Peter 1:1–2.

The first matter has to do with literary form or genre. When God chose to communicate the message of the gospel to the world, he chose human beings as his instruments. And those human beings in turn made use of those means of communication that were available to them in their day. Had God sent his Son into our own world, those entrusted with the good news might well have communicated it through radio announcements, TV "infomercials," and a "Good News Home Page" on the Internet. In the first century world, the ambassadors of the gospel used synagogue sermons, market-place discussion groups, and standard forms of writing—such as the letter.

Letters were a popular means of communication in the ancient world and ranged from brief "send money" notes from children to their parents to carefully crafted treatises designed for publication. The New Testament letters fall somewhere in the middle of this spectrum. With the possible exception of Philemon, they are more than private notes, since they are written by public figures (apostles and other accredited messengers) to (usually) a collection of individuals or churches. But they lack the literary polish and general address of most of the ancient treatise-type letters.

Second Peter fits neatly into this middle-of-the-road type of ancient letter. And, like the other New Testament letters, it employs many of the forms usual in ancient letters. We are used to receiving letters that begin with the sender's name and address in the letterhead, then the addressee's name and address, and finally a brief salutation, "Dear Doug." Ancient letters, written in the days before zip codes, usually began more simply: "X to Y, greetings." This is the precise form we find at the beginning of the letter sent by the apostolic council to the churches of Syria and southern Asia Minor: "The apostles and elders, your brothers, To the Gentile believers in Antioch, Syria and Cilicia: Greetings" (Acts 15:23).

But the New Testament letter writers, while using the customary form, adapt it to their own needs. They identify sender and receiver, but instead of the word "greetings" (Greek *chairein*), they use a related word that fits better the message of the gospel: "grace" (Greek *charis*). And they expand on each of these items and so begin, even in the letter opening, to communicate something of the message they want to get across. The bottom line: We make a big mistake simply to skip over these verses as if they were a mere formality. They set the tone for what follows by mentioning some of the foundational experiences that writer and readers share in common. "Grace," the grace revealed in Christ, binds them together and is the context in which everything in the letter must be understood.

The second matter to discuss here to understand better the real force of these verses is the first-century relationship between Jews and Gentiles. God, of course, had long ago made Israel his special people, and this was a unique privilege that the Jews were jealous to guard. During the intertestamental period, the Jews put increasing stress on practices such as circumcision, Sabbath observance, and proper diet in order to wall themselves off from Gentiles. Most Jews in Jesus' day looked forward to a messianic kingdom in which Jews would have ruling positions and Gentiles would be either excluded or given only the most menial positions. But, as we know, God sent his Son into the world to bring into being a people who would honor him as Lord from "every tribe and tongue and nation." Luke tells us in Acts 6–15 how the early Christians gradually came to accept this idea of the kingdom.

But the full membership of Gentiles into the new covenant people of God—and the terms on which they would be accepted—was the biggest theological issue the early Christians faced (see, for instance, the book of Galatians). When Peter, therefore, briefly reminds his Gentile readers that they enjoy "a faith as precious" as that of Jewish Christians, he is touching on a matter that most of us assume but which was of recent and overwhelming significance for him and his readers. And we should not forget that it was Peter himself whom God used to bring about this full inclusion of Gentiles. God sent Peter a vision to help him understand that Gentiles could not be excluded; and God used Peter to bring to faith the first Gentile convert (Acts 10). And it was Peter, with his impeccable Jewish credentials, who spoke out decisively in favor of allowing Gentiles to enter the new covenant on the basis of faith alone (15:7–11). We can better appreciate the phrase "to those who ... have received a faith as precious as ours" when we hear the echoes of this struggle in the background.

WHAT PETER SAYS in these verses that most requires our attention today is what he says about "knowledge of God and of Jesus our Lord" as the means by which we might enjoy "grace and peace in abundance." It is no accident that Peter returns to this same concept of "knowledge" at the end of his letter (3:17–18):

> Therefore, dear friends, since you already *know* this, be on your guard so that you may not be carried away by the error of lawless men and fall from your secure position. But grow in the grace and *knowledge* of our Lord and Savior Jesus Christ. To him be glory both now and forever! Amen.

The biblical writers often draw attention to a particular idea or word by "framing" their argument with it (the technical word is *inclusio*). For Peter, in other words, "growing in knowledge" is a key idea in this letter. In the Bible, "knowing" is a very personal activity. The Old Testament writers use the word to describe intimate relations between one person and another, including sexual relations. The New Testament also uses the word this way, as when Paul asserts that "Jesus knew no sin" (2 Cor. 5:21).[9] Therefore, when Peter begins his letter by referring to "the knowledge of God and of Jesus our Lord," he is saying that the readers of the letter will only enjoy "grace and peace in abundance" as they grow in their relationship to God and to Jesus.

But we must be careful not to evacuate the biblical concept of "knowing" of all cognitive value. "Knowing God" does mean having a warm, intimate relationship with our Creator; but it also means understanding who he is, with all its implications. Peter, we remember, is warning his readers about some heretical teachers. To avoid their errors, these Christians must not only have

---

9. The NIV translates "had no sin," but the Greek verb is *ginosko*, "know."

a "warm and fuzzy" feeling toward God; they also need to know some specific things about him, what he has done, and what he demands of us. One of the things they need to know, Peter hints, is that Jesus is God (v. 1; see explanation above).

In our day we are rightly warned about the danger of a sterile faith, of a "head" knowledge that never touches the heart. But we need equally to be careful of a "heart" knowledge that never touches the head! Too many Christians *know* too little about their faith; we are therefore often unprepared to explain how our "God" differs from the "God" of Mormonism or of the Jehovah's Witnesses. Again and again the New Testament makes plain that our very salvation can depend on confessing truth about God and his revelation in his Son. The biblical writers demand a "knowledge of God" that unites head and heart. We must be careful not to sacrifice the head in favor of the heart.

2 Peter 1:3–11

HIS DIVINE POWER has given us everything we need for life and godliness through our knowledge of him who called us by his own glory and goodness. ⁴Through these he has given us his very great and precious promises, so that through them you may participate in the divine nature and escape the corruption in the world caused by evil desires.

⁵For this very reason, make every effort to add to your faith goodness; and to goodness, knowledge; ⁶and to knowledge, self-control; and to self-control, perseverance; and to perseverance, godliness; ⁷and to godliness, brotherly kindness; and to brotherly kindness, love. ⁸For if you possess these qualities in increasing measure, they will keep you from being ineffective and unproductive in your knowledge of our Lord Jesus Christ. ⁹But if anyone does not have them, he is near-sighted and blind, and has forgotten that he has been cleansed from his past sins.

¹⁰Therefore, my brothers, be all the more eager to make your calling and election sure. For if you do these things, you will never fall, ¹¹and you will receive a rich welcome into the eternal kingdom of our Lord and Savior Jesus Christ.

MOST NEW TESTAMENT letters, following their secular models, feature a thanksgiving immediately after the opening. Peter takes a different tack here. He wastes no time in preliminaries, but instead gets right to the heart of what he wants to communicate to his readers. We have seen in 1:2 how Peter highlights the idea of "knowledge." That same idea is central in 1:3–11, which forms, in fact, a "mini-sermon."[1] Its theme is the need for Christians to grow in their knowledge of Jesus Christ (see vv. 3 and 8). Like many good sermons, it has three points:

(1) God has given Christians all that they need to become spiritually mature (vv. 3–4).

---

1. The Greek text of v. 3 begins with a conjunction, *hos* ("as"), which does not normally introduce a new paragraph. Some commentators therefore think that vv. 3–4 should be attached to vv. 1–2, with v. 5 initiating a new paragraph (Mayor, *The Epistle of St. Jude and the Second Epistle of St. Peter,* 83).

---

(2) Christians must actively pursue spiritual maturity (vv. 5–9).

(3) Christians must pursue spiritual maturity if they expect to be welcomed into God's eternal kingdom (vv. 10–11).

God's Provision (vv. 3–4)

SPIRITUAL MATURITY BEGINS with God's provision (vv. 3–4). It is "his divine power" that has given to us Christians all that we need both for new spiritual life and for "godliness." Normally we would think that the "his" in "his divine power" refers to God the Father.[2] But Peter has already called Jesus God in verse 1. And Peter uses the word "power" (*dynamis*) later on in this same chapter to describe the appearance of Christ at his transfiguration. While a decision is not easy—and perhaps not ultimately important—I tend to think that Peter is referring to Christ's divine power.[3] This power is not so much Christ's intrinsic power, which he has by virtue of his Godhead; more likely it refers to his power to reclaim lost sinners, unleashed through his death and resurrection. See especially Romans 1:4, compared to 1:16, for this idea:

> who [Christ] through the Spirit of holiness was appointed to be "Son-of-God-in-*power*" by his resurrection from the dead. (1:4)[4]

> I am not ashamed of the gospel, because it is the *power* of God for salvation of everyone who believes. (1:16)

"Godliness" is prominent in this opening sermon of 2 Peter. It translates a Greek word that means, literally, "good worship" (*eusebeia*). This is a relatively rare word in the New Testament, occurring once in Acts (3:12; interestingly, in a speech of Peter's), ten times in the Pastoral Letters (1 Tim. 2:2; 3:16; 4:7, 8; 6:3, 5, 6, 11; 2 Tim. 3:5; Titus 1:1), and three other times in 2 Peter (1:6, 7, 11). The word is Hellenistic in its flavor and is often translated "piety." It is a general word, and the biblical authors use it to summarize the behavior expected of Christians who have come to know the God of Scripture. Thus, Peter reminds us, God has made available to us all that we require to lead lives pleasing to him.[5]

---

2. Kelly, *The Epistles of Peter and of Jude*, 300.

3. See, e.g., Green, *The Second Epistle General of Peter and the General Epistle of Jude*, 62–63; Bauckham, *Jude, 2 Peter*, 177.

4. The translation is my own, reflecting, I think, a more accurate interpretation of the verse than is suggested by the NIV rendering, which links "with power" with the verb "declared."

5. Many commentators (e.g., Bauckham, *Jude, 2 Peter*, 177) think that the "divine power" is Jesus' rather than God the Father's.

But God has made this power available in a specific way: "through our knowledge of him who called us." As in verse 2, "knowledge" refers to an intimate and informed relationship that is the product of conversion to the gospel. Based on biblical teaching elsewhere, we would expect "him who called us" to refer to God, since it is God the Father who is usually pictured as the one who "calls" people into relationship with himself (cf. Rom. 8:28–29; 9:12; Eph. 1:18). But we have already seen (2 Peter 1:1–2) how much emphasis Peter puts on the role of Jesus Christ in this letter; and elsewhere in the letter he usually makes Christ, rather than God the Father, the object of knowledge (see 1:8; 2:20; 3:18; in 1:2, it is both "God" and "Jesus our Lord"). Probably, then, "him who called" is Jesus.

A few commentators think those whom Christ has called are the apostles (= "us").[6] But there is nothing in this context to suggest so restricted a reference. Though unusual in the New Testament, Peter here links Christ with the Father in calling Christians into salvation.[7] This calling is not, as some might want to take it, a general invitation—as if Peter is saying no more than that Christ invites people to accept the gospel and be saved. This calling is, rather, an effective summons—an act by which God (or Christ) brings people into relationship with himself. Note how Peter in his first letter uses the language of calling as a simple way of describing Christians (1 Peter 1:15; 2:9, 21; 3:9; 5:10; see also Rom. 1:7; 8:28; 1 Cor. 7:17–24). Calling, in fact, is another way of speaking of God's election, since the relevant Greek words are closely linked (*kaleo* and *ekloge*, which come from the same root).

Peter adds that Christ calls us "by his own glory and goodness." In his first letter, Peter notes that God "gave [Christ] glory" (NIV "glorified him," 1 Peter 1:21); and, again, in 2 Peter 1:17, referring to the Transfiguration, Peter says that Christ "received honor and glory from God the Father." The Greek word for "glory" (*doxa*) originally meant "reputation" or "fame." But the New Testament use of the word is decisively influenced by the Septuagint (the Greek translation of the Old Testament), which used this Greek word to render the Hebrew *kabod*. This term refers to the majestic presence of God. It is this glory of God that Isaiah sees in the temple and that forces him to his knees in terror and worship (Isa. 6). Christ, as God himself, partakes of that same glory (e.g., 2 Cor. 4:4; Eph. 1:12; Phil. 3:21; Heb. 1:3; 2:7; 1 Peter 1:21).

Christ's glory is often associated with his resurrection (see 1 Peter 1:21), and Peter may be implying that connection here as well. But it is not just through the strength of divine power that Christ calls us. For sinners to be

---

6. E.g., Kelly, *The Epistles of Peter and of Jude*, 300–301.

7. See, e.g., Mayor, *The Epistle of St. Jude and the Second Epistle of St. Peter*, 85; Bigg, *The Epistles of St. Peter and St. Jude*, 253–54; Bauckham, *Jude, 2 Peter*, 178.

put into right relationship with a holy God required an act of redemption, an act that could be accomplished only by one who was himself morally perfect. Hence Peter notes that Christ called us also "by his own . . . goodness." Some scholars think the Greek word used here (*arete*) means "power," but Peter's other uses of the term in this context (v. 5) point to the meaning "virtue," "excellence of character." Christ lived a sinless life and went to the cross in obedience to the Father. It was through this "active" and "passive" obedience (as the theologians put it) that he was qualified to offer himself as a sacrifice on our behalf.

The connection between verses 3 and 4 is not immediately clear. The NIV preserves the ambiguity of the Greek by translating "through these." But what is the antecedent of "these"? "God and Jesus our Lord" (v. 2)? Or "everything we need for life and godliness"? Or "his own glory and goodness"? Probably the last, for it is closest and makes good sense.[8] Christ's attributes of divine majesty and moral goodness have been instrumental in giving believers not only what is needed for a godly life (v. 3) but also those "very great and precious promises" that enable us to participate in the "divine nature" itself.

Peter's language here is elliptical: In saying "through these he has given us his very great and precious promises," he really means that through these attributes, Christ has provided for the *fulfillment* of these promises. As Phillips paraphrases, "God's greatest and most precious promises have become available to us." The promises Peter has in mind are not qualified here in any other way. He is probably thinking of those many promises in the Old Testament about a new era of salvation and blessing that God would bring into being through his Messiah. Christians now experience the fulfillment of those promises and thus have the remarkable privilege of enjoying intimacy with the God of this universe—or, as Peter puts it, "that you may participate in the divine nature."

Peter's language in this phrase is strong and controversial. "Divine nature" has a mystical or pantheistic ring—in Peter's day and in ours. What he seems to mean is that believers come to share in some essential qualities that are characteristic of God himself. Just what those qualities are Peter does not say here; and it is necessary to search the New Testament carefully to determine what they might be (and, just as importantly, what they might *not* be!). At this point, however, we can say simply that Peter must have in mind those divine qualities that enable believers to "escape the corruption in the world caused by evil desires."

---

8. I agree, therefore, with Mayor, *The Epistle of St. Jude and the Second Epistle of St. Peter*, 87; Bigg, *The Epistles of St. Peter and St. Jude*, 255; Green, *The Second Epistle General of Peter and the General Epistle of Jude*, 64.

The Bible makes clear that our ultimate separation from "corruption" (*phthora*) will come only with the resurrection of the body. Peter uses the word in this eschatological sense in 2 Peter 2:10; and this may be what he means by the phrase "escape the corruption in the world."[9] But the reference to "evil desires" at the end of the verse, along with Peter's focus on godliness in this passage, suggests rather that escaping corruption has to do with the renouncing of sin in this life.[10] Note that Peter also uses *phthora* with this moral sense (2:20). I think, then, that Peter sees our participation in the divine nature as consisting especially in the new ability to resist sin through our union with Christ and the indwelling of the Spirit.[11]

The Believer's Responsibility (vv. 5–9)

IN VERSES 3–4, Peter has laid the groundwork for his main sermonic point by reminding his readers that God has provided Christians with the power to live godly lives. In verses 5–9 he gives us that key point itself: *Christians need to live godly lives.* And, just in case we might miss the connection between these two sections, Peter spells it out for us: It is "for this very reason"—that is, God's provision of all that we need—that we are to seek spiritual maturity.

Peter uses strong language to emphasize just how strenuously we need to pursue this goal. "Make every effort," he says. The word "effort" can also be translated "earnestness," "haste," "zeal." Peter is fond of this word, using it again in 1:10, 15 and 3:14. The last verse is especially interesting, for it repeats the basic exhortation that we have here and thus serves to "round off" the letter: "So, then, dear friends, since you are looking forward to this, *make every effort to be found spotless, blameless and at peace with him.*" Peter's point is clear: Spiritual growth is not a matter that Christians can treat lightly; it is a goal to which we need to give ourselves body and soul, every day of our lives.

Rather than summarizing this goal in a single word, Peter chooses to describe it as a series of ascending steps. Verses 5b–7 describe, like the steps in a staircase, eight Christian virtues that must be added, one to the other, as we move upward in our pursuit of spiritual maturity. Some commentators, and especially popular writers and speakers, make much of the sequence of the steps here—as if we must make sure to add these virtues exactly in the order that Peter sets them forth. But this reading of the passage, while superficially convincing, fails to take account of the literary form that Peter is using (see "Bridging Contexts" section). Once we see that Peter is using a pop-

---

9. See, e.g., Bauckham, *Jude, 2 Peter,* 183.

10. See Mayor, *The Epistle of St. Jude and the Second Epistle of St. Peter,* 88.

11. For further discussion on the idea of participating in the divine nature, see the "Bridging Contexts" and "Contemporary Significance" sections.

ular device of his day, we will recognize also that the order in which he puts these virtues may be somewhat haphazard. All of them are important; but we doubt that Peter intends to say that we must pursue them in the precise order he gives them.

Having said this, however, it is significant that Peter begins where he does (with "faith") and ends where he does (with "love").[12] Faith, of course, is the foundational Christian virtue (or, better, gift; see v. 1); with it we respond to God's call and come to know him and his Son, the Lord Jesus (v. 3). But true Christian faith, as James especially reminds us (James 2:14–26), always leads further. Consequently, Peter calls on us to add "goodness" to our basic response to God's work. "Goodness" (arete) is the same word Peter used at the end of verse 3 to describe God's quality of moral excellence. Peter here borrows again from the wider Greek world, where the word meant, broadly, "virtue" (the word occurs elsewhere in the New Testament only in Phil. 4:8 and 1 Peter 2:9).

The third term in Peter's list is likewise a general one. "Knowledge" can apply to almost any arena of life. Here, obviously, it has a religious application. Since it comes in the middle of this list rather than at its beginning, it probably does not refer to that basic, intimate knowledge of God that defines who we are in Christ (cf. vv. 2 and 3). Here, it most likely refers specifically to the ability to discern God's will and orient one's life in accordance with that will.[13]

"Self-control" comes next in Peter's list of Christian virtues (v. 6). Greek philosophers prized self-control, viewing it as the ability of the human being to act entirely of one's own free will without being subject to the whims and pressures of other people, competing philosophies, or one's own emotions.[14] Peter and the other New Testament writers who use this term (see also Acts 24:25; Gal. 5:23) do not, of course, use the word in this philosophic sense. For them, self-control, an aspect of the fruit of the Spirit (Gal. 5:23), enables believers to avoid falling prey to the temptations—especially sexual—that are so unavoidable in the world we live in.

But just as constant as the enticement of sinful pleasures is the sorrow of afflictions of all kinds. And if "self-control" helps the believer battle the former,

---

12. See also Bauckham, Jude, 2 Peter, 185.

13. It is worth noting that the Greek word for "knowledge" here is gnosis, whereas Peter has used the compound form epignosis in vv. 2 and 3. While not clearly the case everywhere in the New Testament, Peter probably sees a distinction between them (see Bauckham, Jude, 2 Peter, 186).

14. See especially Aristotle's description of the self-control (enkrateia) in his Nicomachean Ethics 7.1–11. Philo, the Jewish Greek-influenced philosopher, also made a great deal of self-control. See, in general, W. Grundmann, "ἐγκράτεια, κτλ.," TDNT, 2.339–42.

so "endurance," the next virtue in Peter's list, helps us to handle the latter. Endurance is the ability to "bear up under" (the Greek word, *hypomone*, comes from two Greek words, "under" and "remain"). The New Testament frequently uses this word to describe the Christian's ability to remain steadfast in his or her faith in times of trial (see Rom. 5:3–4; 2 Cor. 1:6; 6:4; 2 Thess. 1:4; James 1:3–4; 5:11; 1 Peter 1:6). We are not surprised, then, to find the word in Revelation, as in 13:10: "This calls for patient endurance and faithfulness on the part of the saints" (cf. also 1:9; 2:2, 3, 19; 3:10; 14:12). Trials come in many forms and face believers at every turn: illness, the desertion of friends, financial pressures, death. The New Testament writers frequently refer to the constant pressure these difficulties put on Christians in this life; thus they are equally insistent on the need to cultivate endurance.

"Godliness" was singled out by Peter in verse 3, along with "life," as that goal to which the believer's knowledge of God should lead. We should not be surprised, then, to find the term reappearing here at the end of verse 6 as the sixth of those virtues that Christians are to be striving to exemplify. While God gives us the ability to become godly, it is our responsibility to use the power he has made available to us and actually work at becoming people who please God in every phase of life.

Much has been written on the different Greek words that the New Testament uses for "love." Many of these writings make the mistake of thinking that the different Greek words are invariable in meaning and always distinct from one another.[15] One often hears, for instance, that *eros* refers to sexual love, *philia* to family love, and *agape* to distinctively Christian love. More than any other, the text that gives rise to such comments is John 21:15–17, where the Lord three times requires Peter to affirm his "love" for him. Unfortunately, matters are more complicated than this. The Greek words for love do not have an invariable meaning and, in fact, overlap quite a bit. Nor is the word *agape* an exclusively Christian word. In fact, it is all but impossible to maintain a consistent distinction between the key terms in John 21; the words are probably used with almost the same meaning.[16] The same is true throughout the New Testament.

Having said this, however, we should also note that it is still possible to differentiate the words—*where the context makes it clear*. And the context of verse 7 suggests that Peter does make just such a distinction. The first word he uses is *philadelphia*, "love of the brother," or, as NIV renders it, "brotherly kindness." In distinction from the second word, the familiar *agape*, *philadelphia* probably

---

15. See, for instance, Richard C. Trench, *Synonyms of the New Testament* (reprint; Grand Rapids: Eerdmans, 1953), 41–44.

16. See, e.g., D. A. Carson, *The Gospel According to John* (Grand Rapids: Eerdmans, 1991), 676–77.

refers to love expressed among fellow Christians.[17] *Agape*, then, is not a completely different love, but embraces "love of the brethren" as one sphere of Christian love in its fullest scope—that Spirit-given act of the will by which we treat other people with active benevolence. Surely it is not by chance that love, the crown of Christian virtues (see 1 Cor. 13), comes at the climax of Peter's staircase of Christian qualities. Note the parallel in Colossians 3:14: "And over all these virtues put on love, which binds them all together in perfect unity." Love is not only the last and greatest Christian virtue; it is also the "glue" that holds all the rest of them together, the quality without which all the others will be less than they should be.

The way in which Peter begins his list of virtues might suggest that he thinks his readers at this point possess only faith and that they have to add all the others. But Peter goes on to show that this is not the case. In verse 8 he implies that they already "possess" these virtues. Indeed, as we have seen, many are gifts of the Spirit that are present to some degree in all Christians. No, the issue is not one of having them or not having them; the issue is one of growing in the degree to which the Christian exhibits them. We must not be content, Peter suggests, with a B– in "goodness" or "knowledge" or "self-control" or "godliness" or "brotherly kindness" or "love." We should not be content until we have an A+ in each one.

Now this is a goal that I don't think any of us will achieve in this life. But Peter's point is that we need to be constantly on the way toward this goal, getting closer to it all the time. For it is only as we move along in this way that we will be able to avoid being "ineffective and unproductive" in our Christian walk. "Ineffective" translates a Greek word used only three other times in the New Testament. Two of these come in Jesus' parable about the workers in the vineyard, where it refers to "idle" workers (Matt. 20:3, 6). A number of English translations, therefore, turn the negative here into a positive, urging Christians to be "active" (TEV; REB). "Unproductive" means, literally, to be "without fruit." One thinks here of Jesus' cursing of the fig tree (representing Israel) for its lack of fruit (Mark 12:12–14, 20–26 and parallels). Too many Christians are content simply with being Christians, happy simply to know they won't go to hell. But the true Christian never rests content with such a minimal (albeit important!) level of Christian experience. True "knowledge of our Lord Jesus Christ" (end of v. 8) should always spark the unquenchable desire to know him better and better and to seek to use that knowledge in the service of others. Indeed, as Peter will suggest in this letter, one cannot be a true Christian without showing the effects of one's relationship with Christ in a renewed lifestyle.

---

17. See Mayor, *The Epistle of St. Jude and the Second Epistle of St. Peter*, 93.

In verse 9 Peter touches for the first time on why, in his reader's own situation, this growth in knowledge of Christ is so important: Spurious Christians, false teachers, were about. Surely Peter has these people—whom he will describe in great detail in chapter 2—in mind when he warns about the kind of person who "does not have them [i.e., the virtues of vv. 5–7]." Peter goes on to describe these people as "nearsighted and blind." This combination of words seems rather strange: If a person is "blind," how can he or she be "nearsighted"? In the Greek the latter word is a participle (*myopazon*) and could be translated "because of shutting one's eyes" (cf. REB, "willfully blind").[18] This translation matches very well the final description of this example of a spurious Christian: He has "forgotten that he has been cleansed from his past sins."

Many think that "cleansing from sin" refers specifically to baptism.[19] This is possible, since the New Testament presents baptism as related to the forgiveness of sins and as a standard part of coming to Christ. But the Bible is fond of the metaphor of "washing" or "cleansing" as a way of depicting the forgiveness of sins. This is probably all that we have here. As is usual in the Bible, the idea of "forgetting" is not a mental process but a practical failure to take into account the true meaning and significance of something. As Peter will make even more clear in 2:20–22, these fake Christians are people who at least claim to have had their sins forgiven by Christ but who are not now living as if that makes any difference to them. Such is the danger that may await those of his readers who fail to grow in Christian virtues, for there is no standing still in the Christian life—one is either moving ahead or falling behind.

The Importance of Godliness (vv. 10–11)

IN THE LAST part of Peter's mini-sermon, he does what a good preacher should always do: motivate the listener to take action based on the truth shared in the message. Peter therefore builds on the warning he has implicitly expressed in verse 9, but he now takes a positive tack. "Therefore" may relate to the danger of spiritual blindness (v. 9),[20] but more likely it refers back to all of verses 3–9.[21] "Be all the more eager" picks up the basic exhortation in verse 5: "Make every effort."[22] That effort is to be directed toward making their "calling and election sure."

---

18. See Green, *The Second Epistle General of Peter and the General Epistle of Jude,* 72–73. The verb occurs only here in the Greek Bible.

19. E.g., Mayor, *The Epistle of St. Jude and the Second Epistle of St. Peter,* 87.

20. Ibid., 87.

21. See also Green, *The Second Epistle General of Peter and the General Epistle of Jude,* 73.

22. The relationship is especially clear in Greek, since a form of the word *spoude* is used in both places.

"Calling" and "election," words closely related in the Greek (*klesis* and *ekloge*, respectively), probably work together to emphasize the single concept Peter has in mind: God's, or Christ's, effective drawing of the sinner to himself for salvation (see v. 3). The Christian must earnestly seek to grow in Christian virtue in order to "validate" this calling of God. Some theologians have difficulty with the idea that Christians must work in order to validate their election and to ensure that they will not fall away. And we must carefully nuance just what this means—and more importantly, what it does not mean (see the "Contemporary Significance" section). But we must not evaporate Peter's language of its seriousness and strength: Striving for spiritual maturity is not an option in the Christian life.

Peter mentions two reasons why it is important for Christians to "make their calling and election sure," one negative and one positive. Negatively, Christians are to respond in this way so that they "will never fall." James uses the word translated "fall" here to mean "sin" (James 2:10; 3:2; NIV translates "stumble"). But it is unlikely that Peter is suggesting believers may attain the position of never sinning; James himself insists that "we all stumble in many ways" (3:2). What Peter may mean is that that the fruitful Christian "will be spared a disastrous coming to grief"[23]—that no serious interruptions on the path to glory will occur. This meaning of the term is certainly possible, since Paul contrasts "stumbling" with "falling beyond recovery" in Romans 11:11. But most commentators think that the "stumbling" here is of a final nature, denoting a fall that prevents one from getting to heaven. They are probably correct. The "stumbling" here is the opposite of "receiving a rich welcome into the eternal kingdom of our Lord and Savior Jesus Christ" (v. 11) and seems to be equivalent to the "falling" that Jude contrasts with being presented faultless before the Lord in the last day (Jude 24).

This leads us, then, to the positive reason why Christians are to "make [their] calling and election sure": to bring "a rich welcome into the eternal kingdom of our Lord and Savior Jesus Christ." Jesus proclaimed the presence of the kingdom, a kingdom that, the New Testament makes clear, came into existence through Christ's death and resurrection. Christians now experience the kingdom, or better reign, of God (see Col. 1:13; 2 Thess. 1:5). But the New Testament also makes clear that this kingdom has a future aspect to it; we pray, "Your kingdom come," because we are dissatisfied with things as they are and long for the day when our sins and trials will be no more (see also 1 Cor. 6:9–10; Gal. 5:21). It is our effusive welcome into this eternal kingdom that should motivate us to move forward in the Christian life.

---

23. Green, *The Second Epistle General of Peter and the General Epistle of Jude,* 74.

PETER'S "MINI-SERMON" IN 1:3–11 is, of course, directed to first-century Christians. And Peter naturally uses tools of communication appropriate for that time and place. Most of these are similar to ones we use today. But two of the strategies Peter employs here may not be.

First, in verses 5–7 Peter uses a certain "literary form" or rhetorical technique. Recognizing when an author is using a certain form is vital if we are to understand his message. All of us are familiar with the importance of recognizing "form" when we read, but because most of the forms we encounter are well known in our day, we identify them almost unconsciously. Several years ago, my children gave me for Christmas a book whose focus was American history. On page 72 of this volume, I read:

> Lincoln's family was poor. He was born in a log cabin. And when we say "a log cabin," we are talking about a cabin that consisted entirely of *one single log*. That is how poor Lincoln's family was. When it rained, everybody had to lie down under the log, the result being that Lincoln grew up to be very long and narrow, which turned out to be the ideal physique for splitting rail.

Now long before I reached this passage I knew the kind of book I was reading. Written by popular humorist Dave Barry, the book is a "spoof," in which the author adds a great deal of humorous fiction to a little bit of fact.[24] But the point is that I needed to know the form of this book if I were to have any hope of understanding it or enjoying it. A person from another culture, or dusting if off to read it two thousand years from now, might not recognize this form and could treat the book as serious history.

New Testament authors similarly adapt various genres and forms from their culture as they communicate the good news of Jesus Christ in their day and age. One of the forms they use is called the *sorites*. This form links virtues or vices together in a series. A good example comes from Romans 5:3–4: "And not only so, but we also rejoice in our sufferings, because we know that suffering produces perseverance; perseverance, character; and character, hope."[25] What is important for us to understand about the *sorites* is that the

---

24. The full title is *Dave Barry Slept Here: A Sort of History of the United States* (New York: Ballantine, 1989). Why my children would have given me such a frivolous book is another matter!

25. Extrabiblical examples occur in the intertestamental book Wisdom 6:17–20; the early Christian book *Shepherd of Hermas*, Mandates 5.2.4 and *Visions* 3.8.7; and the rabbinic Mishnaic tractate *Sotah* 9:5.

ancient writer did not always intend the order in which he put the vices or virtues to be the actual order in which they must always occur. In the Romans text cited above, it is possible, judging from the logical sequence in these verses, that Paul does expect believers to manifest these virtues in these stages. But in 2 Peter 1:5–7, such a logical sequence is not at all clear: Why, for instance, should "godliness" lead to "brotherly kindness," rather than the other way around? And surely Peter does not intend to suggest that we cannot show brotherly kindness to others until we have developed self-control.

Once we recognize, then, this "form" in verses 5–7, we will be reluctant to insist that the order of virtues in Peter's list must correspond to the order in which we are to produce them. Peter knows that all of them are important and that entrance into God's kingdom requires that we be exhibiting these qualities "in increasing measure."

A second rhetorical strategy we find in these verses has to do with the words Peter chooses rather than the form into which he puts those words. Dominant in Peter's world was the culture and set of ideas that originated in the heyday of classical Greek culture in the fifth and fourth centuries B.C. Alexander the Great took this culture and these ideas with him when he conquered much of the ancient Near Eastern world in 333–323 B.C. The upshot was that Greek ways of thinking and Greek cultural institutions became dominant in this part of the world. We use the term *Hellenism* (derived from the Greek word for "Greek," *hellen*) to describe this worldview. So influential was Hellenism that it was not displaced by the Romans when they conquered much of this territory in the century just before Christ. Rome may have conquered Greece in a military sense, but Greece conquered Rome in a cultural sense. Historians therefore speak of the years from about 300 B.C. to A.D. 300 as "The Hellenistic Age."

In 2 Peter, Peter uses many terms that were popular in Hellenistic religion and philosophy. Many of them have a semitechnical ring, like the words "deity" or "new age" today. We bring up this point here because 1:3–4 contain some of the most striking of these Hellenistic religious terms. Take the word "knowledge," as in the phrase "the knowledge of him who called us" (v. 3). The language of *knowing* God has, to be sure, strong biblical and Jewish roots. But few words or concepts were as widespread in the Hellenistic world as that of knowledge. In the second Christian century, the first major heresy adopted it as its watchword and so is known to us as "Gnosticism" (from the Greek *gnosis*, "knowledge").

But probably the most striking Hellenistic expression we find anywhere in 2 Peter comes in verse 4, where Peter says that Christians participate in "the divine nature." The Greek word translated "divine" (*theios*) was common in the Greek world but relatively rare in the Bible. In fact, it occurs only one other place in the New Testament outside this passage—significantly, in Paul's speech to the well-educated Greek Athenians (Acts 17:29). This Greek word is almost as broad as our English word "divine." It could be applied to virtually any kind of "god" that ancient people imagined.

But even more startling is Peter's use of the language about Christians "participating in the divine nature" and so escaping "the corruption that is in the world." For these ideas were characteristic of certain mystical traditions in the Greek world, which preached the need for human beings to become "divine" in order to avoid the contagion of the material world (note the similarity to the teachings of some contemporary Eastern religions). The philosophical flavor of the language can be seen in the following quotation from the Jewish philosopher Philo:

> For how could the soul have conceived of God, had He not breathed into it and mightily laid hold of it? For the mind of man would never have ventured to soar so high so as to grasp the nature of God, had not God Himself drawn it up to Himself, so far as it was possible that the mind of man should be drawn up, and stamped it with the impress of the powers that are within the scope of its understanding.[26]

What are we to make of such language? As we noted in the introduction, some scholars are convinced that the presence of this language in 2 Peter shows that Peter, the fisherman from Galilee, could not have written this letter. Others think that the language suggests that Peter is guilty of expressing some less-than-Christian ideas. But we are not required to come to such extreme conclusions. A good communicator knows his audience and puts the message in a way that fits that audience. This is exactly what Peter is doing. We can surmise that his readers were in the habit of using such terms or that the false teachers were using this language to make their points. So Peter accommodates himself to his audience, adopting their way of speaking so that he can communicate to them more effectively.

For example, we have good evidence that some of the ideas that eventually developed into the system of Gnosticism were already around in Peter's day. And we suspect that the frequency of the word "knowledge" in 2 Peter owes something to the fact that Peter knew it was being used a lot by his readers. So he picks up their term—but fills it with Christian content. Similarly, "participating in the divine nature" will not mean the merging of one's personality into the person of the Godhead. Put in its Christian context and worldview, it is a vivid way of reminding believers that they have the Holy

---

26. *Allegorical Interpretation* 1.38 (vol. 1 of *Philo* from the Loeb Classical Library, trans. F. H. Colson and G. H. Whitaker [Cambridge, Mass.: Harvard University Press, 1949]).

Spirit residing in their hearts and that they can therefore begin to manifest some of those qualities that are characteristic of God himself: holiness, love, compassion, godliness.

When we interpret such language, then, we can make a serious error by assuming that it has the same technical meaning as it did in the context where it first originated. Many words and expressions that are virtually technical terms in certain environments have a more general meaning as they are used in everyday discourse. The expressions Peter uses fit into this category. We would seriously misunderstand Peter's message if we were to insist that the language must mean in Peter what it does in some of these other sources. In my own teaching, for instance, I will deliberately bring in the phrase "new age" in order to make a point of contact with those in my audience who might be caught up in some aspect of this amorphous movement. But I fill the phrase with its biblical meaning (the time of fulfillment that dawned with the coming of Christ).

Missionaries, of course, are engaged in such "contextualizing" all the time. Consider Don Richardson's famous use of the "peace child" analogy to communicate the gospel to the Sawi people in Papua, New Guinea.[27] Richardson found in the culture he was trying to reach a certain tradition that he could effectively use to communicate an essential point of the gospel. But his listeners would go astray if they were to assume that every element of that "peace child" tradition in their culture was also true of the Christian gospel message. So, as we read 2 Peter, it is important for us to ask just how the language Peter may be borrowing from his world functions within his own letter and general Christian worldview. We must recognize where he is "contextualizing" the gospel for his day and make appropriate allowances as we "recontextualize" it for ours.

One other issue of interpretation that this text raises also merits discussion. As we argued in our comments on verse 7, many commentators, teachers, and preachers have "over-interpreted" the different Greek words for "love" in the New Testament. The mistake they make is to think that each Greek word has an invariable meaning that is always distinct from other words that have roughly the same meaning. In fact, as experts in the field of lexical semantics have repeatedly told us, few words in any language are so specific and invariable in meaning as this kind of interpretation suggests. For one thing, words quickly lose any technical meaning they may have originally had. We often forget, when interpreting ancient texts that, for instance, as much time separates Aristotle from the apostle Peter as does Shakespeare from T. S. Eliot. Yet who would presume to think that a word with a specific meaning in *Hamlet* continues to have that same meaning in *The Wasteland*?

---

27. See his book *Peace Child* (Glendale, Calif.: Gospel Light, 1974).

Another important consideration is style. Authors often vary the words they use, not because they want to suggest a subtle shift in meaning, but because of the kind of construction in which they are using the word or for the sake of variety. As I write this commentary, for example, I sometimes speak of "scholars," other times of "interpreters," and still others of "commentators." In most instances, my reason for using one term or the other is purely stylistic; I don't want my readers to grow bored with one particular term. But this does not mean that I will never use these words quite deliberately. I may, for instance, be about to use the word "scholar" when I remember that the poor quality of the work in question might argue that this is not an appropriate designation of the author; and so I switch to "interpreter." But the point here is that we can never simply assume, in any given context, that two words with similar meanings will always be intended by their biblical author to have different meanings. We have to do our homework, looking carefully at how the words are used elsewhere and paying close attention to the context in which they are used. When all is said and done, good interpretation of the Bible, in this as in so many other matters, comes down to common sense: interpreting the text before us just as we would an article in the morning newspaper or a column in *Sports Illustrated*.

 PARTICIPATING IN THE **divine nature**. In the previous section, we have been looking at some of Peter's language in 1:3–11 and noting the importance of correctly identifying its contextual meaning *for Peter* and then correctly "recontextualizing" it. The contemporary significance of this process will become clear if we look more closely at Peter's assertion that Christians "participate in the divine nature."

About ten years ago, I was invited to speak in a church that was becoming divided over a certain view of the Christian life propagated by one of its members. This individual made a great deal of Peter's claim that Christians have a "divine nature." He insisted that this meant that a Christian was given an entirely new nature, basically incapable of sinning. After all, he reasoned, God's "nature" is obviously a sinless one; if we had his nature, then it stood to reason that we could not sin! The whole matter "hit the fan" in this church when he counseled a Christian woman to "submit" to her non-Christian husband's demands that she have sex with him and another man at the same time—after all, she had a "divine nature" that could not be touched by such sin!

As most of us will recognize, this particular teacher made two mistakes in his interpretation of 2 Peter 1:4. First, he did not pay close enough attention to the context. Peter does not say that we *have* a divine nature; he says that we *participate* in the divine nature.[28] In other words, there is some sense in which Christians experience a quality or qualities that God has—but there are certainly many qualities of God that we do not share! Just what these shared qualities might be is not completely clear from the context. Some commentators think that Peter may have in mind God's immortality, arguing that this is what Peter means when he goes on to say that Christians "escape the corruption in the world." Christians, by virtue of their union with Christ, are assured that their bodies will be raised and that they will live forever in these incorruptible bodies.[29] Other commentators think that participating in the divine nature means that Christians share in God's own holy character. "Escaping the corruption in the world" will refer, then, to the need for Christians to separate themselves from the moral corruption that is so much a part of our fallen world. Context favors this second meaning: Peter is talking here about growth in holiness rather than about eschatological deliverance. But, whichever meaning Peter intends, he clearly does not say that we possess "the divine nature" in its totality and are therefore sinless.

The second error made by this modern-day false teacher lies in failing to reckon with the point we were making in the "Bridging Contexts" section. Peter, we explained, is picking up a phrase from his own world in order to communicate, in terms they would understand, a truth about God to his first-century readers. As we have pointed out, we must avoid thinking that Peter is giving the language exactly the same meaning that it had in its original context. Certain philosophers and religious teachers in Peter's day undoubtedly thought that "having the divine nature" meant becoming a veritable god. But we have no reason to think that this is what Peter meant by the phrase, and much to show that this is not what he meant.

"Participating in the divine nature" is, then, a great and precious privilege: Through our union with Christ and the indwelling of the Holy Spirit, we share in something of God's own holy nature, separated from the corrupt world around us. And it is precisely "for that reason" (v. 5) that we called on to progress in holiness and godliness. But the very fact that Peter goes on to encourage us to make such progress shows that participating in the divine nature does not bring us into a state of sinlessness or even into a situation in which we can lay back and simply enjoy our new status.

Too many popular portrayals of the Christian life assume that the Bible views human beings in what we might call "ontological" terms. That is, they assume that terms like body, soul, spirit, flesh, etc., refer to actual "parts" of

---

28. The Greek here, in fact, uses a noun rather than a verb: We are "participants," "sharers in" (*koinonoi*) the divine nature.

29. See the "Original Meaning" section.

the human being. When, therefore, the Bible speaks of Christians as "a new creation" in Christ (2 Cor. 5:17) or as participating in the "divine nature," they immediately suppose that Christians have actually become, in a total sense, a new creation or that they have a divine nature in place of the old sinful nature, with the assumption being that Christians cannot really sin anymore or that all Christians need to do in the battle against sin is do "what comes naturally." In reality, the Bible uses most of these terms not in an ontological sense but in a relational sense. To be a new creation means to have a new, vital, and determinative relationship to Christ, not to have a new being that has replaced the old. The biblical authors, including Peter, know that Christians still sin; that is why they issue a lot of commands to fight the battle against sin. We must not err in taking away the significance of the language of transformation that the New Testament uses.

Having noted one particular application of this passage, let me now turn to the text as a whole. As we explained in the "Original Meaning" section, Peter uses the opening section of his letter (vv. 3–11) to get to the heart of his concern. Using an effective homiletical strategy, he (1) reminds his readers of the awesome spiritual power available to them (vv. 3–4); (2) exhorts them to use those resources to grow in godliness (vv. 5–9); and (3) promises them that this pursuit of godliness will usher them into God's eternal kingdom (vv. 10–11). He calls his readers to godliness because he is worried about the influence on them of false teachers, who are marked by an ungodly lifestyle (see chap. 2).

Contemporary application of this basic concern is obvious and straightforward. As in Peter's day, the church contains many people who fail in various ways to display the kind of godly behavior that God wants of us. Such a lackadaisical attitude toward godliness can infect even the most dedicated believer. We find it so easy to presume on God's grace by becoming satisfied with simply "being saved." Many Christians begin slipping into the attitude expressed by the French skeptic Voltaire, "God will forgive; that's his job." Peter wants to sound a clear warning against this spiritual slackness.

Balance in the pursuit of godliness. But the very strength of Peter's exhortation raises two related theological/practical questions in our minds. First, how does Peter's stress on our own effort to become godly (v. 5) fit with the New Testament emphasis on the Spirit as the one who sanctifies us? Does not Paul claim that the qualities of godliness are produced by the Spirit working within us (cf. Gal. 5:22–23)? To put it theologically, is not our sanctification something that God does in us by his Spirit? How can Peter, then, make it seem that our own effort is crucial?

The answer to these questions comes in finding the right biblical balance between God's contribution and our own in the process of becoming holy. The New Testament makes crystal clear that both are necessary if we are going to make any progress at all in godly Christianity. Thus, on the one hand, God's new covenant with his people is marked above all by a new and empowering presence of the Spirit. Poured out at Pentecost on those first believers, God's Spirit comes to reside in the heart of everyone who acknowledges Jesus as Lord and Savior. Each believer experiences the fulfillment of Jeremiah's prophecy about the new covenant, in which God's law is "written on the heart" (Jer. 31:31–34; see Heb. 8:8–12). This means that obedience to God, in contrast to the situation under the old covenant, is a matter of the heart and of God himself producing that obedience from within us. God's part in our growth in godliness is basic and essential, and the New Testament repeatedly emphasizes it:

> The "righteous requirement of the law" is "fully met in us, who do not live according to sinful nature but according to the Spirit" (Rom. 8:4);
> "It is God who works in you to will and to act according to his good purpose" (Phil. 2:13);
> "Both the one who makes men holy [Jesus] and those who are made holy are of the same family" (Heb. 2:11).

Some Christian teachers put great stress on these and similar passages. They conclude that becoming holy is really God's job and that we are basically passive in the process; our job is simply to "let go and let God."

But there is another side to the picture. Peter, as we have seen, focuses on the need for our own effort in becoming holy; and he says the same thing elsewhere as well:

"As obedient children, do not conform to the evil desires you had when you lived in ignorance. But just as he who called you is holy, so be holy in all you do; for it is written, 'Be holy, because I am holy'" (1 Peter 1:14–16). Peter is not alone in bringing in the human side of sanctification. The same Paul who wrote the texts quoted above also says:

> "Therefore, brothers, we have an obligation—but it is not to the sinful nature, to live according to it. For if you live according to the sinful nature, you will die; but if by the Spirit you put to death the misdeeds of the body, you will live" (Rom. 8:12–13);
> "You were taught ... to put off your old self ... and to put on the new self" (Eph. 4:22–24).

There are other Christian teachers who latch on to these texts and tend to present the Christian life as kind of military boot camp. Our job is to go out and discipline ourselves, work hard, take orders, and—presto, we will be holy.

What should be obvious to all of us is that, to be fair to *all* of Scripture, we must make room in our understanding of sanctification for both the divine and the human side. We must insist both that it is God, by his Spirit, who makes us holy *and* that it is we, ourselves, who have the job of becoming holy. Peter naturally emphasizes human responsibility because he is confronting a situation where people are in danger of becoming lax about holiness. But he would certainly not want us to take what he says in these verses as the whole truth. He would be the first to insist that our own "effort" to become godly is doomed to failure if God by his Spirit is not already working in us to produce just that godliness.

Practically, then, we can conclude with several suggestions for following Peter's injunction to grow in godliness. (1) We must make sure that we are Christians to begin with and remember that we have at our disposal the Holy Spirit to enable our growth. Some people deceive themselves at just this point, thinking that they are Christians because they grew up in a Christian home or walked down the aisle at an evangelistic crusade. They find themselves frustrated at every turn when they try to live as God wants them to— and no wonder! One might as well try to use a computer that is not plugged in as try to become holy apart from God's Holy Spirit.

(2) We must use all the means at our disposal to cultivate the Spirit's power in our lives: Bible study, prayer, Christian worship and fellowship, and so on. People might be born with natural athletic ability, but they will not have much success running an Olympic marathon unless they have cultivated that ability over much time. As Richard Foster has put it,

> We today lack a theology of growth. And so we need to learn how we "grow in the grace and knowledge of our Lord and Savior Jesus Christ" (2 Peter 3:18). In particular, we need to learn to cooperate with "the means of grace" that God has ordained for the transformation of the human personality. Our participation in these God-ordained "means" will enable us increasingly to take into ourselves Christ's character and manner of life.[30]

(3) We must take responsibility to make our lives conform as best as we can to the godly image presented in Scripture. We know we don't do it in our own power, but we are still supposed to do it. There are many practical things we can do day in and day out to work at producing Christian virtues.

Making our calling and election sure. A second theological/practical issue raised by Peter's introductory sermon surfaces especially in the last two verses (vv. 10–11). Here Peter seems to say that our very election depends

---

30. Richard J. Foster, "Becoming Like Christ: What Is Supposed to Happen in the Christian Life," *Christianity Today* (Feb. 5, 1996), 28.

on our own efforts and that, if we are not diligent enough, God will not welcome us into his final salvation.

Many Christians, though perhaps troubled by the bald way I have expressed it, would not be unduly bothered by what Peter seems to be saying. But others would be—I am thinking here of Calvinists, those who look to the Reformer John Calvin as expressing perhaps more plainly than any theologian the sovereignty of God in salvation. Calvinists claim that God chooses human beings to be saved on the basis of his own eternal decision, and they cite biblical texts to support their view. For instance, in Romans 11:5–6, Paul asserts, "So too, at the present time there is a remnant chosen [or elect] by grace. And if by grace, then it is no longer by works; if it were, grace would no longer be grace." If, indeed, what Paul says here is that a person's election depends entirely on God and his grace, how can Peter exhort us "to make your calling and election sure"? Calvinists also think that Scripture teaches what some call "eternal security"—that a person who has genuinely been saved will *stay* saved and that they cannot lose their salvation. But, again, does not Peter suggest that if we do not do the things listed in verses 5–9, we may "fall" and not "receive a rich welcome into the eternal kingdom of our Lord and Savior Jesus Christ"?

Now I cannot hope even to begin to settle the differences between Calvinists and Arminians here. But I must say a little about these matters—not only because the text raises these issues, but because I would like to defend, however briefly, the Calvinism that I myself happen to profess! Calvin himself tried to avoid any problems from 2 Peter 1:10 for his theology by arguing that "making sure" of one's election meant simply to make one's election certain in one's own mind. Peter was not thinking, according to Calvin, of a person's objective *status* but only of that person's subjective *awareness* of the status. The problem with this explanation, of course, is that Peter's language does not seem to suggest any such subjective viewpoint. Let me suggest another way of viewing the matter, one that picks up again the concern for biblical balance that we introduced in talking about the first issue.

As I indicated, the Scriptures do teach what is usually called the "Calvinist" view of salvation: that God, by his free and eternal decision, calls certain people to be saved; that he reaches out in his grace to bring those people into his salvation; and that he makes sure that those whom he has saved reach heaven in the end. But I think that Calvinists have often been guilty of so emphasizing these points that they lose sight of the obvious biblical emphasis on human response throughout this process. God elects; but I must believe. God preserves me until the end; but I must "put to death the misdeeds of the body" if I hope to find eternal life (Rom. 8:13, quoted above). Both are taught in Scripture, and we must affirm both if we are to remain biblical.

In 2 Peter 1:9–10, then, I think that Peter is simply reminding us of this human side of salvation. Our effort in responding to God's grace in our lives is essential if we are to confirm that God has truly chosen us as his people and if we are to receive God's royal welcome into heaven. As a Calvinist, I would add that those whom God has truly chosen will always, because he gives us his Spirit, so respond to God and thus confirm their election and get to heaven. In faithfulness to Scripture, we face here what some call an "antinomy": truths that are not contradictory but which we cannot neatly reconcile either. God chooses us and ensures that we get to heaven. We need to choose God and live godly lives so that we can reach heaven.

Peter's situation, of course, calls on him to stress this human side of the situation. And, before leaving this text, we should come back to what his emphasis is here. Whether we finally put the data of Scripture together into a Calvinist or an Arminian framework, we ought to see Peter's emphasis here, that we must pursue godliness if we expect to receive God's welcome. May we not presume on his grace!

2 Peter 1:12–15

SO I WILL always remind you of these things, even though you know them and are firmly established in the truth you now have. ¹³I think it is right to refresh your memory as long as I live in the tent of this body, ¹⁴because I know that I will soon put it aside, as our Lord Jesus Christ has made clear to me.¹⁵And I will make every effort to see that after my departure you will always be able to remember these things.

THIS PARAGRAPH IS transitional. Peter has introduced the letter (1:1–2) and its central purpose (vv. 3–11). In verses 16–21, he will begin to explore the specific issues that have led him to write this letter—the erroneous ideas and practices of certain so-called Christians. But before Peter launches into these specifics, he does two things: (1) He commends his readers for their spiritual maturity (v. 12), and (2) he lets them know that he writes to them as one who is himself near death (vv. 13–15). Both points reinforce the strength of his appeal. The first removes the possibility that his readers might be offended by his warnings, while the second gives to his words a "death-bed" earnestness that reinforces the seriousness of what he is saying.

The "so" at the beginning of verse 12 creates a connection between verses 3–11 and verses 12–15. Peter seems to suggest that it is because the believers' ultimate reward (v. 11) depends on earnestly striving for godliness (vv. 5–9) that he will continue to "remind" them of "these things."¹ The theme of reminding frames this passage, being found again at its conclusion: " . . . you will always be able to remember these things" (v. 15b). Peter realizes that what he is saying to these Christians is not new. The missionaries who first brought the gospel to them would have insisted that they live out the implications of Christ's Lordship in their lives. And Peter himself, whether he was one of those first missionaries or not, has also made the same point to them— perhaps in person and perhaps also in a previous letter he wrote to them (see 3:1). It is somewhat surprising that he speaks of this reminding as taking place in the future ("will . . . remind").² However, as he does again at the

---

1. See Bauckham, *Jude, 2 Peter*, 195.

2. The Greek construction uses the future tense of *mello* with the infinitive *hypomimneskein*—literally, "I am about to remind." A few commentators think that the construction

end of the paragraph, Peter probably refers to the permanent effect he hopes his words in this letter will have.

Not only have his readers heard already about the importance of pursuing godliness; they have also been obedient to the exhortation. As Peter puts it, they "are firmly established in the truth." Yet Peter knows well how prone believers are to lose the fine edge of their zeal for godliness, for the world keeps trying to "squeeze us into its mold" (cf. Rom. 12:2 LBP), and false Christians arise to propagate their own brand of faith without fervor. So, Peter says (v. 13), he will continue to exhort his readers "as long as I live in the tent of this body." This last phrase—"tent of this body"—is the NIV's paraphrase of what in Greek is a single word: *skenoma*, "tent." The NIV undoubtedly intends that the word "body" defines "tent": this tent, that is, this body of mine. The Greek word has this metaphorical significance, particularly when an author wants to distinguish the (physical) body from the soul, or spirit, of a person.[3] Paul, for instance, uses a related term in a similar context: "Now we know that if the earthly tent [*skenos*] we live in is destroyed, we have a building from God, an eternal house in heaven, not built by human hands. . . . For while we are in this tent, we groan . . ." (2 Cor. 5:1, 4a). Thus, it is an appropriate word for Peter to use in this context (he also uses it in v. 14, although NIV simply translates "it"), since he is thinking of his death, when he will "put aside" his (earthly) body.

But what Peter wants especially to stress in this paragraph is that the time available for him to continue his ministry of exhortation is limited. He knows he will soon be putting aside his earthly body.[4] How does he know this? Because "our Lord Jesus Christ has made it clear to me." Commentators speculate about when and how Christ mentioned this to Peter. Some think he must have communicated it to Peter in a prophecy or vision that is no longer available to us. A few have thought that Peter may be referring to so-called "Quo Vadis" legend found in the apocryphal book, *The Acts of Peter*. According to this story, Peter, leaving Rome to escape arrest, is confronted by Jesus. Peter asks the Lord, "Where are you going?" (Latin *quo vadis*), to which the Lord replies that he is going to Rome to be crucified. Peter therefore turns back to Rome to be crucified. But the story is first attested about A.D. 180; and see-

---

might indicate preparedness (cf. ASV: "I shall be ready to . . . "), but this is unlikely (see ibid., 195).

3. The Greek word occurs elsewhere in the New Testament only in Acts 7:56, where it has a literal significance, referring to the desert "tabernacle" of the Israelites.

4. A few commentators (e.g., Green, *The Second Epistle General of Peter and the General Epistle of Jude*, 79) think that the Greek word *tachine* might mean "sudden" rather than "soon" (as the NIV translates). But this is unlikely.

ing this account as the backdrop for 2 Peter 1:14 virtually requires that Peter not be the author of this letter.

It is therefore simplest to think that Peter refers to the prophecy about his death that we find at the end of John's Gospel. Jesus, after forcing Peter three times to assert his love for him, says to him: "'I tell you the truth, when you were younger you dressed yourself and went where you wanted; but when you are old you will stretch out your hands, and someone else will dress you and lead you where you do not want to go.' Jesus said this to indicate the kind of death by which Peter would glorify God" (John 21:18–19a). Jesus' words refer to Peter's death by crucifixion as a martyr.[5] Some commentators do not think Peter can have this prophecy in mind, since it refers only vaguely to Peter's death as an old man. And how could he know from this statement that death was imminent now?[6] But we can surmise that Peter found himself in a situation where persecution had arisen and that he had drawn the conclusion that the Lord's prophecy about his death was shortly to be realized. Moreover, the Greek word that connects Peter's assertion about his imminent death and the reference to Christ (*kathos*) is one that normally indicates a correspondence ("just as") rather than a cause ("because").[7] So Peter may simply be noting that his expectation of death is in keeping with Jesus' prediction about his end.

Faced with imminent death, then, Peter makes a last appeal to his readers. But he trusts that the force of this appeal will go on "after [his] departure" (v. 15).[8] How does he expect this to happen? He may be referring to the Gospel of Mark, since reliable tradition has it that Mark wrote down Peter's preaching. Or Peter may be thinking of additional teaching he is hoping to give them, either through his personal presence or through another letter. But it is best to think that he has in view the letter of 2 Peter itself. By recording his exhortations and warnings in written form, Peter hopes that what he has said will have an enduring ministry in the lives of these Christians.

---

5. "Stretching out the hands" probably refers to the custom whereby condemned prisoners were forced to carry the horizontal piece of the cross to the place of execution (see D. A. Carson, *The Gospel According to John* [Grand Rapids: Eerdmans, 1991], 679).

6. Mayor (*The Epistle of St. Jude and Second Epistle of St. Peter*, 101–2) therefore thinks that Peter refers to an unknown saying.

7. See, on this, Bauckham, *Jude, 2 Peter*, 199.

8. "Departure" translates the Greek word *exodos*, which Luke uses to describe Jesus' death in his Transfiguration narrative (Luke 9:31). Since Peter goes on in this context to describe the Transfiguration, some think that he alludes to this text. But quite apart from the problem of dating, the word is too common to make the allusion probable (Bauckham, *Jude, 2 Peter*, 202).

THIS PASSAGE AGAIN raises the issue of the literary form of 2 Peter. As we mentioned in the Introduction, many scholars classify it as a "testament" or at least think that it has many of the characteristics of a testament. This word takes its literary sense from the legal sphere: A "testament" (from Latin *testamentum*) refers to the arrangement one makes for the disposition of one's property at death. The word has then been applied by modern scholars to a book, or part of a book, in which a person makes a final speech from his or her deathbed. The most famous biblical example is the speech in which Jacob confers blessings on and makes predictions about each of his sons in Genesis 48:8—49:27. But it was particularly during the intertestamental period that Jews began using this form extensively. We therefore find in the collection of Jewish books called the Pseudepigrapha a "Testament of Job," a "Testament of Moses," a "Testament of Solomon," a "Testament of Adam," and, best-known and most influential, a "Testament of the Twelve Patriarchs." Typical features of these testaments are:

(1) The speaker knows (sometimes by prophecy) that he is about to die.
(2) The speaker gathers around him his children or a similar audience.
(3) The speaker often impresses on his audience the need for his hearers to remember his teaching and example.
(4) The speaker makes predictions of the future.
(5) The speaker gives moral exhortations.

Each of these features is present in 2 Peter. Peter announces that he is near death (1:12—15); he addresses an audience that is close to him; he asks his hearers to remember his example and teaching (1:12—15; cf. 3:1—2); he predicts the future (cf. 2:1—4; 3:3); he issues moral exhortations (throughout the letter). We should not, therefore, be surprised that scholars identify 2 Peter as a testament.

There is, however, one important difference between 2 Peter and these Jewish testaments. As the titles of these books indicate, they claim to be the farewell discourses of well-known figures in Israel's history. Yet, as all recognize, they were written from 200 B.C. to about A.D. 300. In other words, the testaments are decidedly pseudonymous, written by an unknown author in the name of a spiritual hero from Israel's past. It is precisely because 2 Peter resembles these testaments that many scholars have concluded it, too, must be pseudonymous. But unlike these Jewish testaments, there can only be a very short period of time between Peter's lifetime and any reasonable date for the letter. Moreover, 2 Peter, as its introduction and conclusion make clear, is, in its basic literary form, a letter, written to a specific audience facing a specific set of circumstances. These factors, along with others we enumerated in the introduction, make it unlikely that 2 Peter is pseudonymous.

But the fact that this letter does not share the particular feature of the Jewish testaments does not diminish the number of parallels that do exist. We can surmise that Peter deliberately chose to write in this literary style as one that was most appropriate for his circumstances (facing imminent death) and purposes (to warn and exhort his readers). What we have, in fact, is a biblical author adapting a form popular in his own culture and "baptizing" it in the service of the gospel.

 A PARAGRAPH LIKE this one that focuses almost exclusively on Peter's own circumstances and his purposes in writing is difficult to apply directly. But two points that Peter touches on carry indirect significance for the church of our day.

(1) The first is Peter's emphasis on "memory." In a recent wide-ranging book entitled *Landscape and Memory*, historian Simon Schama argues that our appreciation of landscape and nature is the product as much of the memory that we bring to the scene as it is of the scene itself. He quotes Henry David Thoreau:

> It is in vain to dream of wildness distant from ourselves. There is none such. It is the bog in our brains and bowels, the primitive vigor of Nature in us, that inspires that dream. I shall never find in the wilds of Labrador any greater wildness than in some recess of Concord, i.e., than I import into it.[9]

All of us have had such experiences of the power of memory. For example, on the flight home after our honeymoon, my wife, Jenny, and I listened to Rachmaninoff's *First Piano Concerto*. After twenty-two years, I can still not listen to that piece of music without seeing, in my mind's eye, the Rocky Mountains beneath me and sensing my wife in the seat beside me, our life together before us.

As this passage suggests, and the Scriptures elsewhere confirm, memory plays an important role in the spiritual realm as well. God called on the people of Israel to "remember" his acts of redemption on their behalf and instituted the Passover as a vivid annual reminder of those saving events (see Ex. 13:3, 9; Deut. 7:18). What the Israelites were to do was not just, in

---

9. The quotation is from Thoreau's *Journal*, August 30, 1856. Schama's book was published by Alfred A. Knopf (New York) in 1995.

an intellectual sense, recall what had happened in the past. They were to "bring it to mind" in a way that informed their entire being: intellect, will, emotions, and behavior. Remembering God's work on their behalf would make it present for them; and so the Jewish family, celebrating Passover, was to identify with that desert generation, sharing in their salvation and making the Exodus events and their corollaries part of themselves.

In a similar way, that is what Jesus calls on his disciples to do in the Supper he instituted, doing it "in remembrance" of him (Luke 22:19). Paul frequently calls on his readers to "remember" his example or the teaching they had received (e.g., 1 Cor. 4:17; 15:1; 2 Cor. 10:7; 2 Tim. 2:14). Perhaps the Pauline text closest to ours comes in the apostle's conclusion to his letter to the Romans (Rom. 15:14—15a):

> I myself am convinced, my brothers, that you yourselves are full of goodness, complete in knowledge and competent to instruct one another. I have written you quite boldly on some points, as if to remind you of them again. . . .

And in one of those many texts that reveals the close relationship between this letter and Jude, Jude 5 expresses a purpose much the same as 2 Peter 1:12–15: "Though you already know all this, I want to remind you that. . . ."

What we find in many of these texts, then, is an acknowledgment that the readers already know the truth being communicated and a repetition of that truth as a "reminder." The biblical authors are clearly concerned that Christians might "forget" even the most basic truths of the gospel—not in a mental sense, but in a volitive and practical sense. I may mentally remember that Christ died for my sins; but I may not make that truth a vital part of my person and behavior and instead become consumed with guilt and dread. I may mentally remember that God calls me to lead a holy life and warns me of the consequences if I do not, but I may still fail to be concerned about leading a holy life.

Ultimately, as Jesus recognized, it takes the ministry of the Holy Spirit to "bring to mind" the truths of the gospel (John 14:26). But God's word, written and proclaimed, is the source of that reminder. And what Peter is indirectly suggesting here is that the repetition of the truths of the gospel, in both word and in acted "memorials" like the Lord's Supper, is a necessary component of a vital Christian experience. We all know of preachers who tend to repeat, Sunday after Sunday, the same basic points—and this is certainly stultifying (and probably indicative of a lack of growth in the preacher). But we also find preachers who are constantly seeking for the new, the novel, the different, and who tend to abandon basic gospel truth in their quest to impress their listeners with how "up-to-date" they are. Such a preaching ministry may be intellectually stimulating; but without constant reiteration of basic biblical truth about God's redemptive acts for us, it will produce Christians with no foundation and no hope for the future.

(2) Another point of contemporary relevance that emerges, indirectly, from this paragraph is the biblical perspective on the fate of the believer at death. First, a little background. In the Greek world of Peter's day, there was a variety of beliefs about the afterlife. Devotees of the Orphic religions viewed death as the time when the divine soul of the person would be released from the prison of the body to enjoy immortal existence. Both Plato and Aristotle also held that some part of the human being (whether the "soul" or "reason") was immortal and would live on after death without the body. But perhaps the view that was most popular among the "Greek-on-the-street" was that found in Homer—that most people (apart from notorious sinners or great heroes) would survive death only as bodiless shades in Hades, without any consciousness or real personal existence.[10]

Almost all Jews asserted, against this typical Greek view, some sort of conscious immortality. Some held a view similar to Plato's, teaching the immortality of the soul (e.g., see The Wisdom of Solomon). But most Jews maintained a view, clearly presaged in the Old Testament, that the bodies of pious persons would be raised after death to enjoy an "embodied" state of bliss with the Lord. Jesus and the New Testament writers adopted and expanded this view. The resurrection of the bodies of believers who had died was basic to the gospel, an implication, Paul points out, of the resurrection of Christ himself (1 Cor. 15). When this resurrection will take place is not so clear. Some texts may suggest that the body is raised immediately at death, the believer "exchanging" his or her earthly body for a heavenly one.[11] But 1 Thessalonians 4:13—18 seems, rather, to teach that believers' bodies will be raised at the time of Christ's return in glory.

What then will be the state of the believer's soul between death and Christ's return? It may simply be "unconscious," held in a kind of suspended animation (i.e., "soul sleep"). But, again, Paul seems to think that his death will result immediately in his "being with the Lord" (Phil. 1:21—23). Most Christian theologians, therefore, conclude that the believer's soul will go immediately into the presence of the Lord at death, with the body being rejoined with the soul at the time of Christ's return in glory.

What Peter says in this passage about his own death may seem, at first sight, to conform to the Greek idea of the immortality of the soul. For he

---

10. See the brief survey in Murray J. Harris, *From Grave to Glory: Resurrection in the New Testament* (Grand Rapids: Zondervan, 1990), 36—40.

11. The text usually thought to teach this view is 2 Cor. 5:1—10.

speaks of his death as causing a "setting aside" (*apothesis*) of the "tent of his body" (v. 14). Nowhere else in the New Testament is this term used to describe death. It is a term that connotes the "taking off" of clothes; and the New Testament uses it, and its cognate verb, to speak of the believer "removing" sinful behavior (see, e.g., 1 Peter 2:1; 3:21). What we have here, then, is another instance in which Peter uses language untypical of the rest of the New Testament and which could be said to have a "Greek flavor." But, as is the case in 1:3—11, we have no reason to think that Peter also adopts the Greek concept along with the word—that is, that he abandons the common early Christian conviction that his "putting aside" of the earthly body will be followed by the taking on of a heavenly one.

The growing popularity of Eastern religions throughout the Western world has brought into prominence quasi-mystical ideas about the afterlife that are often a part of these religions. Many people today look at their death as a time when their soul becomes merged with a god, or with "Mother Nature," or with *geia* (the Greek word for "earth," used for a mystical "goddess" concept in some New Age religions). And Christians, consciously or not, are influenced by such ideas. I have heard believers describe their hopes for the afterlife in language that sounded a lot more like Shirley MacLaine than the apostle Paul.

Faced with such influences, we need to reaffirm that the body is central to the afterlife. For those of us who die before the Lord returns, death will, as we have suggested, lead first of all to a bodiless experience of the presence of the Lord. But the biblical writers make clear that this is only an "intermediate state"; we need to continue to set our hopes on that time when we will possess a body suited for life in the Spirit (cf. 1 Cor. 15:44). Such hopes have relevance for the present time also. For downplaying the place of the body in the life after death can lead us to depreciate its significance for the present. The Corinthians did just that, dismissing the importance of the body and justifying all kinds of immoral behavior because the sins involved were "only" bodily sins. Against such a view, Paul reminds us that the body, being a permanent part of us, is a "temple of the Holy Spirit" and that we must "honor God with [the] body" (1 Cor. 6:19—20).

2 Peter 1:16–21

WE DID NOT follow cleverly invented stories when we told you about the power and coming of our Lord Jesus Christ, but we were eyewitnesses of his majesty. ¹⁷For he received honor and glory from God the Father when the voice came to him from the Majestic Glory, saying, "This is my Son, whom I love; with him I am well pleased." ¹⁸We ourselves heard this voice that came from heaven when we were with him on the sacred mountain.

¹⁹And we have the word of the prophets made more certain, and you will do well to pay attention to it, as to a light shining in a dark place, until the day dawns and the morning star rises in your hearts. ²⁰Above all, you must understand that no prophecy of Scripture came about by the prophet's own interpretation. ²¹For prophecy never had its origin in the will of man, but men spoke from God as they were carried along by the Holy Spirit.

 IN 1:12–15, PETER has underscored the importance of what he had to say by characterizing this letter as a sort of last will and testament. Peter wants to leave with his readers a last—and lasting—"reminder" of what he has taught. Fittingly, then, in verses 16–21 he turns to the doctrinal issue that he thinks his readers are most in need of remembering in their present circumstances: the return of Christ in glory and judgment at the end of history. Peter highlights this matter by returning to it again at the end of the body of the letter (3:1–13), thereby creating a frame around the central part of the letter.

Why does Peter focus so narrowly on this one doctrinal point while ignoring or saying little about matters such as Christ's atoning death, his victorious resurrection, and the work of the Holy Spirit? Clearly, because the false teachers were attacking Christian truth at precisely this point. Peter makes this clear in 3:3–4, where he warns his readers of "scoffers" who say, "Where is this 'coming' he promised?" We have no such direct allusion in the present paragraph. But Peter hints that he is also here thinking about the false teachers and their agenda by denying that the apostles' teaching about Christ's return come from "cleverly invented stories" (1:16). In the light of

3:3–4, we can assume that the false teachers were dismissing the truth of Christ's return by attributing the apostles' teaching to fables or myths.

We do not know precisely why, or on what basis, the false teachers were denying the truth of Christ's return. In 3:4–13, Peter puts particular stress on the radical change in the created world that will accompany Christ's return. Probably, then, the false teachers thought that the world would continue on as it now was and denied that there would be any kind of eschatological climax in which good would be rewarded and evil punished. That this was the case seems to be confirmed by Peter's emphasis on the certainty of judgment (see, e.g., 2:3b). And the false teachers' eschatological skepticism was undoubtedly tied to their immoral lifestyle: With no prospect of future judgment, one did not have to worry much about living a righteous life.

We can only speculate about the sources of these false teachers' denial of future eschatology. Certainly many Greek thinkers of Peter's day scorned any notion of a divine providential control of history and of life after death.[1] And these errorists may also have been influenced by a "spiritualized" eschatology of a type that Paul also had to deal with: Christians who thought that the final form of the kingdom had already arrived (cf. 1 Cor. 4:8) and that the resurrection had already taken place (see 2 Tim. 2:18).

Peter attacks this eschatological skepticism by reaffirming "the power and coming of our Lord Jesus Christ" and by citing two reasons why Christians can be sure that this coming will take place: (1) the eyewitness testimony of himself and other apostles who had seen the transfiguration of Jesus (vv. 16–18), and (2) the reliability of the prophecies of Scripture (vv. 19–21).

Peter's Eyewitness Testimony to the Parousia (vv. 16–18)

GRAMMATICALLY, THE MAIN assertion in verse 16 is that "we told you about the power and coming of our Lord Jesus Christ." Significantly, Peter shifts from the first singular person he used in verses 12–15 ("I will remind you . . . I think it right . . . I will make every effort") to the first person plural in verses 16–18 ("we told you . . . we were eyewitnesses . . . we ourselves heard this voice . . . when we were with him"). This "we" must refer to Peter and other apostles, since it was only they who were eyewitnesses of the Transfiguration. Peter's point is that the fact of Christ's transfiguration, and thus also the belief that he will come again, rests on the testimony of several apostolic eyewitnesses.

When Peter associates some of these other apostles with himself in telling his readers about Christ's return, he does not necessarily mean that other apostles had personally told them of this truth—although that is certainly

---

1. Jerome Neyrey has suggested that Epicurean philosophy may lie, at least indirectly, behind the eschatological skepticism in 2 Peter (see *2 Peter, Jude*, 122–28).

possible. Probably Peter simply means that Christ's coming again in glory was a part of the basic gospel message preached by the apostles and that the readers of this letter had received that message. Evangelistic appeals from Peter himself delivered early in the life of the church confirm that Christ's return was a staple of early Christian proclamation. In Acts 3, addressing a crowd of Jews at the temple, Peter calls on his hearers to repent, "that times of refreshing may come from the Lord, and that he may send the Christ, who has been appointed for you—even Jesus. He must remain in heaven until the time comes for God to restore everything, as he promised long ago through his holy prophets" (Acts 3:19–21). Again, speaking before Cornelius and his household, Peter testified that Jesus was "the one whom God had appointed as judge of the living and the dead" (10:42).

"The power and coming" can, of course, refer to two distinct things: Christ's inherent power and his coming again in glory. But the two words probably form a hendiadys; that is, they together refer to a single entity: Christ's "coming in power" (cf. TEV: "mighty coming"). Peter could here be referring to Christ's first "coming": his incarnation and powerful redeeming ministry.[2] But the word "coming" is used throughout the New Testament as almost a technical term for Christ's return in glory—so much so that the underlying Greek word, *parousia*, has passed into our theological vocabulary. The word can mean simply "presence" (as it does at least three times in the New Testament: 2 Cor. 10:10; Phil. 2:12; 2 Thess. 2:9), but it usually means "arrival" or "coming." The Greeks used the word to refer to the special "presence" or even "coming" of a god. Some Jewish writers also used the term in this way; Josephus, for instance, uses it to depict the terrifying appearance of God to Moses on Sinai.[3] Especially significant perhaps for the New Testament use of the word is the application of *parousia* among the Greeks to the official visit of a ruler.[4] Hence, as in verse 16 here, the word occurs seventeen times in the New Testament to refer to Christ's return in glory.

Peter's reminder about the apostolic proclamation of the return of Christ may be the center of the verse grammatically, but the key point he wants to get across comes in the contrasting qualifications of this assertion: The apostles made known the return of Christ not in following "cleverly invented stories" but in being "eyewitnesses of his majesty." "Stories" translates the Greek word *mythos* (from which we get "myth"). This Greek word had a broad range of meaning, but the meaning most relevant to our verse is the

---

2. See, e.g., Calvin, *The Epistle of Paul the Apostle to the Hebrews and the Second Epistle of St. Peter,* 338.

3. Josephus, *Antiquities* 3.80.

4. See the survey of usage in A. Oepke, "παρουσία," *TDNT,* 5.858–71.

sense "fictional account, fable." Jewish authors used the word with this meaning to depict pagan fictions about the creation of the world and of the behavior of the gods.[5]

Enhancing this meaning here is Peter's addition of the modifier *sesophismenois*, "cleverly invented," "deceitfully concocted." The closest biblical parallel to the phrase comes in Paul's references in the Pastoral Letters to "myths and endless genealogies" (1 Tim. 1:4) and to "myths and old wives' tales" (1 Tim. 4:7; cf. also 2 Tim. 4:4 and Titus 1:14). Peter may have been led to deny that the apostles followed such clever fables in proclaiming the return of Christ in order to distinguish their teaching from the teaching of the heretics. But it is more likely that his denial came because the false teachers were accusing the apostles of inventing the whole idea of the Parousia and the judgment it would bring. Perhaps they thought the apostles had introduced the idea to lend weight to their moral strictures: "Behave in a godly way or you will be judged."

But Peter is not content simply to deny that the apostles' teaching about Christ's return was built on a myth; he asserts, positively, that the teaching is the direct product of eyewitness testimony. "Eyewitnesses" may be another of those distinctly Hellenistic religious words of which Peter is so fond, for it was used in his day to describe a certain kind of initiate into the mystery religions. But the word is also used quite generally, so we cannot be sure of this particular nuance.[6] Peter claims, with others, to have been "eyewitnesses of his [that is, the Lord Jesus Christ's] majesty." "Majesty" translates a word (*megaleiotes*) that has divine associations; and here, as the following two verses show, the reference is specifically to Christ's glorious appearance at the time of the Transfiguration.

It was on that occasion, as Peter puts it, that Christ "received honor and glory from God the Father." "Honor" (*time*) and "glory" (*doxa*) may simply form an hendiadys to denote the majesty of Christ's appearance. But the terms may have specific individual significance, "honor" referring to exalted status and "glory" to Christ's splendid appearance.[7] For on that occasion, the Gospel writers tell us, Christ's "face was changed" (Luke 9:29), shining "like the sun" (Matt. 17:2), and his "clothes became dazzling white, whiter than anyone in the world could bleach them" (Mark 9:3; cf. Matt. 17:2; Luke 9:29). Bright, shining, or white clothing often symbolizes purity and victory and is associated in Jewish apocalyptic with the coming of Messiah. And

---

5. See Philo, *On the Account of the World's Creation Given by Moses* 1; Josephus, *Antiquities* 1.22.

6. See the discussion in Bauckham, *Jude, 2 Peter,* 215–16.

7. See Kelly, *The Epistles of Peter and of Jude,* 319.

Jesus' shining face reminds us inevitably of the glow on Moses' face after he had been with the Lord on Mount Sinai (Ex. 34:29–30). Unlike Moses' face, however, which only reflected the glory of God, Christ's face shone with the glory that was intrinsic to him as both Messiah and God.

Christ's exalted status is indicated in the Transfiguration events especially by the accompanying signs and by the voice from heaven. Several elements in the narrative—the "high mountain," the cloud that "enveloped them" (Mark 9:7)—point to the event as a theophany (a manifestation of God). But most decisive, of course, is the voice from heaven, proclaiming Jesus as God's beloved Son. And it is this voice that Peter highlights in his account: "The voice came to him from the Majestic Glory, saying, 'This is my Son, whom I love; with him I am well pleased.'" "Majestic Glory" is a substitute for the name of God, a practice common among the Jews who held the names of God in such high regard that they rarely pronounced them.

Peter's version of the voice that came from heaven at the time of the Transfiguration does not agree exactly (in the Greek) with the version we find in any of the Gospels, though it is closest to Matthew's wording: "'This is my Son, whom I love; with him I am well pleased. Listen to him'" (17:5).[8] Scholars have accordingly debated the source of Peter's wording. But it is surely simplest, when we remember that Peter was on the mountain to hear the voice (cf. the next verse, in which he stresses this very fact), to think that Peter is quoting the words from memory.

What is obviously of greatest importance is the import of the words. They gain their impact from allusions to two key Old Testament texts. "This is my Son" alludes to the language of Psalm 2:7, in which God addresses the messianic King; and "with whom I am well pleased" is language drawn from the first "Suffering Servant" song in Isaiah (42:1). The voice from heaven, therefore, identifies Jesus as both Messiah and Suffering Servant. More important, perhaps, for Peter's purposes, are the implications of Jesus as Son of God. As this conception is developed in the New Testament, it becomes clear that far more than an "official" status is intended by the designation; Jesus is, in some manner, identified with God the Father in a more essential, or even ontological, way (see particularly John 10:30; 14:5–11).[9]

In verse 16, Peter stressed that he was an "eyewitness" of this event. Now, in verse 18, he reminds his readers that he was an "ear-witness" also:

---

8. The NIV of the portions that Matthew and 2 Peter have in common is identical; in the Greek, however, there are several minor differences.

9. On the "Son of God" title in the New Testament, see especially I. Howard Marshall, *The Origins of New Testament Christology* (Downers Grove, Ill.: InterVarsity, 1976), 111–25; and Martin Hengel, *The Son of God* (Philadelphia: Fortress, 1976).

"We ourselves heard this voice." As the Gospel accounts make clear, the "we" here includes Peter, James, and John (see Mark 9:2 and parallels). Jesus selected these three from among the apostolic band so that they might be "with him on the sacred mountain." Many scholars think that the phrase "sacred mountain" reflects a time in the second or third generation of Christianity when the sites of Jesus' life had been hallowed by tradition. But there is no need for such an assumption. "Sacred" translates *hagios*, which can also be rendered "holy." Some think Peter denotes the mountain as "holy" because the Transfiguration itself had made it a place "set apart."[10] Others think that Peter may be reinforcing the allusion to the experience of Moses at Sinai that is so prominent in the Gospel accounts. But Bauckham notes that Sinai is never called the "holy mountain," whereas Psalm 2:6 uses precisely this phrase just before the words to which the voice from heaven alludes:

> "I have installed my King
> on Zion, my *holy hill*."
> I will proclaim the decree of the LORD:
> He said to me, 'You are my Son. . . .'

Peter thus accentuates the notion of Jesus' kingship revealed in the Transfiguration experience.[11]

Before we leave this paragraph, we need to tackle one other issue, central to its function in the letter: Why does Peter allude to the Transfiguration to confirm the truth of Jesus' return in glory? Why not, for instance, refer to Jesus' resurrection or ascension, at which time an angel promised that Jesus would come back (see Acts 1:9–11)? Several unconvincing answers to this question have been offered, the best known being that the Transfiguration is really a post-resurrection appearance of Jesus that the early church read back into the life of Jesus. But in addition to suffering from a number of specific problems, this explanation is obviously incompatible with what the Bible says of the experience. The most likely explanation is that the Transfiguration experience had an intimate relationship to the Parousia of Jesus from the start.

We find a number of pointers in this direction. (1) The Synoptic Gospels preface the Transfiguration narrative with Jesus' prediction that some of the apostles would not die before they saw that glory of the kingdom (Matt. 17:1; Mark 9:1; Luke 9:27). The most natural interpretation is to find this prediction fulfilled in the Transfiguration, when only a few of the apostles (Peter, James, and John) saw Jesus' intrinsic glory. (2) The Synoptic Evangelists usu-

---

10. Green, *The Second Epistle General of Peter and the General Epistle of Jude*, 85.

11. Bauckham, *Jude, 2 Peter*, 221.

ally use the word "glory" in connection with the Parousia. (3) Later Christian tradition connected Jesus' transfiguration with the Parousia.[12] (4) As its name suggests, the Transfiguration involves a transformation in Jesus' appearance, but it is a transformation that reveals his true nature. It is this glorious and majestic nature, hidden, as it were, during his earthly life, that will be revealed to all the world at the time of his return. Put simply, the Transfiguration reveals Jesus as the glorious King, and Peter was there to see it. He therefore has utter confidence that Jesus will return as the glorious King and establish his kingdom in its final and ultimate form.

The Testimony of the Prophets to the Parousia (vv. 19–21)

THE RELIABILITY OF revelation is the idea that links verses 16–18 and verses 19–21. Peter, James, and John can testify to the revelation of Christ's glory in the Transfiguration. But also testifying to Christ's glorious appearance at the end of history are the prophets.

"We have the word of the prophets made more certain" (v. 19a) is somewhat unclear. (1) Who is included in the "we"? Peter and the other apostles, as in verses 16–18?[13] Or Peter and his readers? It is probably the latter, because Peter goes on in this verse to address his readers directly ("you will do well to pay attention . . . "). This suggests that Peter's focus has turned away from the apostles and to his own readers.

(2) What is the "prophetic word"? It could be the Transfiguration itself, an event, as we have just seen, that is prophetic of Christ's coming again in glory.[14] But the language Peter uses would be a most unusual way to describe an event, however much it may carry future reference. Probably, then, the "prophetic word" is a collection of oral or written prophecies. Some think that Peter might have in mind the entire Old Testament or even Old and New Testament prophecy. But the context suggests rather that he refers specifically to Old Testament prophecies about the kingdom to be established by the Messiah at the end of history. This, as we have seen, is the point at issue in 2 Peter.

(3) What does Peter mean with the comparative "made *more* sure"? "Sure" translates a Greek word (*bebaios*) that refers to the certainty and reliability of promises and agreements (see, e.g., Rom. 4:16; Heb. 6:16, 19). Peter may be saying, then, that the Old Testament prophecies are an even more certain basis for belief in the Parousia than eyewitness testimony about the

---

12. See Jerome Neyrey, "The Apologetic Use of the Transfiguration in 2 Peter 1:16–21," *CBQ* 42 (1980): 509–14.

13. Bauckham, *Jude, 2 Peter*, 224–25.

14. Neyrey, *2 Peter, Jude*, 179.

Transfiguration.[15] But the Greek probably cannot bear this meaning. We think, rather, that Peter is suggesting that his testimony about the Transfiguration gives to the prophetic word an even greater certainty than it had before. The prophets predicted that Messiah would establish a universal and glorious reign. Some in the early church may have so spiritualized these prophecies that they eliminated any future reference. The Transfiguration, an anticipation of Christ's ultimate kingdom glory, shows that the words of the prophets, at this point at least, must be taken with full literal force. Thus Christians can be even more confident of their fulfillment.

Confidence in the reliability of the prophetic word should lead to a firm adherence to its teaching. Consequently, Peter urges his readers to "pay attention to it, as to a light shining in a dark place." The comparison of God's word to a light is common in Scripture, one of the more famous instances being Psalm 119:105: "Your word is a lamp to my feet and a light for my path." In the darkness of this present world, God's word casts light on his purposes and plans and so enables believers to live as those who are "in the day" (see Rom. 13:11–12). In this text in Romans, Paul picks up from the Old Testament prophets the idea of "the day of the Lord"—that time when God will intervene decisively in history to save his people and judge his enemies. As the Romans text demonstrates, New Testament writers proclaimed that, with the death and resurrection of Christ, God had fulfilled his promises about that day. But they were equally insistent that these past redemptive events did not include all that God has intended to do in saving his people and judging his enemies. The "day of the Lord" still awaits its culmination.

It is this as yet unfulfilled aspect of the day that Peter here picks up: He wants his readers to pay attention to the prophetic word "until the day dawns and the morning star rises in your hearts." The "day," as we have seen, is an Old Testament metaphor for the eschatological climax. "Morning star" translates a word that means, literally, "light-bringer" (*phosphoros*). People in the ancient world usually used the word to denote the planet Venus, which often appears just before dawn. Some commentators think that it cannot have this meaning here, since Peter refers to it *after* the dawning of the day. But Peter is probably not intending a chronological order in the phrases. The dawning of the day refers generally to the eschatological climax, whereas the rising of the morning star in the heart refers to the effects of that climax in the life of the believer. "Morning star" may refer to Christ himself, since Scripture elsewhere uses "star" as a messianic reference (Num. 24:17; Rev. 22:16). The clause, then, "is a pictorial description of the way in which, at His coming, Christ will dissipate the doubt and uncertainty by which [believers']

---

15. Bigg, *The Epistles of St. Peter and St. Jude,* 268.

hearts are meanwhile beclouded and will fill them with a marvelous illumination."[16]

But what is it that believers know? There are two main possibilities, well represented by the NIV translation on the one hand and the REB rendering on the other:

NIV: "no prophecy of Scripture came about by the prophet's own interpretation"

REB: "No prophetic writing is a matter for private interpretation."

These quite different interpretations are created by three ambiguities in the Greek text.

(1) The verb in this sentence (*ginetai*) is vague in meaning. The NIV translation "came about" and the REB translation "is a matter of" are both fair renderings.[17]

(2) Critical for the differing interpretations is the Greek word *idias*, which means "one's own." The NIV takes this to refer to the prophet. It therefore suggests that the issue in verse 20 is the *origin* of prophecy: It did not come about through the prophet's own fallible and quite possibly mistaken notions about the visions he saw or the words he heard. Rather, as verse 21 asserts, it came about through the sovereign work of God in his Spirit.[18] The REB, on the other hand, applies "one's own" generally to any particular individual. It therefore sees verse 20 as a statement about the *interpretation* of prophecy: It should not be given whatever meaning a particular individual (who may have his own ax to grind) wants to give it. Peter would then be suggesting either that there is only one true interpretation of prophecy[19] or that the church at large, rather than self-appointed individuals, should be responsible for its interpretation.[20]

(3) The Greek construction connecting verses 19 and 20 (a participle) can indicate a close relationship between the verses or an indirect one. Most English versions put a period after verse 19 and begin verse 20 with a new sentence. This could match either of the interpretations of verse 20. But if the NIV interpretation is adopted, it is tempting to connect the verses more

---

16. Kelly, *The Epistles of Peter and of Jude*, 323.

17. Admittedly, the past tense in the NIV rendering ("*came* about") is a bit questionable. The Greek verb is in the present tense; and while Greek verbal tenses do not always indicate the time of an action, it is somewhat unusual to translate a Greek present indicative with an English past tense. But the choice of text does not significantly affect the meaning here.

18. Excellent detailed defenses of this interpretation can be found in Green, *The Second Epistle General of Peter and the General Epistle of Jude*, 81–91; Bauckham, *Jude, 2 Peter*, 230–31.

19. Mayor, *The Epistle of St. Jude and the Second Epistle of St. Peter*, 112–14, 196–98.

20. Bigg, *The Epistles of St. Peter and St. Jude*, 269–70.

closely, giving the participle a causal meaning: Believers are to pay attention to the prophetic word (the main point of v. 19) *because* they know first of all that it does not originate from human beings (v. 20), but from God (v. 21).

A decision between these two interpretations of verse 20 is difficult. Each fits well into the context. An emphasis on the origin of prophecy fits well with Peter's concern in verse 19 to get his readers to pay closer attention to prophecy. But a reminder that prophecy is not a matter of private interpretation would make a fitting response to the false teachers, who were probably twisting Scripture to suit their own purposes. In the last analysis, however, we think the interpretation reflected in the NIV should be accepted. It suits the immediate context best, affording a natural basis for the command in verse 19. Moreover, the word "interpretation" also points in this direction. The Greek word means, literally, an "untying" or "unraveling," and it was widely used to denote the explanation of mysterious events, visions, and sayings. One Greek version of the Old Testament, for instance, used this word to describe Joseph's interpretations of the baker's and butler's dreams in Genesis 40 and 41.[21] Thus the word is better suited to describe the prophet's own interpretation of the visions and revelations given to them than to characterize the interpretation of the prophets' words by believers in Peter's day.

If verse 20 is about the correct interpretation of prophecy, then Peter presumably intends verse 21 as indirect support: People must not interpret prophecy according to their own whim and fancy because the prophets spoke what the Holy Spirit intended them to speak.[22] But the allusive nature of this connection in itself gives further support to the interpretation of verse 20 that we argued above. On this view, then, Peter in verse 21 reinforces what he has said about the origin of prophecy in verse 20. The prophets' predictions did not arise from their own private ideas about what the visions they received meant; "for," as he now explains further, what the prophets said did not have "its origin in the will of man, but men spoke from God as they were carried along by the Holy Spirit."

The belief that the prophets spoke for God is, of course, basic to the Scriptures. As the Lord said to Jeremiah when he protested that he did not know what to say to the people of Judah, "'I have put my words in your mouth'" (Jer. 1:9). False prophets, on the other hand, were those who "follow their own spirit" (Ezek. 13:3) and "speak visions from their own minds, not from the mouth of the LORD" (Jer. 23:16).

---

21. The Greek version is Aquila; for a summary of the evidence, see J. T. Curran, "The Teaching of 2 Peter I.20," *TS* 4 (1943): 351–52.

22. See, e.g., Bigg, *The Epistles of St. Peter and St. Jude,* 270; Kelly, *The Epistles of Peter and of Jude,* 325.

Peter's reassertion of this standard biblical teaching may have been sparked by the false teachers. At a later date, the Ebionites, radical Jewish Christians, claimed that the prophets spoke "of their own intelligence and not the truth."[23] It may be that the false teachers Peter is fighting held similar views. In any case, Peter insists that the prophets were God's spokesmen, "carried along" by the Holy Spirit. Many commentators find a sailing metaphor in these words; as Green puts it, "The prophets raised their sails . . . and the Holy Spirit filled them and carried them along in the direction He wished."[24] Peter may well intend the allusion, since the verb he uses here can refer to a boat "driven along" by the wind (see Acts 27:15, 17). But the verb is a common one, and it certainly does not usually refer to sailing. More relevant, then, is the fact that Peter has used this same verb in verses 17 and 18 to describe the divine voice that "came" from heaven. The words Peter and the other apostles heard from heaven at the Transfiguration and the words that the prophets spoke came from the same place: God himself.

The prophets, then, speak God's words. But do they also speak their own words? Some theologians have so emphasized God's role in prophetic (and biblical) inspiration that they have viewed the prophets themselves as passive mouthpieces. But note what Peter says here: "*Men* spoke from God." He is not denying that the prophecies were genuinely the words of the prophets themselves, men who consciously chose their words in accordance with their own vocabulary, style, and circumstances. What Peter does affirm, however, is that the words they chose to use were *also* the words that God wanted them to use to communicate the message he intended.

RELEVANT AND APPROPRIATE application of this section must be especially sensitive to the wider biblical context on three matters: the Transfiguration (vv. 16–18), the imagery of "the day" (v. 19), and the inspiration of the Scriptures (vv. 20–21).

The story of Jesus' transfiguration comes at a critical juncture in each of the Synoptic Gospels (Matt. 17:1–8; Mark 9:2–8; Luke 9:28–36). Matthew, Mark, and Luke agree in placing it shortly after Peter's confession of Jesus' exalted status and of Jesus' subsequent announcement that he would be going to Jerusalem to suffer and to be crucified (Matt. 16:13–28; Mark 8:31–9:1; Luke 9:18–27). Indeed, the Evangelists are at pains to make clear that the Transfiguration occurred shortly after these events, providing a rare note of

---

23. The words are from the late fourth-century theologian Epiphanius (*Panarion* 30.1.5).
24. Green, *The Second Epistle General of Peter and the General Epistle of Jude*, 91.

specific chronology: "after six days" (Matt. 17:1; Mark 9:2; Luke has "about eight days after" [9:28]). At the level of the first disciples, therefore, the experience served to bolster their confidence in Jesus. For Jesus' solemn warning about his coming death must have perplexed them. If Jesus was truly the Son of God, the Messiah, would he not be going to Jerusalem to be crowned rather than crucified? Thus the revelation of Jesus' glory, along with the endorsement from heaven itself in the divine voice, served to reassure Peter and the others.

But especially important for Peter's use of the story is the thoroughly eschatological flavor of the narratives. As we noted above, each Evangelist places just before the Transfiguration a prediction from Jesus that some of his disciples would see "the kingdom of God" (Luke 19:27)/"the Son of Man coming in his kingdom" (Matt. 16:28)/"the kingdom of God come with power" (Mark 9:1)—the fulfillment of which comes in the Transfiguration. Other elements in the story point in the same eschatological direction. The presence of Elijah reminds us of the prediction of Malachi (applied in the New Testament to John the Baptist) that God would "send you the prophet Elijah before the great and dreadful day of the LORD comes" (Mal. 4:5). And Moses, while most famous as Israel's lawgiver, also has eschatological significance, based especially on the promise that God would "raise up for you a prophet like me [Moses]" (Deut. 18:15). That this role of Moses is in view is suggested by the heavenly voice, which in its command to "listen to him" echoes Moses' demand that the people listen to this coming prophet like him. Pointing in the same direction are the mention of the cloud, which often has eschatological associations (see, e.g., Ps. 97:2; Isa. 4:5; Ezek. 30:3; Dan. 7:13), and Peter's desire to erect "booths," probably alluding to the Feast of the Tabernacles, or "Booths," a celebration filled with allusions to God's final intervention in history.[25]

These many allusions show how justified Peter was in using the Transfiguration event as evidence for the Parousia. Clearly Peter and the other apostles did not know how the timing would work out; even after his resurrection, Jesus had to warn them that they would not know "the times or dates" when the kingdom would be restored to Israel (Acts 1:6–7). But the apostles could be certain that the Parousia would occur; they had, in effect, already seen it.

A second allusion in this paragraph can also be better appreciated when

---

25. On the significance of the Transfiguration, see especially Walter L. Liefeld, "Theological Motifs in the Transfiguration Narrative," in *New Dimensions in New Testament Study*, ed. Richard N. Longenecker and Merrill C. Tenney (Grand Rapids: Zondervan, 1974), 162–79.

we set it in its larger biblical context: Peter's reference to the dawning of "the day." As noted above, Peter undoubtedly here alludes to the widespread concept of "the day of the Lord." We must explore that concept further. The roots of this concept go back to passages in the Pentateuch that speak of a certain "day" when God would visit his people for judgment or deliverance (see, e.g., Deut. 30:17–18). Several of the prophets use the phrase with this reference, treating it as a concept well-known to the people. This comes out especially clear in Joel, who warns the people who were looking forward with anticipation to "the day" that their sins will make it for them a time of sadness and distress rather than joy (Joel 1:15; 2:1–11). Yet for the remnant, those "who call on the name of the LORD," the day will bring salvation (2:28–32; see also 3:14–16, where the "day" brings judgment on the nations but deliverance for Israel).[26] Most interpreters agree that "the day" in the Old Testament refers both to times of judgment and deliverance within Israel's history (e.g., the Exile) and to a climactic visitation from God at the end of history.[27]

Granted the early church's understanding of Jesus, we should find it as no surprise that the New Testament speaks not only about "the day of the Lord" or "the day of God" but also about "the day of the Lord Jesus," or some such variant.[28] But, as in the Old Testament, this "day" is pictured both as a time of judgment ("the day of wrath" [Rom. 2:5; cf. also 2:16; Eph. 6:13; 1 Thess. 5:4]) and as a time of vindication and deliverance for the saints (e.g., Eph. 4:30; Phil. 1:10; 2:16; 2 Thess. 1:10). But, unlike the Old Testament, the New Testament writers use the phrase consistently to refer to the end of history, to the time when Jesus Christ will return in glory and power.

We cannot fully appreciate Peter's reference to "the day," however, unless we recognize a second level of metaphor—a level that comes out clearly in Romans 13:12–13a, where Paul uses "the day" as both a theological reference and as a metaphor for godly moral conduct: "The night is nearly over; the day is almost here. So let us put aside the deeds of darkness and put on the armor of light. Let us behave decently, as in the daytime. ..." In the ancient world, darkness was the time for evil marauders to come out and was thus to be feared, as well as the time when sins of the flesh were especially common (in the Romans text just quoted, Paul goes on to warn about "orgies and drunkenness ... sexual immorality and debauchery ... dissension and jealousy"). Thus darkness and nighttime became widespread as metaphors for evil, while

---

26. Similar references are found in Isa. 11:11; 13:6, 9; 22:5; 34:8; Jer. 46:10; Ezek. 7:10; 13:5; 30:3; Amos 5:18–20; Obad. 15; Zeph. 1:7, 8, 14–18; Zech. 14:1.

27. On the "day of the Lord" in the Old Testament, see Walter C. Kaiser, Jr., *Toward an Old Testament Theology* (Grand Rapids: Zondervan, 1978), 186–91.

28. In fact, the New Testament uses eighteen different variations of this basic expression.

their contrasts, light and daytime, were applied to purity and upright behavior. In the New Testament, John is especially fond of the "light/darkness" imagery (cf., e.g., John 3:19–21).

Finally, "light" and "day" also can refer to revelation, as God's word, or Christ himself ("the light of the world"), illuminates the darkness of this present evil age.

Peter's main reference here is clearly to the first of these associations, since he speaks about the *coming* of "the day." But we can detect a train of thought in which he brings into his context the two metaphorical associations of the language. The revelatory allusion is seen, of course, in his reference to the "word of the prophets" as a "light shining in a dark place." And, while less clear, the rising of the morning star in the hearts of believers may allude to the completion of God's morally transforming work in the lives of his people.

Central to this paragraph is a debate about the return of Christ in glory—the Parousia. The debate is not just about when the Parousia will take place or what will happen in what sequence when it does, but about whether it will happen at all. On the one side are those who claim that the idea of the Parousia is based on "cleverly invented stories" (cf. 1:16). While Peter does not name the perpetrators of this accusation, they are clearly the false teachers whom he describes in chapter 2. On the other side of the debate are Peter and his fellow apostles, who are sure that Christ will return in glory because they have seen the eschatological glory of Christ with their own eyes (vv. 16–18) and find the Parousia predicted in the authoritative Word of God.

The underlying issue that this paragraph raises, therefore, is the issue of authority. What is our basis for believing that certain things—like the return of Christ in glory—is true? In order to enhance our application of this passage, we propose in this section to use what Peter says in these verses as a jumping-off point to explore the biblical teaching about authority.

We begin with the negative side of the issue: myth. From verse 16 we can infer that the false teachers were accusing Peter and the other apostles of basing their teaching about the Parousia on "cleverly invented stories [myths]."[29] We cannot understand what this accusation really means until we sort out the meaning of the slippery term *myth*. Today we often use this term to denote a story or fact that is not true. Thus, for instance, we might hear a sportscaster say, "The story that the coach plans on retiring is a myth." But we are also familiar with the term as a designation of ancient stories about gods and goddesses; hence, we speak of "Greek mythology." When used in this way,

---

29. It is possible, though less likely, that Peter is accusing the false teachers of basing their own deviant ideas on myths.

myth still carries the assumption that the stories are untrue, but there is an additional idea: The stories contain important information about the religious, cultural, and intellectual beliefs of the Greeks. In other words, while not "true" in the historical sense, these myths tell us a great deal about the Greeks' view of the world. Aristotle, for instance, claims that "the mythical form is chosen to make apprehension possible for the masses, for their religious and ethical instruction."[30] In the nineteenth and twentieth centuries, certain biblical critics extensively utilized this concept of *myth* as a useful way to retain religious significance for the New Testament even as they dismissed as unhistorical most of its narratives.[31]

We must reckon with this widespread use of the term *myth* in Hellenistic philosophy and religion to appreciate the New Testament reaction to it. In contrast to almost all other religions of the time, Christianity had a stubbornly historical basis. The apostles insisted that the truth of what they preached about Jesus, while extending far beyond the historical realm, was nevertheless dependent on actual time and space events. The theological significance of Jesus' resurrection is not a historical datum; but without a real resurrection in "space and time," there can be no theological significance at all—we are "still in [our] sins" (1 Cor. 15:17).

We are not surprised, then, in finding that the Greek word *mythos* has a consistently negative nuance in the New Testament. It occurs only four other times, all in the Pastoral Letters. Paul may possibly be referring there to speculative stories about Old Testament events and people such as we find in the Midrash, labeling them "Jewish myths" (Titus 1:14; cf. also 1 Tim. 1:4, with its reference to "endless genealogies"; also 4:7; 2 Tim. 4:4). But the important point for our purposes is that Paul contrasts these myths with "the truth" (2 Tim. 4:4). In these letters at least, myths convey no positive spiritual significance.

As we suggested above, Peter seems to use *mythos* in a similar way. The false teachers are denying the reality of Christ's return in glory by accusing Peter and the other apostles of basing their teaching on myths. It could be argued, of course, that the false teachers were suggesting that there was a kernel of truth in the story of the Parousia—that, like the religious myths we mentioned earlier, the story, though untrue, had some religious benefit. But Peter says nothing to indicate this; and in calling them "cleverly invented" myths, he suggests a more consistently negative meaning.

Set in contrast to these myths as the authority for Peter's prediction of the

---

30. Aristotle, *Metaph.* 11.8.

31. David Fredrich Strauss was the key figure here; see his *The Life of Jesus Critically Examined* (London: SCM, 1973; the German original was published in 1835–36).

Parousia are eyewitness testimony and the "word of the prophets." The testimony of people who had "been there" is, of course, directly related to the historical basis for the Parousia. Peter, James, and John *saw*—not in a vision or a dream, but at a specific time and place in history—Jesus' Parousia glory. And Peter wants us to believe that Christ will come again in glory because he did see this. He is not alone in claiming authority for eyewitness testimony. Paul, in the famous resurrection chapter (quoted above), insists that the Corinthians accept the truth of resurrection because Peter, "the Twelve," "five hundred of the brothers," James, "all the apostles," and, finally, Paul himself saw the resurrected Christ (1 Cor. 15:3–8). And John also claims he is proclaiming what "we have heard, which we have seen with our own eyes, which we have looked at and our hands have touched" (1 John 1:1).

The second authority Peter claims for his teaching about the Parousia is "the word of the prophets" (v. 19). In order to make sure that his readers appreciate the strength of this authority, he reminds them that this word, or message, is not the prophets' alone—it is also God's. In verses 20–21, Peter develops this point and gives to us one of the more important biblical testimonies about the inspiration of Scripture.

"Inspiration" means "breathed in"; and Christian theologians use this word to describe the quality of Scripture according to which it is the product of God's "breathing" his words into it. Perhaps the classic text is 2 Timothy 3:16: "All Scripture is God-breathed and is useful for teaching, rebuking, correcting and training in righteousness." "Scripture" here is, of course, the Old Testament; but the text establishes that whatever appropriately be considered "Scripture" carries the quality of being "God-breathed."[32] Jesus attests to the same idea, when, in response to Satan's temptation, he cites Deuteronomy 8:3: "'Man does not live on bread alone, but on every word that comes from the mouth of God'" (Matt. 4:4). Likewise, the author of Hebrews begins his letter by noting that "in the past God spoke to our forefathers through the prophets," and he repeatedly attributes the words of the Old Testament to God (e.g., 4:7; 8:8) and the Holy Spirit (e.g., 3:7; 10:15).

In fact, both Old and New Testaments are permeated with the notion that the words of the prophets and the Scriptures are words from God. Thus, Peter's claim that the "word of the prophets" is not the product of their own

---

32. The Greek word here, *theopneustos*, has sometimes been taken in an active sense: Scripture as "breathing" out God's own words. But the passive meaning is to be preferred: Scripture is the product of God having breathed into it. Similarly, some would view the word as an attributive adjective: "All God-breathed Scripture is. . . ." But the predicative function of the adjective, reflected in the NIV translation, is better. On these issues, see, e.g., George W. Knight III, *The Pastoral Epistles: A Commentary on the Greek Text*, NIGTC (Grand Rapids: Eerdmans, 1992), 446–47.

infallible imagination (v. 20) but of God himself and that the prophets were "carried along" by the Holy Spirit as they spoke (v. 21) is nothing new.

But two points in these verses require a closer look. (1) What does Peter include in "the word of the prophets"? Some theologians think that the reference is to the entire Old Testament Scriptures. They note that the Jews could occasionally use the category of "prophecy" to describe the Scriptures as a whole.[33] But in the New Testament at least, "prophecy" does not usually have so broad a meaning. Peter is most likely referring specifically to the prophetic parts of the Old Testament. Some might therefore want to conclude that Peter attributes divine influence only to the prophetic part of the Old Testament. But this goes far beyond the evidence of the text. We think it more likely that, while speaking specifically about the prophets (for this was Peter's need in this context), Peter would apply his ascriptions to the Old Testament as a whole.

(2) A second controversial matter is the way in which God spoke "through" the prophets. In the Hellenistic world of Peter's day, the idea of people "inspired" by a god and speaking his words was widespread. And, often, the human being involved in the process was thought to be almost entirely passive: The god took possession of the person and used his or her organs to communicate the divine message. Some Christian theologians have come close to adopting this model in their explanation of biblical inspiration. Gregory the Great, for instance, compared the authors of Scripture to the "pen of the Spirit";[34] and one can find similar metaphors throughout the history of the church. This view of inspiration is often called the "dictation" theory. But most theologians have recognized the need for a better balance between the human and the divine author in the production of Scripture. As we noted above, "*men* spoke from God." The words of Scripture throughout bear the imprint of the human authors: in style, background imagery, genre, etc. Scripture is, at the same time, the product both of human beings and of God.

This human-divine interplay is called "concurrence." In this process, we believe, God prepared specific human beings, through birth, environment, etc., to communicate his word. These human beings genuinely spoke their own words. But the words they used were also just those words that God wanted them to use. Imbalance on this point is fatal. To deny the human element in Scripture is to ignore the reality of the individual personalities, writing styles, situations, etc., that make up much of the richness of God's

---

33. E.g., Millard J. Erickson, *Christian Theology* (3 vols.; Grand Rapids: Baker, 1983), 2.210; Wayne Grudem, *Systematic Theology: An Introduction to Biblical Doctrine* (Grand Rapids: Zondervan, 1994), 75.

34. See Migne, *Patrologia Latine* 75.517.

Word. But to deny the divine element or to reduce it simply to a vague influence is to deprive the words of Scripture of their truthfulness and, therefore, ultimately, of their authority.

 JOHN STOTT HAS called on Christians to devote themselves to "BBC": basic, balanced Christianity. To be sure, balance can sometimes become an excuse for not thinking hard enough about issues—to come down in the middle because it is easier than really working through the alternatives to discover where the truth lies. But balance, as long as it is the product of careful thinking and not of superficiality, is a valuable commodity in the Christian faith. Heresies usually begin with imbalance. In applying 2 Peter 1:16–21, I would like to look at two issues that demand just such balance.

On the inspiration of Scripture. As we mentioned at the end of our treatment in the previous section on inspiration, the claims of the Bible itself demand that we fully acknowledge both that specific human beings, with all their individual idiosyncracies, wrote the words of Scripture, and that God caused the words he wanted to be written to be written. We noted that some theologians in the course of church history have emphasized the second point at the expense of the first, leading to a "mechanical dictation" theory of inspiration. The human author, on this view, becomes nothing more than the dictaphone that passively has transmitted God's words to others. I have found that this kind of error is still present in the church. Christians who are rightly concerned about the authority of Scripture will often resist the idea, for instance, that commands in Scripture may be intended for only a limited audience.

An example of this is the requirement in 1 Corinthians 11 that a woman wear a "sign of authority" on her head (we will leave aside here the question of whether this refers to a veil or a hairstyle). Some Christians believe this passage requires women always to wear some sort of veil in the public worship service. But most Christians, correctly I think, believe that Paul is giving advice about a form of dress particular to that century and that its application in our time may take a different form.

An even better example might be the differences in word meanings that we find within Scripture. For instance, it is well known that John consistently labels Jesus' miracles as "signs" in his Gospel; recall the famous summary: "Jesus did many other miraculous signs [Greek *semeia*] in the presence of his disciples, which are not recorded in this book. But these are written that you may believe that Jesus is the Christ, the Son of God, and that by believing you might have life in his name." The writers of the first three Gospels, on the other hand, use "sign" in a negative sense: When the Pharisees ask Jesus for a "sign," Jesus responds: "A wicked and adulterous generation looks for a miraculous sign [*semeion*, the same Greek word as in John], but none will be given it except the sign of Jonah" (Matt. 16:4).

Occasionally when I have pointed out this difference in the nuance of the Greek word *semeion* in classes, students find the difference troubling, thinking that such a contrast might detract from the truthfulness of Scripture. But I see this simply as an aspect of the human element of Scripture. God, while ensuring that each of the Evangelists wrote what he wanted them to write, left the writers free to choose their own vocabulary. The contexts in which they used words make it clear enough that John gives a different meaning to *semeion* than do the Synoptic Evangelists. For the former, a *semeion* was a miracle that pointed to Jesus' true significance; for the latter, it was a "command performance," a circus trick that people expected of Jesus in order to be convinced of who he was. But the point is that our doctrine of inspiration should have no difficulty accommodating these kinds of phenomena.

It is obvious, however, that the bigger problem in our day lies in an imbalance in the other direction—giving the human element of Scripture so much attention that the divine element is eliminated or constricted. For many, the Bible is "inspired" in only the loosest sense—as, for example, some might think Wordsworth was "inspired" as he wrote *The Prelude*. But among confessing Christians also we sometimes encounter those who insist that God must have "accommodated" himself to the human writers of Scripture. The result, they suggest, is that we still have errors in the Bible. Writers such as Paul Jewett suggest, for instance, that we need not take as authoritative what Paul says about the ministry of women in 2 Timothy 2:11–15 because Paul was reflecting the male prejudice of his day.[35] Here, I would argue, we have an imbalance in which the divine author of Scripture is given too little place. God, by nature, does not lie; he cannot utter a falsehood. If, then, the words of Scripture are genuinely God's words (cf. our survey of the biblical evidence in the previous section), then the words of Scripture must be without error.

And this debate is no mere academic quibbling, for the authority of Scripture to challenge our beliefs and actions is directly dependent on its full truthfulness. Allow mistakes in the Bible (even in matters of history, dating, geography, etc.), and we have no way of limiting those mistakes. We possess no "red letter" editions of the Scriptures that highlight those sections that are *really* true. If we did, people would inevitably view the truthfulness and author-

---

35. Paul K. Jewett, *Man as Male and Female* (Grand Rapids: Eerdmans, 1975), 112–47.

ity of Scripture through the lenses of their own culture and personal tendencies. Homosexuals seeking to avoid biblical condemnation for their lifestyle will suggest that the biblical authors were simply reflecting the homophobia of the Jewish culture and will dismiss the texts in which we find such condemnations. American Christians, wanting to maintain their luxurious and wasteful lifestyle, will suggest that biblical passages about wealth reflect lower-class prejudices. The list can be extended indefinitely.

We do not deny that the strongest doctrine of Scripture imaginable still leaves us with many questions of interpretation. But we maintain that an appropriate recognition of the Bible as a divine book, bearing necessarily throughout the imprint of God's utter truthfulness, will act as an important defense against explaining away some of the "hard truths" of Scripture.

An apologetic method. A second matter requiring balance implied in this passage is an apologetic method. How are we to establish the truthfulness of the claims of Christianity and convince people to respond appropriately? We can find Christian apologists at two ends of a spectrum. At one end are those who are called "evidentialists": They think that good apologetics will seek to win converts by arguing on the basis of the historical evidence. Examples of this approach (though not necessarily extreme examples) are J. N. D. Anderson, *The Evidence for the Resurrection*, and Frank Morrison's *Who Moved the Stone?*[36] On the other side are those who argue that the non-Christian cannot be argued into the kingdom and that evidences will do little to convince a hardened sinner whose mind is blinded by Satan of the truthfulness of Christianity. Cornelius van Till and his disciples are the most famous exponents of this apologetic approach, which focuses on revelation and the work of the Spirit.[37]

We cannot here describe fully each method, the many variations of each, or their respective merits. But we would note that Peter's appeal to eyewitness testimony in this paragraph suggests the appropriateness of the appeal to evidence. He is, of course, writing to Christians—people already converted. But he certainly has one eye also on the false teachers, and his appeal to the evidence of what he had seen is therefore significant apologetically.

I certainly think that Van Til and others have an important point: Without the work of the Spirit to renew the mind and soften the heart, all the evidence in the world will be useless to bring people to Christ. We must give full credit to Paul's warning that "the man without the Spirit does not accept

---

36. Frank Morrison, *Who Moved the Stone?* (London: Faber, 1930); J. N. D. Anderson, *The Evidence for the Resurrection* (London: InterVarsity, 1950).

37. See, for instance, John Frame, *The Doctrine of the Knowledge of God* (Phillipsburg, N.J.: Presbyterian & Reformed, 1987).

the things that come from the Spirit of God, for they are foolishness to him, and he cannot understand them, because they are spiritually discerned" (1 Cor. 2:14). But neither can we ignore the many passages, like 2 Peter 1, that appeal to the evidence of events in history as a basis both for apologetics to unbelievers and edification of believers. Peter, preaching to a crowd of Jews on the first Pentecost, proclaims: "God has raised this Jesus to life, and we are all witnesses of the fact. Exalted to the right hand of God, he has received from the Father the promised Holy Spirit and has poured out what you now see and hear" (Acts 2:32–33). Evidence without the work of the Spirit, sought through prayer and the Word, will be of no use; but a refusal to appeal to evidence flies in the face of both the historical nature of revelation and the witness of the early Christians themselves.

2 Peter 2:1–3

BUT THERE WERE also false prophets among the people, just as there will be false teachers among you. They will secretly introduce destructive heresies, even denying the sovereign Lord who bought them—bringing swift destruction on themselves. ²Many will follow their shameful ways and will bring the way of truth into disrepute. ³In their greed these teachers will exploit you with stories they have made up. Their condemnation has long been hanging over them, and their destruction has not been sleeping.

WITH THESE VERSES, Peter introduces the subject that will occupy the rest of the letter body: a denunciation of false teachers. Peter hinted at the existence of these false teachers in 1:16, implying that they were accusing him and the other apostles of basing their prediction of the Parousia on "cleverly invented stories." Now he turns full attention to them.

Peter begins simply by introducing them and briefly characterizing them (2:1–3). The key word in these verses is "destruction/destructive": the false teaching itself is destructive (v. 1) and will bring destruction on the false teachers themselves (vv. 1, 3). He develops the theme of condemnation in 2:4–10a, citing biblical examples of judgment to make his case. Then come two paragraphs of further characterization (2:10b–16 and 17–22). Finally, the argument comes full circle as Peter returns to the issue of the Parousia, showing that the false teachers' skepticism is unwarranted (3:1–10) and urging his readers to live in light of the coming day of judgment (3:11–13).

Introduction of the False Teachers (v. 1a)

THE "ALSO" IN verse 1 suggests a close connection between this verse and what has preceded in chapter 1. This connection is to be found in the topic of "prophets." Because God himself speaks reliably through his prophets, we must pay close attention to their words (1:19–21). "But," Peter reminds us, "there were also false prophets among the people." Indeed, the history of God's people in the Old Testament is strewn with examples of people who claimed to be speaking for God but were really advancing their own ideas or programs. As Richard Bauckham has noted, these Old Testament false prophets regularly shared three characteristics: (1) they did not speak with divine authority; (2) their message was one of "good news," promising peace and security in contrast to the warnings about judgment given by true prophets; and (3) they were shown to be worthy of condemnation.[1] Peter applies all three characteristics to the "false teachers" he denounces. And we should especially take note that these false teachers, like the false prophets of old, scorn the idea of a judgment to come (see 3:2–10).

Two points about Peter's initial reference to these false teachers should be noted. (1) Peter refers to them as "false teachers" rather than "false prophets." The latter designation would have seemed more likely, both because Peter has already used that phrase to describe their Old Testament counterparts and because it was widely used in Jewish, New Testament, and early Christian predictions about the future (cf. Matt. 7:15; 24:11, 24; Mark 13:22; Luke 6:36; Acts 13:6). "False teachers," on the other hand, are never explicitly mentioned elsewhere in the New Testament, although Paul does refer, in a passage similar to this one, to "teachers" who "say what [people's] itching ears want to hear" (2 Tim. 4:3; cf. also 1 Tim. 4:1). If the phrase is not simply a stylistic variant of "false prophets," then "false teachers" may have been deliberately chosen by Peter because he knew that these people did not claim prophetic authority.[2]

(2) Peter uses the future tense: "there *will* be false teachers among you." And this is no stray reference or slip of the pen, for Peter continues to describe them with this future tense in verses 1–3: "they *will* secretly introduce destructive heresies"; "many *will* follow their shameful ways and *will* bring the way of truth into disrepute"; "these teachers *will* exploit you." These references should be compared with 3:3: "in the last days scoffers *will* come. . . ." Why the future tenses here? Three explanations have been offered.

(a) The unknown author of 2 Peter, writing after Peter's death, quotes predictions from the apostle Peter about the rise of heresy in the last days, which the author applies to the situation he is addressing. This explanation, of course, assumes that 2 Peter is a pseudonymous letter, a view we have found good reason to reject (see the introduction).

(b) Peter wants to warn his readers about false teaching that has not yet affected his readers but which he knows to be present elsewhere and suspects will be bothering them shortly. But this explanation does not account satisfactorily for the realistic description of the false teachers in verses 10–22 and in 3:4–13, where Peter uses the present (e.g., 2:11, 17, 18) and aorist tenses (3:15) to describe them.

---

1. Bauckham *Jude, 2 Peter,* 238.
2. Ibid.

(c) I prefer, then, to think that Peter is himself "quoting" early Christian prophecies about the rise of false teaching. Jesus himself warned his followers about such false teaching (see esp. Matt. 24:11, 24; Mark 13:22). Since these predictions of Jesus come in the Olivet Discourse, some interpreters think that they have relevance only to the period just before the end of history. But, in fact, the section of the Olivet Discourse from which these predictions are taken is better seen as a description of the entire period between Jesus' first coming and his second. Jesus is warning his disciples not to be surprised at the deviant teaching that will quickly begin to compete with the true teaching of the gospel. Paul sounded similar warnings as he addressed church leaders (e.g., Acts 20:29–31; 2 Tim. 3:1–6). Thus Peter refers his readers to these predictions as a means of indicating to them that the false teaching infecting their communities should be no surprise.[3]

A Profile of the False Teachers (vv. 1b–3)

IN THE REST of this opening paragraph, Peter gives a brief profile of these false teachers. He avoids specifics at this point, painting with broad brush strokes to impress on his readers the seriousness of the threat they pose for the community. He makes eight points, in rapid succession.

(1) They are *devious* in their manner. Realizing that an open resistance to apostolic teaching would be useless, they introduce their false ideas "secretly." Paul used a form of this same word to characterize the Judaizing false teachers who had "infiltrated" the ranks of some believing communities (Gal. 2:4).[4] Since Peter accuses the false teachers of arrogance later in the chapter, he probably does not mean that they are hiding what they are teaching. Rather, he suggests, they are covering up the degree to which their teaching differs from the accepted apostolic teaching.

(2) They are perpetrating a *serious error*: "even denying the sovereign Lord who bought them." "Sovereign Lord" translates *despotes* (from which we get our word "despot"), a term applied to God or Christ only four other times in the New Testament (Luke 2:29; Acts 4:24; Jude 4; Rev. 6:10). It carries a strong sense of commanding authority, and Peter probably uses the title here to underscore the seriousness of the false teachers' denial. As in Jude 4, a somewhat parallel text, the "sovereign Lord" is here probably Christ—an identification suggested also by the qualifier "who bought them." As the New Testament testifies elsewhere, Jesus paid the price of his life at the cross

---

3. Green, *The Second Epistle General of Peter and the General Epistle of Jude*, 93.

4. The Greek verb in 2 Peter is *pareisago*, while Paul uses an adjective (*pareisaktos*). The words do not always connote a secretive "bringing in," but probably do in both these contexts (see BAGD).

that he might buy out, or "redeem," human beings from their slavery to sin (the same verb, *agorazo*, describes this transaction in 1 Cor. 6:20; 7:23; Rev. 5:9; 14:3–4).

But how were these false teachers "denying" the Lord? Was it a theological denial, related to their skepticism about Christ's return in glory? Or was it a practical denial, according to which their licentious lifestyle amounted, in effect, to a denial of the Lord? The parallel in Jude 4 and the reference to their "shameful ways" in verse 2 suggest that the latter was part of the picture. But Peter also emphasizes their teaching in this context. Probably, then, the denial involved both teaching and practices that were incompatible with acknowledging Jesus as Lord.[5]

(3) The *outcome* of their teaching is destruction (a fair paraphrase of the Greek here, rendered "destructive [heresies]" in the NIV). This word here (and in v. 3) refers to eschatological condemnation. As a metaphor for judgment, the word does not carry the literal meaning of "annihilate" or "cease to exist," but, with "salvation" as its opposite (2 Cor. 2:15), denotes the eternal loss of fellowship with God (see also John 12:25; Rom. 14:15; 1 Cor. 1:18; 8:11; 2 Cor. 4:3; 2 Thess. 2:10).

The NIV reinforces the seriousness of the false teachers' doctrine by labeling it "heresies." But this translation may go too far. In the New Testament period, the Greek word Peter uses (*hairesis*; our English "heresy" is taken from it) generally means "party, sect" (Acts 5:17; 15:5; 24:5, 14; 26:5; 28:22), or "faction" (1 Cor. 11:19; Gal 5:20). Only in the late first century A.D. does the word come to have the technical sense "heresy": deviation from orthodox teaching. So while the NIV certainly captures the basic point, a translation such as "destructive opinions" (NRSV) may be more accurate. In any case, Peter's point is clear enough: Those who follow the theology of the false teachers will be led not to final salvation but to condemnation.

(4) The *destiny* of these false teachers is, like those who follow them, "destruction." In saying that this destruction will be "swift," Peter may mean that the eschatological judgment will soon take place. And certainly such an idea of imminence, in the sense of a conviction that the last day *could* come at any time, is widespread in the New Testament. But rather than predicting the time of the judgment, "swift" probably indicates its certainty. Peter makes the same point at the end of verse 3: "Their condemnation has long been hanging over them, and their destruction has not been sleeping." The false teachers may think that they will not have to reckon with God's judgment, since they hold the view that this world will continue indefinitely as it is now (see 3:2–5). But "destruction" for leading others to "destruction" is inevitable.

---

5. See, e.g., Calvin, *Hebrews and 1 & 2 Peter*, 316.

(5) The *popularity* of these false teachers is great. "Many will follow their shameful ways." Sadly, there are always those within the church who are attracted to new and different teaching, especially if, like the ideas peddled by these false teachers, it removes the bounds of moral constraint and accountability to a holy judge.

(6) Their *impact* on the Christian movement is disastrous. For by following this erroneous teaching and lapsing into the kind of licentious behavior that Peter ascribes to the false teachers in 2:10–22, professing Christians bring "the way of truth into disrepute." The New Testament writers borrowed the term *way* from the Old Testament and Jewish world to summarize the Christian way of life—the beliefs and practices that characterized followers of Jesus (see esp. Acts 9:2; 19:9, 23; 24:14, 22). When believers deviate from that way, and especially when they live immoral lives while professing Christ as Lord, they cause the Christian movement to be "blasphemed" (*blasphemeo;* NIV "bring ... into disrepute"). Paul expressed a similar concern about the effect of false teaching (1 Tim. 6:1; Titus 2:5), and Peter himself, in his first letter, urged believers to lead exemplary lives before unbelievers so that their "blasphemies" against the Christian way would be shown to be groundless (1 Peter 4:4).

(7) The false teachers are *motivated by greed* (v. 3). Peter alludes to this motivation later in the chapter as well, comparing the false teachers to Balaam, "who loved the wages of wickedness" (2:15; cf. v. 14: "experts in greed"). The ancient world was filled with wandering teachers who had the reputation of propagating almost any doctrine that would earn them a living. So the false teachers, Peter claims, are "exploiting" the believers, trading in "stories that they have made up."

(8) This phrase brings us to the final characteristic of the false teachers: The *basis* of their teaching is "stories they have made up." Peter probably intends us to see here a contrast with 1:16: It is the false teachers, not the apostles, who build their doctrine on the basis of "cleverly invented stories," that is, on fabrications and forgeries.[6]

 PETER'S DESCRIPTION OF the false teachers in these verses is so general that it might seem we could apply what he says to almost any group of false teachers in the history of the church. However, we need to examine two issues before we can so confidently make such appli-

---

6. Josephus uses the Greek word Peter uses here (*plastos*) to refer to "forgeries" (*Life* 177, 337).

cation: the eschatological setting of the false teaching; and the seriousness of the teaching.

(1) As argued above, Peter uses future tenses to describe the false teachers because he is paraphrasing early Christian predictions about deviant teaching that will arise "in the last days." Perhaps the most important text comes in Jesus' own words in Matthew 24:4–5, 10–11, 23–24:

> Jesus answered, "Watch out that no one deceives you. For many will come in my name, claiming 'I am the Christ,' and will deceive many.... At that time many will turn away from the faith and will betray and hate each other, and many false prophets will appear to deceive many people.... At that time if anyone says to you, 'Look, here is the Christ!' or, 'There he is!' do not believe it. For false Christs and false prophets will appear and perform great signs and miracles to deceive even the elect—if that were possible."

Many interpreters question whether Peter can be quoting this text as relevant to his own day, because they think that in Jesus' Olivet Discourse (where these words occur) he predicts only what will happen at the very end of history, when he returns in glory. Jesus' return in glory is, indeed, the climax of this discourse (see Matt. 24:29–31). But the earlier part is devoted to a description of what will prevail *before* his return (see the transition in v. 29: "immediately after the distress of those days"). At this point, we must remember that, from Jesus' perspective, the time period of this situation is undefined. Not knowing "the day or the hour" of his glorious return (see v. 36), Jesus likewise does not know how much time will elapse before the end. This being the case, we doubt that he is thinking in verses 4–28 of a period of time at the end of history, distinct from the rest of the time between his ascension and the Parousia. Rather, Jesus is predicting the situation that his followers will be facing throughout the "church age."[7]

What we need to do, I think, is to adjust our thinking about eschatology (teaching about the end of time). The New Testament certainly predicts that a short time of special distress will immediately precede the return of Christ (see, e.g., 2 Thess. 2:3–11). But the New Testament writers more typically portray the entire period from Jesus' ascension to his second coming as a time of various kinds and degrees of tribulation. John reminds us that while a climactic Antichrist will come at the end of the world, even now "many antichrists have come" (1 John 2:18). The apostles and early Christians were convinced, in other words, that they were already living in "the last days" (see,

---

7. For a brief, clear defense of this view of the Olivet Discourse, see D. A. Carson, "Matthew," *EBC*, ed. F. Gaebelein (Grand Rapids: Zondervan, 1984), 8:488–95.

e.g., Acts 2:16–21). Eschatology was not just future; it was also a present reality. From this perspective, we see how natural it is for Peter to apply Jesus' predictions to the false teachers disturbing the security of the church in his day. At the same time, we in our day, still living in these last days, should not be surprised at false teaching that continues to crop up on all sides—for Jesus has warned us to expect it.

(2) If we are to apply Peter's strong denunciation of and warning about false teachers, we also need to have some idea about what kind of teaching he has in mind. For Peter would not want his strictures to apply to every case of doctrinal disagreement or moral failure. The New Testament allows diversity among believers on certain issues. The most famous examples are the disputes about eating meat sacrificed to idols in 1 Corinthians 8–10 and about "kosher" food in Romans 14:1–15:13. In each passage, Paul urges that the disagreeing parties learn to live with one another without insisting on a uniform belief or practice.

Balance at this point is essential. It is contrary to the New Testament, on the one hand, to lump every detail of doctrine and practice into the category of Christian essentials. One thinks in this regard of those Christians who insist, for instance, that everyone must read the same version of the Bible or believe exactly the same things about the sequence of events at the end times. On the other hand, it is fatal to allow complete tolerance on every issue that comes along. Christianity would then be evaporated of its essence and consist of little more than a vague reverence for "God." Certain strands of the ecumenical movement err in just this direction. In the interests of Christian unity, they reduce the faith to its lowest possible common denominator.

So how do we achieve the right balance? How do we know when to apply Peter's denunciations? The answer is simple, although not always easy to put into practice: We must determine what the New Testament deems essential. Once we have done that, we must hold tenaciously to what it requires while, at the same time, practice tolerance about what it does not. What makes this principle difficult in practice, of course, is disagreement about what the New Testament plainly requires and what it does not. Some Christians, for instance, are convinced that the Scriptures plainly teach a pretribulation rapture of the church. They will therefore have difficulty extending tolerance to those who hold a different view. Other Christians, however, do not think the biblical data on this matter are at all clear, and they are happy to work with those who hold different views. But regardless of disagreements over what is essential and what is not, we must begin by agreeing to let the Word stand over us in such matters.

And we have one other resource to help us make decisions about what is essential and what is not: the voice of history. Without subscribing to the

Roman Catholic view that elevates church tradition to virtually an equal status of authority with the Word, we may still learn a great deal from the decisions reached by other Christians in other times and places about what is "orthodox" and what is not. Special attention is often given in this regard to the ecumenical councils of the early church—those gatherings of theologians in the first six centuries that were regarded as representative of the Christian church as a whole. Scripture must, of course, stand as the ultimate arbitrator in these matters; but we Protestants, especially, have too often neglected the rich resource of orthodox tradition that is available to us.

Now Peter makes clear that the false teaching he is countering is a serious doctrinal and practical error. These teachers are "denying the Sovereign Lord who bought them," are teaching matters that lead to eternal condemnation, and are themselves bound for that same condemnation. His words, therefore, are appropriately applied only to teaching that clearly runs counter to what the New Testament requires Christians to believe and to do.

 PETER'S WARNINGS ABOUT false teachers are, unfortunately, as appropriate today as they were in his time. Indeed, as we have seen, our Lord has warned us to expect such deviations from the faith. The church will always have to contend with both the outright opposition of those who reject Christ entirely as well as the more subtle threats of those who claim the name of Christian but twist and distort the Christian message. Indeed, precisely because they are more subtle, the latter threat is often the more dangerous one.

We can argue that the danger of false teaching is greater in our day than it has ever been. Why? Because we live in an era that is deeply suspicious of absolute truth. It used to be that people would argue about what religion, philosophy, or system of ethics was "right." English literature classes in college debated about the "correct" interpretation of Charles Dickens's *Our Mutual Friend*. However, college classes today discuss differing perspectives—often mutually contradictory—that one might validly see in Dickens's great novel. The idea of "a correct interpretation" is dismissed at the outset. And when people discuss religion these days, they usually content themselves with a claim such as, "It works for *me*," or, "It's not for everybody, but it's *my* road to spiritual fulfillment."

Our society has embraced pluralism and tolerance as its new gods. Observers of society and its intellectual movements have dubbed this new viewpoint "postmodernism," signaling the shift from the typically modernist pursuit for truth to the current preoccupation with "whatever works for you."

Basic to this new way of approaching reality is an "incredulity towards meta-narratives."[8] "Translated, this means: distrust any voice that purports to tell you that 'that's the way it is.'"[9] We live at a time when everything is tolerated—except intolerance. In such a climate of opinion, Christians often find it both uncomfortable and difficult to take a stand for absolute truth. "What right do you have to impose your morality, or your religion, on me?" people will ask when we take a stand for the faith.

As a result, many Christians have conceded the debate over truth and increasingly rely on a defense of the faith more congenial to our age: that of utilitarianism. "Our witness today is witness to our own faith, and in affirming its validity we may become less interested in its truthfulness that [sic] in the fact that it seems to work."[10] It is not hard to imagine the disastrous consequences of this move for the Christian faith. For the Scriptures claim Jesus Christ is "*the* way" to the Father, not one among many others. Absolute truth is built into the warp and woof of Christianity.

The implications of this "paradigm shift" (as some are calling it) for the topic that Peter addresses in this paragraph are not hard to figure out. As Christians focus more and more on defending their faith on the basis of practicality—going to church has helped my family; my commitment to Christ has given me a better self-image—they will be less and less concerned to know the truth. Feeling replaces thinking. Such a situation provides a golden opportunity for false teachers to enter our ranks and prey on those who simply do not know much about what they believe or why.

The challenge is especially great because, as Peter reminds us, false teachers are often deceptive, mixing enough truth with their error so that well-meaning but uninformed Christians will be taken in by them. I think at this point of some of the more radical "health-and-wealth" gospel advocates on TV and radio. They constantly harp on genuine biblical promises such as, "If you believe, you will receive whatever you ask for in prayer" (Matt. 21:22). They make their message sound very biblical. But they can do so only by selective quotation. The problem is one of balance, but it is not a problem that those who do not know their Bibles well will spot. Most sects and cults operate in just this way.

Perhaps, then, the most significant point of application to emerge from this paragraph in our own day is the assumption Peter makes about the utterly

---

8. F. Lyotard, *The Postmodern Condition: A Report on Knowledge* (Minneapolis: Univ. of Minnesota Press, 1984).

9. Kevin J. Vanhoozer, "Exploring the World; Following the Word: The Credibility of Evangelical Theology in an Incredulous Age," *TrinJ* 16 (1995): 7.

10. David F. Wells, *No Place for Truth, or Whatever Happened to Evangelical Theology?* (Grand Rapids: Eerdmans, 1993), 173.

disastrous consequences of false teaching. The false teachers who have embraced and are propagating these heresies, says Peter, are "bringing swift destruction on themselves" (v. 1); "their condemnation has long been hanging over them, and their destruction has not been sleeping" (v. 3). The heresies themselves, says Peter, are "destructive": Any who buy into them find themselves on the road to eternal condemnation.

The specific false teaching Peter is addressing seems to have had its basis in a doctrinal error—denial of the return of Christ in judgment (see 1:16–21; 3:3–10)—and to have led to serious moral failings (see the "shameful ways" of 2:2, 10–22). But application of Peter's warnings should not be confined to this one particular "heresy." As we suggested in the previous section, it is hermeneutically appropriate to extrapolate from this particular false teaching to other false teachers. Any denial of clearly revealed biblical truth falls under the strictures that Peter gives here. Thus, as much as we may respect the moral seriousness of Mormons, for instance, their denial of the deity of Christ puts their doctrine into the category that Peter discusses here. Examples can be multiplied endlessly; and false teaching, while taking many similar forms throughout history, is always emerging with new nuances and permutations of errors. But it is the broad principle that we must latch hold of here: What we *believe* matters—and matters eternally.

What we are advocating is not a "heresy hunt"—becoming so ultrasensitive to every fine nuance of expression that we read people out of the kingdom on the basis of the most subtle theological differences. Of this kind of unbiblical intolerance we have tragic examples from the past. Yet as much as we may deplore the way some Christians have been too eager to brand those who disagree with them as heretics, we should at least recognize that they have a sense of the importance of truth.

2 Peter 2:4–10a

FOR IF GOD did not spare angels when they sinned, but sent them to hell, putting them into gloomy dungeons to be held for judgment; ⁵if he did not spare the ancient world when he brought the flood on its ungodly people, but protected Noah, a preacher of righteousness, and seven others; ⁶if he condemned the cities of Sodom and Gomorrah by burning them to ashes, and made them an example of what is going to happen to the ungodly; ⁷and if he rescued Lot, a righteous man, who was distressed by the filthy lives of lawless men ⁸(for that righteous man, living among them day after day, was tormented in his righteous soul by the lawless deeds he saw and heard)—⁹if this is so, then the Lord knows how to rescue godly men from trials and to hold the unrighteous for the day of judgment, while continuing their punishment. ¹⁰This is especially true of those who follow the corrupt desire of the sinful nature and despise authority.

Original Meaning

THE IDEA THAT God reserves evil people for judgment is the key idea in this paragraph. Characteristically, Peter mentions the idea both at the beginning ("held for judgment," v. 4) and at the end ("hold . . . for the day of judgment," v. 9) of the section. The concluding words of 2:3 announce this theme: "Their condemnation has long been hanging over them, and their destruction has not been sleeping." Recognizing this relationship, many commentators attach this warning to verses 4–10 and end the first paragraph with verse 3a.[1] In fact, the warning is transitional. It both concludes verses 1–3a and introduces verses 4–10.

The structure of 2:4–10a is simple: Peter writes one long conditional sentence. The protasis (the "if" part of the sentence) is long, extending from verses 4 through 8. The NIV helps the reader of the English text to make sense of it by breaking it up into four parts and repeating the word "if" (the Greek word for "if" appears only in v. 4):

"If God did not spare angels . . . [v. 4]

---

1. E.g., Bauckham, *Jude, 2 Peter*, 245, who notes the shift from the future tenses of vv. 1–3a to the present tenses in v. 3b. See also Neyrey, *2 Peter, Jude*, 196.

if he did not spare the ancient world ... [v. 5]
if he condemned the cities of Sodom and Gomorrah ... [v. 6]
if he rescued Lot ... [vv. 7–8]
then [v. 9a]:
the Lord knows how to rescue godly men ...
and to hold the unrighteous for the day of judgment. ... [vv. 9–10a]"

In the four "if" clauses Peter reminds his readers of events in the Old Testament that he uses to draw his conclusions in the "then" clause in verses 9–10a (and note that Peter mentions the Old Testament events in their canonical order). The first three examples are negative; Peter cites famous instances of God's judgment in order to establish his second conclusion, that God knows how to condemn evil creatures. The fourth example, the reference to Lot in verses 7–8 (as well as the reference to Noah in v. 5b), establishes Peter's first conclusion, that God knows how to rescue the righteous. The parallel section in Jude 6–7 lacks any reference to God's rescue of the godly. Perhaps Peter includes this point because his readers are getting frustrated and discouraged at the need to resist the false teachers. Thus he encourages them by reminding them of God's sovereign protection of the righteous in times of trial and adversity.

Examples of God's Judgment (vv. 4–8)

IN VERSES 4–6, Peter cites three traditional examples of God's judgment to illustrate his claim that God will swiftly (cf. v. 1) and certainly judge the false teachers who are beginning to make their appearance. Two of these examples are well known from the Old Testament: the Flood in Noah's day (v. 5) and the spectacular destruction of the cities of Sodom and Gomorrah (v. 6). But the first illustration, God's judgment of "the angels that sinned," does not immediately bring to mind any particular Old Testament incident. In fact, nowhere does the Old Testament cite an unambiguous reference to God's judgment on angels.

Some interpreters have thought that passages such as Isaiah 14:12–17 and Ezekiel 28:11–19 may refer to a fall of Satan and other disobedient angels from heaven before the creation of the world and that Peter is alluding to this punishment.[2] But a more likely candidate for Peter's reference emerges when we consider Jewish tradition. A number of writers in the intertestamental period developed a story about angels who sinned and were punished by God at the time of the Flood. The story finds its most developed form in the pseudepigraphical book 1 Enoch, but it is alluded to in several other

---

2. E.g., Calvin, Hebrews and 1 and 2 Peter, 348.

writings as well. This tradition was not simply made up from whole cloth; the writers were elaborating on Genesis 6:1–4, a passage that tells about "sons of God" who were attracted to the "daughters of men," married them, and had children with them. In the Jewish tradition we are referring to, the "sons of God" were angels, and their cohabiting with women was a basic reason why God judged the world of Noah's day.

I think it is likely that Peter has this story in mind. (1) An allusion to the Jewish tradition fits the apparently chronological order of Peter's examples in verses 4–7: the fall of the angels (Gen. 6:1–4), the Flood (6:5–8:22), Sodom and Gomorrah (chap. 19). (2) In a passage that has many parallels with this one, Jude explicitly quotes *1 Enoch* (Jude 14–15; cf. v. 6). (3) Peter probably refers to this same tradition in his first letter when he announces that Christ "went and preached to the spirits in prison" (1 Peter 3:19).[3] (4) Peter seems to echo the wording of that tradition in his language describing the angels' punishment. See, for instance, *1 Enoch* 10:4: "Bind Azazel [a disobedient angel] hand and foot and throw him into the darkness." Although not clearly taught in the Old Testament, the story is one that Peter seems to assume is familiar to his readers.[4]

God punished these sinful angels, Peter claims, by "putting them into gloomy dungeons." The NIV rendering quoted here is not the only possible one; the TEV, for example, says that the angels were "kept chained in darkness" (cf. also KJV and NRSV). The difference is a single Greek word: The NIV accepts the word *sirois*, which means "pits" or "caves," while the TEV reads *seirais*, "chains." The latter word is what we find in the parallel passage in Jude, where the author speaks of the angels as "bound with everlasting chains for judgment on the great Day" (v. 6). But this very parallel is what suggests the unlikelihood that Peter wrote the same word. For the scribes who copied the manuscripts of the New Testament tended to assimilate the wording of parallel passages. In this case, then, the word *seirais*, "chains," has possibly been inserted into 2 Peter by a scribe familiar with Jude in place of the rarer word *sirois*.

In any case, Peter probably does not want us to think of the angels as literally confined in dark caves or dungeons. The language is metaphorical; he is using a popular ancient conception of the afterlife to denote God's judgment. Perhaps the metaphor is intended to suggest that God has

---

3. Many scholars doubt that Peter is referring to this tradition here (see esp. Wayne Grudem, *The First Epistle of Peter: An Introduction and Commentary*, TNTC [Grand Rapids: Eerdmans, 1988], 157–62, 203–39). But we think that the case in favor of this interpretation is strong (see, e.g., Kelly, *The Epistles of Peter and of Jude*, 152–57; J. Ramsay Michaels, *1 Peter*, WBC [Waco, Tex.: Word, 1988], 205–11).

4. For further discussion of Peter's use of Jewish traditions in this paragraph, see the "Bridging Contexts" section.

restricted the scope of the (evil) angels' activity as a result of their sin.

The presence of a metaphor here is further suggested by the Greek word that lies behind the NIV's "but sent them *to hell*." This word is *tartareo*, "consign to Tartarus." In Greek mythology, Tartarus was the subterranean abyss to which disobedient gods and rebellious human beings were consigned. The NJB captures the idea rather literally: "sent them down into the underworld." Other Jewish writers had already borrowed the language to describe the place were the ungodly were punished.[5] The translation "hell," while accurate enough in some ways, may be misleading. For Peter makes clear that this consigning of the angels to Tartarus is only a preliminary punishment; they are being "held for judgment." Tartarus in Peter's conception appears not so much to represent a place of final and endless punishment (as our "hell" often does), but the limitation on sphere of influence that God imposed on the angels who fell.

Peter's next warning example comes from the most famous judgment of God found in the Old Testament: the Flood in Noah's day (v. 5). Peter uses similar wording to connect these first two examples: God "did not spare" the angels who sinned, and he "did not spare" the "ancient world" either.[6] Peter quickly reminds us that Noah and his family were an exception to this "[world of] ungodly people"; thus God "protected Noah, a preacher of righteousness, and seven others." The Old Testament makes no mention of Noah's preaching, although intertestamental Jewish tradition does.[7] But the Old Testament gives a sound basis for this tradition because, as Calvin remarks, "[Noah] tried to bring a degenerate world to a sound state of mind, and because he did so not only by teaching and exhortations to holiness but by his constant and anxious toil for a hundred and twenty years in building the ark."[8]

Peter's reference to the "seven others" who were saved with Noah is intriguing. He makes a similar point in his first letter: After speaking about the "spirits in prison who disobeyed" in Noah's day, he adds that "in [the

---

5. "Tartarus" does appear as a name for hell in the Septuagint (Job 40:20; 41:24; Prov. 30:16) and in a few Jewish writings (*1 Enoch* 20:2; *Sibylline Oracles* 4.186; Philo, *Moses* 2.433; *Rewards and Punishments* 152). This is another example of Peter's penchant for using Hellenistic terminology (see the "Bridging Contexts" section of 1:3–11).

6. The phrase "ancient world" may suggest that Peter is thinking here of a universal flood that submerged the entire globe. But in the latter part of the verse, Peter uses the word we translate "world" again (*kosmos*), but this time he qualifies it as "the world of ungodly people" (NIV does not translate this second *kosmos*). As often in the Bible, "world" refers to human beings rather than to the earth itself. Whether the Flood was universal or not is a matter that will have to be decided on the basis of other texts.

7. See, for example, Josephus, *Antiquities* 1.74; *Sibylline Oracles* 1.148–98, esp. 1.129, and others.

8. Calvin, *Hebrews and 1 and 2 Peter*, 379.

ark] only a few people, eight in all, were saved through water" (1 Peter 3:20). The "eight" were Noah, his wife, his three sons, and their wives (see Gen. 6:18; 7:7, 13). In this first letter, the word "only" suggests that Peter's purpose in referring to the number is to encourage Christians who are being persecuted by reminding them that the godly are often in the minority. This may be his purpose here as well. The false teachers may be attracting quite a following, and some of Peter's readers may be discouraged about that. They need to remember that the godly are often few but that God is always faithful to preserve them.

We should not be surprised that Peter moves from the Flood to Sodom and Gomorrah in order to illustrate God's judgment; the pairing of these two famous disasters was well established. Jesus himself used these two events to warn about God's sudden judgment on sensuous people (Luke 17:26–29):

> Just as it was in the days of Noah, so also will it be in the days of the Son of Man. People were eating, drinking, marrying and being given in marriage up to the day Noah entered the ark. Then the flood came and destroyed them all.
>
> It was the same in the days of Lot. People were eating and drinking, buying and selling, planting and building. But the day Lot left Sodom, fire and sulphur rained down from heaven and destroyed them all.

Peter's description of God's judgment on the cities of Sodom and Gomorrah (v. 6) is straightforward enough, although we discern again the influence of tradition. According to the Old Testament, God destroyed these sinful cities by raining down sulfur on them (Gen. 19:24). Peter chooses to focus on what was undoubtedly the result of this sulfurous deluge: The cities were "burned . . . to ashes." The word Peter uses (*tephroo*, "reduce to ashes") was also used by Dio Cassius to depict Pompeii after the eruption of Mount Vesuvius in A.D. 79. More to the point, Jewish writers before Peter had described the destruction of the two wicked cities in the same terms. For example, Philo, the first-century Alexandrian philosopher, says that God "consumed the impious and their cities, and to the present day the memorials to the awful disaster are shewn in Syria, ruins and cinders and brimstone and smoke."[9] And as Philo calls the site of the disaster a "memorial," so Peter also brings out the lasting implications of the terrible destruction; God "made them an example of what is going to happen to the ungodly."

But, like the Flood narrative, the story of Sodom and Gomorrah also has a positive side. God "rescued Lot, a righteous man" from the disaster, just as

---

9. Philo, *Moses* 2.56 (quoted from *Philo*, vol. 6, ed. F. H. Colson, LCL [Cambridge, Mass.: Harvard Univ. Press, 1935], 477).

he rescued Noah and his family (v. 7). Describing Lot as a "righteous man" may seem like a bit of a stretch. The Old Testament portrays him as, at best, weak and compromising. He was rescued almost against his will, the credit going not to his own virtue but to God, who graciously intervened at the request of Abraham (see esp. Gen. 19:29). Again, however, Peter's description of Lot lines up with some Jewish traditions, which also portrayed him as "righteous."[10]

Yet Peter's brief characterization of Lot is not without basis in the Old Testament text. As Peter points out, Genesis 19 suggests that Lot did not participate in the rampant homosexuality that characterized the cities and was, indeed, "distressed" by it. While certainly far from perfect, Lot never lost his basic orientation to the Lord. The word "righteous" that Peter uses need mean no more than this. In the New Testament, this word often refers to a person's status before the Lord rather than to one's innate moral virtue. Moreover, it is important to note that Peter does not say that the Lord rescued Lot *because* he was a righteous man. Similarly, it will be not by virtue of their inherent goodness that God will deliver Christians in Peter's day, or in ours, from the judgment that he will bring on the ungodly. Rather, it will be because of their "knowledge of God and of Jesus our Lord" (2 Peter 1:2) and because they are distressed, as Lot was, at the rampant sin around them.

The importance of this last point is evident from Peter's elaboration of Lot's "distress" in verse 8. The NIV rightly makes this verse a parenthesis (as does also KJV, NRSV, NASB). Lot "was tormented in his righteous soul by the lawless deeds he saw and heard." The NIV correctly links what Lot "saw and heard" with "their lawless deeds." But it obscures the fact that in the Greek, the verb "torment" is in the active voice: Lot "tormented his righteous soul." I want to avoid making more of this than the text warrants. But we recall that Lot ended up in Sodom by his own choice. And Genesis makes clear that Sodom was already a notoriously sinful place when Lot made this choice (see Gen. 13:11–13). Perhaps, then, Peter has used the active voice here to suggest that Lot was himself considerably responsible for the anguish that his "righteous soul" experienced.

The Application of the Examples (vv. 9–10)

WITH VERSE 9, we come to the end of Peter's long conditional sentence. The NIV helps the English reader understand this relationship by adding the phrase "if this is so" at the beginning of the verse. If, in other words, the Old Testament shows again and again how God has intervened to judge sinners

---

10. Greek *dikaios*. See especially Wisdom 10:6; 19:17. In other Jewish traditions, however, Lot is portrayed as a notorious sinner.

and save the righteous, "then the Lord knows how to rescue godly men from trials and to hold the unrighteous for the day of judgment, while continuing their punishment."

Peter's readers are invited to put themselves in the category of "godly men." They need to be reassured that their sacrifices in living by God's rules in an ungodly environment will be rewarded. But what are the "trials" from which they will be rescued? The NIV takes some liberty here, translating a Greek word that is singular (peirasmos) with a plural English word. The Greek word has two distinct meanings. It can mean "temptation," the inner enticement of sin—as in 1 Timothy 6:9 (where Paul warns that "people who want to get rich fall into temptation")—or it can mean "trial" or external affliction—as in 1 Peter 4:12 ("Dear friends, do not be surprised at the painful trial you are suffering").

If the word means "temptation" here, then Peter is probably promising rescue from temptation to sin, such as Lot experienced in Sodom (see NASB).[11] But Peter's two other uses of peirasmos both mean "trial" (1 Peter 1:6; 4:12), and this is the more common meaning in the New Testament. Some commentators who adopt this meaning think that Peter is referring to the great trial of faith that will occur at the end of history.[12] There is much to support this idea; as Bauckham notes, "Since the Flood and the judgment of Sodom and Gomorrah are prototypes of eschatological judgment, the situations of Noah and Lot are typical of the situation of Christians in the final evil days before the Parousia."[13] But while Christians are no doubt in the last days, I think Peter would at least have allowed those days to go on for some time. Thus I think he includes in the "trial" here all those challenges to faith that Christians experience in this world.

In the second part of the verse, Peter draws his negative moral from the Old Testament examples he cites in verses 4–8: "The Lord knows how ... to hold the unrighteous for the day of judgment, while continuing their punishment." Along with most contemporary English versions, the NIV finds Peter here promising not only a future judgment for the unrighteous but also a punishment that is already underway. This is not the only way to take the Greek here, however, and the KJV, for instance, speaks only of future judgment: "The Lord knoweth how ... to reserve the unjust unto the day of judgment to be punished."[14]

---

11. Bigg, The Epistles of St. Peter and St. Jude, 277; Kelly, The Epistles of Peter and of Jude, 335.

12. See, e.g., Green, The Second Epistle General of Peter and the General Epistle of Jude, 102; Bauckham, Jude, 2 Peter, 253.

13. Bauckham, Jude, 2 Peter, 253.

14. The ambiguity in the Greek lies in the participle kolazomenous, "being punished," which modifies terein, "to keep." The NIV understands the participle to be denoting action

Many commentators think this latter option is correct.[15] But two points favor the interpretation assumed by the NIV. The Greek word "being punished" is in the present tense, most naturally suggesting that the punishment is taking place at the same time as the keeping. Furthermore, the combination of present, preliminary punishment and future, final judgment is found also in verse 4, where Peter says that disobedient angels have been put into gloomy dungeons "to be held for judgment."[16] If this is what Peter means, how is that punishment of sinners now being carried out? I will tackle this issue in the "Contemporary Significance" section.

The NIV again follows most English versions by splitting verse 10 into two sentences, putting the first one with verses 4–9 and the second with verses 11ff. This is a good decision. The first part of verse 10 is tied grammatically to verse 9, as Peter gives an example of those "unrighteous" who will be judged. But verse 10b, which is not tied grammatically to the first part, shifts the focus to a more extended description of these unrighteous people.

In verse 10a, then, Peter brings us back to the beginning of the chapter. In verses 1–3, he warned about false teachers; in verses 4–9, he cited Old Testament examples to support his claim that they would be condemned; now he suggests that prominent among these false teachers destined for condemnation are the very people who are disturbing his readers' churches. Peter contents himself with two general characteristics of these unrighteous false teachers: They "follow the corrupt desire of the sinful nature," and they "despise authority."

The NIV rendering of this first description is too mild. Peter piles up some very strong words; a literal rendering is "going after flesh in a passionate longing for defilement."[17] The reference is to sexual sin, probably including, in light of Peter's reference to Sodom and Gomorrah in verse 6, homosexuality.[18]

The second general characteristic of these false teachers is more difficult to understand. Specifically, what kind of "authority" were these teachers despising? We outline four options. (1) In the second part of verse 10, Peter claims that they "slander celestial beings." This translation (NIV) is an interpretation of another difficult Greek word, but it is probably correct. The

---

taking place at the same time as the verb it modifies: "keep while punishing." The KJV, however, assumes that the participle has a future reference: "keep to be punished."

15. E.g., Bauckham, *Jude, 2 Peter*, 254; Green, *The Second Epistle General of Peter and the General Epistle of Jude*, 103.

16. For this interpretation, see also Kelly, *The Epistles of Peter and of Jude*, 324.

17. The NIV often translates the Greek word *sarx*, "flesh," with "sinful nature." This may be a somewhat helpful paraphrase in some places. But here the rendering misses the specific sexual associations that the word "flesh" would better convey in English.

18. Green, *The Second Epistle General of Peter and the General Epistle of Jude*, 103.

singular "authority" in verse 10a may then be an unusual way to refer to angelic beings.[19] (2) Peter may be referring to the "authority" of the church, which the false teachers were refusing to heed as they pursued their own heretical ideas.[20] Yet there is little in the context to support the identification. (3) The most important "authority" for Christians is, of course, the Lord. And many interpreters think that it is this authority that the false teachers are despising.[21] (4) This third option may be correct, but I prefer a more general reference. In both this verse and in the similar Jude 8, we find the accusation that the false teachers are despising "authority" followed immediately by the charge that they "slander celestial beings [angels]." It makes good sense, then, to see this second accusation as a specific example of the former. "Despising authority," in other words, is a general charge to the effect that the false teachers are self-willed and rebellious. Peter is not thinking of any specific authority; he is thinking of the principle of authority.

THE MAIN IDEA in these verses comes across clearly: God judges those who obstinately disregard his commands while he protects those who stay faithful to him. But some of the details Peter uses to communicate this point are not so clear. One issue in particular can create difficulty for the interpreter: the influence of Jewish traditions on Peter's use of the Old Testament. This issue raises a larger hermeneutical question: How, and to what degree, do books that are not in the Bible influence what the New Testament authors believed and wrote? In the following paragraphs, I want briefly to investigate this matter so that we can better understand the details of this passage.

The use of the Old Testament in the New Testament is one of the perennial issues in biblical theology and interpretation. In the past, scholars gave a great deal of attention to the quotations of the Old Testament in the New. More recently, interest has turned to the many places where the New Testament takes up Old Testament themes and passages without directly citing a text. The New Testament writers were so thoroughly versed in the Old Testament that the words and themes from the Scriptures are woven into the very

---

19. The word Peter uses (*kyriotes*) may support this view. It is rare, occurring only four times in the New Testament: here, in Jude 8 (which is closely parallel), and twice in Paul, where it refers to angelic beings (Eph. 1:21; Col. 1:16). See Mayor, *The Epistle of St. Jude and the Second Epistle of St. Peter*, 127.

20. Green, *The Second Epistle General of Peter and the General Epistle of Jude*, 103–4.

21. See TEV, "those . . . who despise God's authority"; NJB, "those . . . who have no respect for the Lord's authority." For commentators, see, e.g., Bigg, *The Epistles of St. Peter and St. Jude*, 279; Kelly, *The Epistles of Peter and of Jude*, 336; Bauckham, *Jude, 2 Peter*, 255.

fabric of what they wrote. Scholars therefore speak of "echoes" of Scripture in the New Testament, in which writers convey certain nuances of meaning by implicitly referring the reader to an Old Testament passage or theme. *Intertextuality* is another term being applied to this phenomenon. It recognizes in perhaps a deeper way than ever before that the Bible is really one book, whose parts can be rightly understood only in light of the whole.[22]

Complicating this intertextual situation, however, are the layers of tradition that stand between the original Old Testament text and the New Testament author. New Testament writers like Peter were, of course, versed in the Scriptures from an early age. They had heard it read, interpreted, and applied in the synagogue and elsewhere from childhood on. And during that time, they had absorbed many particular ways of reading the Old Testament. Their reading was, of course, decisively transformed by their commitment to Jesus as the fulfillment of the Old Testament. But the new perspective that faith in Christ brought, while transforming their reading of the Scriptures, did not erase every interpretation they inherited from their Jewish background. Many of these traditions play a role in the New Testament interpretation of the Old Testament.

Second Peter 2:4–10a offers a good case in point. In my comments above, I noted at least four places where Peter was apparently influenced in his use of the Old Testament by Jewish traditions:

(1) God's judgment of the "angels who sinned" (v. 4) probably refers to the Jewish elaboration of Genesis 6:1–4.
(2) Noah's "preaching" (v. 5), not mentioned in the Old Testament, is recounted in several Jewish books.
(3) The language Peter used to describe the destruction of Sodom and Gomorrah ("reduced to ashes" in v. 6) is closer to Philo and some other Jewish writers than to the Old Testament.
(4) Peter's claim that Lot was "righteous" (v. 7) duplicates the description of Lot found in at least one intertestamental Jewish book (Wisdom of Solomon).

I am not suggesting that Peter specifically knew and quoted each of these books or writers—although he could certainly have been aware of most of them. It is rather a case of Peter's referring to popular teaching that he was familiar with and which is attested by these books. We know that the Jews elaborated Old Testament passages and stories as they handed them down and as preachers and teachers sought to apply them. Some of these elaborations

---

22. A brief, though seminal, introduction to this approach can be found in Richard B. Hays, *Echoes of Scripture in the Letters of Paul* (New Haven: Yale University Press, 1989), 14–33.

became widespread and were perhaps regularly associated with the Old Testament passages on which they were based. These traditions surface in the intertestamental books mentioned above, and Peter presumably became acquainted with them during his years in the synagogue.

The last three allusions to Jewish tradition are uncontroversial. In each case, the Jewish tradition simply brings out more explicitly a point that is already present or hinted at in the Old Testament stories. But the first allusion is controversial indeed, for here we find Peter referring to a Jewish tradition about angels that is based on what many contemporary evangelical scholars think is a misinterpretation of Genesis 6:1–4. Before I examine this issue, let me expand on the tradition and its basis.

Genesis 6:1–4 reads:

> When men began to increase in number on the earth and daughters were born to them, the sons of God saw that the daughters of men were beautiful, and they married any of them they chose. Then the LORD said, "My Spirit will not contend with man forever, for he is mortal; his days will be a hundred and twenty years."
>
> The Nephilim were on the earth in those days—and also afterward—when the sons of God went to the daughters of men and had children by them. They were the heroes of old, men of renown.

Critical is the identification of "the sons of God." Most Jews during the intertestamental period thought that these "sons of God" were angels. This tradition of interpretation is found in many places but appears most clearly and most often in the apocalyptic book *1 Enoch*. In 6:1–2 of this book, we read:

> In those days, when the children of man had multiplied, it happened that there were born unto them handsome and beautiful daughters. And the angels, the children of heaven, saw them and desired them; and they said to one another, "Come, let us choose wives for ourselves from among the daughters of man and beget us children."

The author of *1 Enoch* goes on to describe how these angels did, in fact, cohabit with "the daughters of men" (7:1). From their union came the giants (cf. the "Nephilim" in Gen. 6:4). Furthermore, the angels brought with them sinful practices that they taught their wives and offspring (7:2–6). Prominent among these practices was the art of magic. *First Enoch* traces the sinfulness of the world to these fallen angels, whom the author often calls "watchers." They, their sin, and their judgment are referred to many times in the rest of the book.[23]

---

23. See 9:6–9; 10:7–15; 12:4–6; 13:1–2; 14:4–7; 15:3–7; 16:3; 19:1; 54:7–55:2; 64:1–69:25. Other intertestamental writings that refer to this tradition are: *Jubilees* 5:1; 10:1–6;

The popularity of this tradition would make it a natural choice for Peter to illustrate God's judgment in the past. And, as we pointed out in the introduction, Peter's readers, while probably Gentiles, were also well acquainted with the Old Testament. Peter's use of this tradition, however, creates a problem for those of us committed to the complete accuracy of the Bible. For if this is what he is doing, he seems to be endorsing a Jewish interpretation of Genesis 6:1–4 that many think is not correct. He, in effect, is citing an example of God's judgment that never took place. And this obviously calls into question the truthfulness of what he wrote.

We have, I think, three possible solutions to this problem. (1) As I have noted in the "Original Meaning" section, Peter may not be referring to this Jewish tradition at all. While the Old Testament does not clearly describe a "fall" of angels, many scholars think that at least two passages might refer to the fall of the chief of the evil angels, Satan: Isaiah's denunciation of the "morning star" in Isaiah 14:12–20 and Ezekiel's prophecy against the King of Tyre in Ezekiel 28:1–19. But it is perhaps more likely that these texts use hyperbole to describe the arrogance and downfall of historical human rulers active at the prophets' time. The much clearer history of the fall of the angels that many of us have in our heads comes not from the Bible but from the great epic poem of John Milton, *Paradise Lost*, in which he develops the theme at great length.

But even if the fall of angels is not clearly narrated in the Old Testament, something like it is clearly assumed. And Revelation 12:7–9 portrays, in visionary form, the casting out of "Satan and his angels" from heaven after a war with Michael and the good angels. Peter may, then, be referring to this "prehistoric" fall of the angels. We need to keep this as an open possibility, since Peter does not explicitly connect his reference to "angels who sinned" to Genesis 6 or to the time of Noah. But I have also given several reasons why I think Peter probably does have the Genesis 6 tradition in mind.

(2) Peter may be referring to the tradition of the angels of Genesis 6 without intending us to conclude that it is an actual, historical occurrence. In effect, he may be doing what many modern preachers do when illustrating their sermons—refer to a popular, well-known story that is not true but which can be used to make a point. I don't think we should dismiss this possible solution, though it does have some problems. The most serious is the clearly historical incidents that Peter uses as his other illustrations. The Flood

---

Josephus, *Antiquities* 1.73; Philo, *On the Giants* 6; *Questions on Genesis* 1.92; see also the *Damascus Document* (CD) 2:18. The quotation from *1 Enoch* comes from James H. Charlesworth, ed., *The Old Testament Pseudepigrapha*, Vol. 1: *Apocalyptic Literature and Testaments* (Garden City, N.Y.: Doubleday, 1983), 15.

in Noah's day (v. 5) and the destruction of Sodom and Gomorrah (v. 6) really happened. It would take a supersensitive reader to guess that the first illustration of God's judgment in the series did not actually take place. Recall, moreover, that Peter is trying to convince his readers of the reality of God's judgment in the face of false teachers who are treating such matters as "myths" or "stories" (see 1:16). For Peter to refer in this context to a tradition of God's judgment that could very well itself be labeled as a "myth" would be a dubious strategy. Still, this possibility remains as one seriously to consider.

(3) The third solution is to assume that the prevalent Jewish interpretation of Genesis 6:1–4 in Peter's day is, in fact, correct: The "sons of God" were angels. Contemporary interpreters of Genesis take three different views of the "sons of God" in Genesis 6:1: that they refer to human beings[24] or human princes, to divine beings, or to angels. The first of these views is, in fact, becoming less popular, as it is recognized that the Hebrew phrase *bene elohim* likely does not refer to human beings here. The second view is popular among interpreters who think that Genesis depends on a widespread ancient myth about the cohabiting of gods and human women.[25] But the third also finds a number of supporters, who cite texts like Job 1:6 and 2:1, where the "sons of God" are clearly angels.[26]

It is admittedly difficult to conceive of angels and human beings having sexual relationships; and this has always been the chief objection to the view that the "sons of God" are angels. Jesus himself seems to suggest that the angels do not engage in sexual relationships (see Matt. 22:30 and parallels). Moreover, Genesis 6:5–8 says nothing about the sin of angels, but it says a great deal about the sin of human beings. Interpreters suggest several ways of getting around these difficulties, but we need not pursue this matter here. What is important is to recognize that, properly nuanced, we need not think it impossible that Genesis 6:1–4 refers to fallen angels who had sexual relations with women.

What may we conclude, then, about Peter's use of Genesis 6? Perhaps this is a case in which we need to give intertextuality full reign. Peter's reference to "angels who sinned," especially in light of 1 Peter 3:19–20, probably depends on a certain reading of Genesis 6. Since we believe that the Bible ultimately speaks with one voice, perhaps we should accept Peter's interpretation as the true interpretation of the enigmatic "sons of God" text.

---

24. See, e.g., C. F. Keil and F. Delitzsch, *Commentary on the Old Testament: The Pentateuch* (3 vols. in one; reprint; Grand Rapids: Eerdmans, n.d.), 127–34.

25. See, e.g., Claus Westermann, *Genesis I-II: A Commentary* (Minneapolis: Augsburg, 1984), 371–72.

26. See G. J. Wenham, "Genesis," in *The New Bible Commentary: 21st Century Edition*, ed. D. A. Carson, R. T. France, J. A. Motyer, and G. J. Wenham (Downers Grove, Ill.: InterVarsity, 1994), 65. Wenham goes on to suggest that the text may refer to sacred prostitution.

Whatever our conclusions on this matter, the text certainly shows how important it is that we interpret Scripture in the light of Scripture, and that we be aware of Jewish traditions that may have played a role in a New Testament author's use of the Old Testament. Everyone should agree with the former principle, as long as we are talking about the interpretation of the New Testament in light of the Old. Christians have always seen the importance of reading the Old Testament in the light of Christ. But what I am suggesting in the argument above is a little more radical: "exegeting" an Old Testament passage according to the New Testament interpretation.

As evangelical Christians, we believe that God preserved Peter from introducing errors into this reading of the Old Testament through the influence of these traditions. But the ancient Jewish interpretation of Scripture may well preserve accurate interpretations that we can still learn much from. The enigmatic Genesis 6:1–4 story may be one such example of this process.

FINDING CONTEMPORARY SIGNIFICANCE in 2 Peter 2:4–10a is not difficult. For the situation addressed is all too similar to the position of the church in the world today. In 2:1 Peter reminded us that "there will be false teachers among you." And his prediction is certainly applicable to the late twentieth century. Everywhere we look, we find people advocating ideas that the Bible clearly condemns, yet claiming that they are the true way to find God, or "meaning in life," or spiritual fulfillment. And these religious teachers are often successful, attracting large followings, making a good living for themselves, and garnering lots of publicity. It is this apparent injustice that Peter is concerned about in this passage. How is it that God stands silent as such false teachers twist his truth and lead his people astray?

Peter's answer is simple: God is not standing silent. Using the examples of the angels who sinned, the world of Noah's day, and the cities of Sodom and Gomorrah, Peter argues that God is both judging sinners now and will finally condemn them in the future. Note how he mentions the two stages of this judgment at both the beginning of the paragraph (v. 4) and at its end (v. 9):

God did not spare angels when they sinned, but sent them to hell, *putting them into gloomy dungeons to be held for judgment.*

The Lord knows how ... *to hold the unrighteous for the day of judgment, while continuing their punishment.*

The Bible everywhere teaches about a great day of judgment to come, when the righteous will receive their eternal reward and the unrighteous will suffer eternal condemnation. The idea of judgment in this life is not so common, but appears often enough. We think, for instance, of Romans 1:18–32. Here Paul three times claims that God "gave over" sinful human beings to the consequences of the sin that they had chosen (vv. 24, 26, 28). Having turned from the true God to worship idols of their own making, these people were "handed over" to sexual impurity, unnatural passions, and a depraved way of thinking. Having stubbornly chosen their own way in opposition to God, God allows them to continue on the road they chose—all the way to its disastrous end. As the German poet Schilling put it, "The history of the world is the judgment of the world."

Peter may have these same ideas in mind as he mentions the present punishment that the unrighteous are experiencing. The very sin these people commit, with all its terrible consequences for the health of mind and body, is a form of punishment. Thus Peter encourages us, as we contemplate the ungodly of our day, to look beyond their superficial happiness and success to the inner anxiety, despair, and frustration that lurks just below the surface.

But Peter's main point is not the means of punishment but its certainty. He wants to assure believers that those who scorn God and teach what is contrary to his truth will not get off scot-free. As Green puts it, "False teaching and false behaviour ultimately always produce suffering and disaster, be it in Lot's day, in Peter's, or in our own."[27] Behind Peter's words is his conviction, shared with all the biblical authors, that God is both righteous and sovereign. Because he is righteous, he cannot let sin go unpunished. And because he is sovereign, he will execute that punishment some day. Indeed, philosophers such as Kant have posited the need for some kind of god precisely in order to ensure ultimate justice in what seems so often to be an unjust world.

There is in all of us that longing for "the right to prevail"; witness the number of books and movies that command huge audiences by portraying the ultimate victory of good over evil. When Luke Skywalker and the rest of the "freedom fighters" finally conquer the evil empire in the last of the *Star Wars* movies, we have a sense of satisfaction and of justice that God himself has planted within us. The psalmist tells us of just this kind of an experience. Asaph begins Psalm 73 by bemoaning the apparent happiness and success of the wicked (vv. 1–12). His reaction is one that many of us can identify with: "Surely in vain have I kept my heart pure" (v. 13a). But then, Asaph tells us, he "entered the sanctuary of God"—he put himself in a place where he could take God's perspective on things (v. 17). And thus he was led to "understand their final destiny": disaster and destruction (vv. 18–28). And lest we think that this is a pre-Christian perspective, listen to what Paul in 2 Thes-

---

27. Green, *The Second Epistle General of Peter and the General Epistle of Jude*, 100.

salonians 1:6, 8–10 tells the Christians in Thessalonica, who are suffering a severe persecution:

> God is just: He will pay back trouble to those who trouble you. . . . He will punish those who do not know God and do not obey the gospel of our Lord Jesus. They will be punished with everlasting destruction and shut out from the presence of the Lord and from the majesty of his power on the day when he comes to be glorified in his holy people and to be marveled at among all those who have believed.

Now some of us may wonder how all this emphasis on judgment fits with other biblical teaching. After all, as Christians, we must guard against a sinful desire for retribution that our Lord warns us about. We are to "love our enemies and pray for those who persecute us" (Matt. 5:44). But we can love so unreservedly precisely because we know that "it is [God's] to avenge; [he] will repay" (Rom. 12:19). God has told us not to worry about seeking vengeance, about righting every wrong—he will take care of that. Love for the unrighteous and satisfaction in God's judgment of the unrighteous go hand in hand in Scripture. Peter's reminder of God's judgment of the ungodly should therefore give us satisfaction in the ultimate rightness of this world at the same time as it provides the foundation for a sacrificial love of sinners.

Satisfaction with God's holy and impartial judgment is, however, only one side of the picture. As Peter reminds us in this paragraph, God not only condemns the ungodly; he also delivers the godly. The Flood destroyed the world, but God rescued Noah and his family. God destroyed Sodom and Gomorrah, but he rescued Lot. So God will always deliver his people from their trials. Not, of course, that he will prevent his people from experiencing trials. The New Testament is realistic about the difficulties and afflictions of all kinds that believers can expect to face in this life (see, e.g., Rom. 5:3–4; James 1:2–4; 1 Peter 1:6; 4:12). The promise Peter makes is rather that God will never allow his people to be overwhelmed by the trial; as Paul promises in 1 Corinthians 10:13:

> No temptation [or trial] has seized you except what is common to man. And God is faithful; he will not let you be tempted [or tested] beyond what you can bear. But when you are tempted [or tested], he will also provide a way out so that you can stand up under it.

This may also be what Jesus teaches us to pray for: "Lead us not into temptation [or trial]" (Matt. 6:13). God brings trials of various kinds; and, like Noah's family and Lot, these trials may come as the result of God's own judgment on the ungodly. God does not promise that his people will be unaffected by such trials, but he does promise that he will deliver them "out of" the trial.[28] In other words, God promises to provide all that is necessary to see that Christians emerge from trials with their faith intact and their salvation untouched. Will trials bring Christians physical harm? Yes. Emotional stress? Certainly. Economic deprivation? Often. Physical death itself? Possibly. The New Testament furnishes plenty of examples of all of these. But God, in his sovereign wisdom and goodness, always gives his people "a way out" of these trials: the means to endure and to emerge spiritually strong.

We live at a time when many Christians are succumbing to the siren voice of the "health and wealth gospel." Christians are promised health and wealth, these preachers proclaim.[29] All you have to do is "claim it in faith and it's all yours!" This "gospel" is certainly a "different gospel" (cf. Gal. 1:6–9). Seizing on certain verses, usually out of context, it ignores the plain teaching of Scripture, that "we must go through many hardships to enter the kingdom of God" (Acts 14:22).

This is not the place to detail all the problems with this movement. But I bring it up because most of us have probably absorbed some of its emphases into the way we look at suffering. We think of difficulties as the exception rather than the norm. As a result, trials can bring a crisis of faith in which we question God's plan, his love for us, or even his existence. Peter's matter-of-fact way of mentioning the trials of Old Testament saints as well as of his own readers should help us shift our perspective and view trials as an expected part of life. And it is then that the marvelous promise of these verses can come home to us: God will rescue us from them. Nothing, Peter says in his first letter, can do us any ultimate harm (1 Peter 3:13). God assures us that he controls whatever comes into our lives. He measures the trials we experience, being careful not to allow them to overwhelm us and make it impossible to maintain our godliness.

A subsidiary point to this issue, but one worth making in light of Peter's emphasis on God's ability to rescue the godly, is the present confinement of the demons. The "angels who sinned," Peter reminds us, have been "sent to hell" and are now confined in "gloomy dungeons" (2 Peter 2:4). Clearly Peter's language is metaphorical; we are not to imagine fallen angels in a physical prison somewhere. But the language does make clear that these angels who fell—the demons—are confined by God in their sphere of activity.

---

28. The Greek preposition Peter uses in v. 9 is *ek*, which often has the meaning "out from the midst of."

29. See, e.g., Kenneth Copeland, *The Laws of Prosperity* (Fort Worth: Kenneth Copeland Publications, 1974); idem, *Prosperity: The Choice Is Yours* (Fort Worth: Kenneth Copeland Publications, 1992); Kenneth E. Hagin, *Obedience in Finances* (Tulsa: RHEMA Bible Church, 1983).

Other biblical passages confirm the same point—most picturesquely Job 1–2, where Satan must ask God's permission to inflict harm on Job. Knowledge that demons are restricted by God in their activities should be great comfort to Christians. This point requires renewed emphasis in our day, for popular Christian authors, most notably Frank Peretti, have drawn our attention to the influence of demons in our world. Surely we need to be awake to the spiritual conflict in which we are engaged. Too many Christians, because they do not understand the spiritual battle we are waging, are woefully unprepared to fight it. But imbalance is always perilously near when we speak of this subject. As J. I. Packer has said,

> When we study demonology, we walk on a knife-edge; at our feet all the time are two yawning chasms of error, into which we can all too easily topple. On the one hand, we can take Satan too seriously, as some in the early church and the Middle Ages did. This will cause us to fall out of the peace of God into morbid fears and fancies . . . and we shall take up a negative view of the Christian life as primarily a course of devil-dodging exercises and anti-Satanic manoeuvres. . . . On the other hand, we can err by not taking the devil seriously enough. . . . Unwillingness to take the devil seriously has two bad effects: it fools men, by keeping them from the knowledge of their danger as objects of the devil's attacks, and it dishonours Christ by robbing the cross of its significance as a conquest of Satan and his hosts (cf. Col. 2:15).[30]

Some Christians in our day are making this first mistake; they live in unnecessary fear of the influence of demons on their lives, homes, and families. Yes, demons exist, they are present, and they are powerful. But, as Peter reminds us, they have been judged and "put on a chain" by God himself. As Christians indwelt by God's Spirit, we need never fear them.

Another point in these verses has a striking application to our own context. Peter goes out of his way to emphasize the strength of Lot's reaction to sin: He was *"distressed* by the filthy lives of lawless men" (v. 7) and *"tormented* in his righteous soul by the lawless deeds he saw and heard" (v. 8). I wonder how many Christians are similarly "distressed" and "tormented" by sin. Perhaps, in seeking to excuse ourselves, we might respond that Lot was faced with a lot more sin than we. But I am not sure that the differences are all that great. The Bible makes clear that the most serious sin of Sodom and Gomorrah was homosexuality.

---

30. J. I. Packer, *God's Words: Studies of Key Bible Themes* (Downers Grove: InterVarsity, 1981), 85–86.

I hardly need point out that homosexuality has, in the space of a few short years, become an accepted lifestyle in the United States. In my morning newspaper on the day I write these words, for instance, I find an article entitled "Oregon Anti-Gay Votes Delayed Until 1998."[31] The impression given is that some bigoted people in Oregon are trying to legalize their hate. But as I read the article, I discover that the initiative these Oregonians are proposing would "define the family concept as 'limited to one man and one woman in a marriage covenant.'" That doesn't sound all that radical! Yet it speaks volumes that citizens in our day have to pass referenda to make legal what almost everyone in America assumed to be proper just a couple of decades ago. The evidence that we live, indeed, in a "post-Christian" age accumulates rapidly.

And what is the reaction of Christians to the increasing abandonment of Christian moral norms? Many, to be sure, and to their credit, are responding vigorously, with a loving but firm restatement of the biblical perspective on sexuality. But many of us, I fear, are simply accepting what is happening without any undue fuss or concern. We are not "distressed" or "tormented" by what we see around us. Oh, we may be disturbed by these developments and deplore those who choose an unbiblical lifestyle. But few Christians experience the "torment of soul" that Lot felt as he faced the ungodliness of his society.

Television illustrates the problem better than anything else. I do not need to tell you that a great deal more sex, foul language, and gratuitous violence are found on network TV than was the case a decade ago—not to mention cable TV! Many of us have continued to watch the programs as the sex and vulgarity have gradually increased. The result? Many of us now watch things on TV without flinching that would have greatly distressed us only a few years ago. We are no longer shocked at it; we have become insensitive to it.

This muted reaction to ever more rampant sin is fraught with danger not only for society but for the church. As Cardinal Newman, the nineteenth-century Roman Catholic theologian, put it, "Our great security against sin lies in being shocked at it." When we are shocked at something, we avoid it at all costs. The sight of a person dying of lung cancer is as potent an argument against smoking as we are ever likely to see. So the sight of sin and the ravages it creates should shock us into avoiding it at all costs. But when sin loses its "shock value," it can too easily become something we tolerate and then fall prey to ourselves.

Why do we not find more Christians "weeping and mourning" for the sin that rages around us? There are two basic reasons. (1) We care too little

---

31. *Chicago Tribune*, June 7, 1996, sec. 1, p. 1.

about the holy standards of God. Lot, for all his faults, was, Peter tells us, a "righteous" man. A righteous person is in right relationship with God— justified by faith, accepted by God on the basis of the work of Christ. But a righteous person is also one who finds the "mind of Christ" becoming more and more dominant in all his or her thinking and acting (see Rom. 12:2). It is as we internalize God's standards and values that our horror at the rampant disregard of those values grows. We are not shocked at sin because we do not sufficiently share God's own horror at it.

(2) We care too little about this world we live in. Lot could not have been distressed at the sin of those around him unless he cared about them. Perhaps the failure of many contemporary Christians to be shocked at sin arises from our disengagement from the world around us. Many social commentators have recently been pointing out the failure of so many modern societies to have any real sense of community.[32]

There is in the West a tradition of the autonomous person, the "rugged individualist," who is strong and whom modern technology has, if anything, made even stronger. And Christians have often succumbed to this privatistic tendency. We rejoice (rightly) at being made right with God. We seek to live righteous lives ourselves; we bring up our families to follow in the same footsteps; we worship with like-minded people. We hear of startling differences in lifestyle in the media and know of work associates or neighbors who live ungodly lives. But because we are not really involved with them and with the larger world, we are not all that bothered by their sin. Having barricaded ourselves in our Christian enclave, we are relatively untouched by what takes place outside. But such a privatistic faith is a far cry from the engagement with the world that being "salt and light" requires. And the more we are engaged with the world, the more we will be distressed at the sin we find there.

---

32. See especially Robert N. Bellah, et al., *Habits of the Heart: Individualism and Commitment in American Life* (Berkeley: Univ. of California Press, 1985).

2 Peter 2:10b–16

BOLD AND ARROGANT, these men are not afraid to slander celestial beings; [11]yet even angels, although they are stronger and more powerful, do not bring slanderous accusations against such beings in the presence of the Lord. [12]But these men blaspheme in matters they do not understand. They are like brute beasts, creatures of instinct, born only to be caught and destroyed, and like beasts they too will perish. [13]They will be paid back with harm for the harm they have done.

Their idea of pleasure is to carouse in broad daylight. They are blots and blemishes, reveling in their pleasures while they feast with you. [14]With eyes full of adultery, they never stop sinning; they seduce the unstable; they are experts in greed— an accursed brood! [15]They have left the straight way and wandered off to follow the way of Balaam son of Beor, who loved the wages of wickedness. [16]But he was rebuked for his wrongdoing by a donkey—a beast without speech—who spoke with a man's voice and restrained the prophet's madness.

Original Meaning

PETER HAS PREDICTED that false teachers would constantly arise to plague the church of Jesus Christ (2:1–3a). He has announced God's condemnation of them, likening them to sinners and rebels in the Old Testament (2:3b–9). In verse 10a, he began to get more specific, introducing a group of people to whom God's condemnation especially applied—most certainly the false teachers that were disturbing the peace of the churches to whom he is writing. In the present paragraph, Peter goes on to describe them in more detail.

Verse 10a, then, is transitional: It rounds off Peter's general discussion of God's judgment with a particular application and it introduces the subject of the next verses. Indeed, this half verse captures the two characteristics of the false teachers that Peter elaborates and condemns in verses 10b–16: their sensuality (they "follow the corrupt desire of the sinful nature") and their arrogance (they "despise authority"). In typical manner, Peter takes these up in reverse order, exposing the false teachers' arrogance in verses 10b–13a and their sensuality in verses 13b–16.

The False Teachers' Arrogance (vv. 10b–13a)

THE REASON MOST translations and commentaries put a break in the middle of verse 10 is because of a change in syntactical construction. The first part of the verse, with the word "especially," continues the sentence begun in verse 4. But the second part of the verse begins a new sentence, where Peter applies two similar words to the false teachers: "bold" (*tolmetai*) and "arrogant" (*authadeis*). It is not easy to find any clear difference in meaning between the two; they function together to draw a picture of "arrogant audacity."[1]

The false teachers' arrogance is manifested in their not being afraid "to slander celestial beings."[2] The NIV rendering "celestial beings" conceals an important ambiguity in the Greek text. The literal translation is simply "glories." Peter uses this same plural form of the word in 1 Peter 1:11 to refer to the glorious events that Christ experienced after his suffering. In the present passage, clearly "glorious *beings*" of some kind are meant. A few commentators (more in the past than in the present) think that local church leaders may be meant.[3] Now, as an elder in my own local church, I would like to be considered a "glorious being," but I am not sure that the idea is a biblical one. More likely, as the NIV suggests and most contemporary commentators agree,[4] Peter is referring to angels. Furthermore, most also agree that *evil* angels are meant, since Peter seems to contrast these "glorious ones" reviled by the false teachers with the "angels" in verse 11[5] (which, since Peter commends their activity, must be good angels). Why is it wrong for the false teachers to slander these evil angels? Presumably because, though fallen, they still bear the impress of their "glorious" origin.

Peter introduces the good angels to contrast their behavior with the disrespectful attitude of the false teachers. Although they are "stronger and more powerful" than the evil angels, they do not "bring slanderous accusations"

---

1. The phrase is Bauckham's (*Jude, 2 Peter*, 262).

2. The syntax here would also allow the translation "they do not stand in awe of angels, blaspheming"; see TEV: they "show no respect for the glorious beings above; instead, they insult them."

3. See, e.g., Bigg, *The Epistles of St. Peter and St. Jude*, 279–80; Green, *The Second Epistle General of Peter and the General Epistle of Jude*, 104–5. Calvin (*Hebrews and 1 and 2 Peter*, 351) thought that civil leaders might be meant.

4. The main problem with this view is linguistic: The Old Testament never calls angels "glories." But some Jewish texts link angels with glory (see, e.g., Ex. 15:11 in the Septuagint; Philo, *Special Laws* 1.45; *Testament of Levi* 18:5; *Testament of Judah* 25:2; see the survey in "δόξα," *TDNT*, 2.251). And we have a few texts that use the term to denote angels (1QH 10:8; 2 Enoch 22:7, 10; *Ascension of Isaiah* 9:32).

5. J. Neyrey is an exception among recent commentators. He thinks that "the glorious ones" are good angels (Neyrey, *2 Peter, Jude*, 213–14); and Mayor thought that angels of any kind were intended (Mayor, *The Epistle of St. Jude and the Second Epistle of St. Peter*, 129).

against these glorious, though fallen, beings. Two interpretive decisions are reflected in this way of paraphrasing verse 11. The Greek text does not at all make clear who it is that the (good) angels are greater than and whom the (good) angels refrain from accusing. I am reflecting the views of most scholars by identifying both with the evil angels. And the NIV agrees with at least the second judgment; its rendering "such beings" clearly refers back to "celestial beings" at the end of verse 10.

Confirming this way of taking the verse is Jude 8–9, which contains a rebuke of false teachers that is similar to that found here in 2 Peter 2:

> In the very same way, these dreamers pollute their own bodies, reject authority and slander celestial beings. But even the archangel Michael, when he was disputing with the devil about the body of Moses, did not dare to bring a slanderous accusation against him, but said, "The Lord rebuke you!"

By referring to the archangel Michael and Satan, Jude makes explicit the contrast between good angels and fallen ones that we have argued is Peter's intention.

So much for the details. How about the larger picture? What, exactly, are the false teachers doing? And where does Peter get his information about the angels? To begin with the second point: Jewish tradition is probably once more Peter's source. In the parallel passage in Jude, Jude quotes from a lost Jewish intertestamental book called *The Assumption of Moses*.[6] Peter may also have this tradition in mind. Another possibility, however, is that Peter is continuing to reflect the story about the "watchers" that he used back in verse 4, which finds its greatest elaboration in *1 Enoch*. In *1 Enoch* 9, the author narrates a scene in which the good angels, hearing the outcry of human beings from the earth as they are being harmed by the evil angels, did not directly intervene, but brought the situation before the Lord. Again, Peter presses into service traditions familiar to his hearers to expose the audacity of the false teachers.

As to the first question (the attitude of the false teachers), we begin with the word *blasphemeo*. Peter uses this word at the beginning of his denunciation (end of v. 10; NIV "slander") and again at the end (v. 12; NIV "blaspheme"), and he uses a form of this same word to describe the judgment that the good angels refuse to bring against the evil angels (v. 11; NIV "slanderous"). This Greek word, which we transliterate into English as "blaspheme," can refer to the reviling of fellow human beings, but it more often denotes words or actions that defame God or people and ideas associated with him. Peter has

---

6. For more detail on this tradition, see the commentary on Jude 9.

already accused these false teachers of causing the "way of truth" to be "blas-phemed" (2:2; NIV "bring . . . into disrepute"). Now he suggests that they are also making light of evil angels.

Since the false teachers seemed to be materialistic and thus skeptical about things like the return of Christ and the judgment to come, this "blasphemy" may have taken a very basic form and involved a general denial of the exis-tence of such beings.[7] Or, since evil angels in particular were being blas-phemed, it is more likely that the false teachers were mocking the possibility that their sins might put them at the mercy of such evil spiritual beings.[8] Other possibilities have been suggested, but the fact is that Peter does not give us enough information to be sure about what the problem was. What is clear, however, is that, though fallen, the evil angels still retain a rank higher than that of human beings (that is why Peter can call them "glorious beings"). In their arrogance, the false teachers were in some way denying this fact.

The beginning of verse 12—"But these"—might imply a shift to a new topic. But since Peter continues to talk about the false teachers' blasphemy, the verse probably continues the topic of arrogance toward evil angels from verses 10b–11.[9] Peter uses the adversative "but" because he is shifting gram-matical subjects back from the angels (v. 11) to the false teachers (v. 10b). This arrogance, Peter suggests, is partly the result of ignorance. Shouldn't this excuse the false teachers, then? No, for ignorance in the Bible is often a will-ful refusal to understand God's truth; and the sharpness of Peter's criticism makes clear that this is what he had in mind here.

Peter goes on to compare the false teachers to animals. If he is thinking especially of the false teachers' libertine lifestyle in this verse, the point of comparison is presumably between the instinctual behavior of animals and the false teachers' lack of concern for moral guidance. They "behave like animals" by following their natural, fleshly appetites without regard for spir-itual guidance. In a word, they are "unspiritual." But if Peter is still referring to the false teachers' arrogance toward evil angels (as I think he is), then the point of comparison is between the animals' lack of rationality and the false teachers' sinful ignorance.

The NIV translation "brute" comes from a Greek word that means "with-out reason" (*alogos*), and this supports the second reading of the comparison. On the other hand, Peter's adjective *physika*, "natural," "unspiritual" (NIV "crea-tures of instinct"), could point to the first, "moral" comparison. Perhaps, then,

---

7. See, e.g., William Barclay, *The Letters of James and Peter* (Edinburgh: Saint Andrew, 1958), 390.

8. Bauckham, *Jude, 2 Peter*, 262.

9. For a different opinion, see Green, *The Second Epistle General of Peter and the General Epis-tle of Jude*, 108, who thinks that the blasphemy here is directed against Christian morality.

Peter uses the comparison with the animals to refer *both* to the false teachers' ignorance and to their immorality.

But the apostle's chief point of comparison between the animals and the false teachers lies in another realm altogether. Picking up a common ancient saying about animals, Peter reminds us that they are "born only to be caught and destroyed." And, he goes on, "like beasts they [the false teachers] too will perish." The NIV rendering here is quite interpretive, reflecting two critical decisions about the Greek text. (1) The word *phthora* (which the NIV does not directly translate) often means "[moral] corruption," as it does, for instance, in the two other places that Peter uses it (2 Peter 1:4; 2:19). If we give the word this meaning, the end of verse 12 then reads, as in the KJV: "shall utterly perish in their own corruption." Moral corruption, Peter would be saying, is the reason why the false teachers are condemned. But the word *phthora* in the first part of the verse means "destruction," not "corruption" ("born only ... to be *destroyed*"); and this is probably its meaning in the second part of the verse also.

(2) How should we relate this word "destruction" to the verb in the sentence, "will perish" (or "will be destroyed")? (a) These words come from the same root, so Peter may be adding the noun to the verb simply to emphasize the idea: "they [the false teachers] *will surely be destroyed.*"[10] (b) "In their destruction" could refer to the evil angels: "The false teachers will be destroyed with the evil angels."[11] (c) "In their destruction" could refer to the animals. If so, Peter is saying either that "the false teachers will be destroyed *when* the animals are destroyed" (see NASB; NRSV), or that "the false teachers will be destroyed *like* the animals" (NIV; REB; TEV).[12] The last of these options is the best, doing justice both to the Greek[13] and to the context. Like unreasoning animals, destined only to be slaughtered, the false teachers, in their unreasoning arrogance and sinfulness, are destined also for the slaughter— the slaughter of God's judgment.

The beginning of verse 13 is also difficult in the Greek text, and commentators suggest two major possible translations: (1) "being defrauded of the profits of their wrongdoing," or (2) "receiving harm for the harm they have caused." Almost all the English translations have some kind of variant of the second option, and they are almost certainly correct. Peter uses a word play here to emphasize the idea of just recompense: The false teachers have

---

10. The construction here would then be a cognate dative (also called "Semitic," because it is common in Hebrew and Aramaic); see Green, *The Second Epistle General of Peter and the General Epistle of Jude,* 108.

11. Bauckham, *Jude, 2 Peter,* 264.

12. See also Mayor, *The Epistle of St. Jude and the Second Epistle of St. Peter,* 131; Kelly, *The Epistles of Peter and of Jude,* 339.

13. The Greek word *zoa,* "animals," is the closest antecedent to the pronoun *auton.*

harmed others; the "reward" they will receive is, in turn, "harm." The NIV has captured the meaning here pretty well, but I think it is wrong to put a paragraph break at the beginning of verse 13. Rather, as with most other English versions, we should make the first part of verse 13 the end of the sentence begun in verse 12. "Being paid back with harm for the harm they have caused" provides a fitting addition to the prediction of the false teachers' ultimate destruction.

The False Teachers' Sensuality (vv. 13b–16)

"SENSUALITY" IS NOT a word that we use all that often, but it is difficult to think of a better one to summarize Peter's second main accusation against the false teachers. *Webster's New Collegiate Dictionary* defines "sensual" as "relating to or consisting in the gratification of the senses or the indulgence of the appetite." This is precisely the quality Peter attributes to the false teachers in verses 13b–16. He draws his picture of sensuality with eight brief characterizations.

(1) "Their idea of pleasure is to carouse in broad daylight." "Pleasure" can, of course, be a neutral or even positive thing; God has himself created many things to give his people pleasure. But the Greek word here for "pleasure," *hedone*, is the word from which we derive "hedonist," one who lives for only pleasure. The Greeks numbered this kind of pleasure among their four "deadly sins," sometimes contrasting it with reason (cf. "unreasoning animals" in v. 12). In Peter's day, as in ours, indulgence of sinful pleasure usually took place under cover of darkness. Practicing such hedonistic activities "in broad daylight" is therefore a sign that the false teachers are completely shameless about their indulgence.

(2) "Blots and blemishes." These are obviously general descriptions. The best way to define them is to recognize their opposites. Thus, in 3:14, Peter encourages his readers, as they look forward to the return of Christ, to "make every effort to be found *spotless, blameless*." Although it is difficult to bring out in English translation, these two italicized words are the exact antonyms of the two words Peter uses here to describe the false teachers ("blot" = *spiloi* and "spotless" = *aspiloi*; "blemishes" = *momoi* and "blameless" = *amometoi*).

(3) "Reveling in their pleasures while they feast with you." Peter creates a connection with the earlier part of the verse by using the verb "reveling," which comes from the same Greek root as the word the NIV translates "carouse." One of Jude's descriptions of his false teachers makes an interesting comparison with this clause in 2 Peter: "These men are blemishes at your love feasts, eating with you without the slightest qualm—shepherds who feed only themselves" (Jude 12a). Peter's reference to the false teachers "feasting with" the Christians to whom he writes suggests the same scenario: the early Christian "love feast" held in conjunction with the celebration of the

Lord's Supper. This "love feast" was a regular part of the early Christian fellowship, and it is generally recognized that Paul's rebuke of the Corinthians in 1 Corinthians 11:17–34 presupposes this practice. While we cannot be sure, then, it is likely that Peter here rebukes the false teachers for indulging their own sinful pleasures even as they continue to join with other Christians in celebrating the atoning work of Christ at the church's fellowship meals.

(4) "With eyes full of adultery, they never stop sinning." Peter's language is more vivid than the NIV translation; he claims that the false teachers have eyes full of "adulterous women." By this he means that the false teachers are so addicted to sex that they look at every woman as a potential partner in their lust.[14] The NIV also fails to make clear that the phrase "never stop sinning" also refers to "eyes"; cf. REB: "They have eyes for nothing but loose women, eyes never ceasing from sin."

(5) "They seduce the unstable." Up to this point, Peter's description of these people has hardly justified the characterization we have been using (based on vv. 1–3) of "false teachers." He has said a great deal about their personal moral failings but little about their influence on others. From here to the end of the chapter, however, the "teaching" aspect of their false Christianity is Peter's focus.

"Seduce" translates a Greek word that has its roots in the world of hunting and fishing; it suggests the bait used to lure a fish to the hook or an animal to the trap. But the word had become used generally of any kind of (especially) moral temptation (see also James 1:14). So we should probably not think that Peter intends a sporting metaphor. The word "unstable" (*asteriktous*) is again striking by virtue of its antonym; Christians, Peter urged in 1:12, need to be people who are "firmly established [*esterigmenous*] in the truth." It is precisely those who fail to become solidly grounded in Christian truth whom false teachers find to be easy prey. Like trees with shallow roots, they are easily swayed and toppled.

(6) "They are experts in greed." Here again the NIV rendering is accurate but loses some of the force of the original, which, literally translated, is "having a heart that has been trained in greed." "Train" is a word drawn from the realm of athletics; it suggests that long, hard, and disciplined struggle to become proficient in a sport. These false teachers, Peter implies, are so devoted and consistent in their greed that they must have worked very hard at it for a long time! And it is their "heart"—the very center of one's being in biblical perspective—that has become so proficient in greed.

---

14. Peter's description may be based on a popular ancient proverb, which held that a shameless man did not have *koras* (a pun—the word can mean both "pupils" and "maidens") in his eyes, but *pornas* ("prostitutes"); cf. Plutarch, *Moralia* 528E.

The word "greed" (*pleonexia*) is a broad term. In Ephesians 4:19, for instance, Paul writes about those who have "given themselves over to sensuality so as to indulge in every kind of impurity, with a continual lust [*pleonexia*] for more." In other words, "greed" need not relate only to money; it can also denote the desire for more sexual pleasure, power, food, and so forth. Since Peter has already used this word to depict the false teachers' love of money (2:3), the "greed" here is also probably mainly directed to financial gain. But we should probably not restrict the word to this sphere.

(7) "An accursed brood!" (lit., "children of curse"). Again the NIV paraphrases; but the paraphrase is legitimate, for the Old Testament and the Jewish world often attributed a certain quality to people by saying that they were "children of" or a "son of" that quality. Judas, for instance, is "the son of destruction," that is, "one destined for destruction" (John 17:12); people apart from Christ are "children of wrath," that is, "people on whom God's wrath rests" (Eph. 2:3); Christians are "children of light," that is, "people characterized by light" (1 Thess. 5:5). Peter has already pronounced his condemnation on the false teachers (vv. 3b–10a). Overwhelmed by the enormity of their sinfulness, he once again interjects this reminder of their ultimate fate.

(8) "They have left the straight way and wandered off to follow the way of Balaam son of Beor." Characterizing a philosophy or a religion as a "way" was common in the ancient world. The imagery suggests a path of belief that one followed. Biblical writers picked up this language; the Christian movement is sometimes simply called "the Way" in the book of Acts (9:2; 19:9, 23; 22:4; 24:14, 22). And the path of faithfulness to the Lord can be called "the straight way" (cf. 1 Sam. 12:23; Ps. 106:7; Prov. 2:16; Isa. 33:15). Those who lose their religious bearings are described as people who "wander off" from God's way; note, for instance, God's warning to the people of Israel: "I am setting before you today a blessing and a curse . . . the curse if you disobey the commands of the LORD your God and turn [or wander off] from the way that I command you today by following other gods" (Deut. 11:26–28).

Peter gives a specific twist to this imagery, accusing the false teachers of following "the way of Balaam son of Beor." Balaam is one of the interesting and enigmatic characters in the Old Testament. He appeared on the scene as the Israelites were camped on the plains of Moab, preparing to enter the Promised Land (Num. 22–24). Balak, king of Moab, desperate to stop the Israelite invasion, sought to hire Balaam, who was some kind of prophet, to curse Israel. Although Balaam consulted God about what he should do, the text makes clear that he was still inclined to go his own way. For though the Lord himself sent Balaam to Balak, he became angry with Balaam as he was going and sent "the angel of the LORD" to block his path. Apparently Balaam's motives in going were not what they should have been. Balaam could not see the angel, but his donkey did, refusing to move forward and eventually rebuking Balaam.

Chastened, Balaam refused to curse Israel but, to the chagrin of Balak, blessed them four times. Particularly significant for Peter's use of the episode is the occurrence twice in the narrative of the language of "the way": in Num. 22:23, "the way of Balaam" is the literal road he was following; in 22:32, the angel rebuked Balaam for taking a "reckless way." Balaam's story made a strong impression on later generations, and he became a prominent negative example in Scripture (see Deut. 23:4–5; Josh. 13:22; 24:9–10; Neh. 13:1–2; Micah 6:5; Jude 11; Rev. 2:14).

Peter introduces a couple of twists to this story in his application. First, he calls Balaam "the son of Bosor" (NRSV; REB; TEV; the NIV and NASB "Beor" apparently follows a poorly attested variant). Balaam is called "son of Beor" in the Old Testament, and this name is not found elsewhere. Some have conjectured that "Bosor" may have been Peter's Galilean pronunciation of "Beor," but it is more likely that we have a play on words. The Hebrew word for "flesh" is *basar*, and various Jewish traditions characterized Balaam as a very fleshly person. Peter may, then, be deliberately modifying Balaam's name to suit his character.[15]

Jewish tradition may also have played a role in another emphasis in Peter's application: Balaam's greed (see the end of v. 15). While hinted at in the Old Testament text, Balaam's willingness to curse Israel for profit became a staple in Jewish stories about him.[16] Moreover, the Jewish stories made Balaam responsible for Israel's rebellion against God in entering into sexual relationships with the women of Midian (Num. 25). While Peter does not explicitly bring out this element in "Balaam's way," it certainly fits perfectly the profile of the false teachers that he has been drawing in verse 13b–14.

In verse 16, Peter highlights the utter foolishness of Balaam by noting how he was rebuked by his own "donkey—a beast incapable of articulate speech." Indeed, Peter concludes, Balaam must have been "insane."[17] And in noting how even Balaam's donkey understood more about the spiritual situation than the prophet, Peter implicitly associates Balaam with the false prophets who are like "brute beasts, creatures of instinct" (v. 12).

Two other points Peter makes about Balaam in this verse also seem to reflect Jewish tradition: emphasis on the donkey's rebuke of Balaam and Bal-

---

15. Bauckham, *Jude, 2 Peter*, 267–68.

16. See, for instance, Philo, *Moses* 1.266–68.

17. NIV "madness." The Greek word is *paraphronian* and is found only here; Paul uses the cognate verb in 2 Cor. 11:23. Scholars speculate that Peter may have used this word to create a verbal play with the word *paranomias*, "wrongdoing," earlier in the verse.

aam's madness.[18] Once again, then, Peter is likely dependent on popular Jewish elaborations of an Old Testament story in his choice of examples. But we should emphasize that the Jewish tradition merely refined and perhaps affected the wording of Peter's use of the Balaam story; the basic points he makes about Balaam are clear enough in the Old Testament narrative itself.

WE OFTEN FIND it difficult to understand and apply the Bible because the author assumes certain information as he or she writes. Some of the information we lack can be discovered by learning about the biblical world. But other information may be lost to us forever, because it involves matters that the writer and the readers both knew about their special situation but which has not been recorded anywhere. In 2 Peter 2:10b–16 we encounter both types of information.

As we noted in the "Original Meaning" section above, we simply do not know how the false teachers were "blaspheming" evil angels (vv. 10b–12). All that we can do is speculate and admit that whatever conclusions we come to must be tentative. Naturally, we would like to know more about the situation so that we could be more precise in our interpretation. Faced with these gaps, we can go in two possible directions.

Some scholars insist on trying to fill up the gaps by spinning more or less plausible theories about the background situation. I do not want to criticize these efforts; study of these backgrounds is laudable and sometimes turns up genuinely valuable information to help the interpreter. But the tendency among some scholars is to build elaborate theories on the basis of slim and uncertain evidence. Then, despite little—or even conflicting—data, they use these theories as a basis to interpret and apply a biblical text. Some recent interpreters call this process "mirror-reading." The mirror is the specific background theory; and when a text is reflected in the mirror of a specific background theory, that theory decisively shapes the text.

Perhaps the best example of this process is the spate of recent interpretations of 1 Timothy 2:11–15, the passage in which Paul tells Timothy that he does not want women "to teach or to have authority over a man." Many of these interpretations assume—rightly—that we must interpret Paul's prohibition in its first-century context. But they then go on to suggest specific background scenarios that usually have little basis in the text of 1 Timothy

---

18. For the donkey's rebuke of Balaam, see several of the Targums (Aramaic paraphrases of the Old Testament); see the discussion in Neyrey, *2 Peter, Jude,* 211–12. For Balaam's "madness," see Philo, *Moses* 1.193.

and sometimes, indeed, little basis in what we know of the first-century world. Yet scholars following this line of "mirror-reading" conclude that Paul's advice is not directly relevant for the church today *because of one of these theoretical background scenarios.*

Now, I do not want to be misunderstood, for background study is necessary and often of basic relevance in understanding the Bible. But the problem is obvious: We had better be pretty certain of the influence of a given background situation before we make it decisive in our interpretation. Otherwise, we can make texts say almost whatever we want them to or dismiss as applicable to us almost any passage of Scripture.

A second response to our ignorance about the background situation in a text is despair: We have lost vital information and can never find what we need to understand and apply the passage. At this point, we must come back to our root conviction about the role of God in producing the Bible. We believe that the very words of Scripture are ultimately God's words, and that he, in cooperation with the human authors, caused to be written what we now have in the pages of our Bibles. What this means, of course, is that God is also in control of what has *not* been written there. Thus we should be confident that God has preserved for us, in the Bible and in the world he has made, all that we need to know rightly to obey his word to us. In the case of 2 Peter 2:10b–12, then, we are responsible for what the text tells us and need not worry about what we cannot find out about it. In the "Contemporary Significance" section below, we will suggest some ways in which we might apply Peter's rebuke of the false teachers for their cavalier attitude toward the evil angels.

Our understanding of this passage can be enhanced, however, by some background information that Peter and his readers would have shared but which many of us may not appreciate fully. I refer to the biblical/Jewish teaching about angels. Peter, as I have argued above, refers in 2:10b–12 to two distinct categories of spiritual beings: evil spirits ("glories" or "celestial beings") and good spirits ("angels"). These two categories of spiritual creatures were familiar to Peter and to his readers. The Bible constantly mentions as factual the existence of spiritual beings who serve God and interact with human beings in various capacities. The most common name for these beings is "angels," although they are also called "sons of God" (Job 1:6; 2:1); "holy ones" (Ps. 89:5, 7); "spirits" (Heb. 1:14); "watchers" (a literal rendering of Dan. 4:13, 17, 23);and, collectively, "the heavenly host" (e.g., Ps. 148:2, 5). Scripture is silent about how or when they came into being, but they have clearly been created (Neh. 9:6: "You have made the heaven, the heaven of heavens, with all their host," NRSV; cf. also Col. 1:16). They are immaterial by nature, but can take on substantial form in order to interact with human beings.

Alongside these good spiritual beings, we also find evil spiritual creatures. The Old Testament has little to say about these beings, although we occasionally encounter "demons" (Deut. 32:17; Ps. 106:37) and several other murky figures that may be demonic in nature: "the hairy ones" (a literal rendering; NIV has "goat idols"—Lev. 17:7; 2 Chron. 11:15; cf. also Isa. 13:21; 34:14), "Azazel" (Lev. 16:8, 10, 26), and "Lilith" (Isa. 34:14).[19] And, of course, we also have references to an outstanding evil spiritual being, the "accuser," Satan (which is the transliteration of the Hebrew word for "adversary": 1 Chron. 21:1; Job 1:6–2:7; Zech. 3:1–2). And, while not identified as such in the Old Testament, the serpent in the Garden of Eden is also, according to Revelation 12:9, related in some way to Satan.

The Old Testament engages in no speculation about the exact nature of these evil spiritual beings or about their origins. However, since God made all things "good," it is safe to assume that they were originally good spiritual beings who rebelled against God and lost their original holiness. This "fall" of the angels must have occurred before Genesis 3, where Satan appears on the scene as the evil tempter.[20]

Angels, demons, and Satan are, of course, prominent in the New Testament. The word "angel" is itself used almost exclusively for good spiritual beings, with only a few possible exceptions.[21] The New Testament authors are interested in the involvement of these beings in the lives of Jesus and his followers and contribute little to our understanding of their nature or origins. The closest we get to such speculation is Revelation 12:7–9, which describes in visionary form the casting down to earth of "Satan and his angels" after a war in heaven.

Jews in the intertestamental period sought vigorously to fill in the gaps of this rather vague biblical picture of the spiritual beings, engaging in considerable speculation about various ranks of such beings, their names, and their functions. They displayed great interest especially in the origin of evil spiritual beings, developing, as we noted in the "Bridging Contexts" section on 2:4–10a, a powerful myth about the fall of angels and the origin of evil (based on Gen. 6:1–4).[22]

---

19. The NIV renders "Azazel" as "scapegoat"; see, however, the footnote. In Isa. 34:14, there is debate about the meaning of the Hebrew word, some versions (cf. NIV) taking the term to refer to an animal rather than to a demon.

20. Among other works on the angels, the summary of Wayne Grudem (*Systematic Theology: An Introduction to Biblical Doctrine* [Grand Rapids: Zondervan, 1994], 397–436) is helpful.

21. Rev. 12:9, referring to "Satan and his angels" is the clearest. See also Rom. 8:38; 1 Cor. 6:3. In 2 Peter 2:4 and Jude 6, the word "angel" is used because the authors are viewing them from the standpoint of their original status.

22. I have argued that Peter refers to this myth when he speaks of the "angels who sinned" (v. 4).

Considerable interest in various spiritual beings was also found in the general Graeco-Roman world of Peter's day. Many people believed that these beings were active in the world, standing behind the powers of government and influencing both one's individual life and the course of history. Angels were also important in many of the Gnostic systems of thought that began cropping up in the second century A.D. The radical cosmological dualism taught by the Gnostics made it difficult for them to conceive of a holy and majestic God having anything to do with this sinful world. They therefore made the angels mediators between God and this world.

In a word, then, talk about spiritual beings was "in the air" in the first-century world. Belief in them was far more a part of people's basic worldview than it is in our day. This is not to say, of course, that such views were necessarily adopted by the New Testament authors. But where they touch on such ideas, we can presume the helpfulness of the background. We should not, then, be surprised to find Paul rebuking the Colossians for paying too much attention to them (Col. 1:16–17; 2:10, 15, 18), or the author to the Hebrews arguing that Christ is greater than them (Heb. 1–2).

Clearly, however, the false teachers Peter is dealing with were moving in an opposite direction, at least with respect to evil spiritual beings. Rather than paying too much respect to them, they were paying too little attention to them. Unfortunately, we can only speculate about the precise form of their "blasphemy" of these evil angels. In bridging from Peter's day to ours, then, we will have to be content with drawing only general parallels between the false teachers' attitudes and those of contemporary Christians.

 "THERE IS NOTHING new under the sun," laments Solomon in Ecclesiastes 1:9. In nothing is this maxim more true than in the case of those who depart from the truth of the Christian faith. Century after century, the same basic doctrinal errors lead people astray, and the same sins gain a hold on them. This paragraph in 2 Peter is a good case in point. Written almost two millennia ago, Peter's sketch of "the false teachers" seeking to lead the church astray in his day (cf. 2:1, 3, 18–19) could have been drawn by someone analyzing the church in our day. But in chapter 2, and in the present paragraph especially, Peter's main preoccupation is not with what these people were teaching, but with how they were acting. Why is this?

We can be certain that these people were actively teaching their false ideas of Christianity. But we can also be certain that a lot of their "teaching" came not in words, either written or spoken, but in actions. We all know the proverb, "A picture is worth a thousand words." The "picture" of Christian living that these people were painting by their actions must have been just as powerful as any formal teaching they could have done. Thus Peter minces no words as he describes their behavior, seeking to show to his readers that the "picture" of Christianity these false teachers were displaying was false and disastrous.

False teaching is often revealed in false living. "By their fruit you will recognize them," Jesus told his disciples as he warned them about false prophets (Matt. 7:16). And so it always is: Following bad doctrine leads to bad practices. The false teachers of Peter's day were propagating wrong ideas about Christ's return in glory and about judgment to come (cf. 1:16–21; 3:3–12). And Peter takes them to task for it. But he also paints this vivid picture of their sinful lifestyle in chapter 2 to show, from another angle, that these people cannot be trusted to represent the true Christian faith.

The test of right behavior is one that we can apply to teachers in our day as well. Of course, the Bible makes clear that no Christian, and no Christian teacher, will be without sin; as James reminds us (as if we needed the reminder!), "We all stumble in many ways" (James 3:2). People can teach right things and still do many wrong things. But when we are faced with a teaching that we are not sure about and that we are having a hard time judging against the standard of Scripture, a careful look at the lifestyle of those who propose such teaching will often prove helpful. Do they teach with humility and love? Do they give evidence of seeking to submit all their conduct to the Lordship of Christ? Do they pray with fervor and sincerity? These are the kind of questions that Scripture encourages us to ask of those who would teach us.

What we have said about the connection between teaching and lifestyle is implicit in what Peter writes in 2:10b–16. I want now to turn to the explicit teaching we find in the paragraph. Four points, in particular, are applicable to our day.

(1) The first of these has to do with the false teachers' attitudes toward spiritual beings. Expanding on his brief reference to the false teachers' arrogance in verse 10a, Peter in verses 10b–13a lambastes them for "blaspheming" evil spiritual beings—the demons. True, we cannot be at all sure what the specific error of the false teachers in Peter's day may have been. But as I pointed out above, people in Peter's day had a lively interest in spiritual beings of all kinds. And, indeed, fascination with the spirit world seems to be endemic in human beings—whether it takes the form of occult practices, seances, ouija boards, or visions. From a Christian perspective, we can understand why this is: God has made us with a spiritual side, and those who do not find it satisfied where it can only finally be satisfied—in a relationship to the only God through his Son Jesus—will seek to satisfy it elsewhere.

Many of our own contemporaries, of course, following the reigning materialistic worldview, are skeptical about the existence of any kind of spirit world. But we also see a renewed interest in spiritual beings. The last few years have seen a spate of books and TV shows about angels. Typical of this latest outbreak of interest in spiritual beings is a focus on good angels who are sent to help us. What people seem to want is a spirit world without any consequences. A vague belief in the existence of good spiritual creatures who are "out there" to help me but who make no demands on me seems the perfect man-made religion.

Against this view of angels, Christians need to reassert biblical teaching at two points. (a) Angels are creatures who do God's bidding; separating them from the God of the Bible is impossible. (b) There are all kinds of spiritual beings—good and evil. To ignore this and to seek contact with angels apart from commitment to God in Christ is to open oneself to the influence of evil spiritual beings. Satan, we are told, "masquerades as an angel of light" (2 Cor. 11:14).

As far as we know, preoccupation with good angels was not one of the errors of the false teachers whom Peter rebukes. Rather, they were taking a superior attitude toward evil spiritual beings. Their error stands as a warning to Christians. In my comments on 2:4–10a, I argued that some Christians in recent days have given too much attention to demons. But the opposite problem is certainly common as well. The materialistic world in which we live exerts a subtle but strong bias against any true belief in the supernatural world. Demons are something we read about in the Gospels, see on the movie screen, and may even pay lip service to at the level of our convictions. But do we really, in the depths of our being, reckon with their influence and allow our belief to guide our day-to-day conduct? Paul warned the Corinthians, who prided themselves on their "knowledge," that their attendance at idol feasts put them in danger of demonic influence (1 Cor. 10:14–22). We need to ask what idols we are toying with, willfully and foolishly ignoring the real spiritual power that may be at work in them.

In talking idly with one of my high-school-age sons, I discovered that he and his friends were reading horoscopes in the newspaper on their lunch hour at school, laughing it up over the foolishness of the whole thing. I did not want to play the heavy-handed father, but I did feel I needed to remind him of the reality of the spirit world and how demons might use the most innocent-appearing things to try to get a foothold in a believer.

I know some of these matters are controversial, and committed Christians will disagree about the presence of demonic influence in many debated practices. But I think Christians need to be cautious about getting involved in the Masons or about role-playing that tinkers with the occult. Reference to the spirit world in such societies and activities may appear to be purely superficial or of simple entertainment value. But we must always reckon with the possibility that below the surface may lurk genuine demonic influence.

Christians will disagree about some of these matters. But no Christian should be in any doubt about the danger we run when we persist in willful sin. Influencing our sinful behavior is the personal power of the Satan and his host. Sins for which we ask and receive God's forgiveness cannot bring us into spiritual danger, for on the cross, Christ "disarmed the powers and authorities" (Col. 2:15). But when we do not seek God's forgiveness for our sins or pretend that our sin is not really sin, we run the danger of putting ourselves at the mercy of the demons. This may have been just the error of the false teachers. Bent on their own pleasure, rejecting God's standards of righteousness, they were, in effect, treating with contempt the evil spiritual beings that stood behind these practices.

(2) If Peter's attack on the false teachers for their arrogance toward evil spiritual beings (vv. 10b–13a) has much to say to contemporary Christians, his attack on their sensuality (vv. 13b–16) has perhaps even more. Peter accuses them of pursuing *hedone*, "pleasure" (v. 13). And "hedonistic" might describe our culture better than any other single word. We live in a society whose god is pleasure. We have defined the "pursuit of happiness," enshrined in the Declaration of Independence, as the pursuit of food, drink, entertainment, wealth, and sex.

Moreover, like the false teachers of Peter's day, who found themselves in a never-ending pursuit of more and more pleasure (cf. "they never stop sinning" in v. 14), people in our day also find themselves caught in one of the "laws of pleasure": diminishing returns. The food that used to satisfy no longer does, so we search for ever more exotic and more expensive dishes. What once entertained us now seems blasé; so we demand new media, bigger TVs, more stations. The spousal sex that used to satisfy our natural urges is no longer enough; as a result, we try sex with others and explore various deviant practices to bring the excitement back. Pleasure, in other words, is a goal never reached; it is always somewhere in the distance, urging one on to new and usually more sinful practices, never quite satisfying.

Pleasure from sex or a satisfying meal or a well-acted play is, of course, not sinful. God built within us the capacity to enjoy these things. The problem comes when the pleasure derived from these activities becomes our dominating goal. That is hedonism—and it is rampant among Christians. One specific manifestation is preoccupation with pornography. Peter touches on this when he accuses the false teachers of having "eyes full of [adulterous women]" (v. 14): in other words, they looked at women as sexual objects. I cannot speak for women, but I know that men are taught in our culture from an early age to look at women just in that way. (And if the references among many women in our day to "hunks" means what I suspect it does, women are catching up fast.)

The opportunities—and therefore the temptations—to view women as sex objects have increased dramatically. When I was an adolescent, boys would have to go out of their way to sneak a peak at *Playboy*. Today, boys can tune in to cable stations when their parents aren't watching or "cruise the net" and view images of women far more explicit than anything *Playboy* ever published. Arguing that this explosion of pornography should not bother Christians, since we have the choice of simply ignoring it, misses the point. The more available the material, the easier it is to give in to this powerful temptation, not to speak of the corrupting influence it has on society at large. So successful was Paul's preaching in Ephesus after a couple of years that people stopped buying the idols of Artemis fashioned by Ephesian silversmiths—so much so that the artisans complained to the civil authorities (Acts 19). Would that our gospel witness was so powerful that pornographers would begin to complain to the government about us!

(3) Another form of hedonism is the desire for money and the pleasures, comfort, and security that money can buy. Peter claims that the false teachers are "experts in greed" (v. 14), imitators of Balaam, who "loved the wages of wickedness" (vv. 15–16). Balaam, you remember, was offered money by Balak to curse Israel. While he piously proclaimed that "I could not do anything great or small to go beyond the command of the LORD my God" (Num. 22:18), he nevertheless invited Balak's emissaries to spend the night so that he could see what the Lord might tell him in the morning (v. 19). Yet God had already explicitly commanded Balaam not to go with them. In his greed, Balaam sought an answer from God on a question that God had already answered. In other words, love of money can deflect and ultimately bring disaster to a ministry. Just ask Jim Bakker, sent to prison because his greed led him to use illegally money donated to his ministry.

But we who earn money by our ministries need to face up to a more subtle form of greed as well. I refer to letting financial considerations play too large a role in what ministry we decide to engage in. I teach in a seminary in which most students, and their families, work hard and live spartanly for three, four, five years or more to earn their divinity degree. It is entirely appropriate that graduating students consider finances when they are examining various ministry opportunities. But finances must always come a long second (or third or fourth) to other considerations. I am old-fashioned enough to believe that God calls men and women to specific ministries; and, yes, finances may be one way that he makes that call clear. But surely God sometimes calls us to ministries where the money may not be all that we would wish; where financial security cannot be guaranteed; where raising support may be necessary. In fact, considering that the greatest need for Christian ministers is in the countries with the least money, we would expect that God would often call his people to just such financially insecure places.

Lest I be accused of lecturing only to others, let me use myself as an example for a moment. One of the surprises that I have had in my ministry of teaching and writing is the number of opportunities I receive. Evangelical publishers are selling a lot of books, and they need people to write them. So now come two offers. One book promises to sell well and bring in steady royalties over a number of years; the other offers no such prospect, but focuses on a message the church needs to hear. Which do I choose and why? My decision should rest on one and only one consideration—considering my gifts and abilities and the needs of the church and the world, which book is God calling me to write? But with five children and a wife committed to a ministry of home-making, I perennially struggle to balance the checkbook. And I am afraid that there have been times when I have let money play too big a role in deciding what ministry opportunities to accept.

In his first letter, Peter warned church leaders that they were not to be "greedy for money," but that they were to be "eager to serve" (1 Peter 5:2). When Paul was engaged in planting a church, he refused to receive money from the people in that city, working by day in his own trade to provide for himself, so that no one could accuse him of preaching for money (1 Thess. 2:1–12). In a very "bottom-line"-oriented world, we need constantly to put money in its place—as one, quite minor, consideration in our decision-making. We will be free to do so only when we can say, with Paul, "I have learned to be content whatever the circumstances" (Phil. 4:11). If we are certain that God has called us to do something, we can be certain he will give us everything he deems necessary for us in that situation.

(4) I have been sketching some negative lessons to be learned from Peter's description of the false teachers. But, as my final point of application, I want to turn from the false teachers to their victims. Peter tells us that the false teachers were "seducing the unstable" (v. 14). This is the way it always is with false teaching. False teachers cannot force their opinions on anybody. They can only persuade people to adopt their ways of looking at things. And false teaching, of course, often has an attractive veneer. People like new ideas; and false teaching, by definition, trades in new ideas. People also like teaching that might make them feel less guilty about their own sins and failings. And certainly the false teaching of Peter's day held out this advantage.

The point is this: False teaching is often going to be naturally attractive to people. Only a solid grounding in God's truth and a genuine love for him will be able to protect people. Only Christians who have not taken the time (or have not had the time; see 2:18) to become solidly grounded in their faith fall prey to false teaching.

At the risk of sounding like a broken record, let me reiterate a point I think is absolutely vital in our present circumstances: Too many of our churches are devoting too much energy to the periphery of Christian ministry and too little to its heart. For at the heart of Christian ministry must always be the molding of people into the image of Christ, and the full and faithful teaching of God's truth is the means the Spirit uses to accomplish this goal. For example, teaching about the various cults in our churches is undoubtedly a useful enterprise and helps Christians understand the errors that are so prevalent in our day. But it is ultimately positive teaching about the Christian faith that will serve as the best protection against heresy, for we can never cover all the possible errors that false teachers might come up with.

Moreover, truth has its own positive impact, in which it strengthens and gives insight to the believer. Faced with false teaching in Ephesus, Timothy is told again and again by Paul to devote himself to "sound [healthy] doctrine" (see esp. 1 Tim. 4:6–8, 11–16). We need more pastors who have devoted themselves to living and teaching "sound doctrine." We need always to show the relevance of Christian truth and to deal with the issues in our culture that people are wrestling with. What will ultimately produce stable, growing Christians is careful, reverent exposition of God's Word. J. C. Ryle, writing over a hundred years ago, made this same point:

> You live in a world where your soul is in constant danger. Enemies are around you on every side. Your own heart is deceitful. Bad examples are numerous. Satan is always labouring to lead you astray. Above all false doctrine and false teachers of every kind abound. This is your great danger.
>
> To be safe you must be well armed. You must provide yourself with the weapons which God has given you for your help. You must store your mind with Holy Scripture. This is to be well armed.
>
> Arm yourself with a thorough knowledge of the written word of God. ... Neglect your Bible and nothing that I know of can prevent you from error if a plausible advocate of false teaching shall happen to meet you. ... You are the man that is unlikely to become established in the truth. I shall not be surprised to hear that you are troubled with doubts and questions about assurance, grace, faith, perseverance, etc. ... I shall not wonder if I am told that you have problems in your marriage, problems with your children, problems about the conduct of your family and about the company you keep. The world you steer through is full of rocks, shoals and sandbanks. You are not sufficiently

familiar either with lighthouses or charts. . . . You are the man who is likely to be carried away by some false teacher for a time. It will not surprise me if I hear that one of these clever eloquent men who can make a convincing presentation is leading you into error. You are in need of ballast (truth); no wonder if you are tossed to and fro like a cork on the waves.[23]

If you are a Christian layperson, I challenge you: Learn Christian truth. If you are a Christian minister, I challenge you: Teach Christian truth. May you be able to say, as Paul did when he left the Ephesian church leaders for what he thought was the last time: "You know that I have not hesitated to preach anything that would be helpful to you. . . . I am innocent of the blood of all men. For I have not hesitated to proclaim to you the whole will of God" (Acts 20:20, 26–27).

---

23. This selection is from a tract of Ryle's, quoted by J. I. Packer, *God's Words: Studies of Key Bible Themes* (Downers Grove, Ill.: InterVarsity, 1981), 41–42.

2 Peter 2:17–22

THESE MEN ARE springs without water and mists driven by a storm. Blackest darkness is reserved for them. [18]For they mouth empty, boastful words and, by appealing to the lustful desires of sinful human nature, they entice people who are just escaping from those who live in error. [19]They promise them freedom, while they themselves are slaves of depravity—for a man is a slave to whatever has mastered him. [20]If they have escaped the corruption of the world by knowing our Lord and Savior Jesus Christ and are again entangled in it and overcome, they are worse off at the end than they were at the beginning. [21]It would have been better for them not to have known the way of righteousness, than to have known it and then to turn their backs on the sacred command that was passed on to them. [22]Of them the proverbs are true: "A dog returns to its vomit," and, "A sow that is washed goes back to her wallowing in the mud."

Original Meaning

PETER'S DESCRIPTION OF the false teachers runs from verse 10 to the end of the chapter. Most commentators and translations rightly put a paragraph break between verses 16 and 17, recognizing a pause for breath at this point. One also detects a shift of emphasis. In 2:10–16, Peter has focused on the false *character* of these heretics: arrogant, sensuous, and greedy. Only in one passing allusion—"they seduce the unstable" (v. 14)—did he say anything about the "teaching" part of their profile. But now, in verses 17–22, their impact on other people takes center stage.

Their teaching, Peter claims, is hollow, arrogant, and deceitful (vv. 17–19). At the same time, he returns to the theme of verses 4–10a as he warns these false teachers about the terrible judgment awaiting them.[1] Indeed, because they have known the way of righteousness but have deliberately turned from it, their fate will be all the worse (vv. 20–22). By ending his polemic on the same note of judgment with which he began, Peter again exhibits the "ring composition" we have noted elsewhere in the letter.

---

1. Neyrey, *2 Peter, Jude,* 217–18, notes how these verses echo many of the words and themes from earlier in the chapter.

Hollow and Deceptive Teaching (vv. 17–19)

PETER'S COMPARISON OF the false teachers to the ignorant and greedy Balaam (vv. 15–16) ends his first round of critical comment. He marks the beginning of his second round with an abrupt return: "These men. . . ."[2] The two opening metaphors in verse 17 vividly capture the hollow and insubstantial nature of the false teachers' message. In the dry climate of the East, a spring of water is a marvelous blessing, giving—and sometimes even saving—life. Imagine the weary traveler's chagrin, then, when he or she finds the spring to be dry. So is the false teachers' message: It disappoints the spiritual pilgrim by promising spiritual vitality but not delivering it. Like the people of Israel, the followers of these impostors "have forsaken me [the Lord], the spring of living water, and have dug their own cisterns, cisterns that cannot hold water" (Jer. 2:13).

We might at first think that the second metaphor, "mists driven by a storm," has a different meaning—perhaps indicating the false teachers' instability, blown hither and yon by any breeze of doctrine. But the word "mist" can also denote the haze left after the condensation of a cloud into rain. But rather than producing life-giving rain, it could dissipate and, indeed, served as a harbinger of dry weather to come.[3] The two metaphors, therefore, combine to characterize the message of the false teachers as hollow and therefore disillusioning.

In language reminiscent of his earlier condemnation (see esp. vv. 4b, 10), Peter adds at the end of the verse a quick sentence of judgment: "Blackest darkness is reserved for them." Some commentators have criticized the sequence of imagery here, noting that it is awkward to think of springs of water and mists being confined to darkness. But authors often shift metaphors without connecting their images; and the image of darkness may, in fact, fit quite well with the accusation that the false teachers are "mists": "In place of the momentary darkness which they now cast, there is prepared for them a much thicker and eternal one."[4]

The "for" at the beginning of verse 18 connects both this verse and the next to verse 17. In these two verses, Peter explains why the false teachers are consigned to the darkness of hell (cf. v. 17b) and how they disillusion and harm people with their doctrine and practice (cf. v. 17a). Peter has already

---

2. The abruptness arises from the lack of any connecting conjunction or particle in Greek (a somewhat unusual phenomenon called "asyndeton"). The Greek for "these men" is *houtoi*. Peter has addressed the false teachers this way already (v. 12); but he does not consistently use the word—as Jude does—as a transitional marker.

3. The Greek word, *homichle*, is rare, found only here in the Bible. The understanding of the word given above is based especially on a description in Aristotle (*Meteor.* 1.346B).

4. Calvin, *Hebrews and 1 and 2 Peter*, 355.

chastised them for their arrogance (v. 10), and he returns to that theme here. The false teachers "mouth empty, boastful words." Peter indulges in some irony here, using the same Greek word for the false teachers' speech (*phthen-gomai*) as he has used to describe the speech of Balaam's donkey in verse 16. Even a donkey "mouthed" better doctrine than these false teachers do!

And this doctrine, while presented with a great show of power and persuasiveness is, in fact, "empty." This word suggests the idea of futility or frustration—of something that can never quite attain its goal. Paul, for instance, uses the word to describe the "futility" to which creation was subjected as a result of the fall of humanity into sin (Rom. 8:20). And words from this same root are used to describe the folly and inherent powerlessness of idolatry and the life of paganism (Acts 14:15; 1 Peter 1:18). The false teachers' words, while superficially attractive, cannot produce the spiritual fulfillment that they promise. Moreover, while the NIV does not preserve the connection, this first clause in verse 18 is linked to what is the main assertion in the verse: The false teachers entice people *"by* mouthing empty, boastful words."[5]

Peter then goes on to add a second clause to this main verb: The false teachers also entice "by appealing to the lustful desires of sinful human nature." The NIV is a rather free paraphrase of a difficult sequence of words in the Greek, which can be literally translated "in desires of the flesh, acts of sensuality." The NIV "by appealing" is a fair and accurate addition. Not so happy is their rendering of the Greek word for "flesh" (*sarx*) with "sinful human nature." As I have argued elsewhere (see the "Bridging Contexts" section after 1:3–11), the use of the word "nature" to translate this phrase can imply a view of the constitution of human beings that is only questionably biblical.

The word "lustful" represents the Greek word *aselgeia*, which Peter has already used twice in the chapter—once of the "shameful ways" of the false teachers generally (v. 2) and once of the "filthy" lifestyle of the people of Sodom and Gomorrah (v. 7). It denotes licentiousness, sensuality, a pleasure-focused lifestyle of sexual promiscuity, gluttony, and drunkenness. The word is plural here and is awkwardly tacked on to the end of the phrase (see our literal rendering above). Commentaries and translations are not certain what to do with this word. Some see it as restating the "desires of the flesh" (cf. NASB, "by fleshy desires, by sensuality"). Others, such as the REB, think it is a second, parallel term: "sensual lusts and debauchery." Most, however (cf. the NIV), take the word as a modifier of "desires." A decision among these alternatives is impossible to make. The idea, in any case, is clear: The false teach-

---

5. I am giving the participle *phthengomenoi* an instrumental force. As to the word "entice," Peter reuses a word that translates the same Greek word as "seduce" in verse 14.

ers appeal to the sinful and licentious desires of people to entice them away from the truth. Thus Peter lists two means that the false teachers use to attract people to their brand of heresy; as Bigg puts it, "Grandiose sophistry is the hook, filthy lust the bait."[6]

But the false teachers, Peter suggests, do not go after just anybody. Clever in picking their targets, they dangle their lure in front of "people who are just escaping from those who live in error." A significant textual variant is found in the Greek that underlies this clause. Some manuscripts read *ontos apophy-gontes*, others have *oligos apopheugontas*. Even without knowing any Greek, one can note how similar these two phrases are and how easy it would be for a scribe to change one of them to the other. If we accept the first alternative, the people whom the false teachers are enticing are those who have "fully escaped" from "those who live in error." The KJV adopts this reading, translating "those that were clean escaped from them who live in error."[7]

But the second reading is adopted by all the contemporary major English translations and should be accepted. It identifies the false teachers' targets as people who had only "recently" or "barely"[8] escaped from "those who live in error"; in fact, the present tense of the participle in this reading suggests that they are still in the process of escaping the entanglements of their past lives. It makes excellent sense to think that the heretics would go after new converts. The word "error" (*plane*) is regularly used in the Bible to describe paganism (see, e.g., Rom. 1:27; Titus 3:3). In other words, Peter pictures these new converts as still in the process of distancing themselves from the values and lifestyle of the pagan society to which they recently belonged and in the midst of which they continue to live.

In verse 19 Peter continues to describe the false teachers' mode of operation. Another tactic to entice recent converts from their faith is to promise them freedom. This is about the only place in the chapter that Peter touches on the false teachers' doctrinal program. Unfortunately, he is not specific: freedom from what? When one considers the evidence from the letter itself, three possibilities deserve to be considered. (1) The false teachers may have been promising freedom from fear of evil spiritual beings. Peter has criticized the heretics earlier in the chapter for their arrogance and unconcern with these beings (vv. 10b–12). (2) The false teachers may have been promising freedom from eschatological judgment.[9] As both 1:16–21 and 3:3–12

---

6. Bigg, *The Epistles of St. Peter and St. Jude*, 285.

7. See also ibid., 287.

8. The Greek word here is *oligos*, "a little measure." It is not clear whether it has a temporal meaning ("for a little while, recently") or a general quantitative meaning ("to a slight extent"). The difference in meaning is slight.

9. Bauckham, *Jude, 2 Peter*, 275–76; Neyrey, *2 Peter, Jude*, 223.

show, the false teachers' basic doctrinal plank was skepticism about the return of Christ and the judgment associated with his return. (3) They may have been advocating freedom from any external moral constraint.[10] Peter has dwelt repeatedly on the false teachers' libertine lifestyle (vv. 13–16, 18). And we have evidence from elsewhere in the New Testament of a tendency to abuse the free grace available in the gospel by turning it into a license to sin (see the warnings in Rom. 6; Gal. 5:13–14; 1 Peter 2:16).

Since any of these views fits well into the broader context of 2 Peter 2, we must ask which fits best in the immediate context. Here the rest of verse 19 helps. Peter points out the irony in the false teachers' situation: While promising others freedom, "they themselves are slaves of depravity." The emphatic "themselves" suggests that the "depravity" to which they are enslaved is closely related to the freedom they promise. But what is this "depravity"? The NIV makes a definite interpretive decision in rendering the Greek word phthora with "depravity." A more neutral translation would be "corruption" (found in most English versions). The corruption may be moral in nature (in which case depravity is a fair rendering) or it may be physical.

Peter has used phthora twice before in this letter, once with each meaning. In 1:4, I argued it has a moral flavor; in 2:12, it refers to eschatological destruction. Neither definition fits very well with the idea that the false teachers promise freedom from evil spiritual beings, so this option should be eliminated. But if the reference is to eschatological destruction, the second option works well: While promising people freedom from judgment, the false teachers themselves are destined for judgment. And if moral corruption is intended, the third also makes good sense: The false teachers reveal the futility of their promise of freedom from moral requirements by living lives enslaved to immorality themselves. I think this last interpretation is slightly better than the other. The language of slavery in this verse and the focus on immorality in verse 20 suggests that Peter is thinking along these lines rather than in terms of eschatological judgment. As Green puts it, "In their quest for self-expression, they fell into bondage to self."[11]

Peter reinforces the point by quoting a proverb: "A man is a slave to whatever has mastered him." Since the proverb originated from the practice of enslaving enemies captured in wartime, some commentators think that it should be given a personal reference: "A person is enslaved to whoever has mastered him."[12] But it is in the nature of a proverb to shift its referents

---

10. This is the most popular view among the commentators; see, e.g., Bigg, *The Epistles of St. Peter and St. Jude*, 286; Kelly, *The Epistles of Peter and of Jude*, 346; Green, *The Second Epistle General of Peter and the General Epistle of Jude*, 117.

11. Green, *The Second Epistle General of Peter and the General Epistle of Jude*, 117.

12. E.g., Kelly, *The Epistles of Peter and of Jude*, 347.

depending on the situation to which it is applied. Here, Peter applies it to the impersonal force of sin; thus, the neuter rendering (found in almost all English versions) is better.

The Serious Plight of the False Teachers (vv. 20–22)

THE NIV PRESERVES the ambiguity of the original by translating simply "they" at the beginning of this verse. What is unclear is the antecedent of this pronoun. We could go back to the end of verse 18: "people who are just escaping from those who live in error." The repetition of the idea of "escape" in verse 20 may point to this connection. In this case, all of verses 20–22 refer to the new converts whom the false teachers have been making the target of their propaganda. The point of these verses, then, would be a warning to these impressionable believers against this false teaching by pointing out the serious consequences that follow any declension from the truth they had been taught.[13]

But the closest antecedent is found in the subject of the immediately preceding verse: the false teachers. And it is these false teachers who have been Peter's focus throughout the chapter.[14] A decision is difficult here, but I lean slightly to this second interpretation. We would expect the chapter to end with a final denunciation of the false teachers; a warning to recent converts seems somewhat out of place.

Peter, then, continues his description of the false teachers. As Bauckham notes, the apostle uses some of the same language that he used early in the letter to characterize Christians. In 1:4, he said that Christians have "escaped the corruption [*phthora*] in the world"; in 1:3, he claimed that they have come to know our Lord and Savior Jesus Christ. The false teachers, he now notes, have also "escaped the corruption [*miasmata*[15]] of the world by knowing our Lord and Savior Jesus Christ."[16] As I noted in commenting on 1:2 and 3, Peter is fond of the language of "knowledge" (in the biblical sense of experiential knowledge) to describe Christian existence. From his perspective at least, then, these false teachers gave every evidence of being Christians.

Yet they run the risk of becoming "entangled" in the corruption of the world again and, indeed, of being "overcome" by it. Green thinks that

---

13. For this view, see Bigg, *The Epistles of St. Peter and St. Jude,* 287; Kelly, *The Epistles of Peter and of Jude,* 247–48.

14. See, e.g., Mayor, *The Epistle of St. Jude and the Second Epistle of St. Peter,* 141–42; Green, *The Second Epistle General of Peter and the General Epistle of Jude,* 118; Bauckham, *Jude, 2 Peter,* 277.

15. The word is found only here in biblical Greek but is closely related to the word Peter has used in v. 10, *miasmos* (NIV "corrupt").

16. Bauckham, *Jude, 2 Peter,* 277.

"entangled" may preserve the fishing imagery Peter has been using to describe the false teachers' strategy ("seduce," "entice," or "lure" in vv. 14 and 18).[17] Setting lures for others, they become entangled in their own nets. Whether or not this is the case, Peter's point is that such a return to the corrupt lifestyle of the world will bring disaster to them: "They are worse off at the end than they were at the beginning." Peter is almost certainly quoting Jesus' saying at the end of his story about the evil spirit in Matthew 12:43–45:

> When an evil spirit comes out of a man, it goes through arid places seeking rest and does not find it. Then it says, "I will return to the house I left." When it arrives, it finds the house unoccupied, swept clean and put in order. Then it goes and takes with it seven other spirits more wicked than itself, and they go in and live there. And the final condition of that man is worse than the first. That is how it will be with this wicked generation.

So it is with people who embrace Christ but then abandon him for the world again: Because they have knowingly and openly rejected the truth, their judgment will be worse than it would otherwise have been.

This is what Peter explains in verse 21. He again uses "way" language to describe Christianity (see the comments on 2:15). Following Christ means to walk the road of right behavior ("righteousness") that he demands of his disciples. It would be better, Peter warns, not even to enter that road than to walk it for a time and then abandon it. Peter's focus on the moral failings of the false teachers surfaces here again. Not only does he use "righteousness" (in a moral sense) to describe the "way" of Christianity, but he also singles out "the sacred command that was passed on to them" as that which they have abandoned. Peter does not have a single "command" in mind here. He uses the singular to summarize the totality of Christian instruction, a traditional body of teaching that was taught (and thus "passed on") to converts. Paul, similarly, refers to "the form of teaching to which you were entrusted" (Rom. 6:17) and "the good deposit that was entrusted to you [Timothy]" (2 Tim. 1:14).

As Bauckham has noted, Peter has composed verses 20–22 almost entirely out of traditional material: a saying of Jesus in verse 20, a "better for them" warning in verse 21 (such as we find elsewhere in the New Testament), and now, in verse 22, two extrabiblical proverbs.[18] In fact, the NIV plural "proverbs" is a bit of a liberty. The Greek word is singular; Peter perhaps uses it because he views the two proverbs as functioning together to make the same point. And combining proverbs that speak of both dogs and pigs also makes good

---

17. Green, *The Second Epistle General of Peter and the General Epistle of Jude*, 118–19.
18. Bauckham, *Jude, 2 Peter*, 273. He notes as parallels to v. 21 Mark 9:42 and 14:21.

sense. Jews viewed both animals negatively. Dogs in the ancient Near East were not "man's best friend." They were not mild-mannered house pets but wild and savage beasts that often stole food and preyed on weak people. And, of course, pigs were anathema, declared "unclean" in the Old Testament and avoided by pious Jews. Dogs and pigs were thus often grouped together as despised animals.[19]

The meaning of the first proverb is clear enough: Returning to the corruption of the world is like a dog returning to eat its own vomit. But the saying about the pig (NIV "sow") can be taken in two different senses, depending on how we put together the Greek syntax. One possibility is to translate, "A sow that washes itself by wallowing in the mire." Peter would then be suggesting that the false teachers, having gotten a taste for depravity, come to enjoy it; they are like pigs who, it is well known, love to wash in mud.[20] But all the major English translations and most commentators opt for the reading represented in the NIV: "A sow that is washed goes back to her wallowing in the mud." This proverb fits precisely the situation of the false teachers as Peter has depicted it in verses 20–21: Having been washed clean by the blood of Christ, they are nevertheless anxious to return again to the filth of the world.[21]

IN THE LAST "Bridging Contexts" section, I argued that "mirror-reading" a New Testament book can force its message into a mold that the original author would never have recognized. The problem, I argued, is that scholars tend to seize on one particular historical, cultural, or philosophical situation and to insist that everything in a given book be explained in light of it. As Samuel Sandmel put it in a famous essay on the general problem, too many scholars assume that ideas in the ancient world flowed in pipelines—passed down pure and intact and independent of any other ideas. In fact, ideas never remain isolated. They are modified in various ways over time, becoming mixed in various degrees with many other ideas that are rattling around.

---

19. Cf. Jesus' command: "Do not give dogs what is sacred; do not throw your pearls to pigs" (Matt. 7:6).

20. Bigg, *The Epistles of St. Peter and St. Jude*, 287.

21. On this reading of the proverb, it might stema from a popular seventh- or sixth-century B.C. book of sayings called *Ahiqar*; in the Arabic version, 8:8 reads "My son, you have been to me like the pig who went into the hot bath with people of quality, and when it came out of the hot bath, it saw a filthy hole and it went down and wallowed in it." See Bauckham, *Jude, 2 Peter*, 279.

The ancient world in this respect is no different than ours. How many people do you know hold to any "pure" form of belief? Do the Democrats you know consistently toe the party line at every point, never entertaining an idea that might be dubbed Republican or socialist? How many pure "existentialists" do you know? People, including professors and theorists, hold and propagate ideas that are always a mixture, to some degree, of many different, and sometimes conflicting, sources.

Cultural context of the false teachers. As we compile our profile of the false teachers from 2 Peter, then, we would do well to ask about some of the different cultural influences that may have led to their particular brand of heresy. In the commentary thus far, I have focused on specific points of their false teaching. But it is worth at least asking whether we can identify any larger ideological movements of the first-century period that may have fed into their particular brew of erroneous ideas.

Peter's claim that the false teachers were "promising freedom" (v. 19) provides us with a good entry point into this question. I have noted how hard it is for us to know just what kind of freedom the false teachers were promising. But Jerome Neyrey has suggested that this promise is best explained as the product of Epicurean thinking. In fact, he argues that all the distinguishing marks of the false teaching, as we can reconstruct them from 2 Peter, fit nicely into the Epicurean mold.[22] I think Neyrey's reconstruction of the situation is well worth considering—not necessarily because I agree with it *in toto*, but because it reminds us of the impact that broader first-century ideologies may at least indirectly have had on the specific beliefs of people like the false teachers in 2 Peter.

Many of us will remember the Epicureans as one of the major philosophical "schools" of the first-century world. And because the word has passed into common parlance, we often associate Epicureans with the idea of the pursuit of pleasure—with unbridled sexual behavior, good eating, and drinking, or the "high life." Here is where the popular conception goes astray. Epicurus (who lived from 341–270 B.C.) and his followers did, indeed, make the pursuit of "pleasure" their goal in life. But they defined pleasure not as the indulgence of the flesh but as the avoidance of pain and distress. They sought mental peace (*ataraxia*); and certain pleasures of life, far from contributing to that peace, would, in fact, disturb it.

But most significant for our purposes was Epicurus's denial of providence. Epicureans believed in the existence of gods but held that they had nothing to do with life on earth. Human beings, made up of a chance combination

---

22. Neyrey, *2 Peter, Jude,* 122–28. See the introduction for a more general discussion of the false teaching.

of atoms, go their own way in this world without interference from the gods. And when they die, the atoms simply disperse again. Epicureans did not believe in the afterlife or in any kind of divine judgment. "Death is nothing to us; for the body, when it has been resolved into its elements, has no feeling; and that which has no feeling is nothing to us."[23] Any interference from the gods or threat of punishment in the afterlife would constitute an affront to human freedom.[24]

We can readily understand how certain elements in this brief and inadequate description of the Epicureans might fit the profile of the false teachers in 2 Peter. The false teachers' skepticism about the coming of Christ in glory and future judgment (1:16–21; 3:3–12) may well reflect Epicurean attacks on the idea of divine providence. The false teachers' promise of freedom may reflect Epicurean concern about the threat to human integrity from any divine interference. And even the false teachers' licentiousness might be rooted in Epicurean ideas. For while the Epicureans prized a restrained and temperate lifestyle, their doctrine could easily provide the perfect basis for a wild and profligate manner of life. One need not fear divine judgment or punishment in the afterlife. And since the body was "nothing" (see the quotation above), one could do with it whatever one wanted. In fact, as Neyrey points out, critics of the Epicureans scolded them for opening the door for just such immorality. Lactantius, a Roman moralist, claimed:

If any chieftain or pirates or leaders of robbers were exhorting his men to acts of violence, what other language could he employ than to say the same things which Epicurus says: that the gods take no notice; that they are not affected with anger or kind feeling; that the punishment of a future state is not to be dreaded, because the souls die after death, and there is no future state of punishment at all.[25]

Neyrey himself is careful about identifying the false teachers of 2 Peter as Epicureans. He thinks they may have been but is more concerned to argue that the kind of skepticism associated with Epicurus and his followers is an important component of the false teachers' arguments. I am a bit more skeptical than Neyrey about a direct relationship between the false teachers and Epicureans. But I think that he is correct to posit this Epicurean-related skepticism about divine providence as an indirect influence on the false teachers.

---

23. Diogenes Laertius, a third century A.D. Epicurean (10.139). Cited in Neyrey, 2 Peter, Jude, 123.

24. For a brief overview of Epicurean thought, see R. W. Vunderink, "Epicureans," in ISBE, rev. ed., 2:121–22.

25. Lactantius, Inst. 3.17; the quotation is taken from Neyrey, 2 Peter, Jude, 123–24.

The problem, of course (as Neyrey admits), is to figure out how indirect the influence may have been. While perhaps originating with Epicurus, the skepticism he advocated had by the first century A.D. filtered its way to various degrees into a variety of strands of teaching and belief. We may say, as it were, that it was one of those ideas that was "in the air" and that the false teachers picked up as an important component of their heretical notions about Christianity.

Theological context of understanding the false teachers. As I have repeatedly emphasized, bringing the message of 2 Peter into the contemporary world requires careful attention to context. But "context" is multifaceted. We use the word most often to denote the *literary* context: the biblical book, or the immediate section of that book, in which the text we are studying is found. But we must also reckon with the *historical* context, or what we often call the "background" of the text—all those circumstances that form part of the original author's world and that have a bearing on what he wrote.

Scholars of any theological persuasion recognize the importance of these two contexts in their interpretation. In fact, the two combine to form the "grammatical-historical" method, the interpretive approach that has become enshrined in modern biblical studies. But evangelicals have always insisted a third context must be added to these first two: the *theological* context. Evangelicals, unlike many other interpreters, believe the Bible is ultimately a single book, speaking with a single voice. This means that any part of the Bible must be interpreted in light of the teaching of the whole Bible. Nonevangelical interpreters can rest content with the interpretation of a passage that brings it into contradiction with other passages of the Bible. Not so evangelical interpreters. Having done our best to exegete a text according to its literary and historical context, we must then move to the next step and ask how our results square with the teaching of the Bible elsewhere on the same topic.

We may conclude that our results fit nicely with what we think the Bible says elsewhere on the matter, and our exegesis may then be at an end. But we may also find that our conclusions on a given text do not immediately match with what we thought Scripture was teaching in other places. We then have further work to do, going back to our exegesis to see if we may have made a mistake. Perhaps we conclude we have not. It may be, then, that our ideas about what the Bible was teaching elsewhere on the subject is in error. Thus we must turn to these other biblical texts to see if we may be mistaken about what they say. This process (what some have called the "spiral of interpretation") is a necessary corollary of an evangelical belief about the unity of the Bible. Evangelical interpretation should always be marked by attention to this theological context. But it is vital to keep listening to the text, so that it can correct our theology as we go.

Any accurate application of 2 Peter 2:20–22 must grapple with this larger theological context. As I have noted, Peter here uses language to describe the false teachers that he elsewhere uses to depict conversion to Christianity. They have "escaped the corruption of the world by knowing our Lord and Savior Jesus Christ" (v. 20). Yet in the same verse Peter claims that if they persist in the heretical path they have chosen, "they are worse off at the end than they were at the beginning." What being "worse off" means becomes clear when we compare what Peter says about their fate in 2:4–10a: They will suffer eschatological condemnation. A first "reading" of these verses, then, seems to teach that genuine Christians can permanently fall away from their faith if they persist in holding heretical ideas and/or in pursuing a sinful lifestyle.

When one reads the commentaries on this passage, one finds different reactions to this reading of these verses. Michael Green, for instance, dismissing a textual variant that adds "away backwards" after "turn" in verse 21, says, "This is small comfort to those who would dogmatically deny the possibility of a Christian apostatizing." He goes on,

> One must still face the fact that these men are said to have known …the way of righteousness and to have escaped, once upon a time, from the world's defilements. The parallels with Hebrews iii. 12–18, vi. 6, x. 26, 38f., 1 Corinthians x. 1–12, Jude 4–6, are clear and unmistakable. Apostasy would seem to be a real and awful possibility.[26]

Edwin A. Blum's comments on the same text are an instructive contrast:

> Is it possible, then, for Christians to lose their salvation? Many would answer affirmatively on the basis of this and similar texts (e.g., Heb 6:4–6; 10:26). But this verse asserts only that false teachers who have for a time escaped from world corruption through knowing Christ and then turn away from the light of the Christian faith are worse off than they were before knowing Christ. It uses no terminology affirming that they were Christians in reality. ... The NT makes a distinction between those who are in the churches and those who are regenerate. ... So when Peter says, "They are worse off at the end than they were at the beginning," the reference is to a lost apostate.[27]

Both authors would probably agree with D. A. Carson's general definition of apostasy: "the decisive turning away from a religious position and stance

---

26. Green, *The Second Epistle General of Peter and the General Epistle of Jude*, 120.
27. Edwin A. Blum, "2 Peter," in *EBC*, 12:282.

once firmly held."[28] But for Green, the apostasy is from full and genuine Christian salvation, and this text makes clear that it can happen. For Blum, on the other hand, "apostatize" means to fall away from whatever (nonsaving) knowledge of Christ one might have had—losing one's salvation, he implies, cannot happen. Neither commentator seeks to justify his reading of the text against the broader sweep of biblical teaching (although both refer to other "warning" passages). I am not criticizing them for this; no commentator can justify every point he or she makes with a full-blown systematic exploration. But what I think is clear is that these two scholars approach 2 Peter 2:20–22 from quite different understandings of what Scripture says elsewhere about "eternal security." That is, they understand the theological context of the passage differently.

My first purpose in raising this issue is simply to point out the necessary role that theological context plays in interpretation. I sometimes hear students at the seminary where I teach express a bias against "systematic theology." "All I want to do," they piously proclaim, "is to study the text and let it lead me wherever it goes."

"Well and good," I respond. "But do you believe that the Bible is true?"

"Of course," they say.

"Can the Bible be true if it contradicts itself?"

"No."

"What happens, then, if your conclusions about one text contradict your conclusions about another text?"

"Then I must harmonize them," they assert.

"And how do you do that without a broad framework of biblical teaching to work from—in a word, systematic theology?"

So I am not criticizing Green and Blum for reading this text in light of their theology. What I do criticize, however, is the interpreter who fails to let the text contribute to his or her "spiral" of theological growth. None of us has anchored securely in Scripture everything we believe. And the danger we run is to impose an unexamined theological predilection on a text, for we then prevent that text from speaking to us. And this leads me to my second purpose in the discussion: to shed light on the theological significance of such warning passages by describing the process I have gone through in grappling with this text.

I bring to this passage a generally Calvinist theological perspective. I was taught eternal security in seminary, and I have since that time found many

---

28. D. A. Carson, "Reflections on Assurance," in *The Grace of God and the Bondage of the Will: Historical and Theological Perspectives on Calvinism*, ed. Thomas R. Schreiner and Bruce A. Ware (2 vols.; Grand Rapids: Baker, 1995), 2:396.

texts that seem to me to confirm its truthfulness. In addition to the well-known passages from the Gospel of John (especially John 6:39–40; 10:28), I am particularly impressed by Paul's argument in Romans 5–8, where Paul mounts an argument for Christian assurance. Those who have been justified, he teaches, will be saved on the last day (5:9–10). Those who have been predestined, called, and justified are glorified (8:30).[29] He asserts what seems to me to be an unbreakable connection between initial justification and final salvation; indeed, his doctrine of justification is itself eschatological, the ultimate verdict of God being rendered over the believer at the moment of conversion.

But then I move to other passages in the New Testament, particularly the many "warning passages." And I don't even have to leave Romans to find them. In chapter 11, Paul warns boastful Gentile Christians: You "wild branches" who have been grafted into the olive tree (the people of God) can be "cut off" again. Here Paul seems to tell genuine believers (they have been grafted into the people of God) that they are in danger of losing their status among the people of God, of forfeiting the salvation they once enjoyed. Many other passages sound the same note of warning, the most famous, of course, being the ones in Hebrews (especially 6:4–6; 10:26–31). And 2 Peter 2:20–22 fits exactly this mold.[30]

I am therefore faced with a series of texts that appears to conflict with my belief in eternal security. What do I do? Because my belief about eternal security rests on serious study of the text, I first seek ways of explaining these texts in a way that can fit my "theological context." Three options come to mind. (1) Perhaps the warnings are only hypothetical. Peter, for instance, says, "*If* they have escaped the corruption of the world . . . and are again . . . overcome, they are worse off." He does not say that they have actually taken this step. On this view, the biblical authors warn true believers of what the consequences of their persistent apostasy will be—knowing all the time that such apostasy is not possible.

(2) Perhaps the people are not really being warned about eschatological condemnation. Peter, again, for instance, says that these false teachers will be "worse off," that they will end up "wallowing in the mud" again. He may mean simply that the false teachers will experience serious problems in this life and maybe "loss of reward" in the next.

---

29. Paul puts this verb in the aorist tense, and I think it is past-referring here. The believer's glorification has already been determined by the Lord.

30. The best general exegetical/theological study of the warning passages from an Arminian perspective is I. H. Marshall, *Kept by the Power of God: A Study of Perseverance and Falling Away* (Minneapolis: Bethany Fellowship, 1969).

(3) Perhaps the people being warned are not really Christians at all. Peter says that the false teachers have a "knowledge" of Christ, but this may be no more than head knowledge. They may be people who have participated in the life of the church, have given every indication of being Christian, but have never actually experienced God's regenerative work.

Most Calvinist scholars take this last tack; note, for instance, Blum's comments above. And I think this approach is far superior to the other two. A hypothetical warning is not of much use. In moments of incoherent anger, when I had to wade for yet another time through oceans of toys to get to my office, I used to warn my children, "If you don't clean up all these toys right now, I am going to give them all away to other kids." I knew very well that I would never do this; and, more important, *they* knew as well that basically soft-hearted Daddy would never do it. So of what value was the warning? Neither is it satisfactory to think that these warning passages hold out only temporal penalties. In 2 Peter 2:20–22, for instance, being in a worse position than before conversion can only refer to eschatological condemnation.

Thus I turn to the third option, that the false teachers were never really Christians at all. But I find a problem here as well: Peter uses "conversion" language ("knowing" Christ) to describe them. True, he may be using the language differently here than he did elsewhere in his letter, where genuine conversion seemed to be indicated. And we must recognize also that the New Testament authors necessarily describe people on the basis of their appearance/profession. As D. A. Carson has shown, the New Testament consistently recognizes a class of people who are not simply pagans (that is, they are part of the church and have come to experience the blessings of Christ), but who are not yet regenerate Christians either (that is, the Holy Spirit has not yet brought them to faith). Such people are difficult to recognize, and they may, indeed, only be known by their perseverance to the end.[31] In other words, New Testament writers sometimes use the language of Christian conversion for such people on the basis of their appearance.

Even this alternative, however, does not ultimately satisfy me at the exegetical level. Peter in the text we are looking at, and even more clearly the author to the Hebrews, gives every indication of describing these people as they really are, not just as they appear to be. At this point, then, I have failed to come up with a natural and convincing interpretation of 2 Peter 2:20–22 that harmonizes it with my "eternal security" theological context. And so I need to go back and reexamine that context; am I sure about those passages that I think teach this doctrine? Yes, I have to say—trying to make every allowance for the effect of tradition and habit—I think they do validly teach eternal security.

---

31. Carson, "Reflections on Assurance," 399–405.

Where, then, does all this leave me? I have, I think, three options. (1) I can abandon my evangelical conviction about the unity of Scripture. But this, for me, is a "nonnegotiable," taught so clearly and brought home to my heart so often that it cannot be contested.

(2) I can admit that I face on this point a biblical "antinomy": a situation in which the Bible asserts two things that appear to be contradictory. I may have to admit that I cannot yet understand (and may never be able to understand) how these two strands of teaching—genuine Christians cannot lose their salvation; genuine Christians can lose their salvation forever—can be harmonized. My responsibility is not to question or to force the texts into unnatural configurations, but simply to believe that both are true. I think we have to live with antinomies in the Bible—though we must be careful not to entertain outright contradictions, for to do so is to forfeit any intelligent and defensible view of the Bible's truth. And believing both ends of the antimony discussed here looks to be just such a flat contradiction.

(3) Thus, I come to the third alternative: that the false teachers of 2 Peter 2:20–22 are not really genuine Christians. I admit that this is not the most natural reading of the text. Or, perhaps I need to say, not the most natural reading of the text in its immediate context. But my point is that the larger context of the passage is the *entire* Bible. And when that context is considered, my hesitant conclusion is that the best interpretation I can now discover is that Peter is not talking about truly regenerate believers. But I will honestly admit that I am not finally satisfied with this conclusion, and I keep coming across warning passages that I struggle to do exegetical justice to. Finally, I certainly do not accord "eternal security" the kind of nonnegotiable status that I attributed above to my view of Scripture. I am in process on this issue, still convinced that eternal security is a biblical doctrine, but less convinced of it than I used to be.

CONSEQUENCES OF TURNING **away from the truth.** My first point of application stems directly from the issue that I just discussed under "Bridging Contexts": Peter's warning about the consequences of turning away from truth (vv. 20–22). I noted in the "Original Meaning" section how difficult it is to decide whether Peter directs his warning to the false teachers or to new converts whom the false teachers are trying to influence. Whichever it might be, however, and whatever view we finally take on the question of eternal security, one point is clear: Willfully turning back from the truth brings terrible consequences.

Peter implies in his warning a point that Scripture makes clear in many places: that the more we know of God when we reject his truth, the greater will be our punishment. When Jesus distinguishes the "blasphemy against the Spirit" from other sins and claims that it cannot be forgiven (Matt. 12:31–32 and parallels), he is probably thinking of the Pharisees' open-eyed refusal to accept the evidence of Jesus' miracles. It was the abundance of evidence available to them that made their rejection so serious and final. John may be thinking of the same kind of willful rejection when he mentions a "sin that leads to death," for which prayers should not be offered (1 John 5:16). The most famous of such warnings, of course, come in the letter to the Hebrews, where the author warns that people who have come to understand who Jesus Christ is and experienced many of the blessings he has to offer and then turn away from the truth will have no opportunity to repent again (Heb. 6:4–6); their doom is sealed (cf. also 10:26–31).

The "rigorism" expressed in these texts became an important and debated point in the first centuries of the church. Many early Christian teachers went to the extreme of arguing that *any* sin committed after baptism could not receive forgiveness.[32] It was for this reason that some early Christians, such as the Emperor Constantine, waited to be baptized until they were on their deathbeds. Other early theologians insisted that it was only certain sins that could not be forgiven after baptism.[33] But the position of Hebrews and other New Testament writings is clear: Only the sin of willful apostasy cannot be forgiven. Peter agrees: The dire consequences he warns about here are for those who have come to know Christ and then turned away from him.

Sensitive believers and even unbelievers are often disturbed by this denial of the possibility of forgiveness. I recently received a telephone call from a man who was in great distress because he thought he had committed the "unpardonable sin." Some years ago, he had been exposed to the gospel. He had begun to sense the Lord's reality and goodness, but he decided to reject the message. He now found himself unable to believe and feared that God would never accept him. I responded with Calvin's wise comfort: The very fact that someone is worried about having committed the unpardonable sin shows that he or she has not. Such concern and desire to believe suggests that the Holy Spirit, far from abandoning this person, is still at work in his or her life. And so we must exercise extreme caution in accusing a person of having committed this sin. Many people refuse to respond to the gospel, sometimes many times. Only God ultimately knows whether those refusals fall into the category of willful apostasy that Peter and the other New Testament writers are talking about.

---

32. For example, Tertullian, Justin, Clement of Alexandria.
33. See *The Shepherd of Hermas, Visions* 5.7; *Mandates* 4.3.16.

But these passages do warn about a serious possibility, and we must not err on the other side and ignore the dire warnings they issue. The principle assumed in these warnings is that greater knowledge brings greater responsibility. "From everyone who has been given much, much will be demanded" (Luke 12:48). The principle lends new urgency to our proclamation of the gospel and people's response to it. We must warn those who have begun to understand and appreciate the gospel that they may never have another opportunity of becoming saved. Their rejection could be final and eternal.

Concern about holiness in life. But we must not limit the principle of "greater responsibility" to non-Christians. To be sure, I am inclined to think that eternal damnation is not a real threat for the Christian. But the danger is that such a theological position will lead to smug satisfaction, a presumption on God's grace. Belief in eternal security must not lead to unconcern about holiness of life. We may believe that God promises to preserve his saints to the end, but we must also recognize that it is in that very perseverance that the saints are recognized (see Heb. 3:6, 14). Thus we Christians are called to respond to the truth about God that we learn and are warned about the consequences if we fail to do so.

Those, like myself, who labor in a Christian academic environment are perhaps most prone to the danger of "barren learning." Fascination with the Greek verbal system can blind us to what the Greek text is saying about God and his ways with us. Concern to organize and present coherently biblical material can eviscerate the text of its passion and practical significance as professors present it.

But this is not a problem confined to academia. "Cheap grace" is endemic among contemporary evangelicals. We constantly hear that God loves us, that Christ's blood covers our sins, that "if we confess our sins, he is faithful and just and will forgive us our sins" (1 John 1:9)—precious promises, not to be toned down for a minute. The problem is that we don't often enough hear that God is holy and terrible in his majesty, that he is just and cannot abide sin, that "we must all appear before the judgment seat of Christ, that each one may receive what is due him for the things done while in the body" (2 Cor. 5:10). The litmus test of our Christianity is not how much we know but the degree to which what we know affects our attitudes and actions. We Calvinists must be extremely careful that we do not allow our belief in or teaching about eternal security to remove or lessen the responsibility that God places on our shoulders to grow in the grace he so richly makes available.

Freedom and servitude. Another point of application emerges from the other side of this tragic "turn" that Peter warns against in these verses. If Christian truth is what these people are turning from, what are they turning toward? "Freedom," they would apparently respond. And here we find a word that resonates positively with most people today. Political freedom is, in most of the world at least, viewed not only as desirable but as worth fighting for. Perhaps more relevantly, modern humanity also prizes freedom from external constraint. Few have gone as far as advocating anarchy, recognizing that society requires at least a minimum of rules and organization. But since the Enlightenment, it has been assumed that to be genuinely human is to be free to make up one's own mind, to decide for oneself what is right and wrong, guided by conscience alone.

The false teachers in Peter's day were apparently promising something like this. Yet, as Peter implies, such "freedom" is an illusion. Scripture makes clear that no person is autonomous in the strict sense. Every person is subject to someone or something; as Paul put it, "You are slaves to the one whom you obey—whether you are slaves to sin, which leads to death, or to obedience, which leads to righteousness" (Rom. 6:16; cf. also John 8:31–36). The false teachers, as Peter points out, have exchanged one master for another: Exulting in their liberation from God's holy requirements, they "are slaves of depravity." This depravity or corruption is, since the Fall, endemic in human beings. It is that tendency to "be curved in our ourselves," as the theologians used to put it, to make as our goal in life the satisfaction of our own desires. Without divine hindrance, this preoccupation with self rules people, determining their ways of thinking and their actions. In the gospel, God provides the only escape from this servitude of self: servitude of Jesus the Lord.

The question we must therefore insistently bring before the people of our generation is this: Which servitude is preferable? Many, attracted by the pleasures of power or of money or of sex, and swayed by the perverse imagery of the media, answer unhesitatingly: of self. These same people sometimes come face-to-face with the destructive results of their catering to self. I think of a woman who continued the pursuit of the "good life" after her marriage. One weekend she got drunk and had sex with two of her friends. When she confessed what had happened to her husband, her marriage was effectively at an end. She came to her counselor on Monday morning, sobbing uncontrollably over the husband and two children she had lost through her catering to the pleasures of self.

Though not a Christian, the Roman moralist Seneca put it well: "To be enslaved to oneself is the heaviest of all servitudes." The indulgence of the flesh leads inexorably to enslavement to the flesh. As Peter puts it, "A man is a slave to whatever has mastered him" (v. 19). In a similar vein, Paul warns the Corinthians, whose watchword was, "Everything is permissible for me," with this maxim, "I will not be mastered by anything" (1 Cor. 6:12).

As stewards of the gospel, we need to be bolder in warning about the terrible consequences of the self-indulgence that rules our culture. Peter minces few words here. He compares sinful self-indulgence to vomit and mud. Many of us probably shy away from such graphic characterizations of sin, fearing that we will be labeled extremists or unloving. But the increasing tendency for people in our churches to dabble in various forms of self-indulgence requires that we use fairly extreme language to help them see the modern promise of free expression for just what it is.

Modern false teachers. Finally, as I have throughout this chapter, I want to suggest some parallels between the false teachers and their modern counterparts. The images Peter uses in verse 17—"springs without water and mists driven by a storm"—make clear that the false teachers were impressive on the outside but hollow on the inside. They gave the appearance of being insightful spiritual mentors but did not have the reality.

We don't know how these false teachers presented themselves or what stratagems they used to convince their listeners they were worth listening to. But we can imagine that they would do whatever was appropriate in that culture to give themselves an aura of authority and reliability. Similarly in our culture, if a person today wants to gain a following, he does not put on a robe and go out into the streets carrying a sign warning about the end of the world. Rather, he buys a closetful of expensive suits, learns to speak with a rhetorical flourish, rents big arenas or builds big churches, and charges people big bucks for getting in on the show. And many people are swept off their feet by such an impressive appearance of affluence and power.

Paul had to battle this problem in Corinth. False teachers, better looking than Paul, better dressed than Paul, and rhetorically more skilled than Paul, had invaded the church. Unlike him, they charged the people for their ministry. They seemed to be "strong"; Paul appeared "weak." From the standpoint of the world, so it was, Paul admits. But what Paul urges the Corinthians to do is not to judge by appearance but by spiritual reality. Indeed, Paul claims, it was through his worldly weakness that God's power could be more fully manifested (see 2 Cor. 10–13).

We must not make the same mistake as the Corinthians. We must not judge Christian leaders, teachers, and pastors by their appearance. We must not judge a Christian conference or seminar on the basis of the slickness of the advertising or the impressiveness of the facilities rented for it. We must not judge the content of a book by the artistry of its cover. God continues today to do his work through people and institutions that are not always the most impressive from the outside. His power is often "made perfect in weakness" (2 Cor. 12:9). We need to judge ministries by the truth they present and by the spiritual reality seen in the lives of the ministers and people who sit under those ministries.

2 Peter 3:1-7

DEAR FRIENDS, THIS is now my second letter to you. I have written both of them as reminders to stimulate you to wholesome thinking. ²I want you to recall the words spoken in the past by the holy prophets and the command given by our Lord and Savior through your apostles.

³First of all, you must understand that in the last days scoffers will come, scoffing and following their own evil desires. ⁴They will say, "Where is this 'coming' he promised? Ever since the fathers died, everything goes on as it has since the beginning of creation." ⁵But they deliberately forget that long ago by God's word the heavens existed and the earth was formed out of water and by water. ⁶By these waters also the world of that time was deluged and destroyed. ⁷By the same word the present heavens and earth are reserved for fire, being kept for the day of judgment and destruction of ungodly men.

PEOPLE GENERALLY FAMILIAR with the Bible normally think "false teachers" when 2 Peter is mentioned. And, as a simple characterization, that is not far off the mark. But we must remember that the letter was not written *to* false teachers; it was written to Christians. The false teachers are the foil against which Peter develops his positive teaching and exhortation. Yet after chapter 2, it is easy to lose sight of this larger purpose. For after warning his readers about "false teachers among you" (2:1), the author devotes the rest of that chapter to these false teachers, describing their many theological and especially moral errors and uttering God's verdict of condemnation over them. Throughout chapter 2, Peter speaks in the third person plural: "they. . . ."

All that changes in chapter 3, where Peter addresses his readers directly again as his "dear friends" (vv. 1, 8, 14, 17) and turns from denunciation to exhortation. To be sure, he does not lose sight of the false teachers, for he talks about their misunderstanding of eschatology and again condemns them in verses 4–7. But the bulk of the chapter contains teaching and exhortation for believers, which bear a close resemblance, in both form and content, to the end of chapter 1. Note the verbal parallels (the Greek is almost identical in both cases):

1:13 - "to refresh your memory"   3:1 - "as reminders to stimulate you"
1:20 - "Above all, you must   3:3 - "first of all, you must understand"
understand"

By using the same constructions here in chapter 3, Peter signals to the attentive reader that he is coming back to the earlier context and emphasis. More important are the similarities in content. As he did in chapter 1, Peter emphasizes the importance of memory (see 3:1–2, 5, 8). Furthermore, his topic is again eschatology. In 1:16–21, Peter combatted skepticism about the "power and coming of our Lord Jesus Christ," but only hints at the presence of false teachers propagating such a view. Here in chapter 3 he is more explicit, citing "scoffers" who have come along and are sarcastically asking, "Where is this 'coming' he promised?" (v. 4). And in the earlier chapter, Peter sought to establish the reliability of his sources of information about the Parousia: his own experience of the Transfiguration and prophecy. In chapter 3, he grounds the credibility of the Parousia more generally in a certain theological view of history and providence.

Dividing the argument of chapter 3 into paragraphs is not easy. Verses 14–18 form the concluding paragraph of the letter, matching in some ways the opening in 1:3–11. The address "Dear friends" in 3:1 and 8 suggests that these verses each open paragraphs. Verses 11–13, finally, with their shift to exhortation, can also be grouped into their own thought unit.

Within the present unit (vv. 1–7), Peter's argument proceeds in three stages:

verses 1–2: Peter urges his readers to *remember* the truth
verses 3–4: Peter warns of scoffers
verses 5–7: Peter rebukes the scoffers for *forgetting* the truth

Note how the idea of "remembering" frames the paragraph. By recalling the words of Christ and the apostles, believers will cultivate "wholesome thinking" (3:1); and because they have forgotten God's providence in history, the false teachers have stumbled into error.

Peter Urges His Readers to Remember the Truth (vv. 1–2)

THE NIV'S "DEAR friends" takes away something of the strength and Christian flavor of the original: *agapetoi*, "beloved ones." This word connotes the loving fellowship among believers secured by the sacrifice of God's own "beloved one," the Lord Jesus ("whom I love" in 1:17 translates this same word). After the harsh indictment of the false teachers in chapter 2, Peter wants to reassure his readers that he has confidence in their own Christian status and dedication. Why write this letter of warning then? Because Peter knows that no Christian can ever be so secure in his or her faith as to pass beyond the need of exhortation to holy thinking and living.

Christians, of course, should always be learning new things about the faith and discovering new avenues of serving the Lord in the way they live. But Christians also need reminders of basic truth, and they never outgrow the need for such reminders. While still resident somewhere in the data banks of our mind, the basics of faith can cease to have an active influence over us. "Remembering" these truths involves more than the mental act of "recalling" what had once been learned. It is the dynamic process of applying the truths to the new situations and problems that the believer confronts.[1]

Through his reminder, Peter wants to "stimulate you to wholesome thinking." "Thinking" translates a noun (*dianoia*) frequently used by some of the Greek philosophers. Plato, for instance, uses the exact Greek phrase, *eilikrine dianoia* ("wholesome thinking"), that Peter has here. Peter may again, then, be appropriating a phrase current in the world of Greek philosophy and religion for application to Christian truth.[2] For Peter, "thinking" is more than a purely mental process. It includes the ability to discern spiritual truth and apply it. Pagans, Paul says, are "darkened in their understanding [*dianoia*]" (Eph. 4:18), and Christians must cultivate an "understanding" that is "pure" (uncontaminated by worldly sentiment or false conceptions of Christianity).

The reminder Peter now gives his readers is not the first one. He has already written to them an earlier letter that covered many of the same points. What is this earlier letter? Most commentators think naturally that it is 1 Peter,[3] and they may be right. But we should remember that Peter undoubtedly wrote more letters than the two that we have in the canon of the New Testament. Paul, for example, refers to at least three letters he wrote that we do not have in the New Testament: his "previous letter" to the Corinthians (1 Cor. 5:9), a "severe letter" to the Corinthians (2 Cor. 7:8), and a letter to the Laodiceans

---

1. On the idea of memory, see the "Contemporary Significance" section on 1:12–15.

2. See Bigg, *The Epistles of St. Peter and St. Jude*, 288: "St. Peter has used philosophic words caught up in conversation and not quite accurately understood." Bigg is wrong, however, to accuse Peter of "inaccuracy" here. The process of taking language from one field and applying it to another goes on all the time. There is no question of inaccuracy, but of shift in focus due to the new context.

3. Those who think that an unknown person wrote 2 Peter in Peter's name usually see the reference as an attempt to lend authenticity to 2 Peter; see, e.g., Horst Balz and Wolf-gang Schrage, *Die "katholischen" Briefe: Die Briefe des Jakobus, Petrus, Johannes, und Judas*, 147; Henning Paulsen, *Der zweite Petrusbrief und der Judasbrief*, 150. But commentators who think that Peter wrote 2 Peter also make the identification (see, e.g., Bigg, *The Epistles of St. Peter and St. Jude*, 288–89).

(Col. 4:16). It would be surprising if Peter had not done the same. We should not immediately assume, therefore, that just because we have only these two letters of Peter in the New Testament, the one must refer to the other.

In fact, Peter's description of the purpose he has in these two letters—stimulating his readers to "wholesome thinking"—does not describe the contents of 1 Peter particularly well. Moreover, while Peter seems to know the readers of 2 Peter pretty well, we do not get the same impression from 1 Peter. It is for these reasons that commentators like Green think that Peter is referring here to a letter unknown to us rather than to 1 Peter.[4] Still, neither of these points is decisive: Peter's description is vague enough that it *could* apply to 1 Peter, and neither letter says much about the degree of Peter's acquaintance with them. So we should probably leave the identification of this earlier letter undecided.

Peter's focus on the idea of "reminder" in verse 1 naturally raises the question: reminder of what? This question Peter answers in verse 2, where he mentions two specific sources for the teaching that he wants his readers to recall and put into action. First is "the words spoken in the past by the holy prophets" (cf. 1:16–21, where Peter cited "the word of the prophets" as reliable testimony to the Parousia). As in the earlier passage, this reference is almost certainly to Old Testament prophets rather than, for instance, to New Testament prophets. "Spoken in the past" can refer to the teaching of the apostles (see the roughly parallel Jude 17). But it can also refer to the Old Testament (see, e.g., Acts 1:16; Rom. 9:29; Heb. 4:7), and the general notion is usually associated with the Old Testament (see Heb. 1:1). The important thing is that while the act of speaking is in the past, the message once spoken and then written down in Scripture continues to have force and relevance. For, as Peter has already made clear (2 Peter 1:21), God himself speaks in the words of these prophecies.

The second source Peter wants his readers to recall is "the command given by our Lord and Savior through your apostles." The words "given" and "through" in the NIV represent an interpretive paraphrase. A literal translation of the Greek is, "the command of your apostles, of the Lord and Savior." The main problem is to figure out the relationship between the two "of" phrases. The KJV follows a variant reading in the Greek text, reading "of us" rather than "of you" (e.g., "your") and then taking the second "of" phrase to modify the first: "the commandment of us the apostles of the Lord and Savior." But that variant reading cannot be accepted.[5] A second way to construe

---

4. Green, *The Second Epistle General of Peter and the General Epistle of Jude*, 123–24.

5. The Greek word *hemon* ("of us") is supported by only one rather late uncial and some minuscules, whereas the word *hymon* ("of you") finds support in many of the best and earliest manuscripts.

the phrases is to take the second phrase as somewhat of an afterthought: "the command of your apostles—that is, of Christ."[6] Or the two may be parallel; Mayor cites as an example the phrase "Shakespeare's speech of Mark Antony."[7] But the interpretation suggested by the NIV and by almost all other modern English versions is probably best. Peter wants to attribute the command to both the Lord Jesus and to the apostles, but in different senses. The Lord is the originator of the command, the apostles its transmitters.

What is this command? Because of the context (vv. 3–4), many commentators think that the "command" refers to the promised return of Christ in glory. But the word "command" (Greek *entole*) is certainly not a natural one to use to refer to a prediction of this kind. In all of its other approximately sixty New Testament occurrences, the word always refers to some kind of demand or requirement. And Peter has used this word just a few verses earlier with this sense (see 2:21). Almost certainly, then, Peter is describing the moral requirements that are placed on believers.

Peter uses the singular form of the word because he is thinking not so much as a series of "dos and don'ts" but of the basic demand that believers conform to the image of Christ, becoming holy even as the God who called them is holy (see 1 Peter 1:15–16). This central demand of the gospel was first laid down by Jesus himself (see Matt. 5:48: "Be perfect, therefore, as your heavenly Father is perfect"). And this same basic demand was passed on and fleshed out by the apostles to Christians all over the world. It was precisely this need for Christians to strive for conformity to the will of God taught by Christ and handed down by the apostles that the false teachers were willfully ignoring. In other words, Peter's concern is that his readers will not fall prey to this false teaching by neglecting the life of holiness.

Finally on verse 2, some commentators insist that the language of this verse renders it impossible for the apostle Peter to have written it. They note two elements. (1) The reference to "command" suggests the idea of Christianity as a "new law," an idea that surfaced only in the late first and early second centuries. But, as we have argued above, Peter is not using this term to *define* Christianity, only to stress one important side of the faith—a concern reflected often in the apostolic period. (2) The phrase *"your* apostles" suggests that the author could not himself have been one of those apostles. Whoever he is, he must be looking back at an earlier apostolic generation. But this does not follow. Peter simply wants to refer to those particular apostles who first

6. Bigg, *The Epistles of St. Peter and St. Jude,* 289–90.
7. Mayor, *The Epistle of St. Jude and the Second Epistle of St. Peter,* 146.

brought the gospel to the Christians he is writing to.[8] They are *their* apostles in the sense that they are the ones with whom his readers have had contact and whose presentation of the moral demands of the gospel Peter wants to recall to their attention.

Peter Warns of Scoffers (vv. 3–4)

HAVING REMINDED HIS readers of the requirements of Christ and the apostles who first preached the gospel to them, Peter goes on in verses 3–4 to suggest why such a reminder is so urgently needed: The false teachers are mocking the idea of Christ's return in glory. Peter finally brings together two of the most important issues in the letter: the false teachers' skepticism about the return of Christ in glory (see 1:16–21) and their disdain for holiness (chap. 2).

Peter wants his readers to understand "first of all" that the appearance of people like this is not a surprise. As he did in 2:1–4, he again uses the future tense to describe these irreverent mockers: "Scoffers *will* come." As we argued there, the use of the future tense does not mean that someone, writing in Peter's name, now quotes a prophecy of the apostle Peter.[9] Peter himself uses the future tense, as in the earlier passage, because he is indirectly quoting the prediction of Jesus himself. He almost surely has in mind texts such as Matthew 24:5: "Many will come in my name, claiming, 'I am the Christ,' and will deceive many." Jesus warned there and elsewhere that the end times would be characterized by apostasy and false teaching.

Paul also picked up on these warnings and passed them on. See, for instance, his words to the elders of the Ephesian church: "I know that after I leave, savage wolves will come in among you and will not spare the flock. Even from your own number men will arise and distort the truth in order to draw away disciples after them" (Acts 20:29–30). And similar to 2 Peter 3:3–4 is 1 Timothy 4:1: "The Spirit clearly says that in later times some will abandon the faith and follow deceiving spirits and things taught by demons." We sometimes read these passages as if they referred to a period at the very end of history that has not yet come. But both 1 Timothy 4 and 2 Peter 3 reveal that the apostles thought that these predictions about the "last days" were already being fulfilled in the false teaching that had arisen in their churches. And 1 John 2:18 couldn't say it more plainly: "Dear children, this is the last hour; and as you have heard that the antichrist is coming, even now many antichrists have come. This is how we know it is the last hour."

---

8. See, e.g., Bauckham, *Jude, 2 Peter,* 287.
9. As, for instance, Bauckham, ibid., 288, argues.

As we pointed out in the notes on 2:1–4, the New Testament writers commonly viewed the period that began with Pentecost as the "last days." They therefore viewed the predictions about those days as already being fulfilled in their time. Thus Peter here finds the scoffers of his day to be one manifestation of those deceitful apostates whom Jesus claimed would arise to plague the Christian community. His readers, who are perhaps being tempted and are certainly being disturbed by these scoffers, need to realize that the appearance of these people is no surprise. The church of Christ can always expect to find in its midst such scoffers.

The "scoffer" or "mocker" is certainly not a new phenomenon in the history of God's people. The psalmist pronounced a blessing on the person of God who does not "sit in the seat of mockers" (Ps. 1:1). And three times Proverbs presents the mocker as someone whose ways are to be avoided by the righteous (Prov. 1:22; 9:7–8; 13:1). Mocking is one all-too-typical response to the truth of God's revelation. Mockers do not so much reason against the truth of God as they disdain and belittle it. Rather than standing under God's Word, mockers, as Peter points out, follow "their own evil desires." "Evil desires" translates a single Greek word (*epithymia*) that Peter uses to encapsulate the ungodly orientation of such people (see 1:4; 2:10, 18). These scoffers, Peter says, insist on "going"[10] their own way rather than following the will of God.

Mockery is a general response to the truth of God. But the mockers or scoffers that Peter is particularly concerned about were not, apparently, mocking the faith generally. Indeed, they claimed to be following the faith (see, e.g., 2:18–22). Rather they were scoffing at one particular teaching of the faith: the belief that Christ will return in glory at the end of history. "Where is this 'coming' he promised?" they kept asking. By putting "coming" in quotation marks and adding the word "this," the NIV rightly suggests that the word has a special reference here. The Greek word is *parousia*, used throughout the New Testament as a technical term referring to the "coming" of Christ in the last day (see the notes on 1:16).

Peter makes clear that this question is not an innocent request for information about the time or the nature of Christ's return. The form of the question itself suggests otherwise, for it imitates a form found in the Old Testament to express unbelief and mockery (cf., e.g., Mal. 2:17: "You have wearied the LORD with your words. 'How have we wearied him?' you ask. By saying, 'All who do evil are good in the eyes of the LORD, and he is pleased with them' or '*Where is* the God of justice?'"; see also Jer. 17:15). In asking where this coming was, the false teachers were implying that it was past due and that it was therefore not going to happen at all.

---

10. The NIV "following" translates a Greek verb that means simply "going" (*poreuomenoi*).

They based this rejection of the coming of Christ on a general belief in the unchanging nature of the world: "Ever since our fathers died,[11] everything goes on as it has since the beginning of creation." Scholars who claim that an unknown Christian wrote 2 Peter after Peter's death have one of their strongest bits of evidence in this verse. As Bauckham notes, the false teachers appear to be arguing, "The Parousia was promised before the death of the fathers. Well, the fathers have died and *still* nothing happens."[12] The assumption here is that "fathers" refers to the first generation of Christians—a generation that, of course, included Peter and the other apostles, who must therefore be dead by now.

This reading of the text is certainly a possible one, but it is not the only one. "Fathers" in the New Testament only rarely refers to an immediate ancestor ("my father was a policeman"). It usually has a spiritual sense, referring to the "ancestors" of the Jewish nation, and especially to the patriarchs, Abraham, Isaac, and Jacob (as in the hymn "Faith of our Fathers").[13] This meaning of the word also makes good sense in this verse. For the false teachers have been at pains to deny, and Peter to affirm, that the promise of eschatological judgment is rooted in the Old Testament itself. We can very well imagine them arguing that ever since God began his work of creating a people for his name—ever since the time of "the fathers"[14] of the biblical people of God—things have gone on much the same.[15]

Either interpretation of the word "father" explains the language of the verse and fits the context. A firm decision, then, should be based not on a specific word but on the general consideration of the authorship of the letter. And we have seen good reason to accept the letter's own claim to have been written by the apostle Peter. The false teachers, then, were apparently scoffing at the idea of Christ's return at the end of history because they could

---

11. The Greek word here is *koimaomai*, "sleep" (see NASB). "Die" may be a legitimate translation, but it is debated. See our comments in the "Bridging Contexts" section.

12. Bauckham, *Jude, 2 Peter*, 290–92; see also Mayor, *The Epistle of St. Jude and the Second Epistle of St. Peter*, 148–49; Kelly, *The Epistles of Peter and of Jude*, 355–56. Advocates of this interpretation usually argue that this is also the meaning of "fathers" in two early Christian texts that closely resemble 2 Peter 3:4: *1 Clement* 23:3: "Wretched are the double-minded, which doubt in their soul and say, 'These things we did hear in the days of our Fathers also, and behold we have grown old, and none of these things hath befallen us'"; also *2 Clement* 11:2.

13. See, for example, the fifteen occurrences of "fathers" in Stephen's speech in Acts 7. The word probably refers to the patriarchs particularly in several of those verses; and it clearly does in Rom. 9:5; 11:28; 15:8.

14. The NIV "our fathers" is potentially misleading. There is no possessive pronoun in the Greek.

15. For this interpretation, see Bigg, *The Epistles of St. Peter and St. Jude*, 291; Green, *The Second Epistle General of Peter and the General Epistle of Jude*, 129.

not imagine the kind of change in the world and in the human situation that the church's teaching about the Parousia assumed.

Can we determine any more precisely what the false teachers were arguing? Can we understand more exactly what kind of view of history they were taking? We saw in the "Bridging Contexts" section on 2:17–22 that certain Epicurean thinkers in Peter's day expressed skepticism about any divine intervention in the world. They denied, in effect, the whole idea of providence. Perhaps the false teachers held this sort of view of history. But if so, it is difficult to understand how they could make any claim to be Christian, for they would have to deny the incarnation and resurrection of Christ as well as his Parousia. And we might have expected Peter to write something about this. Perhaps, then, they held to a milder form of historical continuity, denying the possibility of any event that would materially change the nature of the world. The Parousia would not, then, fit into their scheme of things because it involved a transformation of both the world and of human beings. If this was their view, it also explains why Peter has chosen the examples of God's intervention in history that he has in verses 5–7.

Peter Rebukes the Scoffers for Forgetting the Truth (vv. 5–7)

THE GENERAL MEANING of verses 5–7 is clear enough. Peter shows his readers why the false teachers are wrong in thinking that "everything goes on as it has since the beginning of creation." On the contrary, Peter notes, God has intervened spectacularly in the course of human history: Having created the world through water and the word (v. 5), God, by that same water and word also destroyed that world in the flood of Noah's day (v. 6). And God will do the same again (v. 7), only this time he will use fire. Clearly, then, the false teachers' assumption about an unbroken continuity in history, without significant divine intervention, is erroneous.

But if the basic argument of the paragraph is easy enough to figure out, many of the detailed points that Peter makes along the way are not. Verse 5 is especially difficult, offering problems both of translation and interpretation. The first translation problem is relatively minor. Should we render the opening words of the verse "They deliberately forget" (NIV; see NRSV; TEV) or "when they maintain this, it escapes their notice that" (NASB; see also REB)?[16] The difference in meaning is slight; but the latter makes better sense of the

---

16. The Greek is *lanthanei autous touto thelontas*. The last word comes from the verb *thelo*, which has here the meaning "maintain [contrary to the true state of affairs]" (see BAGD, 355).The question is whether the participle of this verb, *thelontas*, modifies *lanthanei* ("forget in a 'willful' way" [NIV]) or stands by itself ("it escapes their notice, as they stubbornly maintain" [REB]).

order of the Greek words.[17] The scoffers, Peter suggests, are not ignorant or naive, but willfully disobedient, maintaining a view of the continuity of human history that blatantly flies in the face of the Old Testament. The Scriptures show that the world is not eternal; it came into existence at a certain point in time.

But the details of Peter's statement of this truth are somewhat obscure. Note the difference here between the translations of the NIV and the REB:

> NIV: "by God's word the heavens existed and the earth was formed out of water and by water."
> REB: "there were heavens and earth long ago, created by God's word out of water and with water."

The NIV has two parallel clauses, the first having "the heavens" as its subject and the second "the earth." The REB, on the other hand, makes "heavens and earth" the subject of the entire sentence. Choosing between these two renderings is difficult; each has its strengths and its weaknesses. This is sometimes the situation we face in translating and interpreting Scripture: to choose the option that has the fewest problems. In this case, I think the second rendering has the fewest problems.

Two points combine to make it likely that Peter is treating "heavens and earth" as a pair rather than separating them in different clauses. (1) Peter is obviously alluding to the story of creation as it is found in Genesis 1. As we all know, that story begins with the words, "In the beginning God created the heavens and the earth." (2) Peter goes on to describe in verse 7 how the "present heavens and earth" will also be destroyed. The continuity of his argument suggests that, as "heavens and earth" go together as a unit there, so they do also in verse 5.[18] What Peter is reminding these false teachers about, then, is the creation of the entire universe. Both the world we can experience through our senses ("the earth") and the unseen spiritual realm ("heavens," or better, "heaven"[19]) were brought into being "by God's word." As Genesis 1 repeatedly makes clear, all of creation is the effect of God's powerful word. He spoke, and it came to pass. "By the word of the LORD were the heavens made" (Ps. 33:6); "the universe was formed at God's command" (Heb. 11:3).

---

17. See Kelly, *The Epistles of Peter and of Jude*, 356–57; Bauckham, *Jude, 2 Peter*, 297; against, for instance, Bigg, *The Epistles of St. Peter and St. Jude*, 292.

18. For this interpretation, see especially Kelly, *The Epistles of Peter and of Jude*, 357–58. Its chief syntactical difficulty is the feminine form of the participle *synestesa*, which implies that it modifies only *ge*, "earth." But participles will sometimes take the form of only one of words they modify.

19. The NIV translates literally, since the Greek word here is plural (*ouranoi*). But the word is plural because the Hebrew word for heaven is a "stylistic" plural; the idea is singular.

Perhaps even more difficult are Peter's references to water as the element "out of which" (ek) and "through which" (dia) the heavens and the earth were formed. Charles Bigg thinks that the first phrase reflects an ancient belief that water was the material element out of which all other things were composed.[20] But it is more likely that Peter is again thinking of the story of creation in Genesis 1, where water plays a significant role. In verse 2, before God begins to organize the chaos that he has brought into being, we read about the Spirit "hovering over the waters." These waters, which are apparently viewed as covering the entire globe, are then separated as God makes the "sky" (Greek ouranos, "heaven") (vv. 6–8). And God makes the dry land by gathering the water together (v. 9). On the basis of the Genesis account, then, Peter's assertion that God created the heavens and the earth "out of water" does not seem far-fetched.

But what are we to do with the second phrase, "by water"? Some commentators think that Peter may be alluding to rain, which God uses to sustain the world that he has created (Gen. 2:6).[21] This is possible, but difficult—Peter would have to be using the same verb to mean both "created" and "sustained." Others suggest that the preposition Peter uses here (dia) may have a local sense: God created the universe "in the midst of" water.[22] But this is not what the preposition means in the parallel phrase in 2 Peter 3:6. Thus we prefer to think that Peter simply expands here on his first phrase, "out of water." As the verses we cited from Genesis 1 show, God used water as an instrument in his creation of the sky. And we must also allow for Peter's rhetorical purpose here. One of the main reasons he introduces the idea of the world as being created "by water" is to prepare for the parallel he will make in verse 6, where God destroys the world "by water."[23]

Lest we become lost in the "forest" as we examine the individual "trees" in Peter's argument, we should note again that Peter's general point in verse 5 is clear: God brought the universe into existence, and he did so by his own creative word and through the use of water. Therefore, the false teachers' assumption of an unchanging universe is without warrant. The very universe they are talking about has not always been here.

But Peter's second point is in some ways even more to the point. That same world that God created he also "destroyed" (v. 6), and he did it in the same way that he created the world: by "water and the word of God." To be sure, the NIV translates here "by these waters" (see also TEV; REB). The problem is that the Greek text has only a plural relative pronoun ("which" [see NASB;

---

20. Bigg, *The Epistles of St. Peter and St. Jude*, 293. He refers to the teaching of Thales.
21. Ibid., 293; Green, *The Second Epistle General of Peter and the General Epistle of Jude*, 130.
22. Mayor, *The Epistle of St. Jude and the Second Epistle of St. Peter*, 151–52.
23. Neyrey, *2 Peter, Jude*, 234.

NRSV] or "which things"), and we cannot be sure about its antecedent. Since Peter has used the word "water" twice in verse 5, the NIV rendering is certainly possible. Yet he has not spoken in verse 5 of "waters" but of the same water accomplishing two different things. Moreover, in the Greek text, the last thing mentioned in verse 5 is "the word of God." Perhaps the most important argument in favor of rendering "by water and the word of God" is the prominent role that God's word plays in this paragraph. In verse 5, God creates the world by his word; in verse 7, he judges it "by the same word." It seems only natural that Peter would complete his parallelism by referring to God's word also as the means by which he destroyed the world.[24]

The reference here is, of course, to the flood of Noah, which Peter has already used as an example of God's judgment (2:5). In that verse, as we argued, God's not sparing "the ancient world" referred to the destruction of ungodly people. Here again Peter refers to the destruction of the world. Since Peter has referred in verse 5 to the creation of the universe, some commentators think that he must be thinking in verse 6 of a destruction of the whole physical universe—an idea found in a few Jewish writers.[25] But Peter's shift from the language of "heavens and earth" (v. 5) to "world" (v. 6) may be significant. The latter often means the "world of human beings," the inhabited and organized human dimension of the universe. I think it probably has this meaning here. Peter is affirming the destruction, through the waters of the Flood, of the ungodly human beings of Noah's day.[26] The example is a particularly apt one, because the false teachers are especially denying the judgment associated with the Parousia. This becomes clearer in verse 7.

The connecting link between verses 6 and 7, on the view we have defended above, is "the word of God": Through God's utterance the world of Noah's day was destroyed, and through "the same word" it will be destroyed again. This time, however, God will use fire rather than water to bring about the destruction. Thus, in response to the false teachers, who view the world as going on in the same way forever, Peter makes clear that God has destined it for a sudden and definite end. "The present heavens and earth are reserved for fire"; the universe that now exists is under sentence of condemnation. It is being "kept" for the day when God will judge the world and sentence ungodly people to "destruction" (*apoleia*).

---

24. See particularly Bigg, *The Epistles of St. Peter and St. Jude,* 293–94; Kelly, *The Epistles of Peter and of Jude,* 359–60; Green, *The Second Epistle General of Peter and the General Epistle of Jude,* 130–31.

25. Kelly, *The Epistles of Peter and of Jude,* 359; Bauckham, *Jude, 2 Peter,* 298–99. They refer to *1 Enoch* 83:3–5; Philo, *Life of Moses* 2.63–65.

26. See, e.g., Bigg, *The Epistles of St. Peter and St. Jude,* 294; Green, *The Second Epistle General of Peter and the General Epistle of Jude,* 131.

As we noted earlier (see the comments on 2:3), the words "destroy" and "destruction," when applied in the New Testament to the judgment of human beings, must not be taken literally in the sense of annihilation. Indeed, some theologians have taken the language in this sense, but this does not fit the general New Testament teaching about "eternal" punishment. However uncomfortable we may be with the idea, it seems clearly taught in Scripture (e.g., Matt. 25:41, 46; Mark 9:43, 48; Rev. 14: 9–11; see the discussion in the "Bridging Contexts" section on Jude 11–13). "Destruction" refers to the cessation of existence in this world and to the final and terrible separation from God involved in condemnation. Earlier Peter cited Old Testament examples of the condemnation of "ungodly people" (2 Peter 2:5–6). His application there was to the false teachers, and we are certainly right to suppose he has them in view here also. The false teachers, who sneer at any idea of judgment to come, will themselves experience its full fury.

This verse has sparked considerable theological controversy. Only here in the entire Bible (and possibly 3:10) do we find a clear reference to the destruction of the world with fire. Because of this, and because it is often suggested that Peter borrowed the idea of a final world conflagration from certain pagan philosophers of his day, some scholars resist the idea that Peter has this teaching here. Michael Green, for instance, noting Peter's focus at the end of the verse on God's condemnation of human beings, suggests that destruction with fire is simply an image of God's judgment.[27]

We will discuss this whole issue more thoroughly in the next section, but we note here that Green's idea is implausible. After referring to the "world" (of human beings) in verse 6, Peter returns in verse 7 to the "heavens and earth" language that he used in verse 5 to denote the entire created universe. We cannot limit his reference to human beings only. Note the comment of the second-century theologian Melito of Sardis, who apparently has this passage in mind: "There was a flood of water. . . . There will be a flood of fire, and the earth will be burned up together with its mountains."[28]

BRINGING THE BIBLICAL message into today's world requires that we understand the context and background of that message—the social, historical, and religious environment of the world in which God inspired men to write his words. And we have sketched various elements of the environment as they affect the meaning and application of Peter's words to us.

---

27. Green, *The Second Epistle General of Peter and the General Epistle of Jude,* 132.
28. Quoted by Green, ibid., 133.

But rightly identifying the meaning of God's Word for us today also demands that we understand exactly how the words that the human authors used to communicate their message function. For words can do many different things. Especially confusing are those words that do not mean what they seem to mean on the surface. Consider the question, "Are you crazy?" We usually think of questions as genuine requests for information. But, in most situations at least, this question is not so much seeking information as it is stating an objection to a course of action (e.g., it could well be the response of a wife whose husband has just said, "I think I'll roller blade down this steep hill"). Or consider the statement, "I am hurt." The person who says this is probably not simply stating a fact; he or she is calling for help.

Even more to the point in our interpretation and application of 2 Peter 3:1–7 is the problem of figurative language. Similes are easy to identify because they usually include a word such as "like" or "as" that makes clear the kind of comparison being made (e.g., "My love is like a red, red rose"). But trickier are metaphors, which are not always easy to identify. "The roof fell in on me" may be literal (a firefighter describing how he was injured) or metaphorical (an office worker telling what happened when the boss caught him playing "Tetris" during working hours). In normal conversation we can almost always tell which is which because we are familiar with the idiom, and we know the context in which the statement is made. But what happens when we encounter such language in the Bible? Because we live so far distant from the Bible times, we are not usually familiar with its idioms and metaphors. And context does not always tell the whole story.

Consider two debated examples of such wording in 3:1–7. In verse 4, Peter refers to false teachers who are claiming, "Ever since the fathers fell asleep, all things remain in the same way as from the beginning of creation" (my own lit. trans.). What are we to make of the word "sleep" in this statement? The context makes it clear that it is not intended literally: The false teachers are certainly not suggesting that a night's sleep for their fathers changed their view of history. So the word is metaphorical in some sense. But what does it *refer* to? Virtually everyone recognizes that it refers to death. And so most modern English versions simply translate (as does the NIV) "ever since the fathers died."

Such a translation does not really lose any meaning from the original— if "fall asleep" is a common euphemism for "die." For the metaphor would then be what we call a "dead" one, and the use of the term to describe death says nothing about the writer's view of the nature of death (cf. our much-used "pass away"). But if the metaphor is a "live" one for Peter, then the prosaic translation may lose some of his intended meaning. Peter may then be suggesting a certain, specifically Christian, perspective on death: For the Christian death is not a final doom but a temporary state from which one will be "awakened" in resurrection.[29] This need not refer to what is called "soul sleep"—the idea that Christians between death and the coming of Christ are unconscious. The point would be, rather, that believers who die, while conscious of the presence of the Lord, have not yet been resurrected.

Those who think that we have here a "dead" metaphor cite evidence that Greeks used the word "sleep" to refer to death ever since the time of Homer and that it is also found in the Old Testament with the same sense.[30] Clearly Christians did not invent the metaphor to connote their particular understanding of death. But we may still conclude that Christian writers appropriated this metaphor because it so perfectly suited their theology of death. In other words, it may not have been a "dead" metaphor for Christian writers, even if it was for others in that culture.

The use of the term "sleep" for death in the New Testament points in just this direction, for it is applied only to the death of righteous people.[31] Particularly significant is John 11:11, where Jesus tells his disciples that Lazarus is "sleeping." His point seems to be to characterize Lazarus' death as a temporary condition, to be miraculously changed by the Lord himself within a short period of time. And so we would do better to keep the word "sleep" in our translations of 2 Peter 3:4—perhaps compromising with some such rendering as "sleep in death."

But a second debated instance of metaphorical language in our text involves us in a larger and much more contentious matter: the language of eschatology. As Stephen H. Travis points out,

> because eschatology deals with what "has never entered the heart of man," it raises in acute form the problem of language. Some kind of picture-language seems inevitable when we are speaking about realities which lie both temporally and spatially beyond our present experience. What is the relationship between that language and those realities (assuming, of course, that they *are* real)? Were the biblical writers able to distinguish between "literal" and "pictorial" or "mythi-

---

29. See, e.g., Green, ibid., 129.

30. See, e.g., 1 Kings 2:10; 11:43; 22:40; and the comments of Ernest Best, *A Commentary on the First and Second Epistles to the Thessalonians*, HNTC (New York: Harper & Row, 1972), 185. Evidence that "sleep" was this kind of "dead" metaphor comes from passages such as this one as well as from the Roman writer Catullus (5.4–6): "The sun can set and rise again, but once our brief light sets, there is one unending night to be slept through."

31. The "saints" resurrected at Jesus' death (Matt. 27:52); Lazarus (John 11:11–12); Stephen (Acts 7:60); David (Acts 13:36); Christians, destined for resurrection (1 Cor. 7:39; 11:30; 15:6, 18, 20, 51; 1 Thess. 4:13–14, 15). See on this point with respect to Paul, Murray J. Harris, *Raised Immortal: Resurrection and Immortality in the New Testament* (Grand Rapids: Eerdmans, 1983), 134–35.

cal" language, or did they use such language without reflecting on its precise relationship to reality? And—whatever may have been the case with them—how are we, with our "modern world-view," to handle the Bible's language about the parousia, about judgment, heaven and hell?[32]

We confront this problem in Peter's assertion that "the present heavens and earth are reserved for fire." What are we to make of this language? We may begin by noting three general directions that scholars have taken in handling such "cosmic" assertions.

(1) The first option is associated especially with the famous and controversial New Testament scholar Rudolf Bultmann. Motivated by a desire to make the New Testament relevant to the modern, scientific era, he argued for a program of "demythologizing" the New Testament—that is, taking the myth out of New Testament language. Bultmann viewed the New Testament authors as necessarily limited in their ideas by their "mythological" worldview. They believed in a "three-story" universe, in God's direct intervention in the world through miracles, and in a literal, catastrophic "end of the world." The discoveries of modern science have rendered such ideas obsolete. But this, to Bultmann, did not mean we have to discard the New Testament. Shorn of its mythological trappings, it speaks a message relevant to modern people. We can, for instance, still find meaning in the idea of the Parousia, with Christ coming to "judge the living and the dead" at the end of history, by getting to the core idea this myth represents: that every person must confront Christ in an encounter that will seal his or her destiny. Bultmann would probably think that Peter really thought that the world would be destroyed by fire, but its meaning for us is, perhaps, that the material universe is not the whole of reality.

Bultmann's demythologizing has been unanimously rejected by evangelical scholars. In assuming that the biblical writers were limited by their own time, he ignores the reality of divine inspiration, intended to preserve the truthfulness of their words. Moreover, his view smacks of what C. S. Lewis has called "chronological snobbery"—the idea that only recent and modern ideas can be right. Science has vastly expanded our understanding of, and our ability to manipulate, the natural world—but it has done nothing to challenge the biblical conviction that God created that world, intervenes in it, and will some day bring it to an end. Demythologizing Peter's language is not an option for anyone convinced of the truthfulness of Scripture.

(2) Another general approach to the language of eschatology is to take the cosmic language the Bible uses quite literally. If the Bible says that in the

---

32. Stephen H. Travis, *Christian Hope and the Future* (Downers Grove, Ill.: InterVarsity, 1980), 14.

last days stars will fall from the sky to the earth (Rev. 6:13), then that is just what will happen. This "straightforward" reading of eschatological texts is deeply rooted in evangelical scholarship and popular imagination. When I first became a Christian (many more years ago than I would like to admit), almost the first biblical teaching I heard was from tapes of Hal Lindsay, giving his detailed and generally literalistic interpretation of end-time events as popularized in his best-selling book, *The Late Great Planet Earth*. A high point every year in the church I first attended as a believer was the prophecy conference, when guest speakers would go over the same ground. If one takes this approach to 2 Peter 3:4, then the conclusion follows without much analysis at all: Peter is predicting that the world will eventually be destroyed by fire. And those of us who live in the nuclear age can certainly understand how such a thing could come to pass.

I find that it is fashionable these days in some quarters to deride this approach to eschatology. Some people treat Christians who hold these views as if they were ignorant bumpkins. I don't think such derision is justified. To be sure, I have my reservations about some aspects of the "entirely literal" approach. Its advocates may assume that certain biblical texts are clear when in fact they may not be. And a focus on prophecy can sometimes turn into an unhealthy preoccupation with the details of future history at the expense of living the Christian life here and now. But it seems to me that any believer committed to the full truthfulness of the Bible should welcome the seriousness with which such an approach treats the biblical text. The bumper sticker that proclaims, "The Bible says it; I believe it; and that's good enough for me" captures a vital truth: Christians should accept whatever the Bible teaches.

(3) But it is precisely here that we come face-to-face with the real issue: What does the Bible teach? Many laypeople and not a few scholars think that eschatological texts in the Bible mean just what they appear to say on the surface. But as we have seen, language is not always this simple. And many scholars think that the eschatological language in the Bible is often metaphorical. This brings up the third general direction in the interpretation of the biblical language about the "last things." Its advocates argue that predictions about the stars falling from the sky to the earth are not intended to describe a literal, astronomical disaster; they are simply figurative language for some kind of spectacular event.

The most important biblical evidence for this approach comes in prophetic passages that appear to use cosmic imagery to describe the historical judgment of God. In Isaiah 13, for instance, the prophet depicts God's judgment on the nation of Babylon in cosmic terms:

The stars of heaven and their constellations
   will not show their light.

The rising sun will be darkened
>and the moon will not give its light. (v. 10)
Therefore I will make the heavens tremble;
>and the earth will shake from its place
at the wrath of the LORD Almighty,
>in the day of his burning anger. (v. 13)

Those scholars who follow a more literal hermeneutic (option 2) would argue that the prophet has here moved from a description of the historical judgment on Babylon to the ultimate judgment of the entire world at the end of history. This may be right, but the prophet's return in verses 17–22 to the situation of historical Babylon creates a problem for this way of looking at the verses. Virtually every instance of this kind of cosmic imagery is debated in just this fashion. But I think we have enough evidence to find at least some degree of metaphor in the eschatological language of the Bible.

Consequently, I do not think that we should approach any given eschatological passage with a clear presumption about the language one way or the other. We have to look at each text and decide whether the language is literal or metaphorical. As we do so, we will ask questions such as, "Is the language used here clearly metaphorical elsewhere in the Bible or in the ancient world?" "*Can* what is described literally happen?" "Are there parallel passages that show that the language is metaphorical?"

We must certainly entertain the possibility that Peter's language about the heavens and earth being reserved for ultimate fiery destruction is metaphorical. As we noted in the "Original Meaning" section, Green suggests this possibility, that Peter may simply be describing God's judgment on human beings in this verse. And, to be sure, God's judgment is often pictured in the Bible in terms of "fire." Note how the following passages highlight fire in various ways as a component of the day of the Lord:

The LORD will cause men to hear his majestic voice
>and will make them see his arm coming down
with raging anger and consuming fire,
>with cloudburst, thunderstorm and hail. (Isa. 30:30)
See, the LORD is coming with fire,
>and his chariots are like a whirlwind;
he will bring down his anger with fury,
>and his rebuke with flames of fire.
For with fire and with his sword
>the LORD will execute judgment upon all men,
>and many will be those slain by the LORD. (Isa. 66:15–16)
Who can withstand his indignation?
>Who can endure his fierce anger?

His wrath is poured out like fire;
 the rocks are shattered before him. (Nah. 1:6)
Neither their silver nor their gold
 will be able to save them
 on the day of the LORD's wrath.
In the fire of his jealousy
 the whole world will be consumed,
for he will make a sudden end
 of all who live in the earth. (Zeph. 1:18)
"Therefore wait for me," declares the LORD,
 "for the day I will stand up to testify.
I have decided to assemble the nations,
 to gather the kingdoms
and to pour out my wrath on them—
 all my fierce anger.
The whole world will be consumed
 by the fire of my jealous anger." (Zeph. 3:8)

While some Christians doubt it, it seems clear that "fire" in these verses (as well as the many where it is applied to judgment in the New Testament) is not literal, but metaphorical (see the "Bridging Contexts" section on Jude 11–13). The biblical writers choose one of the most spectacular and painful of human disasters to convey some notion of the terrible nature of God's judgment.

In other words, it is certainly possible that Peter uses "fire" in this verse simply as a metaphor for human judgment. But two points in the passage make this interpretation questionable. (1) Peter's main point in verses 5–7 has to do with the continuity of the universe as a whole. He cites creation and the Flood—which, while directed against human sin, certainly affected the physical world. A reference to the judgment of humans only in verse 7 would be out of place. (2) Peter's use of the phrase "heavens and earth" seems deliberately chosen to refer to the physical universe (see v. 5). We incline, then, with most commentators, to find in the verse a prediction of the ultimate destruction of the world by fire.

But before we leave the point, we should mention one objection to this conclusion. The idea of a final world conflagration was widespread in Peter's day. One particular philosophical school, the Stoics, made this idea important in their thinking. And some scholars argue that Peter would not have taught an idea that was rooted in such a pagan philosophy. But I don't think we can be so dogmatic. God may use even pagan ideas to lead the authors of Scripture into the truth he wants to transmit.

Furthermore, that Peter derived his thinking from Stoicism is unlikely. The Stoics taught that the world be destroyed by fire and then recreated many times—a notion quite distant from what Peter teaches. A more likely influence is Jewish teaching in his day. A number of Jewish theologians had also begun to predict the destruction of the world with fire, and a careful reading of the Old Testament passages cited above shows that at least the germ of the idea is found in the Scriptures themselves. Peter may be the first explicitly to state this idea, but the Old Testament certainly hints at it.

 WHAT SIGNIFICANCE DOES this teaching about the end of the world have for Christians today? Peter has much to say about the importance of "memory" here, and readers should consult the "Bridging Contexts" section on 2 Peter 1:12–15 for discussion of this matter. Peter himself draws out some of the consequences of what he says here about eschatology later in the chapter; we will explore the issue at that point.

Law and gospel. But two other points Peter makes in this section are especially worthy of further application to our times. The first is his rather passing reference to the "command given by our Lord and Savior through your apostles" (v. 2). As we noted in the "Original Meaning" section, the word "command" cannot refer to the promise of the second coming of Christ. One of the most important contributions Martin Luther made to our understanding of God's Word was his distinction between "law" and "gospel." "Law," said Luther, was "what we are to do and give to God"; "gospel" is "what has been given us by God."[33] In Luther's terms, Peter is here speaking about "law," not "gospel." He wants his readers to recall that they, the apostles who first brought the good news of Jesus Christ's death and resurrection, also relayed to them their Lord and Savior's demand to give themselves in obedience to God.

The church in our day is in great confusion when it comes to this demand of our Lord. The confusion relates to two specific matters: (1) Where are we to find the "law" that we are to obey? (2) What is the place of this "law" in the Christian life?

(1) When one surveys the history of Christian theology and looks over the current scholarly landscape, one finds three basic answers to the first question: (a) the love command; (b) the Old Testament law as fulfilled in Christ; and (c) the teaching of Jesus and the apostles.

(a) The prominence of love in the New Testament is well known. Jesus singled out love for "the neighbor" (Lev. 19:15) as the heart of the law and

---

33. Martin Luther, "How Christians Should Regard the Law of Moses," in *Luther's Works*, ed. E. Theodore Bachmann (Philadelphia: Fortress, 1960), 162.

made it the linchpin in his ethical teaching (Matt. 22:34–40; Mark 12:28–31; Luke 10:25–28; John 13:34–35; 15:12). And we find the same focus on the love command throughout the New Testament (Rom. 13:8–10; Gal. 5:13–15; James 2:8; 1 John 2:7; 3:11–20; 4:11, 19–21; 2 John 5). We can understand, then, why some theologians and ethicists have argued that the New Testament "replaces" law with love. The popular modern incarnation of this viewpoint is called "situational ethics." As taught by writers like Fletcher, situational ethics disdains any moral absolutes. In any situation, all the Christian needs to do is the "loving thing." And, according to Fletcher, what is "loving" will vary from situation to situation.

Now there is a sense in which Fletcher and others like him are absolutely right: Christ calls on his followers to love, and he suggests (as does Paul) that the believer who loves will invariably do what is right, thus fulfilling all the other commandments (see, e.g., Mark 12:28–31; Rom. 13:8–10). But what "situational ethics" advocates ignore is that the New Testament also gives definite guidance about how love is to be worked out. Indeed, New Testament writers warn against the sort of "situational" approach that Fletcher proposes. Thus, for instance, when the Corinthians begin going off the rails morally, Paul reminds them that "what counts is keeping the commandments of God" (1 Cor. 7:19). Love is certainly the most important of all the commands that we Christians are to obey; we could even say that it is basic to them all. But the New Testament does not countenance any *replacing* of law with love.

(b) Probably a majority of contemporary evangelical scholars would argue for the second option we listed above: that Christians are obliged to obey the law of Moses as fulfilled in Christ. According to the Puritans, the law of Moses has two distinct functions: As a "covenant of works," it condemns the sinner who disobeys it; as an expression of God's holy will, it directs the conduct of the people of God. For the Christians, the first of these functions is at an end, and this is what Paul means when he asserts that Christians are not "under the law" (Rom. 6:14–15). But the second of these functions remains fully in place, as Paul also suggests when he claims that the gospel "establishes the law" (3:31).

In other words, Christians are to continue to obey the law of Moses—although in its "fulfilled" form. Christ's coming means those parts of the law that were to prepare for Christ are no longer obligatory: Believers do not need to observe the Old Testament sacrifices and rituals (the "ceremonial" law) or the rules for life in the land of Israel (the "civil" law). But Christ himself required continued obedience to the "moral" law (Matt. 5:18–19):

I tell you the truth, until heaven and earth disappear, not the smallest letter, not the least stroke of a pen, will by any means disappear from the Law until everything is accomplished. Anyone who breaks one of the least of these commandments and teaches others to do the same will be called least in the kingdom of heaven, but whoever practices and teaches these commands will be called great in the kingdom of heaven.

On this view of the situation, then, the "command" that Peter is thinking about in 2 Peter 3:2 will be the Old Testament law as Christ and the apostles interpreted and applied it. If asked where this "moral" law is to be found, theologians who follow this line of thinking usually focus on the Ten Commandments.

(c) This traditional Puritan interpretation of law is extremely influential in contemporary evangelicalism. But I question whether it is correct. I certainly do not want to be known as somebody who speaks against the Ten Commandments! But in fairness to the New Testament, I think we must say that the commandments that Christians are now to obey are found in the New Testament rather than in the Old. We referred above to Paul's statement that Christians are not "under the law"; what gives us the right to limit that statement to a certain function of the law or to some part of the law? Nothing in the context suggests any kind of restriction. Nor does Jesus' endorsement of the law in Matthew 5:18–19 settle the matter: Taken at its surface meaning, it demands that believers obey the entire law of Moses—sacrifices, ceremonies, and all.

Clearly, then, something else is going on here. And that "something else" is expressed in verse 17: Christ came to "fulfill" the law. As this word "fulfill" is used in Matthew, it refers to a new covenant reality anticipated by the Old Testament. Applied in this context, this means that Christ's own teaching is the "fulfillment" of the law. What he demands of his disciples is what the Old Testament law was all along pointing toward. But the point is that it is Jesus' teaching, not the Old Testament law, that is the focal point for Christian obedience. This is confirmed at the end of the Sermon on the Mount and at the end of Matthew's Gospel, when it is Jesus' own words and teaching that are made the focus of new covenant ethics (Matt. 7:24–27; 28:19–20).

Obviously, then, I favor the third major interpretation of New Testament "law": that believers are *directly* obliged to obey the teaching of Jesus and the apostles. This "law of Christ" (see Gal. 6:2) is the new covenant equivalent to the old covenant law of Moses. True, this whole matter is complex, and what I have said about it here only scratches the surface.[34] And I think it is

---

34. For detailed defense and critique of each of the major evangelical viewpoints on this question, see especially Wayne Strickland, ed., *The Law, the Gospel, and the Modern Christian* (Grand Rapids: Zondervan, 1993).

especially important to point out that the *practical* difference between these views is small. After all, nine of the Ten Commandments are clearly affirmed and repeated in the New Testament and thus made part of "the law of Christ" (the exception is the Sabbath command).

(2) In some ways, then, of more practical importance is the place that obedience to this law of Christ has in Christian discipleship. Here we find constant pressure toward two extremes: an excessive focus on rules and requirements versus a complete disregard of any rules—that is, legalism versus libertinism. The fundamentalist strain in evangelical Christianity has contributed to the first tendency. Fundamentalists have typically established rules about social conduct, dress, hairstyle, and so forth, loosely derived from biblical principles but very important in maintaining their identity.

In fairness to fundamentalists, we must note that they will strenuously deny any taint of legalism; their rules are not presented as a means of salvation but as a way of honoring God in daily life. But the effect is often to make conformity to rules of essential importance to Christian experience. In the seminary in which I teach, I have often encountered students raised in such a fundamentalist context. And among many of them, I have observed the opposite tendency: reacting against what they see as an excessive emphasis on rules in their early environment, they "throw the baby out with the bath water" and reject "law" altogether. Rightly celebrating the grace of God in Christ, they pooh-pooh any notion of rules; rightly recognizing the centrality of the Spirit for the Christian life, they resist any external norm.

If we are to attain a biblical balance on this matter of "the law of Christ," we need to listen carefully to the teaching of all Scripture. The starting point must be God's new covenant work of grace, in which he plants within the believer his own Spirit, who produces "fruit" in us that is pleasing to himself (cf. Gal. 5:16–26). Any teaching about the Christian life that does not make central this internal work of transformation misses the whole point of the new covenant. Ministry that is faithful to the New Testament will then seek to help Christians realize and work out the potential of this new life within. Jesus used an organic image to describe the process: A good tree produces good fruit (Matt. 7:16–20).

Unfortunately, however, people are not trees. A tree cannot uproot itself from good soil and plant itself in swampy, foul ground. A tree cannot refuse to ingest the fertilizer applied to it. But people, in effect, can. Even the believer, living under the power of grace and with the Spirit within, can resist the work of the Spirit. The Spirit does not instantly erase the programmed thoughts and behavior patterns acquired over ten, or twenty, or thirty years of immersion in the world. Thus it is easy for us to identify our own selfish desires with the promptings of the Spirit; to identify the "loving" action with the action that we really want to do; to think we have the "mind of Christ" when we really have the "mind of this world."

In other words, without taking away anything from the centrality of the Spirit and the demand of love, the New Testament writers insist that there is an external code of conduct to which Christians must still conform. This code, the "law of Christ," is neither detailed nor comprehensive. It focuses more on principles and attitudes than on specifics. It is not spelled out in one long document, but comes to us scattered within the pages of the New Testament. And it is not there to *produce* conduct pleasing to God, but to *guide* it. God is at work, through his Spirit, reprogramming our minds (see, e.g., Rom. 12:1)—Christian conduct is produced from within. But God has also through Christ and the apostles revealed to us his will for our behavior so that we can test the accuracy of that reprogramming and make sure that it is not our own agenda that is being installed. As a result, Christians never move beyond the need to "recall ... the command given by our Lord and Savior through your apostles" (2 Peter 3:2).

God's role in history. Peter touches in this passage on a second matter worth noting in our post-Christian environment. He accuses the false teachers of promulgating the notion that "everything goes on as it has since the beginning of creation" (v. 4). This general attitude is similar to the ruling paradigm in our own world, which is the heritage especially of evolutionary theory. Many Christians struggle with the issue of evolution with respect to its assumptions about creation—and this debate is no doubt an important one. But perhaps even more destructive in the long run is the evolutionary assumption that history operates through blind chance and through uniform processes that are basically invariable from one age to the next. What evolution dismisses is any idea of a personal God who intervenes in the course of history. If the scoffers of Peter's day were alive today, they would be talking about the "invariable laws of nature."

It is this assumption that Peter contests in his references to God's intervention in creation, the Flood, and the end of the world. Green quotes Plumptre: 'The words [of Peter] are a protest against the old Epicurean view of a concourse of atoms, and its modern counterpart, the theory of a perpetual (i.e. unbroken) evolution."[35] Christians, even those who adopt theistic evolution as model of creation, cannot accept the larger evolutionary worldview. Yet we are prone to pick up, unconsciously, this way of viewing the world. We can easily succumb to the reigning paradigm of a "closed" universe and leave little, if any, room for God to act and to reveal himself.

---

35. Green, *The Second Epistle General of Peter and the General Epistle of Jude,* 130.

To be sure, we must guard against the temptation to think we can precisely identify what God is doing in every event in history. Some Christians are far too prone to pontificate on everything that is reported on the evening news. An earthquake becomes a judgment of God against a certain sin in a certain part of the world, a favorable economic report a sign of God's favor, and so on. But a Christian worldview affirms that God is constantly active in the events of our lives and in the history of the world. We may not be able to determine the significance of each one. But God has not stepped off the throne of the universe, nor has he stood aside to let events take their course. We need to recapture the biblical worldview, in which all of life is filled with the presence and activity of a personal, holy, and loving God, who is guiding history toward a definite end.

2 Peter 3:8–10

🔥

BUT DO NOT forget this one thing, dear friends: With the Lord a day is like a thousand years, and a thousand years are like a day. ⁹The Lord is not slow in keeping his promise, as some understand slowness. He is patient with you, not wanting anyone to perish, but everyone to come to repentance.

¹⁰But the day of the Lord will come like a thief. The heavens will disappear with a roar; the elements will be destroyed by fire, and the earth and everything in it will be laid bare.

PETER CONTINUES TO deal with the disturbance created by the appearance of "scoffers" within the church. These false teachers have poured scorn on the idea of a second coming of Christ and the judgment associated with it (vv. 3–4). In verses 5–7, Peter rebuked them directly: "*They* deliberately forget. . . ." Now he turns to the faithful Christians: "But do not *you* forget this one thing, beloved. . . ."[1]

Peter uses the word "forget" to mark the two stages in his argument. In its first stage, he reminded the false teachers of an elementary point: The Old Testament reveals many occasions on which God intervened in his world in a direct and dramatic way. How foolish to think that God cannot judge and even destroy the world (v. 7) when he himself has created it (v. 5) and "destroyed" it once already (v. 6)! But Peter realizes that even faithful Christians have questions about the return of Christ. So in this paragraph he turns to them and makes two arguments: (1) We cannot interpret God's timetable by our human reckoning of time (v. 8); and (2) we must understand God's positive purpose in delaying the Parousia (v. 9). Peter concludes the paragraph (as he did vv. 5–7) by reiterating the truth of the return of Christ to judge (v. 10).

The false teachers, Peter makes clear, were guilty of a deliberate "forgetting." They turned their backs on a truth that was self-evident and were therefore guilty of willful disobedience. But there is another kind of "forgetting" that is not so sinful. Even faithful Christians can fail to maintain a truly biblical worldview, inadvertently picking up ideas from the surrounding

---

1. My own literal rendering of the Greek, which captures the contrast between *autous* ("them") in v. 5 and *hymas* ("you") in this verse.

culture that do not square with God's truth. They can also be disturbed by questions and issues raised by false teachers. Consequently, Peter realizes that the true saints also may require reassurance about Christ's return to wrap up human history.

One of the points on which Peter's audience needed reassurance was the issue of timing. Excited about the new faith they had embraced, often experiencing severe persecution, many early Christians looked eagerly for Christ to return and take them to glory. Jesus had warned his followers to be prepared for his coming, which could take place at any time (e.g., Matt. 24:36–25:30). Peter himself encouraged believers to recognize that "the end of all things is near" (1 Peter 4:7). It is easy to see how such an emphasis could lead to disappointment when Christ did not return as soon as some believers hoped. Was God unfaithful to his promise? Peter understands that some of his readers may be bothered by this question. Thus he makes two points in response to this problem of the apparent "delay" of the Parousia.

(1) Christians must realize that our perception of time is not the same as God's: "With the Lord a day is like a thousand years, and a thousand years are like a day" (v. 8b). The words are an adaptation of Psalm 90:4: "For a thousand years in your sight are like a day that has just gone by, or like a watch in the night." The point of this verse in Psalms is that God, being eternal, does not experience time as we do. What seems like long ages to us is a mere blip in time to him.

Many Jewish and early Christian interpreters used this verse to predict the course of world history. History, they thought, would imitate creation and last for seven "days," the last of which—the Sabbath—would be the messianic age ("the day of the Lord"). Did not Psalm 90:4 prove that a "day" in the Lord's reckoning lasted a thousand years? This line of argument helped lead to the doctrine of "chiliasm," or what we would now call premillennialism—the teaching that Christ's return would usher in a thousand-year period of earthly bliss (see Rev. 20:4–6).[2]

But all this is far from Peter's intention.[3] Peter does not say that God's days equal a thousand years; he says that in God's perspective, a day is "like" (hos) a thousand years, and a thousand years like a day. God views the passing of time from a different perspective than we do. We are impatient, getting disturbed and upset by even a short delay; God is patient, willing to let centuries and even millennia go by as he works out his purposes. Peter is not

---

2. E.g., Justin, *Dialogue* 81; *Epistle of Barnabas* 15.4; Irenaeus, *Against Heresies* 5.23.2; 5.28.3.

3. The fact that Peter shows no consciousness of this meaning of the verse may suggest an early date for 2 Peter, since these ideas were popular in the second century. See Bigg, *The Epistles of St. Peter and St. Jude*, 295–96; Green, *The Second Epistle General of Peter and the General Epistle of Jude*, 134–35; idem, *2 Peter Reconsidered* (London: Tyndale, 1961), 19.

telling his readers that they are wrong to believe that Christ's return is "imminent." What he is telling them is that they are wrong to be impatient when it does not come as quickly as they might like or hope.

(2) Peter's second response to the problem of the apparent delay in Christ's coming has to do with God's purpose in delaying the return. This argument comes at the end of verse 9. The beginning of verse 9 is a transition between the first argument (v. 8) and the second: "The Lord is not slow in keeping his promise, as some understand slowness." The "Lord" may be Christ, since the New Testament writers usually think of the Lord in the phrase the "day of the Lord" (v. 10) as Christ.[4] But the "Lord" in verse 8, referring to Psalm 90:4, is, of course, Yahweh. Consequently, the "Lord" here in verse 9 is also probably God.[5] "His promise" refers to the promise of Christ's return in glory (see v. 4).

"Some," Peter suggests, interpret what they think to be God's "slowness" in fulfilling this promise to be an indication that the whole idea should be rejected.[6] These "some" may be Christians who have been disturbed by the false teachers.[7] Peter is then exhorting these believers not to fall into the heresy of the false teachers. But the word "some" has a polemical edge. It is more likely that Peter is thinking of the false teachers themselves.[8] They view the delay in the fulfillment of God's promise as a sign of God's weakness or uninvolvement with history. God is not really concerned with what is happening here on earth, they may have argued, so that any idea of a real end of this world or of judgment is foolish. This being the case, people might as well do whatever they want, for no accounting for actions before a just God is to come.

Peter directly counters this heretical skepticism: Rather than being a sign of God's lack of concern, his delay in sending Christ in judgment is a sign of his deep concern for human beings. For in God's infinite patience, he is waiting for people to repent before it is too late. He does not want "anyone to perish, but everyone to come to repentance."

Peter's main idea is clear enough, an idea echoed throughout the New Testament (e.g., Rom. 2:3–5; 1 Tim. 2:4; 1 Peter 3:20). But what is hotly debated are the implications of this teaching. If it is God's will that "everyone" should repent, why is it that many do not? For Peter himself has made clear in this letter that there will be people on the day of judgment who will

---

4. Bigg, *The Epistles of St. Peter and St. Jude*, 296.

5. Kelly, *The Epistles of Peter and of Jude*, 362.

6. We find here again possible allusion to Hellenistic debates about God's providence and judgment; Plutarch says, "God's slowness [to judge] undermines our belief in providence" (*Moralia* 549b).

7. Kelly, *The Epistles of Peter and of Jude*, 362.

8. Bigg, *The Epistles of St. Peter and St. Jude*, 296.

suffer eternal destruction because they have refused to embrace God's salvation in Christ (e.g., 2:3–10; 3:6–7).

The answer to this problem depends on how one understands the biblical doctrine of election. By making election dependent on (foreseen) human faith, Arminians maintain that God genuinely and fully wills that all people come to repentance and faith. The reason that all people do not is because God gives people the freedom to decide either for or against him. Obviously Arminians have found in this verse very important support for their view that the only reason human beings fail to experience God's salvation is because of their own choice.

For this reason, of course, this verse is troublesome to Calvinists, who believe that God has chosen only some people to be saved. Most Calvinists have explained the verse along the lines laid down by Calvin himself:

> No mention is made here of the secret decree of God by which the wicked are doomed to their own ruin, but only of His loving-kindness as it is made known to us in the Gospel. There God stretches out His hand to all alike, but He only grasps (in such a way as to lead to Himself) whom He has chosen before the foundation of the world.[9]

In other words, we must distinguish two "wills" in God: his "desiderative" will (what God desires to happen) and his "effective" will. God desires and commands that all people repent, but he effectually makes it possible for only the elect to repent.

Whatever the merits of these two views (and the issue is far more complex than we have suggested), I wonder whether we have to choose between them. For, as Bauckham points out, what Peter says here is similar to a popular Jewish teaching according to which God withholds his judgment while he waits for his people to repent.[10] In this verse, the statement about God wanting "everyone to come to repentance" is preceded and governed by the statement that "he [the Lord] is patient with *you*." In other words, it is God's patience *toward the believers* to whom Peter writes that is the main idea here. We should perhaps, then, qualify the "everyone" at the end of the verse in terms of this leading idea: God is patient with you, wanting everyone *of you* to repent before the end comes. False teachers have arisen in the Christian community. They have begun to infect others with their dangerous views. Rather than bringing judgment on them instantly, God withholds his wrath, patiently waiting for his people to repent and to get right with him again before it is too late.

---

9. Calvin, *Hebrews and 1 and 2 Peter*, 364.
10. Bauckham, *Jude, 2 Peter*, 312.

With verse 10, Peter moves from argument to assertion.[11] God may be delaying the Parousia for his own beneficent purposes, but "the day of Lord will come like a thief." The "day of the Lord," as we explained earlier (see the notes on 2:9), was a popular phrase of the Old Testament prophets, which indicated the time of God's decisive and final intervention in history to judge his enemies and to save his own people. The rest of the verse suggests that the idea of judgment is dominant here, though verse 12 shows that Peter can also use the language about the "day" with a positive focus.

Peter's addition of the phrase "like a thief" to his promise of the coming of the day of Lord is significant. Jesus (Matt. 24:43; Luke 12:39) and Paul (1 Thess. 5:2) also used the analogy of the coming of the thief to explain that the coming of the Lord would be unexpected. Peter clearly opposes those Christians who insisted that Christ had to return within a certain short period of time after his resurrection. But he by no means opposes the idea of imminence itself. For him, as for Jesus, Paul, and the rest of the New Testament writers, the time of Christ's coming cannot be calculated. Like a thief, he can appear at any time.

As in verse 7, Peter here also portrays the coming of Christ with cosmic imagery: "The heavens will disappear with a roar; the elements will be destroyed by fire, and the earth and everything in it will be laid bare." Each of these clauses presents problems of translation and interpretation, with the difficulties increasing as we move through them.

The "heavens" (as in vv. 5, 7) denote that part of creation that is unseen—the spiritual realm. And, as in verse 7, Peter suggests that the day of the Lord will bring destruction to these heavens themselves. The problem in this clause is the word the NIV has translated "with a roar." The word usually refers to a whistling or whizzing sound; it is used of the sound made by an arrow passing through the air. Hence the REB translates "with a great rushing sound"; TEV, "with a shrill noise." But since fire is so prominent in this context, the word is best taken to refer to the "crackling roar" made by a huge fire.[12] In this case, the NIV rendering is apt.

The second clause poses the difficulty of how to translate the Greek word *stoicheia*. The NIV takes a literal but ambiguous approach, rendering it simply "elements." But what are these "elements"? We have three possibilities. (1) They may be the basic elements of the physical universe: according to most ancients, fire, water, air, and earth.[13] (2) They may be the heavenly bodies:

---

11. This is why many English versions, like the NIV, put a paragraph break between vv. 9 and 10.

12. Kelly, *The Epistles of Peter and of Jude*, 364.

13. Neyrey, *2 Peter, Jude*, 243.

sun, moon, stars, planets (see TEV, "the heavenly bodies").[14] (3) They may be spiritual beings.

The last of these options is unlikely since the meaning "spiritual beings" for *stoicheia* is attested only in three hotly debated Pauline texts: Galatians 4:3; Colossians 2:8, 20. Nor does a reference to spiritual beings fit the context here in 2 Peter, which focuses on the physical universe. But either of the first two options fits this emphasis well; and either also fits well with Peter's use of the same word in verse 12, where he predicts that "the elements will melt in the heat." Richard Bauckham thinks the second should be preferred, since Peter seems to be picking up language from Old Testament passages that predict the eradication of the heavenly bodies in the time of the end. See, for instance, Isaiah 34:4:

> All the stars of the heavens will be dissolved
>   and the sky rolled up like a scroll;
> all the starry host will fall
>   like withered leaves from the vine,
>   like shriveled figs from the fig tree.[15]

However, in verse 12, Peter mentions only the "heavens" and the "elements." And this suggests that "elements" and the earth are closely related, favoring the first option. Although we cannot be sure, we think that "elements" refers to the basic building blocks of the earth. In verse 7, Peter announced that the totality of God's creation—"heavens and earth"—were "reserved for fire." Now he moves on one step further, claiming that the elements of the earth will actually be destroyed by fire.

The third clause in verse 10 presents the greatest difficulty, as the following representative translations suggest:

> NIV: "the earth and everything in it *will be laid bare*" (see also NRSV)
> NASB: "the earth and its works *will be burned up*" (see also KJV; NJB)
> TEV: "the earth with everything in it *will vanish*"

The main problem is the verb at the end of the verse. For one thing, the Greek text has several textual variants. That is, the many manuscripts that we use to construct our Greek text differ in the word that they have here. Editors of the Greek New Testament cannot therefore be absolutely certain about which word Peter himself actually wrote. The NASB and TEV renderings certainly make good sense—especially the NASB "burned up," since Peter has

---

14. Most commentators; see, e.g., Bigg, *The Epistles of St. Peter and St. Jude*, 297; Kelly, *The Epistles of Peter and of Jude*, 364.

15. See also Isa. 13:10; Ezek. 32:7–8; Joel 2:10; Matt. 24:29; Mark 13:24–25; Rev. 6:13. See particularly Bauckham, *Jude, 2 Peter*, 316.

been talking in this passage about the final destruction of the heavens and the earth by fire.[16]

But it is just for this reason that we should be a bit suspicious of this reading. For the scribes who transmitted our Greek New Testament often substituted easier words for ones that seemed more difficult. The editors of the Greek New Testament that most scholars use today have therefore decided that Peter probably wrote the word *heurethesetai*.[17] A literal rendering of this word is "will be found," and many scholars do not think Peter could possibly have written this because it makes no sense.[18] But the word can have the connotation "be manifest," and the passive form of the verb probably has the nuance here of "be manifest before God." That is, the earth and "all its works" will be manifest, disclosed in their fullness to God, at the time of judgment. While we cannot be certain, this seems to be the best alternative.[19]

If we adopt this general translation, two possible interpretations remain to us. (1) Peter may be referring to the judgment of human beings, with their "works." The Bible elsewhere speaks of God's revealing and judging the "secrets" of human hearts (e.g., Rom. 2:16), and Peter's language may be describing God's searching assessment of the motives and thoughts of every person. They will all be "laid bare" before him.[20] (2) Peter may be referring to the judgment of the physical earth, with all its works (e.g., buildings, etc.). The former has much to be said for it, but Peter's language and the context support the latter. "Heavens" and "earth" refer to the physical universe throughout this passage (see also vv. 5 and 7). And the continuation of Peter's thought in verse 11 also suggests that physical dissolution has been his point in verse 10.

---

16. The NASB rendering assumes the reading *katakaesetai*, found in the uncial A and several other manuscripts. The TEV translation is based on the word *aphanisthesetai*, read by one manuscript.

17. In addition to being "the most difficult reading," this word also has the strongest manuscript support, being found in two of the most important uncials and in several other manuscripts.

18. Although they accept the reading *heurethesetai* as the best available, the editors of the United Bible Societies *Greek New Testament* also note that the reading "seems devoid of meaning in the context" (Bruce M. Metzger, *A Textual Commentary on the Greek New Testament* [New York: United Bible Societies, 1971], 706).

19. See esp. Bauckham, *Jude, 2 Peter*, 319–20. We may mention here two other interpretations that adopt this same reading. Kelly treats the word as a question: "Will it be found?" e.g., "Will the earth be found after God's judgment is through with it?" (Kelly, *The Epistles of Peter and of Jude*, 365–66). And Al Wolters thinks that the word is shorthand for the idea "be found genuine (see 1 Peter 1:7); Peter is not speaking here of world annihilation but of world purification" ("World View and Textual Criticism in 2 Peter 3:10," *WTJ* 49 [1987]: 405–13).

20. See esp. Bauckham, *Jude, 2 Peter*, 319–21.

WE SHOULD NOT be surprised that Peter had to respond to a false view about the time of the return of Christ. The New Testament teaching on this matter is controversial and easily misunderstood. We will better be able to understand and apply Peter's corrective on this issue if we have a grasp of the general New Testament teaching.

In the Doctrinal Statement of the Evangelical Free Church of America, which, as a teacher in the denomination's seminary, I gladly affirm every year, is the statement that Christ's coming is "imminent." Well and good. But what does it mean to say that Christ's return is "imminent"? Free Church historians and theologians themselves disagree about this. And the same controversy is duplicated in many other denominations, churches, and academic discussions. Many people use the word "imminent" to describe the timing of Christ's return, but they mean different things by it.

We can begin by surveying the New Testament evidence. The belief that Christ's return is imminent comes from the many texts that claim that the Parousia, or the Day of the Lord, is "near." Some of the most important are:

> Matthew 24:33: "When you see all these things, you know that it [or he]
> is near [*engys*], right at the door." (cf. Mark 13:29)
> Romans 13:11b: "Our salvation is nearer [*engyteron*] now than when we first
> believed."
> Philippians 4:5b: "The Lord is near [*engys*]."
> James 5:8b: "The Lord's coming is near [*engiken*]."
> 1 Peter 4:7: "The end of all things is near [*engiken*]."

Do these verses mean that the early Christians definitely expected Christ to return within a few years? Many scholars answer, "Yes." They note three verses from the Gospels in which Jesus seems to make just such a prediction:

> Matthew 10:23b: "'I tell you the truth, you will not finish going through
> the cities of Israel before the Son of Man comes.'"
> Mark 9:1 (and par.): "'I tell you the truth, some who are standing here will
> not taste death before they see the kingdom of God come with
> power.'"
> Mark 13:30 (par. Matt. 24:34): "'I tell you the truth, this generation will
> certainly not pass away until all these things have happened.'"

And Paul seemed to share this expectation as well. In 1 Thessalonians 4:16–17, for instance, he wrote as if he would be alive when Christ returned in glory:

> For the Lord himself will come down from heaven, with a loud command, with the voice of the archangel and with the trumpet call of

God, and the dead in Christ will rise first. After that *we* who are still alive and are left will be caught up together with them in the clouds to meet the Lord in the air.

Therefore, on the basis of Jesus' teaching, the first generation of Christians believed that Christ would return very shortly. After some time, however, that expectation began to fade. Christ's failure to return as soon as expected led some to throw out the idea of a Parousia altogether (e.g., the false teachers Peter is opposing). Other, orthodox Christians argued in response that Christ would certainly come but that he may be delayed for a long time (this would be Peter's view here). Scholars who adopt this paradigm thus trace a development in the idea of imminence in the New Testament writings, from an enthusiastic certainty of a coming within a few years (Jesus, the "authentic" Paul) to a more "realistic" expectation of perhaps long delay (the Pastoral Letters; 2 Peter). For these scholars, "imminence" characterizes the first of these views and refers to the certainty of an immediate Parousia.

But we question the premise of this whole scenario—that Jesus or Paul predicted that the Parousia would take place within their generation. The verses we have cited above, commonly used to prove this, are better interpreted otherwise. The "coming of the Son of Man" in Matthew 10:23 may refer to the fall of Jerusalem; or Jesus may have expanded his vision here from the original Twelve to disciples generally. Mark 9:1 and parallels, as we argued in our interpretation of 1:16–18, refers to the Transfiguration. And "all these things" in Mark 13:30 (par. Matt. 24:34) probably does not include the Parousia itself ("these things" in the previous verse certainly does not). That Paul hoped to be among those alive when Christ returned is clear, but he never taught that this would necessarily be the case. Despite its widespread acceptance in the scholarly community, the idea that Christ would return within a few years of his death and resurrection does not have clear New Testament support.

What we find, on the contrary, are three related strands of teaching. Christ's coming:

is "near" (see the texts above);
may be delayed (Luke 19:11–27; 2 Peter 3:8–9);
is temporally uncertain (Mark 13:32, 35 and par.; 1 Thess. 5:2; 2 Peter 3:10).

We can easily weave these three strands together into a single, coherent teaching. Not even Jesus himself knows the time of his return in glory (Mark 13:32). It has been set by God and revealed to no one. He may, for his own purposes, choose to delay or to speed up the timetable (see 2 Peter 3:12, below). Christians must always reckon with the *possibility* that it can take place at any time. Imminence, defined biblically, means that the return of Christ and the culmination of history are always impending. The Parousia is the next event in salvation history; it may be preceded by signs (Matt. 24:29; 2 Thess. 2:3–7), but the signs come so shortly before the end or are themselves so ambiguous that they give no help in "date-setting." The Christian must always live in expectation that human history may suddenly come to an end.

 ONCE WE UNDERSTAND the New Testament idea of "imminence" as it applies to the Parousia, we can better appreciate what is going on in 2 Peter 3. Clearly the false teachers have assumed a radical and unbiblical interpretation of imminence, thinking that it required Christ to return shortly after his resurrection. Since he did not come when they expected, they rejected the idea altogether. Peter responds by reminding his readers that God's timetable is not ours and that what we might think is an intolerable delay is a mere moment from God's perspective. Peter is not, as scholars think, correcting an earlier, more radical, New Testament view of imminence; he is reasserting the biblical perspective against the misunderstanding of the false teachers.

If the view of imminence as I have outlined above and as Peter defends here is accurate, then an obvious point of contemporary significance is the error of "date-setting." Date-setters have arisen throughout the history of the church. Claiming to have received a vision from God or to have solved the prophetic puzzle, these folks predict an exact date for the Rapture, the Parousia, or, more generally, the end of the world. We mentioned above those Christians who interpreted Psalm 90:4 and 2 Peter 3:8 to predict a thousand-year messianic age and who were therefore certain that Christ would return in A.D. 1000. The fervor caused by the Reformation sparked several other such movements. And in our own day we have lived through Edgar Whisenant's 88 Reasons Why the Rapture Will Be in 1988, while the Korean church was deeply affected (and sadly disappointed) by similar predictions in the early 1990s.

We may be thankful that such self-appointed prophets remind us that Christ could return at any time. But we must deplore and reject their assumption to know what Christ himself did not know. Many sincere Christians have been led astray by these date-setters. Convinced that the end of history is just around the corner, Christians have sold property and houses, quit jobs, and generally dropped out of society. The failure of the predicted world's end has meant for them not only spiritual uncertainty but economic disaster.

But we also meet this general approach in a much milder guise. Tim LaHaye, for instance, has written an article in which he clearly and repeatedly affirms the biblical truth that no one can know the day or the hour. But he also claims that "our generation has more legitimate reasons for believing [that Jesus will return in our generation] than any previous generation."[21] And, interestingly, one of his "twelve reasons" for thinking this is the ancient rabbinic tradition that interpreted the days of creation as outlining the course of world history, with each "day" a thousand years in length. According to LaHaye, this would make the year 2000 the approximate time for Christ's return.[22] True, LaHaye is cautious about all of this, and he plainly refuses to set dates. But he does suggest we can "set limits." He repeatedly notes developments that make it possible—for the first time—for certain of the biblical prophecies about Christ's return to be fulfilled. Implicitly, therefore, generations before ours could not view the Lord's coming as imminent. But this flies in the face of the clear New Testament teaching to the contrary.

LaHaye's article illustrates, it seems to me, one of the persistent problems in Christians' attitude toward the return of Christ: the tendency to tie belief in imminence to certain signs. By doing so, they imply that Christ's return can be imminent only if the signs—as they interpret them, of course—are in place. But this is not the New Testament perspective. It usually affirms the truth of imminence apart from signs. And where signs are mentioned, they are quite general. For instance, Jesus tells us that "when you see all these things, you know that it [or he] is near" (Matt. 24:33). In this context "all these things" include wars, famines, earthquakes, persecution, false christs, and prophets (vv. 4–25)—things that are present throughout the church age.

The danger in the view I am contesting is that Christians will adopt the appropriate eschatological mindset only in times of crisis. The Gulf War against Iraq in 1991 sparked renewed eschatological fervor among believers. And I guess that is a good thing. But how about the years when we are not facing such an obvious international crisis? What happens to our longing for Christ's return then? We believe that Christ's coming is "imminent" because the New Testament affirms it. We are called constantly to live in the light of the end of history, even if we can see no obvious signs of its end in the world around us. God can certainly use the world around us to wake us up and help us see the truth. But when all is said and done, we walk "by faith, not by sight."

---

21. Tim LaHaye, "Twelve Reasons Why This Could Be the Terminal Generation," in *When the Trumpet Sounds: Today's Foremost Authorities Speak Out on End-Time Controversies,* ed. Thomas Ice and Timothy Demy (Eugene, Ore.: Harvest House, 1995), 429.

22. Ibid., 442–43.

2 Peter 3:11–13

SINCE EVERYTHING WILL be destroyed in this way, what kind of people ought you to be? You ought to live holy and godly lives ¹²as you look forward to the day of God and speed its coming. That day will bring about the destruction of the heavens by fire, and the elements will melt in the heat. ¹³But in keeping with his promise we are looking forward to a new heaven and a new earth, the home of righteousness.

Original Meaning

IN 3:3–10, PETER has focused on teaching Christians what to believe about the return of Christ in glory. Now, in verses 11–13, he turns to what Christians should do about it. Reminders about the coming of the Lord and the response that Christians should have toward it are common in the last sections of New Testament letters (e.g., 1 Cor. 15:58; Eph. 5:10–16; Phil. 4:5; Col. 4:5; 1 Tim. 6:14; 2 Tim. 4:1–5; 1 Peter 5:1–10). But since the false teachers are attacking orthodox Christian doctrine at just this point, scoffing at the idea of a history-ending Parousia, Peter finds an eschatological exhortation especially important. He must not only correct this false teaching but demonstrate to believers its practical significance.

In the first part of verse 11 Peter ties his exhortation to the coming destruction of the world, as presented in verses 5–10, but he goes on to give also a positive eschatological grounding to his imperative: the hope of a "new heaven and a new earth" (v. 13). The Parousia brings both destruction and renewal. Christians should live holy and godly lives, then, not only because this world is not going to last but also because a new world is going to take its place. They should pursue righteousness, both to distance themselves from this decaying and doomed world and to prepare for the next, "the home of righteousness" (v. 13).

The connection of verse 11 with verse 10 is especially close, since Peter uses the same verb in both, *lyo* ("will be destroyed"). The future rendering of this verb in verse 11 in the NIV is certainly possible. But technically the verb is in the present tense, and Peter may have chosen this tense to suggest that the destruction of "everything" is even now in process (cf. NJB: "Since everything is coming to an end like this").¹ Just as the bodies of Christians are

---

1. See, e.g., Mayor, *The Epistle of St. Jude and the Second Epistle of St. Peter*, 161; Kelly, *The Epistles of Peter and of Jude*, 366.

"wasting away" (2 Cor. 4:16), so the very universe is in process of decaying (Rom. 8:21). God did not build this world to last forever.

That being the case, Peter asks, "What kind of people ought you to be?" The Greek word for "what kind" (*potapos*) can sometimes have the nuance, "How wonderful, how glorious" (see Mark 13:1; 1 John 3:1). Such a nuance would certainly fit well here,[2] but it does not have this meaning often enough to make the idea certain. Yet even if the nuance is neutral (as in most modern English translations), Peter makes the point clear enough by immediately answering his own question: "You ought to live holy and godly lives."

The NIV is a legitimate paraphrase of the Greek, which literally translated reads, "It is necessary for you to live in holy conducts and godlinesses." The plurals, which are awkward in the Greek and impossible in English, bring out the manifold ways in which believers need to exhibit holy and godly conduct. All we do should be "holy"; that is, it should reflect God's own character of "set-apartness" from this world—a point Peter made in his first letter: "But just as he who called you is holy, so be holy in all you do; for it is written, 'Be holy, because I am holy'" (1 Peter 1:15–16). And all that we do should be "godly"; that is, it should reflect the God we have come to know in Jesus Christ. Peter has made this quality of "godliness" a central ingredient in his initial exhortation to believers in this letter (2 Peter 1:3, 6–7). As we noted there, Peter ends his letter by returning to some of the key ideas introduced at its beginning.

Having begun his exhortation to holy living with an eschatological reminder, Peter concludes it with another: "as you look forward to the day of God and speed its coming" (v. 12a). The attitude of expectancy suggested by the word "look forward" is often mentioned in Scripture as particularly appropriate for God's people (see, e.g., Hab. 2:3–4; Matt. 11:3; Luke 7:19–20). Peter uses the verb three times in verses 12–14, and it therefore becomes a key theme in these verses. Christians need the motivation of the forward look. They need to recognize that God has a plan, that it unfolds just as he wants it to, and that it culminates in blessing for his people. What Christians look forward to is "the coming of the day of God" (NASB, a more literal rendering than NIV here).

We have encountered the word "coming" (*parousia*) twice already in 2 Peter (1:16; 3:4), a word used throughout the New Testament to denote the coming of Christ in glory. But this is the only place in the New Testament where the word is not followed by a personal reference. And the phrase "day of God" itself is unusual; "the day of the Lord" (see the notes on 2:9 and 3:10) is the customary scriptural designation of the end times ("day of God"

---

2. Kelly, *The Epistles of Peter and of Jude*, 366–67.

occurs elsewhere only in Jer. 46:10 and Rev. 16:14). This unusual wording naturally raises the question about a peculiar focus he wants to bring to us. Perhaps he wants to maintain the more "cosmic" flavor of end events, typical of his treatment in this chapter.[3] On the other hand, Peter is famous for unusual words and constructions, so we should be cautious about reading too much into this one.

Christians, says Peter, are not only to "look forward" to this "day of God"; they are also to "speed its coming." The verb used here (*speudo*) can also mean "strive," "make an effort," "be eager." Peter uses a form of this word with this meaning in 1:5; and if it has this meaning here, we would translate something like the NIV margin note: "as you wait eagerly for the day of God to come." But this word has the sense of "hastening" in its other New Testament occurrences (Luke 2:16; 19:5, 6; Acts 20:16; 22:18), and the idea that believers may actually "hasten" the end of history, while at first sight strange, is in fact deeply rooted in Jewish and Christian teaching.

The rabbis claimed that the Messiah would come if only all Israel would repent or obey the law perfectly for one day—a teaching found in different forms in Jewish literature.[4] Peter himself reflects this tradition in his sermon in the temple precincts (Acts 3:19–20): "Repent, then, and turn to God, so that your sins may be wiped out, that times of refreshing may come from the Lord, and that he may send the Christ, who has been appointed for you— even Jesus." We may think that the idea of Christians hastening the coming of Christ takes away from the sovereignty of God, for doesn't the Bible make clear that God determines the time of the end? We have here another instance of the biblical interplay between human actions and God's sovereignty: Human acts are significant and meaningful, but God is nevertheless fully sovereign. As Bauckham argues, what Peter is suggesting is that God graciously factors his peoples' actions into his determination of the time of the end.[5]

If we ask for further details on how Christians can hasten Christ's return, Peter gives no explicit answer. But he has already claimed that the apparent delay in the Parousia is because God wants everybody (or, as we argued, all God's people) to repent—the same point made in the temple sermon just quoted. God's people can hasten Christ's return by their sincere and complete rejection of the hold of sin on their lives. By connecting what he says here about hastening the coming of the day of God with his exhortation in verse 11b, Peter also suggests that the holy living of God's people is a way to speed up the eschatological timetable. And we can include evangelism; recall Jesus'

---

3. Ibid., 367.
4. See Bauckham, *Jude, 2 Peter*, 325, for a helpful list and discussion of the Jewish texts.
5. Ibid., 325.

words: "This gospel of the kingdom will be preached in the whole world as a testimony to all nations, and then the end will come" (Matt. 24:14). Finally, we may also add to the list the prayers of God's people, for we have been taught to pray "Your kingdom come" (Matt. 6:10).

In the last part of verse 12, Peter describes again the cosmic effects of the day of God: "The heavens will be destroyed by fire, and the elements will melt as they are burned" (a more literal rendering of the Greek than the NIV). "Heavens" refers again to the unseen spiritual dimension of the universe (see 3:5, 7, 10). "Destroy" (Greek *lyo*) occurs again as a key verb (see also vv. 10–11). The word "elements" (*stoicheia;* see comments on v. 10) is either the heavenly bodies or the basic physical components of the earth—more likely the latter. Peter is then here announcing the destruction of the entire universe—heavens and earth (see also vv. 5 and 7). The word "melt" is a particularly appropriate one in this context, for it was used in the Old Testament to depict the cosmic disasters that will accompany the Day of the Lord:

> Look! The LORD is coming from his dwelling place;
> > he comes down and treads the high places of the earth.
> The mountains melt beneath him
> > and the valleys split apart,
> like wax before the fire,
> > like water rushing down a slope. (Mic. 1:3–4; see also
> > > Isa. 63:19–64:1, LXX)

But Christians do not "look forward" only to destruction of the universe; they also "look forward" to its renewal. God has promised a "new heaven and a new earth." The promise Peter has in mind is almost certainly the one in Isaiah 65 and 66, the only Old Testament passage in which this idea is mentioned:

> Behold, I will create
> > new heavens and a new earth.
> The former things will not be remembered,
> > nor will they come to mind. (65:17; see also 66:22)

The same image is picked up in Revelation 21:1 in the description of the eternal state that follows the Millennium and the judgment of God.

Peter's intertwining of predictions about the destruction of the universe and its renewal raise questions about the exact nature of what we are to envisage happening in the last day.[6] But the important point here for Peter is not speculation about the exact nature of this "new heaven and earth," but

---

6. We take up this issue briefly in the "Bridging Contexts" section.

that it will be "the home of righteousness."[7] We live in a world where wrong often prevails; a world in which faithful Christians are often persecuted for doing God's will, while evil people enjoy the rewards of their sin; a world in which innocent lives are ripped from wombs and God's laws are flaunted and mocked. All that will be eradicated in the next world. As John puts it in Revelation 21:3–4:

> Now the dwelling of God is with men, and he will live with them. They will be his people, and God himself will be with them and be their God. He will wipe away every tear from their eyes. There will be no more death or mourning or crying or pain, for the old order of things has passed away.

THE FOCUS ON eschatology in 2 Peter 3 is, of course, not unusual in the New Testament. The early Christians were joyfully convinced that they were participating in the "last days" (see the "Bridging Contexts" section on 2:1–4). But they never allowed their joy in the present to dim their hope for the future. For, while experiencing the blessings of the "age to come," Christians also continue to suffer the difficulties of "this age": sickness, persecution, struggles with temptation, and sin. Thus, "the last things" were never far from their thinking, and we find frequent reference to the Parousia and associated events throughout the New Testament.

But what does stand out as distinctive in 2 Peter 3 is the cosmic orientation of the discussion of the last things. New Testament authors typically focus on the personal dimension of the return of Christ: judgment of sinners and transformation (through rapture and resurrection) of believers (see, e.g., Rom. 8:18–30; 13:11–14; 1 Cor. 15; 2 Cor. 5:1–10; Phil. 3:10–11, 20–22; 1 Thess. 4:13–5:10; 2 Thess. 2:1–9). Only in Revelation do we have the kind of emphasis on the effects on the physical world of the return of Christ that we find in 2 Peter 3. And, as we have noted, Peter is the only biblical author explicitly to predict that the universe will be destroyed by fire (3:7, 10, 12; see the discussion in the "Bridging Contexts" section on 3:1–7).

Peter repeatedly emphasizes that the Day of the Lord/of God will bring destruction to the material universe. But at the same time, he predicts the coming of a "new heaven and a new earth" (v. 13). What is the relationship between these two ideas? Does Peter think that the new heaven and earth

---

7. Literally, Peter says, "in which righteousness dwells."

will *replace* the current material universe? Or does he envision a *transformation* of the existing world? These questions are not just academic ones, for the answer we give will have an effect on a number of issues, ranging from our hope for resurrection to our stance on environmental issues.[8]

Peter does not give a clear answer to these questions, though his language—"disappear," "destroy," "melt"—certainly tends toward the idea of replacement. But other biblical passages give us pause. Jesus speaks of the time when he will sit on his throne and the apostles with him at the "renewal [or rebirth, *palingenesia*] of all things" (Matt. 19:28). Peter himself probably alludes to a similar idea in his sermon in Acts 3. We quoted verses 19–20 from that sermon above; in verse 21, he goes on to say, "He [Messiah] must remain in heaven until the time comes for God to restore everything, as he promised long ago through his holy prophets." Debate focuses on the word the NIV translates "restore," which can also mean "consummation" or "establishment."[9] But "restoration" is a better translation here.[10] Restoration suggests not destruction, but transformation. And Peter's claim that this restoration will fulfill the promises of the prophets also points in this direction, since the Old Testament typically envisages the last days in terms of a transformed earth.

Perhaps the most important passage tending in this direction is Romans 8:19–22. These verses come in the midst of Paul's reassuring message about the certainty of the believer's hope. Believers, who share Christ's sufferings, can be fully confident that they will also share his glory (v. 17). This glory far outweighs our earthly struggles (v. 18); indeed, it is the signal for the transformation of creation. Note how Paul puts this idea in verse 21: "The creation itself will be liberated from its bondage to decay and brought into the glorious freedom of the children of God." What Paul seems to be anticipating is not the simple destruction of the present universe, but its transformation.

Complicating this issue is the place of the Millennium in the whole scheme. If one adopts a premillennial eschatology (as I do), then we must allow for an "interim" period of earthly blessing following the return of Christ but before the eternal state. Could the prophecies about transformation find fulfillment during the Millennium, with the prophecies of destruction coming to pass after? This distinction may help us in some texts, but it does not finally resolve the tension. For one thing, most of the New Testament eschatological texts simply do not allow us to distinguish between the Millennium and the eternal state. Furthermore, we often find a tension between

---

8. We discuss some of these in the "Contemporary Significance" section.

9. See F. F. Bruce, *The Book of Acts*, NICNT, rev. ed. (Grand Rapids: Eerdmans, 1988), 84–85.

10. See, e.g., I. Howard Marshall, *The Acts of the Apostles: An Introduction and Commentary*, TNTC (Grand Rapids: Eerdmans, 1980), 93–94. He points to the cognate word in 1:6.

transformation and replacement in the same text. In John's vision of the eternal state, for example, he sees, "a new heaven and a new earth, for the first heaven and first earth had passed away" (Rev. 21:1), which certainly sounds like replacement. But just four verses later, he quotes the Lord as saying, "'I am making everything new!'" (v. 5), which sounds like transformation.

Another way of accounting for this tension is to assume that the language of "passing away" and "burning" refers not to annihilation but to purification. Fire is certainly often a purifying agent in Scripture. The most relevant text here is 1 Corinthians 3:13–15, in which Paul predicts that each person's "work" will be tested "by fire" and that some believers will be saved "through fire." Peter, then, may be predicting the purification of the world through fire, not its destruction. The problem with this view, as we have seen (see the "Bridging Contexts" section on 3:1–7), is the specific language of "destruction" that Peter uses.

We face here, then, a tension that cannot apparently be resolved. It is not that the Bible speaks in contradictory terms about the end of the world. It is rather that it must, in the nature of the case, seek to describe what is unique and quite beyond our experience—the transition from the temporal world to the eternal state—with language and analogies drawn from our own world. Such analogies always fall short of matching the reality; each can, at best, capture only one side of the full picture. What the Bible does make clear, we think, is that the destruction of this present universe at the end of history does not mean the end of the material world. There is continuity as well as discontinuity in the shift from the present heavens and earth to the new heaven and earth.[11]

AS WE LOOK back at Peter's discussion of eschatology in 3:3–13, three points merit particular attention by Christians today.

(1) Christians need to remember the ultimate, "bottom-line," purpose of biblical eschatology: to make us better Christians here and now. Careful study of eschatological passages in the Bible is, of course, appropriate and necessary. And our own human curiosity naturally leads us to speculate about just how and when the events those passages teach will actually take shape in history. But we must not study eschatology for its own sake or for the gratification of our curiosity. Christians bitten by the "eschatological bug" usually end up with vision problems—a tunnel vision

---

11. I am greatly indebted throughout this section to Murray Harris, *Raised Immortal: Resurrection and Immortality in the New Testament* (Grand Rapids: Eerdmans, 1983), 168–70.

in which all they see is "the last days." We must never forget, as Peter makes clear in verse 11, that biblical eschatology is to stimulate in believers a holy and godly lifestyle. In fact, you will find no passage in the New Testament on eschatology that does not have that kind of specific, practical focus.

(2) Christians need to understand the nature of this intimate relationship between eschatology and exhortation, between teaching about the world to come and living in the present world. We have all heard the criticisms directed against Christianity, that it promises only "pie in the sky, by and by," and that Christians are so "heavenly minded that they are no earthly good." Karl Marx made a similar point when he called Christianity "the opium of the masses." He saw Christians as people who were so focused on the life to come that they simply could not get excited about changing their current world. The faith lulled people to sleep and left them content in the midst of injustice and oppression. Liberation theologians in our day make much the same point, arguing for a serious recasting of the Christian faith so that it can become a truly revolutionary movement.

But, as the historian Barbara Tuchman has observed, "Revolutions produce other men, not new men."[12] Only a force from outside this world can change this world. And Christians find that force in the grace of God and in the Holy Spirit. But does a robust eschatology have to dampen Christian ardor to change the world?

It must be admitted that it can, and it has. And there is, of course, a sense in which Christians will always be pessimistic about this world, for Scripture makes clear that no real and permanent transformation can be expected until Christ returns. Some Christians, therefore, give up on this world, pursuing their own private path of holiness and letting the world literally "go to hell." But the "holy and godly life" that Peter calls on us to lead in light of the world's end certainly must include zealous evangelism and the kind of concern for social justice that Jesus said so much about. The scriptural model of the world to come, "the home of righteousness," should stimulate us to make that model as much a reality here and now as possible.

It is at this point that the balance between replacement and transformation as sketched in the "Bridging Contexts" section becomes important. The replacement model is, as we have seen, the one that 2 Peter 3 tends most to support. Peter connects the destruction of the world with his call to holy and godly living (v. 11). The replacement focus reminds Christians to sit fast and loose to all things earthly, for they are not lasting.

I well remember a student I taught many years ago, a new convert with all the beautiful zeal of someone who was bowled over with the grace of Christ.

---

12. Barbara W. Tuchman, *The First Salute* (New York: Alfred Knopf, 1988), 300.

I mentioned that I was going on vacation and was frustrated that I did not have a decent telephoto lens for my camera. He appeared not long after on my doorstep with a very expensive telephoto lens that he insisted I borrow. I told him I didn't think I could do that because I wasn't sure I could take good care of it. "That's OK," he replied. "It's all going to burn anyway." I thought then, and I think now, that this young man embodied a thoroughly Christian attitude toward material possessions. The old adage that "you can't take it with you" is no less true for being repeated so often. Western Christians especially need to put material things in their place—to see them as means to spiritual and ministry ends and to keep them at a distance from our hearts and souls.

If, however, we stop with the replacement model and go no further, we are in danger of ending up with an unbiblical dismissal of this world as of no account before God. The transformation model reminds us that the world, though "subject to decay," will ultimately be liberated (Rom. 8:21). This suggests that the world God created, fallen though it is, is still valuable in his sight. I think this insight holds significance for a Christian response to the environmental movement. Many Christians I know, rightly offended by radical environmentalists' deification of nature and their dismissal of human beings as the pinnacle of God's creation, have written off the whole movement. Some imply that Christians should not bother about nature, because, after all, "it's all going to burn."

But this is the wrong lesson to draw from Peter's teaching about the fiery end of the world. It is one thing to display a lack of attachment to material things by, for instance, loaning an inept and clumsy professor a telephoto lens; it would be quite another to leave the lens out in the rain to get ruined. Thus, while Christians recognize that the planet we now inhabit is not destined to last forever and must, therefore, be given a relative value, we should recognize that it does have value. A commitment to preserve it as best we can seems eminently appropriate in light of the transformation model.

(3) A final point of application in this text comes from the balanced approach to imminence that Peter encourages Christians to adopt. Calvin, commenting on verses 11–13, notes the balance that Peter achieves on this issue in this passage:

> Almost all of us labour under two very different evils, too much impatience and too much laziness. In our impatience we snatch at the day of Christ as something expected imminently, but in our carelessness we push it far off. Therefore just as the apostle has earlier corrected our reckless ardour, so now he shakes our sleepiness off us, so that we may look expectantly for the coming of Christ at any time.[13]

---

13. John Calvin, *Hebrews and 1 and 2 Peter*, 365.

Peter's reminder that "with the Lord one day is like a thousand years" is a rebuke to those who want to "snatch at" the Parousia—the kind of people Paul seeks to calm down in 2 Thessalonians 2. As we noted above, we still find a few people like this around in our day: setting dates for the return of Christ and disappointed when their dates pass without incident. But surely far more of us fall into the second category: sleepy Christians who have settled down into the world and who would be positively irritated if Christ were to come along and take us out of it. As C. S. Lewis has said, "Prosperity knits a man to the World. He feels that he is 'finding his place in it,' while really it is finding its place in him."[14] Prosperity, what so many people think to be an unadulterated good, can be a serious problem for the Christian. A realization that Christ can return at any time will help us to keep our prosperity in perspective.

---

14. C. S. Lewis, *The Screwtape Letters* (New York: Macmillan, 1961), 132.

2 Peter 3:14–18

S O THEN, DEAR friends, since you are looking forward to this, make every effort to be found spotless, blameless and at peace with him. ¹⁵Bear in mind that our Lord's patience means salvation, just as our dear brother Paul also wrote you with the wisdom that God gave him. ¹⁶He writes the same way in all his letters, speaking in them of these matters. His letters contain some things that are hard to understand, which ignorant and unstable people distort, as they do the other Scriptures, to their own destruction.

¹⁷Therefore, dear friends, since you already know this, be on your guard so that you may not be carried away by the error of lawless men and fall from your secure position. ¹⁸But grow in the grace and knowledge of our Lord and Savior Jesus Christ. To him be glory both now and forever! Amen.

Original Meaning

PETER NOW BRINGS his letter to a close by giving final exhortations to the faithful. He marks the transition to a new paragraph by using the summary conjunction "so then" (*dio*) and by addressing his readers as "dear friends," or "beloved ones" (*agapetoi*; cf. the same expression in vv. 1, 8). The use of this same form of address in verse 17 implies another break, though it is not as strong there, for Peter is resuming his exhortation of verses 14–15a after his parenthesis about Paul and his letters (vv. 15b–16). In vv. 14–15a, Peter uses language and alludes to concepts that have been prominent in his discussion of eschatology in chapter 3; "looking forward" (cf. v. 14a with vv. 12–13) and the fact that God delays the Parousia because he patiently waits for people to repent and to be saved (cf. v. 15a with v. 9). Clearly, Peter in verses 14–16 ties his exhortations closely to the eschatological perspective that he has outlined in verses 3–13.

But Peter's exhortation in these verses ultimately reaches beyond this immediate context. Note how two of the exhortations here pick up language that Peter used early in the letter:

3:14: *"make every effort* to be found spotless, blameless and at peace with him"

1:5: *"make every effort* to add to your faith goodness ..."

3:18: "grow in the grace and *knowledge of our Lord and Savior Jesus Christ*"	1:3: "His divine power has given to us everything we need for life and godliness through *our knowledge of him* who called us by his own glory and goodness"

By returning to some of the key ideas at the beginning of the letter, Peter creates a kind of "inclusio." These ideas and exhortations frame the contents of the letter, setting its tone and suggesting its overall purpose: to make the knowledge of Christ his readers enjoy fruitful in holy living.

Though short, this paragraph divides into four basic parts:

Concluding eschatological exhortation (vv. 14–15a)
Appeal to Paul for confirmation (vv. 15b–16)
Concluding general exhortation (vv. 17–18a)
Doxology to Christ (v. 18b)

Concluding Eschatological Exhortation (vv. 14–15a)

CHRISTIANS ARE TO "look forward" to the "day of God," when he will destroy and renew the entire universe. They need constantly to look beyond the circumstances of this life and to gauge every thought and every action in light of the eternal state that Christ's return in glory will introduce. For on the day that Christ returns, believers will "appear before the judgment seat of Christ, that each one may receive what is due him for the things done while in the body, whether good or bad" (2 Cor. 5:10). In light of all of that ("since you are looking forward to this"[1]), Peter urges, "make every effort to be found spotless, blameless and at peace with him."

"To be found" has judicial overtones. It conjures up the scene of the court of law, where the judge "finds" defendants guilty or innocent. Peter, we suggested, used this same verb in a similar manner in verse 10, speaking about the whole physical earth being "found" before God—that is, "laid bare" to his searching and infallibly correct judgment.

The NIV rendering obscures the fact that in the Greek "spotless and blameless" are associated closely together. Peter used similar language about Christ in his first letter, calling him a lamb "without blemish or defect" (1:19).[2] This 1 Peter reference suggests the original context for the language: sacrifice. The Old Testament regularly demands that the sacrifices offered to the Lord be

---

1. The NIV singular "this" translates a plural Greek word *tauta*, "these things," designating the various components of the Day of God as Peter has outlined them in the previous verses.

2. The Greek in 2 Peter 3:14 is *aspiloi kai amometoi;* in 1 Peter 1:19 it is *amomou kai aspilou.* The Greek words *amomos* and *amometos* are variants of the same term.

"without spot or blemish." How much of this original sacrificial association clings to the words in verse 14 here is difficult to say, for the terms had by this time become regularly used of moral purity.

In any case, Peter's point is clear: Motivated by the Day of the Lord that is coming, believers should work hard to be found perfectly pure and blameless when God in Christ assesses our lives. They should strive to be the opposite of the false teachers, who are "blots and blemishes" (2:13). Remember, however, that this is a goal we are to strive for, not a condition that we will finally be able to achieve.[3] For the New Testament makes clear that the believer will always have sin to confess (1 John 1:8) and that our struggle with sin will never finally end until our bodies themselves are "redeemed" (see Rom. 8:23). But this realization should not diminish our sincere effort to get as close to that goal as possible.

As noted above, the Greek text associates "spotless" and "blameless." "At peace," then, stands apart as something of an afterthought. This "peace" may be the peace of a satisfied conscience, the tranquillity that the true believer can enjoy at the time of the judgment, knowing that Christ has taken care of the sin problem.[4] But the "peace" that Peter has in mind is probably the peace of reconciliation—the restored relationship that the believer enjoys with God through the mediation of Christ (see, e.g., Rom. 5:1–2).

The command in verse 15 is parallel to the one at the end of verse 14.[5] As Christians look forward to the end of history, they are not only to strive for holiness, they are also to "bear in mind that our Lord's patience means salvation." Christians are therefore to adopt an attitude toward the apparent delay in Christ's return that is exactly opposite to that of the false teachers. The latter considered (NIV, "understand") the delay to be a sign of God's "slowness" (v. 9), concluding that judgment may never come; they were, therefore, quite unconcerned about having to answer for their immoral conduct. Christians, on the other hand, are to "consider" the delay as an opportunity to pursue salvation.[6] As Peter has pointed out already (v. 9), God's delay in sending Christ to judge the earth is a reflection of his "patience."

The relationship between verses 14 and 15, as well as the flow of thought in verses 12–15 ("day of God"; "his promise"; "our Lord"), therefore, shows that the "Lord" in verse 15 is God, not Christ.[7] Christians are to use the

---

3. See Calvin, *Hebrews and 1 and 2 Peter*, 366.

4. Green, *The Second Epistle General of Peter and the General Epistle of Jude*, 143–44.

5. Verse 15 begins with a *kai*, "and," untranslated in the NIV.

6. The NIV obscures the relationship between v. 9 and v. 15 by using two different verbs ("understand" and "bear in mind"), but the verb is the same in the Greek (*hegeomai*, "consider").

7. See, e.g., Kelly, *The Epistles of Peter and of Jude*, 370; against, e.g., Bigg, *The Epistles of St. Peter and St. Jude*, 299.

opportunity afforded by the delay in Christ's coming to pursue "salvation" (v. 15a). This may mean that they are to be zealous in evangelism, seeking to bring as many to a knowledge of Christ through the gospel as possible before it is too late. But Peter may also be thinking of the opportunity for Christians to secure their own salvation. The language of salvation in the New Testament usually refers to the ultimate deliverance from sin and death at the very end of life (Peter's four other uses of the word "salvation" all have this reference [1 Peter 1:5, 9, 10; 2:2]). Peter would not be writing as he does to these believers if some of them, at least, were not in danger of succumbing to the false teachers' pernicious influence. As a result, he wants them to consider the time they have before Christ's return as an opportunity to secure their relationship before the Lord.

Appeal to Paul for Confirmation (vv. 15b–16)

WITH THE "JUST as" in the middle of verse 15, Peter appeals to the writings of Paul to confirm what he has just told his readers in verses 14–15a.[8] The way Paul is here addressed ("our dear brother") has led many scholars to conclude that Peter could not have written this letter. For were not Paul and Peter at loggerheads, representing opposite viewpoints on issues such as the law and the inclusion of Gentiles in the Christian community? How could Peter, the doughty defender of a traditional Jewish Christianity, have been so flattering to Paul, that champion of law-free Gentile Christianity?[9]

The hostile relationship between Paul and Peter suggested in these questions is deeply entrenched in biblical scholarship, and often in the popular imagination as well. This interpretation rests, of course, primarily on Galatians 2:11–14, where Paul describes a conflict between himself and Peter over just such issues. But this is the *only* evidence for a conflict between the two that we possess. From what we can tell from the New Testament as a whole, Peter and Paul were on the same side theologically (see, for instance, Acts 11:2–18; 15:7–11; note too that the probable amanuensis of 1 Peter, Silvanus [= Silas, 1 Peter 5:12], was from the circle of Paul's coworkers [Acts 15:40; 1 Thess. 1:1]). Calling Paul his "dear brother" would be perfectly natural for Peter and fits well with early Christian usage, for "brother" is often used to refer to coworkers in the gospel ministry (see 1 Cor. 2:13; Phil. 2:25; 1 Thess. 3:2; 1 Peter 5:12).

---

8. Mayor, *The Epistle of St. Jude and the Second Epistle of St. Peter*, 165, insists that the "just as" must refer only to v. 15a. But such a restriction is without basis, since vv. 14 and 15a are so closely related.

9. For an example of this argument, see Kelly, *The Epistles of Peter and of Jude*, 370. He argues that the language used here is similar to late first- and early second-century descriptions of the apostles (e.g., *1 Clement* 5:3–7; Ignatius, *To the Romans* 4.3).

We still need to analyze the pronouns Peter uses in this clause. (1) Why does he refer to Paul as "our" beloved brother rather than "my" beloved brother? The plural could be "editorial," with a singular meaning; but, as Bauckham notes, this usage is almost nonexistent in the New Testament.[10] The "our" may then refer to Christians generally[11] or, perhaps more likely, to fellow apostles (see v. 2).[12]

(2) Who is included in the "you" to whom Paul wrote? Scholars who think that 2 Peter was written long after Peter's death usually think that it includes all Christians, who now possess the canon of Paul's letters.[13] But this kind of argument is weak; the "you" clearly refers to the recipients of 2 Peter, and the letter was clearly not addressed to all Christians. All that we can conclude from this reference, then, is that the readers of 2 Peter have received one or more letters of Paul.[14] But since we cannot be sure where the readers of the letter lived, we cannot decide which of Paul's letters Peter may have in mind. Nor does Peter's identification of the subject matter of the letter(s) help.[15] As we have seen, the connection "just as" indicates that Paul wrote to the readers the same thing that Peter has just said in verses 14—15a. But the point he has made is very general—Christians need to live holy lives in light of the coming of Christ—and Paul touches on this subject in virtually every letter he wrote.

Paul himself often claimed to minister on the basis of the "grace given to me" (Rom. 12:3; 15:15; Gal. 2:9; 1 Cor. 3:10; Eph. 3:2, 7; Col. 1:25). Peter varies the formula, referring to the "wisdom that God gave him."[16] Paul refers to his ministry generally as a work of God's grace in and through him; Peter's language focuses more on the basis for what Paul wrote. What he wrote in his letters came not from his own study or imagination; it came from God himself, who gave Paul the wisdom to understand and apply the gospel in his generation.

But it was not only in what Paul wrote to the readers of 2 Peter that he stressed the connection between the Parousia and godly living. "He writes

---

10. Bauckham, Jude, 2 Peter, 327.

11. Mayor, The Epistle of St. Jude and the Second Epistle of St. Peter, 164.

12. Bauckham, Jude, 2 Peter, 328.

13. Kelly, The Epistles of Peter and of Jude, 372.

14. See Bauckham, Jude, 2 Peter, 330.

15. Various scholars have proposed all kinds of scenarios based on the hints that Peter gives here. Mayor, for instance, thinks that 3:15 must refer to Romans, because it speaks so prominently of God's patience as leading to repentance (2:5) (The Epistle of St. Jude and the Second Epistle of St. Peter, 164). But, as we have seen, Peter is thinking about more than just v. 15a in his reference to Paul.

16. The Greek actually uses a passive construction; as NASB translates, "the wisdom given him." But the verb dotheisan is almost certainly a "divine" passive, with God as the implied agent of the action. The NIV is an acceptable paraphrase.

the same way in all his letters, speaking in them of these matters" (v. 16a). Again, critics of the Petrine authorship of 2 Peter think that the reference to "all" Paul's letters requires a date in the late first or early second century, when Paul's letters had been gathered together.[17] But these critics are guilty once again of an over-interpretation. Peter says no more than that Paul wrote in the same way in all the letters *that Peter has seen.* The language does not imply that all of Paul's letters had been written or that they had been put together into a corpus. Similarly, a sportswriter might say, "In all the Bulls' games, they played great defense." If written in mid-season, "all the Bulls' games" would obviously mean "all the games they have played so far"; it would certainly not have to mean "every game of the season."

Peter now comments further on the letters of Paul generally. He makes one explicit point and one implicit point, both of which are fascinating. *Explicitly,* Peter remarks that the letters of Paul contain "some things that are hard to understand" and are therefore misinterpreted by "ignorant and unstable people." "Hard to understand" translates a word that was sometimes applied to Greek oracles—notoriously ambiguous and difficult to apply. The most famous oracle was the Delphi oracle's reply to a king who wondered if he should go to war or not: "If you go to war, you will destroy a great nation." Whether this nation was the one the king was attacking or his own was, of course, unclear. So, Peter suggests, Paul's letters contain passages that can take on more than one meaning.

Many of us feel relieved and comforted when we read Peter's words here. We do not feel so badly about our problems in interpreting Paul if Peter, a fellow apostle, had the same difficulty! But the context suggests that Peter is making a slightly different point. It is not so much that what Paul wrote was obscure; rather, it could be easy, by looking at what Paul said in the wrong context or in an unbalanced way, to get the wrong meaning out of it.

The letters of Paul themselves reveal situations in which people whom he had taught seized on one of his teachings, took it out of context, and drew the wrong conclusion from it.[18] When, for instance, the Corinthians claimed as their slogan, "Everything is permissible for me" (1 Cor. 6:12), they were probably quoting Paul himself. As Paul goes on to show, however, their mistake was in failing to recognize other significant truths along with that one. The letter of James may reflect a similar scenario, as James corrects his readers' misinterpretation of Paul's teaching about "justification by faith."

In other words, Peter is fully aware of "ignorant and unstable" people who "distort" the meaning of what Paul wrote and bring destruction on themselves. Almost certainly he is referring to the false teachers whom he has been

---

17. E.g., Mayor, *The Epistle of St. Jude and the Second Epistle of St. Peter,* 165.
18. See esp. Bauckham, *Jude, 2 Peter,* 331.

rebuking throughout the letter. He uses the same word of them in 2:14 ("unstable," *asteriktos*) as he uses here. What Peter suggests, then, is that these false teachers are "twisting" Paul's own writings as support for their heresies. Peter may be thinking of their faulty eschatology. But he is more likely thinking of their lawless and licentious conduct, which he castigates in chapter 2. We know that not too long after this time, various heretics appealed to passages in Paul to support just such unbridled behavior.

The *implicit* point Peter is making emerges from his claim that the false teachers distort Paul's letters "as they do the other Scriptures." The word "other" (*loipos*) shows that Peter considers the letters of Paul to belong to the category of "Scripture."[19] Some scholars think that this means no more than that Peter considered Paul's writings to be authoritative.[20] But the word "Scriptures" (*graphai*) always refers in the New Testament to those writings considered not only authoritative but canonical—in a word, it refers to the Old Testament (see "Bridging Contexts" section, below). Peter therefore implies that the letters of Paul have a status equivalent to that of the canon of the Old Testament itself.

Here again, scholars object that such a view of Paul's letters is impossible as early as A.D. 63 or so, when 2 Peter must have been written if the apostle Peter is its author. But we have other evidence at about this time that some New Testament material was beginning to be viewed this way. In 1 Timothy 5:18, for instance, Paul introduces as "Scripture" a verse from the Old Testament and a saying of Jesus.[21] And there is no doubt that the authors of the New Testament claimed from the first to be speaking from God in a way that put their writings on a par with the Old Testament.

Concluding General Exhortation (vv. 17–18a)

PETER IS AWARE that his reference to the letters of Paul has led him off into a detour from his main line of teaching at this point of the letter. So, addressing his readers again as his "dear friends" (*agapetoi*, "beloved") he resumes the exhortations he began issuing in verse 14. Now, however, they are not so clearly tied to eschatology; Peter looks back and brings to bear on his read-

---

19. A few scholars have suggested that the phrase might not mean this; that Peter might be saying only that people distort the letters of Paul as they do the Scriptures (this interpretation is suggested, though not clearly adopted, by Bigg, *The Epistles of St. Peter and St. Jude*, 301–2, and Green, *The Second Epistle General of Peter and the General Epistle of Jude*, 147–48). But this interpretation simply does not do justice to the word "other."

20. E.g., Bauckham, *Jude, 2 Peter*, 333.

21. See also *2 Clement* 2.4; *Epistle of Barnabas* 4.14; Polycarp, *Philippians* 2.1. Critics of Petrine authorship, of course, respond that 1 Timothy is also pseudonymous, written by someone in Paul's name long after his death. See further discussion of this in the "Bridging Contexts" section.

ers the message of the entire letter. Thus, the negative exhortation in verse 17 reflects the warnings about false teachers in chapter 2, while the positive exhortation in verse 18a reiterates a key idea from chapter 1.[22]

The "you" (hymeis) is emphatic, standing in contrast to the "ignorant and unstable" in verse 16. Bauckham and others who think that 2 Peter is pseudonymous interpret the phrase "since you know all this" as a reference back to the apostle Peter himself; that is, the unknown writer of the letter is reminding the readers of what Peter had taught them.[23] But what they know is something much more than what Peter taught; it refers to the "words spoken in the past by the holy prophets and the command given by our Lord and Savior through your apostles" (3:2), and perhaps to the letter of 2 Peter itself.

If, as we think, Peter is writing this letter, he is then referring generally to the early Christian teaching about eschatology and its moral implications that his readers had received. Peter's point is that the readers have been amply warned about the danger of false teaching. Forewarned should mean that they are forearmed—ready to resist the perverse attractions of the false teachers' heresies.

Christians need constantly to "be on [their] guard" (the present tense of the imperative in Greek suggests a constant state of watchfulness). Otherwise, they run the risk of being "carried away by the error of lawless men" (athesmon, a word Peter applied to the false teachers in 2:7). "Error" (plane) can also be translated "wander," and it is not clear whether Peter is thinking of the false teachers' own "wandering" from the faith or to their causing others to "wander" from their faith. Perhaps we need not choose; certainly both have been prominent in the letter.[24] The danger in any such "wandering" is that it may cause a believer to "fall from" his or her "secure position."

Conversion to Jesus Christ provides a solid foundation, a security, for spiritual vitality in this life and glory in the next. The word Peter uses implies that Christians can have confidence in this foundation. But he also, of course, warns about "falling from" that foundation. We discussed briefly in our comments on 1:3–11 the whole problem of "eternal security" that warnings like this raise (see the "Contemporary Significance" of 1:3–11). Here in 3:17 we again find the typical New Testament combination of security and warning. Clearly Peter is concerned that believers not view their "security" in Christ (however understood) to condone a careless attitude toward the struggle with sin. Confidence in our status with Christ should never lead to a presumption on God's grace that leads us to toy with the danger of false teachers or that negates serious striving after holiness.

---

22. Kelly, The Epistles of Peter and of Jude, 374.
23. Bauckham, Jude, 2 Peter, 337.
24. Ibid., 337.

After his final warning, Peter issues a final positive exhortation: "Grow in the grace and knowledge of our Lord and Savior Jesus Christ." If we are to find a single "key verse" for all of 2 Peter, this would probably be it. Here Peter summarizes his root concern: that his readers, resisting the heresy of the false teachers, continue to grow spiritually, becoming more and more like the Christ whom they confess.

Peter spelled out this growth in holiness in some detail in 1:5–10. The NIV takes both "grace" and "knowledge" to depend on "our Lord and Savior Jesus Christ" (they signal this by using a single article before "grace"). In this case, the "grace of Jesus Christ" will mean the grace that he bestows on us. But "knowledge of Jesus Christ" can mean either the knowledge that Jesus Christ gives us (see 1:5–6), or our knowledge of, our relationship to, Jesus Christ (see 1:2–3, 8). While the Greek word Peter uses here can point to the former interpretation,[25] the sweeping nature of the exhortation and the relationship to chapter 1 suggest that the second is correct. This would mean, however, that "of our Lord and Savior Jesus Christ" relates to the words "grace" and "knowledge" in different ways—describing the source of the former and the object of the latter. This is not impossible; but it may be easier to sever the word "grace" from "of our Lord and Savior Jesus Christ" (e.g., see the REB rendering: "Grow in the grace and in the knowledge of our Lord and Saviour Jesus Christ").[26]

Doxology to Christ (v. 18b)

MOST NEW TESTAMENT letters end with greetings, references to fellow work-ers, a request for prayer, and/or grace wishes. Doxologies (ascriptions of glory [Greek *doxa*]) at the end of these letters are unusual—we find them only here, in Romans 16:25–27 (assuming, as I do, that these verses are original), Philippians 4:20, and Jude 24–25. Why Peter has chosen to end his letter in this way is unclear. The absence of some of the usual epistolary features may suggest that he is sending this letter along with others or that he is writing to a number of churches.

Another unusual feature of the ending is that the doxology is to Christ. Normally glory is ascribed to God; only here, in 2 Timothy 4:18, and in Revelation 1:5–6 do we find doxologies directed to Christ—although we do

---

25. The word here is the simple *gnosis*, which Peter uses elsewhere in the letter to depict our own "knowledge" (1:5–6). When Peter refers to our knowledge directed to Christ, he uses the compound *epignosis* (1:2–3, 8; 2:20). See Bigg, *The Epistles of St. Peter and St. Jude*, 303–4; Green, *The Second Epistle General of Peter and the General Epistle of Jude*, 150–51.

26. See, e.g., Mayor, *The Epistle of St. Jude and the Second Epistle of St. Peter*, 170; Kelly, *The Epistles of Peter and of Jude*, 375; Bauckham, *Jude, 2 Peter*, 337–38.

find a "blessing" of Christ, as God, in Romans 9:5. But this certainly fits the high view of Jesus Christ that Peter presents from the very beginning of his letter (see esp. 1:1).

The doxology is unusual in one other way. New Testament authors usually ascribe to God glory "forever and ever" (Greek *eis tous aionas;* see, e.g., Jude 25). But Peter uses a different expression—literally translated, "unto the day of eternity" (see NASB; NRSV). The NIV takes this as a way of referring both to the present and the future: "now and forever" (see also KJV; REB; TEV). But this is certainly not the most natural way to interpret the Greek. Better, in light of Peter's focus on this subject in chapter 3, is to give "day" an eschatological meaning: the "day of the Lord/of God." Christ's coming will inaugurate the eschatological age—a "day" that will last forever. We glorify Christ, looking to this day and earnestly waiting for it.

PETER'S SUGGESTION THAT Paul's letters belong in the category of "Scriptures" cannot be properly understood without some understanding of the formation of the canon of the biblical books and of the significance of this formation.

The word "canon" means a "measuring rod." Early Christians applied it to those books that they considered the authoritative "measuring rod" by which one could determine what was orthodox and what was heretical. The matter is vigorously debated, but there is good evidence that by the time of Jesus, Jews were already operating with at least a de facto canon of authoritative books.

The New Testament uses the word *graphe,* usually in the plural, *graphai,* to refer to these authoritative Jewish Scriptures. Used fifty times in the New Testament, the word always refers to the authoritative writings that we call the Old Testament. The plural is more usual, indicating the collection of books (e.g., Luke 24:27: "And beginning with Moses and all the Prophets, he [Jesus] explained to them what was said in all the Scriptures concerning himself"). The singular usually denotes a single text from the Old Testament (e.g., James 2:8: "If you keep the royal law found in Scripture, 'Love your neighbor as yourself,' you are doing right"). Some scholars claim the word is also applied to passages not found in our Old Testament, but the claim cannot be substantiated.[27] The New Testament authors' restriction of the word "Scripture"

---

27. Most controversial is James 4:5, because we have nothing in the context that represents an actual quotation from the Old Testament. Many scholars think, therefore, that the reference is to an apocryphal tradition. But James is more likely referring to the Old Testament teaching about the jealousy of God (see Douglas J. Moo, *The Letter of James: An Introduction and Commentary,* TNTC [Grand Rapids: Eerdmans, 1985], 146).

to those books we now call the Old Testament suggests that they were operating with an implicit, closed canon.[28]

Other evidence tends to confirm this conclusion. For instance, New Testament writers never quote as an authoritative source any book that is not found in the Old Testament canon. To be sure, Jude does cite passages from the Pseudepigrapha (vv. 9 and 14–15). We will deal with this passage in the commentary below, but suffice to say here that it is not clear that Jude refers to either of these texts as authoritative, nor does he cite them as Scripture or with the kind of introduction we usually find when Scripture is quoted.

An incidental confirmation of the existence of a canon of Scriptures in Jesus' day that looked much like ours is Matthew 23:35: "And so upon you will come all the righteous blood that has been shed on earth, from the blood of righteous Abel to the blood of Zechariah son of Berekiah, whom you murdered between the temple and the altar." Abel is, of course, mentioned in the early chapters of Genesis. The martyrdom of Zechariah son of Berekiah, on the other hand, is described in 2 Chronicles 24:20–21. The point is this: In the Hebrew Bible, 2 Chronicles is the last book. The order in which Jesus cites these martyrs, therefore, suggests that he was familiar with a Bible in which Genesis comes first and 2 Chronicles last—exactly what we now have in our Old Testament.[29]

It is against this background, then, that we must assess Peter's suggestion that Paul's letters also belong in the category of Scripture. The first thing to note is that Peter does not straightforwardly call Paul's letters Scripture. He is much less direct, associating Paul's letters with Scripture rather than identifying them as Scripture. We find the same kind of indirect association in 1 Timothy 5:18, the other relevant New Testament passage: "For the Scripture says, 'Do not muzzle the ox while it is treading out the grain,' and 'The worker deserves his wages.'" Here we also find a New Testament text (Luke 10:7) associated indirectly with an Old Testament passage (Deut. 25:4).

Such indirect allusion is just what we might expect at this point in time. As with most doctrines, the idea of New Testament books as Scripture developed only over time, as these books were used and found to be profitable by the early Christians. In fact, it took a couple of centuries before the process of recognizing and accepting a New Testament canon was complete. Peter was certainly not at the point where he could formulate a full-blown concept of the New Testament canon.

---

28. For a good recent argument for this conclusion, see Roger Beckwith, *The Old Testament Canon of the Christian Church and its Background in Judaism* (Grand Rapids: Eerdmans, 1985).

29. The Jewish historian Josephus, who wrote in the years A.D. 75–95, enunciates a similar canon of authoritative books (*Against Apion* 1.37–43).

If, then, we had the opportunity to ask Peter to clarify and elaborate his point, what might he have said? Would he have argued that the letters of Paul should be added to the canon of authoritative books? This would have been difficult, for, as we have seen, New Testament evidence points to a "closed" first-century canon of Scriptures. Perhaps, then, he would have had to suggest the creation of an additional canon alongside the existing one—in effect, an Old and New Testament. But the fact is that we do not know, and Peter himself had undoubtedly not thought through matters to this extent. What is important is that he suggests that Paul's letters are like the Old Testament Scriptures.

For Peter, this would have meant two things. (1) Paul's letters are inspired by God. In this very letter, Peter enunciates this idea of inspiration (see our discussion of 1:20b–21). Paul's letters also, Peter infers, are the product of God's Spirit, carrying Paul along so that he wrote what God wanted him to write. Paul likewise made clear that inspiration is an integral quality of Scripture: "All Scripture is God-breathed and is useful for teaching, rebuking, correcting and training in righteousness" (2 Tim. 3:16).

(2) Paul's letters are authoritative. Authority is the byproduct of inspiration. Precisely because God, by his Spirit, speaks in them, Paul's letters are to be heeded as if they were the words of God himself. It is this important and practical point that Peter is most interested in. He has been trying to convince his readers to accept the truth about Christ's Parousia and so to devote themselves to a holy life. And he wants them to know that Paul supports his own view of things, not that of the false teachers (as the false teachers were perhaps claiming). Associating Paul's letters with Scripture gives them an authority that his readers should recognize and obey.

Ultimately, of course, Peter writes with the same kind of authority as does "our dear brother Paul." How he viewed his own writing, whether he had begun to entertain any notion that it, too, was Scripture, is impossible to know. But this does seem to be the implication of what Peter says here about the letters of his fellow apostle Paul.

ONE OF THE difficulties for us in formulating a New Testament canon is the lack of any authority after the New Testament to endorse New Testament books. For the Old Testament, we have the New Testament. But we have, of course, nothing comparable for the New Testament.[30] It is for this reason that the implications of passages such

---

30. Roman Catholics, of course, would appeal at this point to the authority of the church's teaching, focused on the Pope.

as 2 Peter 3:15–16 are so important, for they give us at least a scriptural toe-hold from which we can build the doctrine of a New Testament canon. We sketched the background for some of this development in the last section, and we drew out the significance of inspired Scripture in the "Contemporary Significance" section on 1:16–21. Here, therefore, we will content ourselves with reiterating the key point.

In the midst of our debates about the nature and implications of inspira-tion, we must not lose sight of this essential truth: The books of the Bible, breathed out by God himself, uniquely have the power to shape our lives and, ultimately, the world. One of the giants of the modern evangelical movement was Frank E. Gaebelein. Known particularly for his editing work (e.g., *The Expositor's Bible Commentary*), Gaebelein exuded an authentic, deeply rooted love for God and for his people. One could detect in him a person in whom the "mind of Christ" was well developed. I remember to this day his response to an interviewer who asked what had been the most formative influence on his life. Daily reading of the King James Version of the Bible, he responded. Prolonged immersion in God's Word has such an effect. Certainly we must read with attention; certainly the Spirit must apply the truth to us. But the Word of God has the power to renew our minds and thus to change our behavior. No other source can do so.

Note the way I put the matter at the end of the last paragraph: "to renew our minds and *thus* to change our behavior." The intimate connection between doctrine and practice, between what we believe and think and what we do has been clear throughout 2 Peter. In 3:14–18, the apostle makes the con-nection clear once again. Specifically, it is "since [we] are looking forward" to the Lord's coming that we will concentrate our efforts on pleasing our Lord (v. 14). Eschatology leads to ethics. The false teachers, dismissing any notion of Christ's return and of judgment, were falling into a lazy, sensual lifestyle. By understanding the truth about Christ's return, believers will be led to develop an energetic, "otherworldly" lifestyle.

It must have been God's providence that led me, at the very time I was commenting on these verses, to go through a scare about my own life. Though undoubtedly magnified by my own hyperactive imagination (it operates on all eight cylinders in the middle of the night), a medical prob-lem I faced posed genuine concern about the possibility of cancer. For three days, for the first time in some years, I confronted my own mortality. I hated it; sleep was difficult and anxiety was constant. But I also found myself think-ing about God and eternity a lot more than usual, reading my Bible with more attention than normal, and caring far less about what I ate and about material things in general. Confronting eternity sharpened my spiritual appetite even as it dulled my sensual impulses. I discovered just today that the medical problem is not cancer, but a relatively minor and easily cured matter. And already I can feel myself slipping back into the usual lackadaisical spirituality.

This seems to me precisely the general point Peter is making here: Serious reckoning with the end of the world puts this world in perspective for us. As Michael Green puts it, "'How will he find me?' is a very searching question for the Christian to ask himself, whether death (1.14) or the parousia be uppermost in view."[31] What we believe about the course of history, and especially its imminent end, affects the way that we live—or at least it should. For the fact is that many Christians will believe all the right things about eschatology but not find them genuinely changing their attitudes or behavior.

Why is this so? Because eschatology is a doctrine we believe but not a reality we feel and experience. Here is the key, I think, to making the connection between teaching and practice effective and fruitful in our lives: internalizing the truth we hear so that we treat it as reality and not just theory. Somehow we must learn to feel the truth. How? Ultimately, we would all probably answer: the ministry of the Holy Spirit. But through what instruments does the Holy Spirit work? Preaching is clearly one of them. The church desperately needs preachers committed to explaining God's Word and doing it so vibrantly, imaginatively, and passionately that the Word comes alive and is genuinely appropriated by its hearers.[32]

Since we are talking especially about eschatology, we might note in passing that the contemporary church seems largely to have turned away from preaching and teaching on eschatology. The old "Prophecy Conferences" have been replaced with "Marriage Seminars" and "Financial Stewardship Workshops." Certainly we need to address issues of marriage and finances in the church. But the problem is one of balance. In a spirit of condescension toward some of the more intricate eschatological debates, too many pastors and Christians have abandoned eschatological preaching altogether. But effective preaching about "the last things" may be one of the best ways to help Christians internalize a worldview that puts eternity and this world in their right proportion.

One other implication of these verses requires attention in our day: the finality of the Parousia. Peter claims that God's "delay" in sending Christ back to earth is to allow time for repentance (v. 9) and thus for salvation (v. 15). Implied in this is that repentance and salvation can occur only until

---

31. Green, *The Second Epistle General of Peter and the General Epistle of Jude*, 143.

32. For some great ideas along these lines from a passionate preacher, see John Piper, "Preaching as Worship: Meditations on Expository Exultation," *TrinJ* 16 (1995): 29–45.

the Parousia. Christ's return or (for those of us who may not live until that day) death marks the end of all opportunity to embrace Christ and thus be saved. In the well-known words of Hebrews, "man is destined to die once, and after that to face judgment" (Heb. 9:27).

Some scholars argue that the New Testament implies the opportunity to respond to God's offer of salvation even after death. But this is not the case. The finality of our decisions in this life is assumed throughout the New Testament and, as we have seen, in 2 Peter 3 as well. Perhaps there are readers of this commentary who have not yet committed themselves in faith to Christ. For them, of course, the implications of this point are clear: Now is the time to decide; death or the Parousia may forever and at any time end all such opportunity. For those of us who do already know the Lord, the implications are also clear: Now is the time to share the good news of Christ—with your neighbor, your coworker, your fellow team member— before it is too late.

Jude 1–2

JUDE, A SERVANT of Jesus Christ and a brother of James, to those who have been called, who are loved by God the Father and kept by Jesus Christ: ²Mercy, peace and love be yours in abundance.

Original Meaning

ANCIENT LETTERS TYPICALLY began with an identification of the sender, an identification of the recipient, and a greeting. Jude follows this convention, but expands and modifies each part. Thus, he not only identifies himself and his recipients, but he provides for each a brief description that helps us understand what this letter is about. Jude writes not as a private individual but as a representative of Jesus Christ, and his readers are people who belong to Jesus Christ. While a typical ancient letter greeting was usually the single word, "greetings" (*chairein*), Jude modifies it by turning it into a prayer-wish that his readers may enjoy the relationship with Christ they have already established. Moreover, his greeting is unusual even when compared with other New Testament letters. It is the only New Testament greeting that does not include a wish for "grace," and it is the only one to include a request for "love."

"Jude" translates a Greek word (*Ioudas*) that occurs forty-three times in the New Testament. Six different men bear the name, but we can be pretty sure that the Jude who writes our letter is the brother of the Lord mentioned in Mark 6:3 (see the introduction for details and argument). We know almost nothing about him. Like Jesus' other brothers, he did not follow the Lord during his earthly ministry. But, as his self-description here indicates, that changed, perhaps during the time of Jesus' post-resurrection ministry. Jude is now "a servant of Jesus Christ."

"Servant" can also be translated "slave"—the Greek word is not *diakonos* ("[household] servant") but *doulos* ("[bond]slave"). The word obviously indicates Jude's subservience to the Lord whom he has come to know and to whom he now gives himself in service. But the title also carries honor. The great leaders of God's people in the Old Testament were also called "servants" of God, such as Moses (Josh. 14:7; 2 Kings 18:12) and David (Ps. 18:1; Ezek. 34:23). We should not overlook the fact that Jude can now put "Jesus Christ" in the place of "God" or "the Lord" in this honorific title.

We can well understand why Jude would identify himself as "a servant of Jesus Christ." Like Paul (cf., e.g., Rom. 1:1) and Peter (2 Peter 1:1), who do the same thing, Jude uses this title to establish his right to address Christians with an authoritative word from the Lord. He does not write as simply a fellow Christian, but as one who serves and therefore represents Jesus Christ himself. Significantly, unlike both Paul and Peter, Jude does not call himself an "apostle."

But if calling himself a "servant of Jesus Christ" makes perfect sense, it is harder to understand why Jude goes on to add the designation "a brother of James." Without any further description, this "James" must refer to the most famous James in the New Testament—the brother of Jesus (Gal. 1:19), who attained a high position in the early Jerusalem church (Acts 15:13–21; 21:18; Gal. 2:9) and who wrote the letter we now have in the New Testament. Perhaps Jude adds this reference to distinguish himself from other early Christians with the same name: He is that Jude who is the brother of the famous James. Or perhaps Jude is writing to Christians who know and have a high regard for James. Perhaps even more interesting is the question as to why Jude does not here claim to be "a brother of the Lord." But, as we have noted, Jude's physical relationship to Jesus did not bring him any spiritual benefit. The title is therefore irrelevant to what he is doing in his letter.[1]

Jude identifies his readers as Christians. The key word in the description is "called" (*kletois*). This word reflects the New Testament conviction that being a Christian is a product of God's gracious reaching out to bring helpless sinners into a relationship with himself. "Call" does not mean, then, "invite"—as if God were asking people to a party and they can either accept or decline. It means "choose" or "select," and God's "choosing"—because it is he, the sovereign Lord, who is doing it—is effective. All this lies in the background. The critical point here is that "those called," like "saints," becomes a standard way to describe Christians, who make up the new people of God (see also Rom. 1:1; 1 Cor. 1:1).

If this much about Jude's description of his readers is clear, not much else is. The Greek of the last part of verse 1 is difficult to piece together, though the general rendering found in the NIV and followed by almost all the other modern English translations, seems best: "[Those] called" is the main designation, and two parallel descriptions elaborate it:

> who are loved by God the Father
> and [who are] kept by Jesus Christ.[2]

---

1. Note that James does not use the title "brother of the Lord" in his letter either.

2. This rendering assumes that the two participles, *agapemenois* ("loved") and *teteremenois* ("kept"), modify *tois . . . kletois* ("the called").

The exact meaning of these elaborations is unclear. Instead of "loved *by* God the Father," we could also translate "loved [or beloved] *in* God the Father" (NASB; NRSV; REB).[3] In this case, Jude is emphasizing not the source of the love we experience—God the Father loves us—but the context in which we experience love—love is the product of our being "in," being in fellowship with God the Father.[4] On balance, the NIV rendering seems preferable, for the alternative does not identify who is doing the loving.[5] As those who are called and therefore who belong to the people of God, we enjoy the experience of God's constant love for us.[6]

The second description poses a similar problem. The Greek construction used here (the dative case) can indicate either that Jesus Christ is the one who is doing the "keeping" (NIV) or that Jesus Christ is the one "for" whom we are being kept (see, e.g., NRSV: "kept safe for Jesus Christ"). Translating "by" is attractive, because it then keeps the two descriptions parallel. But perhaps the other option is better.[7] Normally God himself is the one who "keeps" Christians, and the idea of being "kept" or "preserved" for Christ is one we find elsewhere in the New Testament. Note 1 Thessalonians 5:23b: "May your whole spirit, soul and body be *kept* blameless at the coming of our Lord Jesus Christ."

"Being kept for Jesus Christ" means that God throughout this life exercises his power on behalf of Christians to preserve them spiritually intact until the coming of Jesus Christ in glory.[8] Believers have much to go through in this life: temptations, trials, and onslaughts from Satan and his minions. But God promises to watch over us at every moment, keeping us safe for Christ's sake. Not, of course, that God's preserving power means we can just relax and leave it all to him. Note how Jude beautifully comes back to this same idea at the end of the letter: "But *keep* yourselves in God's love as you wait for the mercy of our Lord Jesus Christ to bring you to eternal life" (v. 21). God "keeps" us, but we must also "keep" ourselves.

---

3. The Greek here uses the preposition *en*, which can have a local meaning ("in") or an instrumental meaning ("by"). The KJV translation *"sanctified* by God the Father," rests on a variant reading in the Greek text.

4. For this view, see esp. Bauckham, *Jude, 2 Peter,* 26. Bigg suggests a variation, taking "in God the Father" with both participles: " . . . called, who in God the Father are beloved and kept unto Jesus Christ" (Bigg, *The Epistles of St. Peter and St. Jude,* 324).

5. See, e.g., Kelly, *The Epistles of Peter and of Jude,* 243.

6. The Greek word for "loved" is in the perfect tense, suggesting a continuing state.

7. See, e.g., Bigg, *The Epistles of St. Peter and St. Jude,* 324; Kelly, *The Epistles of Peter and of Jude,* 243.

8. The participle (*teteremenois*) is again in the perfect tense, implying that "being kept" is a continuing state that believers are placed in through their faith in Christ.

Jude loves to group what he says into "threes." In verse 1 he has described Christians as "called," "loved," and "kept." Now in verse 2 he prays that his readers may be filled with "mercy," "peace," and "love." "Filled with" is a more literal rendering of the Greek than we have in the NIV, though "be yours in abundance" certainly captures the idea. "Mercy" is not often found in New Testament prayer-wishes (see, however, 1 Tim. 1:2; 2 Tim. 1:2; 2 John 3); "grace" is usually found in its place. But the meaning is much the same: God's unmerited favor bestowed on sinners for their salvation. By "peace," Jude may mean the inner contentment that comes from a restored relationship to God in Christ—the "peace *of* God." But it more likely means our "peace *with* God," that is, the new status of reconciliation that God provides in his Son for us. Similarly, then, "love" means not our love for others, but God's love for us.[9]

Jude knows, of course, that believers enjoy these wonderful blessings in Christ. But his prayer is that they may truly appreciate them and benefit from them in their day-to-day lives.

THE GOAL OF the translator is to render an ancient text into a modern language in such a way that the impact on the modern reader is the same as it would have been on the ancient reader—a goal that can never be attained. Why? Because the original text is part of a whole world that the ancient readers were a part of but which the modern readers are not. This is why even the best translations are ultimately inadequate and must be supplemented by commentaries, dictionaries, encyclopedias, and so on, all designed to fill in the ancient background so that the modern reader can "experience" the full meaning of the original. But even with all these resources, we will never really be "in" the ancient culture the way the original readers were, though we must try to convey something of what the language meant for them.

Consider in this regard the simple phrase "servant of Jesus Christ." The meaning is pretty clear and does not seem to need much explanation. Perhaps it is useful to note that (as we have done) the Greek word carries connotations of "slavery." But persons from that culture who knew the Old Testament (as Jude's readers apparently did) would have detected an important overtone in this phrase that we can easily miss. For, as noted, "servant of the LORD"/"servant of God" is a standard Old Testament phrase. When Jude puts "Jesus Christ" in place of "the Lord" or "God," then, he is communicat-

---

9. See, e.g., Kelly, *The Epistles of Peter and of Jude*, 244, against Green, *The Second Epistle General of Peter and the General Epistle of Jude*, 158.

ing something of immense importance about Jesus—that he has a relationship to Jude similar to the relationship of the Lord to Moses and David.

This was an amazing step for a Jew like Jude, steeped in his people's strict monotheism. But his associating Jesus with God is all the more impressive when we remember that Jude had grown up in the same household as Jesus. Surely an event as spectacular as the Resurrection was necessary to have led Jude to view his own brother as one who was in some sense equal to God.

We must, of course, not press the implications of Jude's "servant of Jesus Christ" too far. We must not imagine that he had worked out all the theological implications inherent in speaking of Jesus in these terms. Jude was not at the point of formulating the doctrine of the Trinity! But when later Christians hammered out the concept of the Trinity, they built their theology on the almost casual kinds of indications that we find in this verse. Early Christians had an experience of Jesus that led them to begin applying to him language they had in the past reserved for God. Only gradually did they work out the theological implications of this transfer of language. But the point, again, is that we need somehow to "hear" these theological overtones in the language Jude uses if we are fully to appreciate the significance of what he says.

THE PROSAIC DETAILS of the opening of a letter would not seem to be fertile ground for contemporary significance. But, as we have seen, Jude provides more than just bare details of identification. His descriptions of himself and of his readers have import for Christians today.

Once we recognize the theological overtones in the phrase "servant of Jesus Christ," we can find in the phrase a reminder of the exalted nature of Jesus. His exalted status is something that, after centuries of orthodox teaching, most of us take for granted. But many do not, and many who do give him a unique status fail to give him "equal billing" with God the Father (e.g., Jehovah's Witnesses; Mormons).

True, we cannot use Jude's description of Christ as a proof text for his deity. But the phrase clearly moves in that direction. It is, in fact, in just this transfer of language about God in the Old Testament to Jesus that we find some of the best New Testament evidence for Jesus' deity. Specific texts in which Jesus is called "God," such as John 1:1; 20:28; Romans 9:5; 2 Peter 1:1; Titus 2:13, and so on, are important. But even more impressive is the abundant New Testament evidence that the early Christians, most from rigidly monotheistic backgrounds, came to act toward Jesus and to speak of him as if he were God. They worshiped him (e.g., Matt. 14:33; 28:9, 17; cf. Heb. 1:6); they applied Old Testament verses about Yahweh to him (e.g., Rom. 10:13); they prayed to him (e.g., Acts 7:59). Though much less direct than a proof text and harder to use in arguing with Jehovah's Witnesses on our doorstep, these indications of how the early Christians viewed Jesus are some of the most valuable arguments for his full deity.

In Jude's description of his readers, I want particularly to focus on the significance of their being "kept for [*or* by; see comments above] Jesus Christ." What Jude says is true of Christians is precisely what Jesus himself prayed for: "I will remain in the world no longer, but they are still in the world, and I am coming to you. Holy Father, protect [*or* keep; *tereson*] them by the power of your name—the name you gave me—so that they may be one as we are one" (John 17:11). We naturally pay great attention to the grace of God in conversion, and we joyfully anticipate the day when God's grace will be manifested again in the return of Christ. But it is easy for Christians to forget about God's grace of preservation, as he is daily and powerfully at work in and among us.

We read about this work of God on our behalf in many places in the New Testament. Peter assures Christians who are being persecuted that they "through faith are shielded by God's power until the coming of the salvation that is ready to be revealed in the last day" (1 Peter 1:5). And writing to Christians who were disturbed by false teachers and apprehensive about their relationship with God, John says, "We know that anyone born of God does not continue to sin; the one who was born of God [= Jesus[10]] keeps him safe, and the evil one cannot harm him."

Christians have many reasons to be anxious. But one thing we do not need to worry about: God's faithfulness in maintaining us in our faith. This is not to say, of course, that we have no part or responsibility in the matter. Jude makes clear that we do (v. 21; see comments there). And note what Peter says in the verse just quoted, that it is "through faith" that we "are shielded by God's power." But we begin, as we always should in the Christian life, with God and his grace. He protects both from human onslaught (persecution) and from spiritual onslaught (Satan). Nothing on earth and nothing in heaven, these verses teach, can "separate us from the love of God that is in Christ Jesus our Lord" (Rom. 8:39).

Such reminders are important because it is easy, in the midst of depression, temptation, or crisis, for the Christian to forget about God's preserving grace. Yet it is this amazing grace, as we sing in the famous hymn, that "hath brought me safe thus far, and . . . will lead me home."

---

10. See I. Howard Marshall, *The Epistles of John*, NICNT (Grand Rapids: Eerdmans, 1978), 252.

Jude 3–4

DEAR FRIENDS, ALTHOUGH I was very eager to write to you about the salvation we share, I felt I had to write and urge you to contend for the faith that was once for all entrusted to the saints. ⁴For certain men whose condemnation was written about long ago have secretly slipped in among you. They are godless men, who change the grace of our God into a license for immorality and deny Jesus Christ our only Sovereign and Lord.

MOST NEW TESTAMENT letters (especially Paul's) move into a thanksgiving and prayer after the initial salutation and greetings. But Jude skips these points, getting right to the heart of what his letter is about. In these two verses, he explains the occasion and theme of this letter.[1] The occasion is the intrusion into the readers' Christian assemblies of false teachers, impious people living and propagating a heretical form of the faith (v. 4). To meet the needs of this occasion, Jude focuses on a single theme: maintaining the truth of the Christian faith as it has been handed down from Christ and the apostles (v. 3).

We have little evidence about who these false teachers were. Jude implies that they claimed to be Christian, for they abused the grace of God in Christ (v. 4). How they did this, we are not sure. But we are sure about their immoral lifestyle, which is the heart of his critique. In verse 4, Jude calls them "godless" (asebeis) men, a word that becomes almost "the keynote of the epistle."[2] Yet Jude's overall purpose, as verse 3 shows, is not negative. It is positive: to encourage true believers to display godliness in the face of the rampant ungodliness around them.

The word "love" plays a central role in the opening of Jude's letter: The readers are "loved" by God the Father (v. 1); Jude prays that they may experience that love more and more (v. 2); and now he addresses them as those whom he also loves: "Beloved" (agapetoi; NIV "dear friends").

---

1. As John White suggests, these verses correspond to the typical epistolary "body opening" (*The Form and Function of the Body of the Greek Letter*, SBLDS 21 [Missoula, Mont.: Univ. of Montana Press, 1972], 18).

2. Mayor, *The Epistle of St. Jude and the Second Epistle of St. Peter*, 26.

In verse 3, Jude explains the situation in which he writes. But we can interpret what he says about this in two different ways. Compare the NRSV and NIV:

> NRSV: "Beloved, while eagerly preparing to write to you about the salvation we share, I find it necessary to write and appeal to you to contend for the faith that was once for all entrusted to the saints."
>
> NIV: "Dear friends, although I was very eager to write to you about the salvation we share, I felt I had to write and urge you to contend for the faith that was once for all entrusted to the saints."

The NRSV translation, by using the word "while," suggests that Jude's writing about "the salvation we share" and his appeal to contend for the faith refers to the same letter—the one we now have before us. In his letter, Jude is accomplishing both these purposes, for by contending for the faith, his readers will be preserving the salvation they have in common. But the NIV, with the word "although," suggests a different scenario. Jude's writing about "the salvation we share" and his appeal to contend for the faith refer to two different letters—the former, one he intended to write, the latter, the one he actually did write (our present letter of Jude).

This second reading is preferable.[3] We are to imagine Jude preparing to write generally and joyfully about the salvation that he and his readers share together[4] when he learns about a new and serious threat to his readers' faith: the false teachers. Consequently, he discards the letter he was about to write in order to warn his readers of this new threat.

The intrusion of these false teachers is what has made it necessary for Jude to "write and urge you to contend for the faith that was once for all entrusted to the saints." Normally in the New Testament, the word "faith" (*pistis*) refers to the act of believing, as when we speak of a person's "faith in Christ." But in a few places the word refers to the content of what a person believes; see, for instance, Galatians 1:23: "They only heard the report: 'The man who formerly persecuted us is now preaching the faith he once tried to destroy.'"

---

3. Why the difference in translation? Neither the word "while" or "although" is in the Greek text; each is an interpretation of the force of the participial construction (*poioumenos*, "making every effort"). Scholars cite some good arguments in favor of "while," but the repetition of the verb "write" favors "although" (see, e.g., Bauckham, *Jude, 2 Peter*, 29; Kelly, *The Epistles of Peter and of Jude*, 245–46).

4. A few commentators think that the "we" in the phrase "the salvation we share" refers to Jews and Gentiles. Certainly the sharing of Jew and Gentile in the messianic salvation is a major note in the New Testament; see our comments on 2 Peter 1:1 ("a faith as precious as ours"). But Jude makes no allusion in the letter to the Jew/Gentile division; and the phrase more naturally means "the salvation that you [the readers] and I [the writer] share." See Kelly, *The Epistles of Peter and of Jude*, 246.

Clearly "faith" has this objective meaning here. It describes what Christians believe—such things as Jesus' atoning death and resurrection, the indwelling of the Holy Spirit, salvation by grace through faith, and (especially in Jude's situation) the holy lifestyle that flows from God's grace in Christ.

These essentials, Jude claims, are not open to interpretation, for this faith "was once for all entrusted to the saints." But this faith has come under attack, and so Jude's readers need to "contend" for it. "Contend" is a strong word. It refers to the exertions of the athlete and is similar to the word Paul used in 1 Corinthians 9:25: "Everyone who *competes* in the games goes into strict training. They do it to get a crown that will not last; but we do it to get a crown that will last forever." Paul later applied this same term to his and his coworkers' energetic defense of the gospel (Col. 1:29; 1 Tim. 4:10; 6:12; 2 Tim. 4:7). Thus Jude urges his readers not simply to resist the false teachers' perversion of the faith; they are actively and energetically to fight for it. Jude himself spells out some of the detailed components of this struggle in verses 20–23.[5]

Why do Jude's readers need to "contend for the faith"? Because (note the "for" at the beginning of v. 2) "certain men ... have secretly slipped in among you." "Certain men" has a contemptuous ring; Jude does not bother to name or even to number them.[6] Perhaps his scorn arises partly from their manner of working. Rather than straightforwardly opposing the faith, these people pursue their agenda by stealth—they have "wormed their way in," as the REB puts it.[7] It is not that they are hidden from the readers, working in secret so the faithful are not even aware of them. Rather, they hide their real nature and purpose. Jesus warned about "wolves in sheep's clothing" (Matt. 7:15)—these false teachers are just such wolves.

Jude leaves us in no doubt about his opinion of these "men." He says four things about them. (1) Their "condemnation was written about long ago." Jude here follows the same pattern Peter used when dealing with the false teachers: to pronounce their condemnation immediately after introducing them (see 2 Peter 2:1–4). Much debate surrounds the phrase "written about long ago." If Jude is using 2 Peter as the basis for his own letter, he may be referring to this passage.[8] "Long ago" may seem to make this view impossible, but the Greek word (*palai*) can mean simply "already" (see Mark 15:44). Still, this is an unusual meaning for the word; and, although I think it possible that Jude is using 2 Peter (see the introduction), I doubt that Jude here refers to this letter.

---

5. Bauckham, *Jude, 2 Peter*, 31–32.

6. Kelly, *The Epistles of Peter and of Jude*, 248.

7. The verb is *pareisdyno*, used only here in the New Testament. The verb Peter uses to describe the false teachers in 2 Peter 2:1 is similar in meaning.

8. Bigg, *The Epistles of St. Peter and St. Jude*, 326.

Another possibility is that Jude is thinking of *1 Enoch*, since he quotes from that Jewish pseudepigraphical book in verses 14–16.[9] But there seems no reason to focus on *1 Enoch* alone when Jude refers to other sources as well. Kelly thinks that Jude may be thinking of the "heavenly tablets," writings kept in heaven on which were inscribed the names of those who deserved punishment as well as those who deserved to be rewarded.[10] The simplest explanation, however, is that Jude introduces the evidence for the false teachers' condemnation that he will adduce in the rest of the letter. He makes his case by citing from the Old Testament (vv. 5–8, 11), from Jewish traditions (vv. 9, 14–16), and from the teaching of the apostles (vv. 17–18).[11] In all these sources, he says, the "condemnation" of these false teachers has long been established.

(2) "They are godless men." As we noted above, "godless" (*asebes*) is an important word in Jude (cf. v. 15; also the cognate noun in v. 18). The author sees it as the single best term to describe the men who have secretly slipped in and are threatening the faith. The word connotes a person who is "without religion," who "fails to worship" (see also Rom. 4:5; 5:6; 1 Tim. 1:9; 1 Peter 4:18; 2 Peter 2:5–6; 3:7). It is broad enough to cover all kinds of sins and errors, but Hellenistic Jews used it especially of irreverence in an ethical sense: "not theoretical atheism, but practical godlessness."[12] Jude clearly applies it in this way, saying almost nothing about the false teachers' doctrinal errors but a great deal about their immoral lifestyle.

(3) They "change the grace of God into a license for immorality." The word "immorality" (*aselgeia*) is another key term that both Peter and Jude use to describe the false teachers. It is a term that connotes especially sins of the flesh: sexual misconduct, drunkenness, gluttony, and so on. As did many before them and many after them, these false teachers twist God's free forgiveness in Christ into an "open sesame" for sinful behavior. It is as if they said, "Wasn't it the essence of God's grace that he took care of our sins completely on the cross? How, then, can there be any penalty for sin any more? We can live as we like." We are not sure whether the false teachers actually reasoned things out this way, or whether this was simply the effect of what they were doing. But the result is much the same.

(4) They "deny Jesus Christ our only Sovereign and Lord." The NIV takes a definite stand on a debated interpretive issue, applying the title "only Sovereign" to Jesus Christ. The Greek is not so clear, and the rendering "the

---

9. Mayor, *The Epistle of St. Jude and the Second Epistle of St. Peter*, 24.

10. Kelly, *The Epistles of Peter and of Jude*, 250.

11. Bauckham, *Jude, 2 Peter*, 35–36.

12. Ibid., 38.

only Lord God, and our Lord Jesus Christ" (KJV) is also possible.[13] But the NIV is followed by almost all the modern versions, and this interpretation does seem to be justified.[14] We have here another instance in which Jude applies language typically used only of God to Jesus Christ.

Exactly how were the false teachers "denying" Christ? They may have been denying him in theory, by contesting his nature or status or by teaching things incompatible with the "faith once for all delivered."[15] But the unique combination "sovereign and Lord" draws attention to Jesus' right to demand obedience from his followers. Probably, then, Jude is thinking of a practical denial of Christ, of people behaving in a manner contrary to what Jesus the Lord demands of his people.[16]

WE WILL UNDERSTAND Jude 3–4 better by paying closer attention to two specific matters: the place of the verses within the argument of the letter and the significance and limitations of tradition in the early church.

Hellenistic rhetoric and the letter of Jude. New Testament authors grew up in a "multicultural" environment. Most were Jews, deeply influenced by the Old Testament and Jewish tradition. Yet they were also citizens of a larger Greco-Roman world, a world formed by the traditions of Greek philosophy and literature and by Roman legal concepts. Scholars debate endlessly about which of these influences was most decisive for the various New Testament writers. Controversy about Paul's place in this multicultural spectrum is especially sharp. When we consider Jude, what immediately strikes us, of course, is his thorough Jewishness. We know he was raised in a Jewish home in Israel. In his letter, he extensively cites and alludes to the Old Testament and Jewish traditions. We might, then, be tempted to conclude that the Jewish influence is the only one that we need to consider when interpreting Jude.

---

13. The main arguments in favor of this rendering are that *despotes* ("sovereign") refers to God in all but one (2 Peter 2:1) of its New Testament occurrences, and that "only Lord" is standard Jewish phraseology for God (see Mayor, *The Epistle of St. Jude and the Second Epistle of St. Peter*, 26–27; Kelly, *The Epistles of Peter and of Jude*, 252).

14. The main argument in favor of this rendering is the single article that governs both *despoten* ("sovereign") and *kyrion hemon* ("our Lord"). See Bigg, *The Epistles of St. Peter and St. Jude*, 327; Bauckham, *Jude, 2 Peter*, 39.

15. Mayor, *The Epistle of St. Jude and the Second Epistle of St. Peter*, 27; Kelly, *The Epistles of Peter and of Jude*, 252–53.

16. Bauckham, *Jude, 2 Peter*, 40.

But this would be shortsighted. Jewish as he was, Jude could nevertheless not escape some influence from the Greco-Roman world of which he was a part. Scholars have shown that any sharp distinction between "Palestinian Judaism" and "Hellenistic Judaism" is impossible. All Judaism in the first century was to some extent "Hellenized"—that is, influenced by Greco-Roman ideas—because all Jews lived in a Hellenistic environment.[17] Thus we must at least be open to the possibility that Jude was influenced by Greco-Roman ideas as he wrote his letter.

One of the most important emphases in this Greco-Roman world was "rhetoric." By "rhetoric," we do not mean literary embroidery (as when we say, for example, that "the rhetorical flourishes of the speaker were most moving"). "Rhetoric" in the ancient world was the art of persuasion. Aristotle had defined some of its classic forms of rhetoric in his *The Art of Rhetoric*, and the Romans, a thoroughly legal people, developed the art extensively.

Many biblical scholars have argued that various New Testament writings, or portions of those writings, follow the standards of ancient rhetoric. These arguments are by no means always persuasive; in many cases, one gets the impression that a form is being forced onto material that does not fit it very well. But F. Duane Watson has made a convincing case that the letter of Jude follows typical ancient rhetorical procedures.[18] A rhetorical perspective places attention on persuasion: Jude is trying to persuade his readers to adhere to his vision of the Christian faith and to reject the view propagated by the false teachers. We should not be surprised if he uses a conventional rhetorical model to accomplish this purpose.

Watson uses typical ancient rhetorical features to outline Jude as follows:

> Verse 3: the *exordium*, which introduces the "case" that the speaker is going to try to make
> Verse 4: the *narratio*, which sets forth the concerns that have led to the issue being addressed
> Verses 5–16: the *probatio*, which attempts to persuade the audience to accept the speaker's point of view by arguments and proofs
> Verses 17–23: the *peroratio*, which repeats the basic case and appeals to the emotions

We can readily see that the body of Jude corresponds to these divisions quite well. This need not mean that Jude self-consciously adopted a particular rhetorical model. It may be that he naturally fell into this general style of argument as it was known to him from his surrounding culture.

---

17. The classic work demonstrating this thesis is Martin Hengel, *Judaism and Hellenism. Studies in Their Encounter During the Early Hellenistic Period*, 2 vols. (Philadelphia: Fortress, 1980).
18. F. Duane Watson, *Invention, Arrangement, and Style.*

At least two elements in verses 3–4 stand out a bit more in light of their rhetorical function. (1) As we have noted, some of the key points in these two verses (and vv. 1–2, what Watson calls the "quasi-exordium") emerge again in the *peroratio* (vv. 17–23):

> love: "loved" and "love" (vv. 1–2), "beloved" (v. 3), and "keep yourselves in God's love" (v. 21)
>
> mercy: "mercy" (v. 2), and "be merciful to those who doubt" (v. 22)
>
> keep: "kept by Jesus Christ" (v. 2), and "keep yourselves in God's love" (v. 21)
>
> the need to adhere to apostolic tradition: "contend for the faith that was once for all entrusted to the saints" (v. 3), and "remember what the apostles of our Lord Jesus Christ foretold" (v. 17)
>
> identification and negative characterization of the false teachers: verse 4 and verses 18–19.

Jude's procedure is typical of rhetorical forms, which usually repeated essential ideas from the *exordium* in the *peroratio*. Rhetorical analysis draws attention to the significance of these points as key ideas in Jude's persuasive strategy.

(2) Rhetorical analysis also helps us understand why Jude uses some of the language he does in verse 4. As both ancient and modern "persuaders" understand, getting people to accept one's point of view can depend as much on emotion as on logic. (Consider the typical political advertising one sees on TV!) Thus good rhetoricians use a lot of emotive language. Note how Jude does this in verse 4: *"certain* men" (contemptuous language); *"secretly* slipped in" (they are underhanded and duplicitous); "godless" (they don't really worship God); "immorality"; "deny Jesus Christ." As Watson notes, the language communicates "urgency and disgust."[19] Jude leaves us in no doubt about what he thinks of these people from the very start, and the strength of his language gets our attention at the outset. What he writes about is no trivial matter.

Tradition in the early church. Contemporary application of these verses also demands that we have some idea of the New Testament teaching on "tradition." Jude touches on this matter in his description of the faith as "once for all entrusted to the saints." Many scholars think that a person living in the apostolic age could not have used such an expression. They insist it smacks of a later period, in the second century perhaps, when the church had come to recognize a traditional body of dogma that had been around for some time. To these interpreters tradition represents a departure from the innovative and vigorous life of the young Christian community. Nor does tradition

---

19. Ibid., 46.

usually have a positive connotation for us. We think of the song from *Fiddler on the Roof*, in which the central Jewish character insists on the old ways by harping on "Tradition." And many of us have worshiped in churches that were tragically closed to innovation because of "tradition" ("but we've always done it this way").

Is this what Jude's expression means? What does the New Testament say about "tradition"? (1) We must recognize that "tradition" plays an important role within the New Testament itself. The most famous example is 1 Corinthians 15:1–8:

> Now, brothers, I want to remind you of the gospel I preached to you, which you received and on which you have taken your stand. By this gospel you are saved, if you hold firmly to the word I preached to you. Otherwise, you have believed in vain.
>
> For what I received I *passed on* to you as of first importance: that Christ died for our sins according to the Scriptures, that he was buried, that he was raised on the third day according to the Scriptures, and that he appeared to Peter, and then to the Twelve. After that, he appeared to more than five hundred of the brothers at the same time, most of whom are still living, though some have fallen asleep. Then he appeared to James, then to all the apostles, and last of all he appeared to me also, as to one abnormally born.

The highlighted word, "passed on," translates the same Greek word that the NIV translates "entrusted" in Jude 3 (*paradidomi*). In other words, Paul himself insists that the truth about Christ's death, burial, and resurrection—central to the gospel message—had been "passed down" to him. Almost from the beginning, it seems, the early Christians formulated a body of essential truths about God's work in Christ that was passed on wherever the gospel was preached.

(2) Paul speaks often about this same "tradition" in the Pastoral Letters. There he insists that Timothy and Titus focus on "sound" or "healthy" teaching (1 Tim. 1:10; 6:3; 2 Tim. 1:13; 4:3; Titus 1:9; 2:1), and he urges Timothy to "guard the good deposit that was entrusted to you" (2 Tim. 1:14). Many scholars think that we have here another example of a late first- or early second-century attitude. But it is perfectly natural to see in this emphasis a concern on the part of Paul, as he reached the end of his life, to pass on intact the gospel as God had revealed it to the apostles. For God gave the apostles a critical role to play in the development of Christian truth. Jesus' promise that the Holy Spirit would "teach you all things and will remind you of everything I have said to you" (John 14:26) probably applies specifically to the apostles, who became the transmitters and guardians of the truth about Jesus.

The point, then, is that already in the New Testament period itself, we can recognize clearly the importance of an established set of beliefs based on the teaching of the apostles. It is this "tradition" that Jude is at such pains to guard against the encroachments of the false teachers.

RECOGNIZING THE RHETORICAL character of Jude reminds us about just what kind of letter the author has written: a passionate argument for a particular point of view. We can easily slip into far too analytical a mode when we read a letter like this one. Careful analysis, of course, is necessary—at least I hope it is, or this commentary has no purpose. But analysis can too easily become an end in itself or have the effect of dulling the real point and power of a letter.

Jude writes with urgency; we need to sense that urgency and pick some of it up as we read the letter. For false teachers are all about in our day, and the "faith once for all entrusted to the saints" is battered and attacked on every side. Do we care? Jude sure did!

Related to his passion is his emotion. He writes no dispassionate analysis of the false teachers; he lambastes and condemns them. We should read Jude sympathetically, allowing his own emotions to stir us to action. For Jude wants his emotional language to persuade us to his point of view. Rhetoric was designed for oral situations: the lawyer pleading a case in court, the politician trying to win over uncommitted voters. Perhaps if we were to read Jude aloud, putting all the emotion he packs into his words into our speech, we could appreciate his message better.

What is Jude so passionate about? In a phrase, "the faith once for all entrusted to the saints." As Charles Bigg puts it, "Jude's language about the Faith is highly dogmatic, highly orthodox, highly zealous. . . . Men who used such phrases believed passionately in a creed."[20]

Creeds are out of fashion in our day, and for two reasons. (1) Many of us attend churches that are not rooted in any creed. The contemporary evangelical movement has fostered many churches that are either nondenominational or only loosely tied to denominations. And it is, of course, in some of the historic denominations that creeds are most important. Yet even in churches that have preserved a strong sense of denominational connection (e.g., many Episcopal, Presbyterian, and Lutheran churches, not to mention Roman Catholicism) there is a tendency today to downplay the role of creeds.

---

20. Bigg, *The Epistles of St. Peter and St. Jude*, 325.

(2) This leads to a second reason for the lack of attention to creeds. The very word has a bit of a "stuffy" ring to it. It conjures up before us the images of musty and dusty church buildings and dry academic disputes. As a result, many modern evangelicals have no roots. Their sense of Christianity goes back no further than their own church (which may have been in existence for only a few years) or no further back than their current pastor.

Now I am certainly not advocating a return to the sad ecclesiastical squabbles—and even wars—that have marred the cause of Christ over the years. Creeds can be narrow and divisive, entrenching certain doctrines at the expense of others and convincing us that our specific view of the faith is the only right one. But the point Jude is making is obvious: There is a set of beliefs, based in the teaching and work of Christ, developed and passed on by the apostles, that is nonnegotiable. To be Christian is to agree with these beliefs; to reject them is to cease to be Christian.

Defining precisely what these beliefs are, of course, is the trick. Many definitions, or creeds, are far too lengthy, including matters that are at best questionable or tangential in the New Testament. But other creeds are far too simple and include far too little. I think in this regard of some of the "confessions" that have emerged in the course of the ecumenical movement. Some of them suggest that you can be a Christian as long as you think that Jesus Christ is somehow significant to your spiritual journey. Any creed we adopt needs to include those matters that the apostolic tradition—the New Testament—makes essential; and it should not include any that are not made essential.

Writing such a creed, of course, is a daunting task; and we must realize that we will never all agree on everything. But I think we can receive help in the task by developing in the evangelical movement a much greater respect for history. I taught a Sunday school class in my church recently in which I took as my subject "orthodoxy." I gave a sketchy overview of "church history," focusing on the way the different periods in history contributed to different doctrines. My purpose was to give these believers, who had never even heard of most of the people and ideas I was talking about, a sense of the oneness of "Christendom": people in every century who have believed basically the same things.

Such a historical consciousness is a tremendous encouragement, reminding us that we stand as part of a great company of people—from all over the world and from every period of time—who have confessed Christ and stood up for the truth. It is also a vital corrective to the over-emphases and blind spots that our culture may bring to our theological vision. For although tradition can stifle growth, lack of tradition often means that a church has no anchor to hold it secure in the faith in the midst of the changing winds of culture and theology.

Finally, I would urge us to recapture the kind of passion for orthodoxy that Jude had. As David Wells and others have pointed out, we live in a time when believers do not get excited about truth.[21] We are narrowly practical in our focus, myopically concentrating on the "bottom line" of behavior to the exclusion of everything else. But one of the points Jude is trying to get across is that truth and practice are linked together. Confessing the right things is vital if we are to live the right way. The truth of God in Christ sets people free. Surely, if we really appreciate the power of the gospel and the blessings it brings to us, we will be more passionate in maintaining and defending it.

---

21. David Wells, *No Place for Truth or Whatever Happened to Evangelical Theology?* (Grand Rapids: Eerdmans, 1993).

THOUGH YOU ALREADY know all this, I want to remind you that the Lord delivered his people out of Egypt, but later destroyed those who did not believe. ⁶And the angels who did not keep their positions of authority but abandoned their own home—these he has kept in darkness, bound with everlasting chains for judgment on the great Day. ⁷In a similar way, Sodom and Gomorrah and the surrounding towns gave themselves up to sexual immorality and perversion. They serve as an example of those who suffer the punishment of eternal fire.

⁸In the very same way, these dreamers pollute their own bodies, reject authority and slander celestial beings. ⁹But even the archangel Michael, when he was disputing with the devil about the body of Moses, did not dare to bring a slanderous accusation against him, but said, "The Lord rebuke you!" ¹⁰Yet these men speak abusively against whatever they do not understand; and what things they do understand by instinct, like unreasoning animals—these are the very things that destroy them.

IN VERSE 3, Jude tells us *what* he is writing—urging believers to cling tenaciously to the truth about Christ that has been handed down to them from the apostles. In verse 4, he tells us *why* he is writing—because false teachers have infiltrated the church and are putting the truth of Christ at risk. Jude returns to the positive thrust that he announced in verse 3 at the end of the letter (vv. 17–23). But in verses 5–16, he elaborates verse 4, describing and condemning the false teachers. These verses fall into three major sections, in each of which Jude cites Old Testament or Jewish traditional material and then applies it to the false teachers. And in each of these sections Jude also uses the word "these" (*houtoi*) to move from his examples to his application.

Section of Jude	Old Testament/Traditional Material	Application
vv. 5–10	vv. 5–7 (9)	vv. 8 ("these") and 10
vv. 11–13	v. 11	vv. 12–13 ("these")
vv. 14–16	vv. 14–15	v. 16 ("these")

Jude's strategy is obvious: By identifying the false teachers with traditional examples of notorious sinners, he moves his readers to reject these infiltrators and, indeed, to regard them with horror.

Many English versions (such as the NIV) and commentators divide verses 5–10 into two separate paragraphs. But the rhetorical pattern just outlined suggests that we should keep together the Old Testament examples of verses 5–7 with their application in verses 8–10. To be sure, this application is complicated by an interruption: Jude's reference to the apocryphal tradition about Michael fighting with Satan for the body of Moses (v. 9). But this allusion seems to be a secondary illustration rather than a new example deserving its own paragraph. Jude's fondness for triads is evident here again. He mentions three Old Testament examples of judgment (vv. 5–7) and three specific sins committed by the false teachers (vv. 8–10).

Three Old Testament Examples of Sin and Judgment (vv. 5–7)

ANCIENT WRITERS OFTEN made their transition from the opening of a letter to its body with what is called a "disclosure formula." It frequently took the form of, "But I want you to know," or, "But let me remind you." Jude's "Though you already know all this, I want to remind you" (v. 5) is a variation on this formula. It introduces verses 5–16 as a whole. "All this" may refer back to what Jude has just said in verse 3: "although you well understand 'the faith once for all entrusted to the saints.'"[1] But the word translated "this" is actually a plural (*panta*, "all these things"), and, that being the case, it more naturally refers to what follows: "although you are already acquainted with the Old Testament and traditional material I am about to share. . . ."[2]

Jude's first example is the desert generation of Israel. Jude reminds his readers that "the Lord delivered his people out of Egypt." We encounter in this statement an interesting textual variant. As noted in the footnote to this verse in the NIV, a number of Greek manuscripts, in place of the word translated "Lord," have the Greek word for "Jesus." Some commentators think that this reading is original and that Jude here thinks of the preexistent Jesus as the one who delivered the people out of Egypt. They point to 1 Corinthians 10:4, where Paul identifies the "rock" that followed the Israelites in the desert with Christ.[3] Others think that "the Lord" is the best reading, but identify this Lord

---

1. Bauckham, *Jude, 2 Peter*, 48.

2. Mayor, *The Epistle of St. Jude and the Second Epistle of St. Peter*, 28.

3. A. R. C. Leaney, *The Letters of Peter and Jude*, CBC (Cambridge: Cambridge Univ. Press, 1967), 88; cf. Neyrey, *2 Peter, Jude*, 61–62.

as Christ.[4] But the flow of the passage shows that whoever delivered and destroyed the people (v. 5) also kept the disobedient angels in darkness (see "he" in v. 6). It is unlikely that Jude identifies Jesus as the one who did all these things. Probably, then, we should read "the Lord" and identify him as "Jehovah" God.[5]

What Jude reminds his readers, then, is that God "delivered his people out of Egypt." He refers, of course, to the Exodus (Ex. 6–14), the event that defined and brought into being the people of Israel. Through the plagues he brought on Egypt through Moses, God forced Pharaoh to "let his people go"; and God then destroyed the armies of Egypt in the "Sea of Reeds" when they tried to follow the escaping Israelites.

However, as Jude's readers and most Christians know, the people whom God delivered from Egypt never got to experience the delights of the Promised Land. Dismayed at the strength of the people already in the land of Canaan, they failed to trust God to give them victory. God therefore sentenced that entire generation of Israelites (with the exception of Joshua and Caleb) to wander in the desert until they had all died off (see Num. 14). Jude emphasizes the tragedy of this rejection by qualifying "delivered" with the word "once for all" (*hapax*, not translated in the NIV) and "destroyed" with the word "afterwards" (*deuteran*).[6] God's deliverance of his people seemed to be decisive and final, yet God still "destroyed" them because of their lack of faith. Jude intends this as a warning to his readers: Don't think, because God has decisively rescued you from your sins, that you can presume on his grace and mercy.

Jude's first (the Exodus generation) and third (Sodom and Gomorrah) examples of God's judgment are well known from the Old Testament. But not so his second (v. 6): "angels who did not keep their positions of authority but abandoned their own home." Many older commentators thought that Jude is referring to the fall of angels that apparently occurred when Satan rebelled against God. A few Old Testament passages may refer to this event, and it

---

4. Bauckham, *Jude, 2 Peter*, 49.

5. See, e.g., Mayor, *The Epistle of St. Jude and the Second Epistle of St. Peter*, 28–29; Kelly, *The Epistles of Peter and of Jude*, 255.

6. There is some debate about this translation, since the word *deuteran* means, literally, "a second time." Some commentators therefore think Jude is referring to the dying off of the desert generation as a "second" destruction after the first, accomplished in Egypt (Kelly, *The Epistles of Peter and of Jude*, 252). Green thinks the reference may be to the second coming of Christ (*The Second Epistle General of Peter and the General Epistle of Jude*, 164). But it is simplest to think that *deuteran*, following *hapax*, means something like "in a second experience after that first one." See, e.g., Bigg, *The Epistles of St. Peter and St. Jude*, 328; Bauckham, *Jude, 2 Peter*, 50.

has become enshrined in western Christian tradition through the splendid elaboration given the event by John Milton in *Paradise Lost*.[7]

But in Jude's day, a far more popular tradition about angels who sinned was associated with the enigmatic reference in Genesis 6:1–4 to "sons of God" who came down to earth and cohabited with "the daughters of men." Jewish interpreters had built an elaborate story on the basis of this text, identifying the "sons of God" with angels and attributing much (or even all) evil in the world to their pernicious influence. These stories find their greatest elaboration in the intertestamental book *1 Enoch*, and since Jude quotes from this very book in verses 14–15, we are almost certainly correct in identifying this story as the one he has in mind in verse 6.[8]

These angels, Jude notes, had been entrusted by God with "positions of authority" (*archen*), that is, heavenly spheres of influence and ministry. But they abandoned their "homes," their "proper dwelling places" (REB), by rebelling against God. God therefore judged them; they are being "kept in darkness, bound with everlasting chains for judgment on the great Day." The "great Day" is a variation of the common biblical "Day of the Lord," the time when the Lord intervenes at the end of history to bring final salvation to his people and eternal judgment to his enemies. These rebellious angels are destined for that judgment.

But God does not wait for that Day to deal with them. Even now, Jude notes, their punishment has begun. "Darkness" is a common way of describing divine punishment in the ancient world; the Greeks used the same word Jude uses here to depict the "underworld," the place of departed spirits. This language is also picked up in *1 Enoch*, as is the reference to "chains." Note the parallels between what Jude says here of the punishment of the angels and *1 Enoch* 10:4–6, which depicts the judgment of one of the chief of the angels:

> And secondly the Lord said to Raphael, "Bind Azazel hand and foot (and) throw him into the darkness!" And he made a hole in the desert which was in Dudael and cast him there; he threw on top of him rugged and sharp rocks. And he covered his face in order that he might not see the light; and in order that he might be sent into the fire on the great day of judgment.[9]

Jude probably has this passage in mind as he writes Jude 6. We can guess he knew that his readers were familiar with these traditions and that a refer-

---

7. For more details on this tradition, see the "Bridging Contexts" section on 2 Peter 2:4–10a.

8. So almost all recent commentators. For details on the *1 Enoch* stories and the interpretation of Gen. 6, see again the "Bridging Contexts" section on 2 Peter 2:4–10a.

9. The quotation is taken from *The Old Testament Pseudepigrapha*, vol. 1: *Apocalyptic Literature and Testaments*, ed. James H. Charlesworth (Garden City, N.Y.: Doubleday, 1983), 17.

ence to them would therefore be persuasive for them. Before we leave this verse, we should note the way in which Jude suggests the equivalence of the angels' sin and their judgment: It was because they did not "keep" their assigned position that God is "keeping" them in darkness. Here we find a negative counterpart to the situation of the righteous, whom God "keeps" (v. 2) and who are therefore to "keep" themselves in God's love (v. 21).

Verse 7 introduces the third of Jude's warning examples: Sodom and Gomorrah, along with "the surrounding towns" (e.g., Admah, Zeboim, and Zoar; cf. Gen. 19:20–22). The striking story of God's judgment of these cities had become almost proverbial; they are mentioned often in Jewish tradition and in the New Testament (see, e.g., Luke 17:26–29). But Jude not only mentions God's judgment; he also tells us why God judged the cities: because, as the NIV translates, they "gave themselves up to sexual immorality and perversion."

The charge of "sexual immorality" is clear and understandable, for according to Genesis 19, the men of Sodom sought to have sexual relationships with the angels who had come to visit Lot. But the second charge that Jude mentions, "perversion," is not so clear. "Perversion" is the NIV rendering of a Greek phrase that, literally translated, is "going after other flesh" (cf. NASB). Most commentators have thought that Jude is condemning the men of Sodom for seeking to have sex with "flesh other than" the flesh of women. That is, the "perversion" they were guilty of was homosexuality. They "abandoned natural relationships with women" (Rom. 1:27) and were hankering after flesh "other" than that which God had commanded them to use.[10] But other commentators think that the "perversion" here is the sin of having sex with angels.[11]

There is some evidence that Jewish tradition associated in this way the sin of the angels (v. 6) and that of the men of Sodom (v. 7). And it would make a neat transition here: As angels are condemned for sex with humans, so the people of Sodom are condemned for seeking to have sex with angels. But Genesis 19 does not imply that the men of Sodom knew that it was angels they were seeking to have sex with. Nor is "flesh" a natural word to apply to angels. Probably, then, the usual interpretation is correct: Jude associates God's judgment on Sodom and Gomorrah with the homosexual practices of their inhabitants.

Jude concludes, then, that these sinful cities on the plain "serve as an example of those who suffer the punishment of eternal fire." Indeed, God's judgment was spectacular and final. According to Genesis 19:24, "the Lord rained down burning sulfur on Sodom and Gomorrah—from the LORD out

---

10. See, e.g., Mayor, *The Epistle of St. Jude and the Second Epistle of St. Peter*, 32.
11. Kelly, *The Epistles of Peter and of Jude*, 258–59; Bauckham, *Jude, 2 Peter*, 54.

of the heavens." Writers contemporary to Jude saw in the topography of the area, with its sulfurous odors, smoke, and terribly desolate appearance, continuing evidence of this awful judgment of God on sin.[12] This is one of the reasons why Jude uses the present tense here at the end of verse, for the cities "serve as an example of those who suffer the punishment of eternal fire." This may also be the reason why Jude does not follow the canonical order in the three examples he lists. Had he done so, we would have expected the angels' sin to come first (Gen. 6), Sodom and Gomorrah second (Gen. 19), and the desert generation third (Num. 14). But by following the order he does, Jude achieves a crescendo in punishment—from physical death (v. 5) to binding in darkness (v. 6) to the "punishment of eternal fire."[13]

Application of the Examples to the False Teachers (vv. 8–10)

JUDE LEAVES US in no doubt about the application of his biblical examples. Though he does not clearly identify who "these dreamers" are, it is clear from the context that he is referring to the "men . . . [who] have secretly slipped in among you" (v. 4). What is significant is that Jude does not focus in his application on the judgment of the false teachers, but on their sin. "In the very same way" suggests that the false teachers are committing the same kinds of sins as did the Israelites (v. 5), the angels (v. 6), and the people of Sodom and Gomorrah (v. 7). Jude does not necessarily mean that the sins are identical. The NIV rendering of the transitional phrase at the beginning of verse 8 is a bit strong; all that Jude implies is that there is a general similarity between the sins.

Jude lists three different sins the false teachers are committing. We give here a literal translation as a basis for our comments. They "dreaming, pollute flesh," "reject authority," and "blaspheme glories." The parallels between these three sins and those of the Old Testament sinners Jude has listed are generally clear. The angels and the Sodomites "polluted flesh" by their sexual perversions; the desert generation, the angels, and the Sodomites all "rejected authority" by refusing to follow the Lord's directives; and the Sodomites "blasphemed glories" by treating with disrespect the angels who had come to visit Lot.[14] But if the general picture seems clear, a number of the details is not. Each phrase requires further investigation.

(1) "Dreaming, they pollute flesh." "Dreaming" seems like an odd word here. A few commentators think it means that the false teachers are living in

---

12. See, e.g., Philo, *Moses* 2.56; see the notes on 2 Peter 2:7.

13. Watson, *Invention, Arrangement, and Style,* 53–54. Bauckham, on the other hand, thinks that the Sodomites come last because their sin corresponds most closely to that of the false teachers (*Jude, 2 Peter,* 55).

14. See Bauckham, *Jude, 2 Peter,* 55.

an unreal world; they were "dreamers" (NIV) in the sense that they imagined God was not displeased with them for their behavior.[15] But most commentators agree that Jude is referring to visionary experiences. The verb he uses here (*enypniazomai*) often refers to the visions that prophets receive, as it does in its only other New Testament occurrence: "Your old men will dream dreams" (Acts 2:17, quoting Joel 2:28). The same verb is used in the Greek translation of the Old Testament to refer to the visions that false prophets claimed to receive (e.g., Deut. 13:2, 4, 6). Apparently, then, the false teachers based their immoral behavior on revelatory visions that they claimed to have received.

By using the phrase "pollute flesh" (NIV, "pollute their own bodies") for the false teachers' immorality, Jude associates them closely with the Sodomites, who went after "other flesh." Whether this means that the false teachers were guilty, as were the Sodomites, of homosexuality is not, however, clear. Jude may mean simply that the false teachers, like the Sodomites, were guilty of sexual immorality.

(2) "They reject authority." Calvin and Luther thought that this meant that the false teachers were rejecting human authority, displaying an arrogant disregard for government and for the leaders of the Christian church. But we can see no good reason to restrict the idea in this way. The word "authority" here (*kyriotes*) comes from the same root as the word "Lord" (*kyrios*), and Jude has already told us that the false teachers "deny Jesus Christ our only Sovereign and Lord [*kyrios*]" (v. 4). Almost certainly, then, Jude means that the false teachers throw off the Lordship of Christ and/or of God.[16]

(3) "They blaspheme glories." As the NIV rendering rightly suggests, "glories" here are "celestial beings," in a word, angels (cf. also REB; note NASB, "angelic majesties").[17] And since Jude calls them "glories" and views the false teachers' blasphemy of them as sinful, we may naturally think that he has good angels in mind. If this is so, just how were they "blaspheming" them? The word "blaspheme" can also be translated "revile," "belittle." It suggests a disparaging attitude and is often applied to speech or behavior that fails to give God or his representatives their due. One can thus "blaspheme" the Holy Spirit by attributing Christ's miraculous signs to the devil (Luke 12:10); "blaspheme" the gospel by claiming that it endorses sin (Rom. 3:8); or "blaspheme" God by failing to live up to his law (Rom. 2:24).

---

15. Mayor, *The Epistle of St. Jude and the Second Epistle of St. Peter*, 33.

16. Some commentators think that the Lordship of God is meant (Mayor, *The Epistle of St. Jude and the Second Epistle of St. Peter*, 34); others of Christ (Green, *The Second Epistle General of Peter and the General Epistle of Jude*, 168; Bauckham, *Jude, 2 Peter*, 56–57); still others of both God and Christ (Kelly, *The Epistles of Peter and of Jude*, 262–63). Since the phrase is so general, the distinction does not much matter.

17. See the "Original Meaning" section on 2 Peter 2:10b for the use of the word "glories" (*doxai*) with this meaning.

The false teachers may, then, be "blaspheming" angels by speaking against them, as did certain Gnostic heretics by claiming that angels served an inferior god. But, although some scholars associate the false teachers in Jude with Gnostics, there is little basis for the identification. Since the Old Testament and Jewish tradition gave angels an important role in the judgment, it may be that the false teachers, by downplaying judgment to come, were, in effect, disparaging the angels.[18] Or the false teachers, by rejecting the authority of God and his law, may have indirectly been attacking angels as well, who were thought to be the mediators and guardians of the law (see Acts 7:38; Gal. 3:19–20).[19]

Either of these last two interpretations makes good sense of verse 8. But I must question whether they make equally good sense in the context. Verse 9 is not an easy verse to interpret, but the most natural explanation for its presence in this context is to serve as a contrast to the behavior of the false teachers. Michael the archangel, Jude notes, did not "bring a slanderous [or blasphemous] accusation" against Satan. This suggests that the false teachers *were* guilty of slandering Satan. If so, then it makes best sense to identify the "glories" in verse 8 with *evil* angels instead of with good angels.[20] As we have argued on 2 Peter 2:10b, this seems to be what Peter means in a similar passage. And, as I pointed out there, the idea of calling evil angels "glories" or condemning people for blaspheming them is not all that strange. For, though fallen, the evil angels still bear the impress of their glorious creation and original status, and they should not be treated lightly.

Perhaps, then, the false teachers were disparaging the evil angels by presuming, apart from the power of the Lord, to dismiss their significance on their own behavior. Perhaps the experience of the Jewish exorcists in Acts 19:13–16 is something of a parallel:

> Some Jews who went around driving out evil spirits tried to invoke the name of the Lord Jesus over those who were demon-possessed. They would say, "In the name of Jesus, whom Paul preaches, I command you to come out." . . . One day the evil spirit answered them, "Jesus I know, and I know about Paul, but who are you?" Then the man who had the evil spirit jumped on them and overpowered them all. He gave them such a beating that they ran out of the house naked and bleeding.

I am not suggesting that Jude's false teachers were trying to exorcise demons on their own. But they may have been guilty in a general way of the mistake

---

18. Neyrey, *2 Peter, Jude,* 66.
19. Bauckham, *Jude, 2 Peter,* 57–58.
20. See, e.g., Green, *The Second Epistle General of Peter and the General Epistle of Jude,* 168–69.

made by these Jewish exorcists: dismissing the power and influence of evil angels without the authority of Jesus to back it up.

As noted above, verse 9 is a notoriously difficult verse. We face two problems: the source for the story Jude refers to, and the application of the story to the false teachers.

(1) The word "archangel," used only one other time in the New Testament (1 Thess. 4:16), refers to the highest rank of angel, as Jews developed these ranks in the intertestamental period.[21] Michael, mentioned three times in the Old Testament (Dan. 10:13, 21; 12:1) and once elsewhere in the New (Rev. 12:7), is always included in this group and often made the most important within this highest rank. The problem is that we do not find anywhere in the Old Testament or in extant Jewish literature the story that Jude refers to here. However, several early Christian fathers tell us about a book that they were familiar with that contained the story. It is variously called *The Assumption of Moses* or *The Testament of Moses*.[22] One of the bases of the story Jude quotes is apparently the vision of Zechariah in Zechariah 3, in which "the angel of the LORD" and Satan dispute over Joshua the high priest:

> Then he showed me Joshua the high priest standing before the angel of the LORD, and Satan standing at his right side to accuse him. The LORD said to Satan, "The LORD rebuke you, Satan! The LORD, who has chosen Jerusalem, rebuke you! Is not this man a burning stick snatched from the fire?" (vv. 1–2)

We can recognize how the tradition that Jude quotes puts the words of rebuke from this vision on the lips of Michael. We, of course, have no way of knowing exactly what Jude thought about this story. He certainly gives no indication that the book from which he quotes had canonical status. But did he think that the story about Michael and Satan was true, that it really happened? Or was he simply quoting a story well known to his readers to illustrate a point? We have no way of telling (for further details, see the "Bridging Contexts" section).

(2) More important for our immediate purposes is the significance of the story for Jude. According to most English translations (including the NIV), the main point is that Michael, archangel though he was, "did not dare to bring a slanderous accusation against him [Satan]." The connection with verse 8, through the idea of "slander," is clear. Presumably, Jude's point is that the false teachers are so presumptuous as to do what even Michael, the archangel,

---

21. Sometimes there are four chief angels, sometimes seven (see Bauckham, *Jude, 2 Peter*, 60).

22. There is considerable controversy over the existence and relationship of these two books and which one Jude may have referred to. An up-to-date survey of the situation can be found in Bauckham, *Jude, 2 Peter*, 65–76.

refused to do: rebuke, without the Lord's authority and backing, Satan or his associates. For Michael did not himself rebuke Satan; he called on the Lord to do so. The false teachers, however, disparage evil angels on their own authority.

With the "these" at the beginning of verse 10, Jude returns to his characterization of the false teachers. We should view verse 9, then, as a quick illustrative interruption in his criticism of these heretics. The NIV unfortunately disrupts the verbal continuity from verses 8 and 9—the verb translated "speak abusively against" is again the verb "blaspheme" or "slander." Thus the first part of verse 10 wraps up Jude's criticism of the false teachers for slandering evil angels: What they do not even understand, they slander.

Oh, yes, Jude goes on, there are some things they do "understand."[23] But they understand them "by instinct, like unreasoning animals." As the parallel in 2 Peter 2:12 suggests, Jude is here describing the false teachers' sexual excesses. Rather than following the "reason" of God's word, they act at the level of pure instinct—like animals, with no moral compass or sense of right and wrong. No wonder that they are "destroyed" by these things. Thus Jude ends his paragraph on the note that has been so important throughout: the eschatological judgment that will strike the false teachers in Jude's churches, just as it struck the desert generation, the angels who sinned, and Sodom and Gomorrah.

 **Bridging Contexts**

AS WE BEGIN to think further about the significance of these verses for the Christian church, two issues in these verses cry out for further exploration: Jude's use of traditional material and his reference to homosexuality at Sodom and Gomorrah.

Use of traditional material. At several points in this commentary, I have looked in some detail at the authors' use of traditional material. This is because 2 Peter and Jude depend heavily on both the Old Testament and on Jewish traditions. And, as I have argued, appreciating the traditions they are using enhances our understanding of what it is they are trying to communicate to their readers. Jude 5–10 is another passage deeply indebted to traditional material. A closer look at the background and significance of some of these traditions will help us to apply these verses more effectively.

(1) We should observe that Jude is not the first to gather together the examples of sin and judgment that he features in verse 5–7. Jewish writers

---

23. Here the NIV creates a word play in English that is not evident in the Greek; the first "understand" in the verse translates the Greek word *oida*; the second a different Greek word, *epistemi*.

before him had used the same combination of examples. Note the following texts:

Sirach 16:7–10	*Damascus Document* 2:17–3:12	*3 Maccabees* 2:4–7
"ancient giants [= angels of Gen. 6] who revolted in their might. He [God] did not spare the neighbors of Lot. . . . He showed no pity for a nation devoted to destruction. . . ."	"the Watchers of the heavens [= angels of Gen. 6] fell. . . . their males [of God's people] were cut off in the desert"	"You destroyed . . . the giants. . . . You consumed with fire and sulphur the men of Sodom. . . ."

Testament of Naphtali 3:4–5	*Mishnah Tractate Sanhedrin* 10:3
" . . . so that you do not become like Sodom, which departed from the order of nature. Likewise the Watchers departed from nature's order."	'The men of Sodom have no share in the world to come. . . . The generation of the desert have no share in the world to come."

To be sure, only Sirach has all three references, and the other texts allude to other examples besides these three. But these texts still demonstrate the general pattern of reference that we find also in Jude 5–7.

What do we gain by observing this pattern? (a) It confirms our conclusion that Jude is referring to the story of Genesis 6 when he mentions "angels who did not keep their positions" (v. 6). Four of the five texts cited above refer to this story, calling these fallen angels "Watchers," as was typical in intertestamental Judaism, or referring to their offspring as the "giants." Since Jews were accustomed to including the "sons of God" story from Genesis 6 along with allusions to Sodom and Gomorrah and the desert generation, we are safe in thinking that Jude does too.

(b) We can guess that the pattern was already known to Jude's readers. They would have been familiar with the tradition that singled out these (and similar) incidents as warning examples about the dangers of sin. They would have known that the people who committed these sins suffered condemnation, that they had "no share in the world to come" (cf. the *Mishnah*). Jude's putting of the false teachers into this same paradigm would therefore have considerable rhetorical effect. By associating them with established groups of notorious sinners, Jude adds emotional strength to his condemnation. It is similar to our labeling a political opponent as a "Benedict Arnold" or accusing a particularly dictatorial boss of being a "little Hitler."

(c) Another byproduct of our recognition of this tradition behind Jude

5–7 is a certain caution in the application of the details of these examples to the false teachers. Jude may mention one or more of these groups of sinners because they were part of the tradition rather than because they displayed characteristics exactly similar to the false teachers. True, he finds a general similarity, but the likeness need not extend to the details. We cannot necessarily conclude, for example, that the false teachers were guilty of homosexuality just because the men of Sodom and Gomorrah were. The parallel between the two groups may involve no more than the flaunting of biblical mandates about sexuality.

(2) Jude's use of traditional material in these verses raises a second issue: How much of the tradition that he cites does he intend to take over? The question comes up, first, in his use of the Jewish tradition about the "sons of God" based on Genesis 6:1–4. As we have noted, this tradition assumed that the "sons of God" were angels who came down to earth and had sexual relationships with human women. The problem with Jude's use of this tradition is that many, perhaps most, evangelical scholars would argue that this is not the meaning of Genesis 6:1–4. In the "Bridging Contexts" section on 2 Peter 2:4–10a, I explore this whole problem. Suffice to say here that a good case for identifying the "sons of God" with angels can be made, and that we must at least ask whether the biblical author is endorsing the truth of the story or is simply citing a tradition that he knows to be popular among his readers.

Here in Jude, as in 2 Peter, this last question is not easy to answer. But we must admit it is difficult to think that Jude viewed the story of the angels in verse 6 any differently than he did the story of the desert generation in verse 5 and the history of Sodom and Gomorrah in verse 7. J. Daryl Charles, however, has argued that, while agreeing with the tradition to the extent of associating a fall of angels with the time of Noah's flood, Jude does not clearly take over the sexual nature of the sin that they committed.[24] Charles makes a good point; biblical authors do not always take over all the details of the Jewish traditions that they use, and we should note that Jude makes no explicit mention of the angels' sexual sin. To be sure, many commentators think that it is implied because of the parallel with the men of Sodom and Gomorrah. But the connection remains implicit, and we should be careful not to make Jude say more than he does.

But the issue of Jude's use of traditional material surfaces as an even greater problem in verse 9. For here Jude does not even refer to a canonical book, but to a story that appears in a book—*The Assumption of Moses* or *The Testament*

---

24. J. Daryl Charles, *Literary Strategy in the Epistle of Jude*, 108–16.

of Moses—that no religious group has ever considered canonical. We have here, I think, two options.

(a) Jude may have viewed this story as a popular "legend" with which both he and his readers were familiar and which he could use to illustrate his point. To use an analogy, he may be doing what the modern preacher does when he says, to illustrate the new world in which Christians live, "as Dorothy said to Toto, 'I don't think we're in Kansas anymore!'" The preacher is not assuming that *The Wizard of Oz* is an authoritative source or even that the story it tells is true. It is a fictional work that serves, at this point, to illustrate a truth.

Could Jude regard the story about Michael and the devil in a similar way? It is entirely possible. His readers evidently held apocalyptic literature like *The Assumption/The Testament of Moses* in high regard, and it would be entirely natural for him to appeal to a story that they knew well.[25] We cannot be sure of this, however; and some would argue that it would have been difficult for Jude's readers to see the difference between this story and the other (Old Testament) examples in this section.

(b) A second option, then, is to assume that Jude believes that this incident really did take place. This does not mean, however, that Jude thinks that the book from which the story is taken is canonical or even totally accurate. It would mean only that Jude believes that this story is true. How would he know that? We must, I think, at this point, fall back on our belief in the inspiration of the Bible. Jude wrote under the direction of the Spirit of God, who led him to this particular passage—and kept him from citing other texts that did not contain true stories.

The issue of homosexuality. Finally, the contentious issue of homosexuality requires some comment. In the next section, we will talk about the contemporary significance of allusions such as we find in Jude 7. Here, we want to sketch briefly the biblical context for the discussion.

The story of Sodom and Gomorrah in Genesis 19 never explicitly identifies the sin of homosexuality as the reason why God destroyed the cities. The Lord tells Abraham before the destruction that "the outcry against Sodom and Gomorrah is so great and their sin so grievous that I will go down and see if what they have done is as bad as the outcry that has reached me" (18:20–21). The angels sent to investigate the situation say much the same thing just before the destruction comes (19:13). But, since the story of the angels' visit focuses on the attempt of the men of Sodom to have sex with the angels, it seems obvious that it is because of this sin, in particular, that God destroys the cities. To be sure, the prophet Ezekiel lists other sins of

---

25. See Roger Beckwith, *The Old Testament Canon of the Christian Church and Its Background in Judaism* (Grand Rapids: Eerdmans, 1985), 401–5; A. Plummer, *The General Epistles of St. James and St. Jude* (London: Hodder & Stoughton, 1891), 424.

which "Sodom" was guilty: arrogance, a luxurious lifestyle, and unconcern about the poor. But in Genesis 19 itself, it is homosexuality, called by Lot "a wicked thing" (19:7), that receives the attention. That homosexuality was the sin that led to the destruction of Sodom and Gomorrah is, of course, the traditional understanding; it led to the use of the words "sodomy" and "sodomite" to denote homosexual activity.

Genesis 19, however, is by no means the only Old Testament text that condemns homosexuality. It is clearly prohibited in God's law to the Israelites:

Leviticus 18:22: "Do not lie with a man as one lies with a woman; that is detestable."
Leviticus 20:13: "If a man lies with a man as one lies with a woman, both of them have done what is detestable. They must be put to death; their blood will be on their own heads."

During the later stages of the intertestamental period, Jews came more and more into contact with the Greek world, where homosexual relationships were common. Indeed, many Greeks valued a loving sexual relationship between males more highly than heterosexual sex. Confrontation with this world led Jewish writers to assert even more strongly the biblical ban on homosexuality. As J. D. G. Dunn accurately summarizes the situation, "antipathy to homosexuality remains a consistent and distinctive feature of Jewish understanding of what man's createdness involves and requires."[26]

We must keep this background in mind when we come to assess the significance of such references as we have in Jude 7 for the practice of homosexuality in our day. We now turn to that matter.

THE ISSUE OF **homosexuality**. In the latest stage in the modern "sexual revolution," tolerance for homosexuality has become accepted in an astonishingly short period of time. Attitudes have changed so rapidly that what would have been assumed without argument only fifteen years ago—that, let us say, an avowed homosexual should not be a school teacher—now has to be strenuously argued and may not, when all is said and done, be agreed to by most people.

Christians, of course, are not immune to these changes. Admit it or not, our attitudes are deeply influenced by movements in the culture of which we are inescapably a part. Thus, Christians are reevaluating their understanding of homosexuality, and some insist we need to revise our view. The church has been wrong, they claim, to brand homosexuality as a sin. The idea that

26. J. D. G. Dunn, *Romans 1–8*, WMC (Waco, Tex.: Word, 1988), 65–66.

homosexuality is sinful is a misunderstanding of what the New Testament teaches on the matter. To apply Jude 7, therefore, we need briefly to evaluate the larger issue of homosexuality in the New Testament.

In addition to the allusion to homosexuality in Jude 7, we find three other passages in the New Testament that condemn homosexuality:

> Because of this, God gave them over to shameful lusts. Even their women exchanged natural relations for unnatural ones. In the same way the men also abandoned natural relations with women and were inflamed with lust for one another. Men committed indecent acts with other men, and received in themselves the due penalty for their perversion. (Rom. 1:26–27)

> Do you not know that the wicked will not inherit the kingdom of God? Do not be deceived: Neither the sexually immoral nor idolaters nor adulterers nor male prostitutes nor homosexual offenders nor thieves nor the greedy nor drunkards nor slanderers nor swindlers will inherit the kingdom of God. (1 Cor. 6:9–10)

> We also know that law is made not for the righteous but for lawbreakers and rebels, the ungodly and sinful, the unholy and irreligious; for those who kill their fathers or mothers, for murderers, for adulterers and perverts, for slave traders and liars and perjurers—and for whatever else is contrary to the sound doctrine. (1 Tim. 1:9–10)

Christians in the past have almost universally thought that these passages condemned all forms of homosexuality as sinful and deserving of God's judgment. But some scholars are now persuaded that these texts teach no such thing. They generally pursue two, sometimes overlapping, lines of argument.

(1) Some suggest that key words Paul uses in these verses have a restricted meaning. For instance, J. Boswell argues that the word translated in the NIV of 1 Corinthians 6:10 as "homosexual offenders" (*arsenokoitai*) refers to male prostitutes who have sex with either men or women (this same word appears in 1 Tim. 1:10 [NIV, "perverts"]). In other words, if the word refers to male prostitutes only, neither text condemns homosexual practice generally.[27] But the meaning of the word that Boswell argues for is unlikely. The term picks up in Greek the language about homosexuality used in Leviticus 18:22 and 20:13; and, as we noted above, both texts speak simply of homosexuality.[28]

(2) Revisionists suggest that while some texts in Paul may seem to con-

---

27. J. Boswell, *Christianity, Social Tolerance and Homosexuality* (Chicago: Univ. of Chicago, 1980), 341–52.

28. See esp. David F. Wright, "Homosexuals or Prostitutes? The Meaning of *Arsenokoitai* (1 Cor. 6:9; 1 Tim. 1:10)," *Vigiliae Christianae* 38 (1984): 125–53.

demn homosexuality, this does not represent Paul's real attitude. Paul is simply picking up his Jewish tradition without endorsing it.[29] But this will not do. How are we to know when Paul agrees with a tradition he cites or not? Virtually anything Paul says can be dismissed by such a procedure.

The bottom line in the New Testament seems to be this. As is the case with many issues, we can expect that the New Testament writers agree with the Old Testament teaching except when they explicitly indicate their disagreement. The Old Testament is clear about the nature of homosexuality: It is a sin. Nowhere does the New Testament disagree; in at least four texts, we have argued, it endorses the Old Testament viewpoint. When we add to this that Jewish teaching was unanimous in condemning homosexuality, then trying to argue any other viewpoint in the New Testament is a clear case of wishful thinking.

The fact that we have so few references does not mean that homosexuality was no big deal to the New Testament writers; it means that they simply assumed the view that was endemic in Jewish culture. As D. F. Wright comments about Paul, "he saw same-sex activity as so self-evidently contrary to God's creative purpose as to allow of such brief—but eloquent—mention."[30] We find on this matter simply another instance in which people are trying to read current societal mores *into* the Bible rather than letting the Bible determine those mores.

We must recognize in this regard the incredibly strong temptation for people to find a value system that will endorse the kind of behavior they have chosen. In his last novel, *Resurrection*, Leo Tolstoy describes just such a situation. The novel focuses on the efforts of a nobleman named Nekhlyudov to redeem a woman, Maslova, whom he had seduced and thus led into a life of prostitution. Nekhlyudov is surprised when Maslova rebuffs his attempts to reform her and when she expresses no shame for the kind of life she was leading. Tolstoy comments:

> And yet it could not be otherwise. Everybody, in order to be able to act, has to consider his occupation important and good. Therefore, in whatever position a person is, he is certain to form such a view of the life of men in general as will make his occupation seem important and good.
>
> It is usually acknowledged that a thief, a murderer, a spy, a prostitute, acknowledging his or her profession to be evil, is ashamed of it. But the contrary is true. People whom fate and their sin-mistakes have

---

29. See, for instance, Robin Scroggs, *The New Testament and Homosexuality* (Philadelphia: Fortress, 1983).

30. D. F. Wright, "Homosexuality," in *Dictionary of Paul and his Letters*, ed. Gerald F. Hawthorne and Ralph P. Martin (Downers Grove, Ill.: InterVarsity, 1993), 414.

placed in a certain position, however false that position may be, form a view of life in general which makes their position seem good and admissible. In order to keep up their view of life, these people instinctively keep to the circle of those who share their views of life and of their own place in it. This surprises us where the persons concerned are thieves bragging about their dexterity, prostitutes vaunting their depravity, or murderers boasting of their cruelty. But it surprises us only because the circle, the atmosphere, in which these people live, is limited, and chiefly because we are outside it.[31]

In other words, we must understand that people caught in the sin of homosexuality will seek to justify their sin; attempts to make the Bible condone such behavior should not be surprising. (We should add that Tolstoy goes on to condemn people generally for such a self-asserting value system. Perhaps we need also to ask whether each of us has not similarly learned to tolerate certain sins by living in a restricted "circle.")

Christians committed to the authority of the Bible must therefore bring to bear the teaching of the Bible on this matter. We must resolutely refuse to allow the culture to shift our values or to compromise on our application of them. Homosexual behavior is sinful, a form of behavior that can exclude people from the kingdom of God (1 Cor. 6:9–10). As stewards of the gospel, we are entrusted with this message.

But we must proclaim this message in the right spirit. The accusation of "homophobia" is being used to criticize anybody who calls into question homosexuality as an alternative lifestyle. And this, of course, is both ridiculous and dangerous—it implies that anyone who speaks against homosexuality is motivated by irrational fear. But we must recognize that genuine homophobia does exist in the church—that some Christians speak out strongly and even harshly against homosexuality for the wrong reasons. We need to speak out, but we need to speak because we are concerned to defend scriptural values and because we love those who are homosexual. For the "loving" act in such a situation is not to keep quiet, mind our own business, and let homosexuals pursue their chosen lifestyle right to the gates of hell. The loving act is to reach out with the gospel to homosexuals.

It is, of course, only the power of God unleashed in the gospel that can break through the circle of approval that Tolstoy describes and transform the homosexual. Current secular theory about homosexuality is placing more and more emphasis on nature, rather than "nurture," as the cause of homosexual behavior. Homosexuals, we are now being told, are genetically predisposed to the sin. But even if this is so—and the jury is still out on the

---

31. Leo Tolstoy, *Resurrection* (New York: Oxford Univ. Press, 1994), 164–65.

scientific data—homosexual behavior is not unchangeable. Many people are predisposed, for all kinds of reasons, to certain sins—this is no excuse in God's eyes. The important point is that the gospel offers people the power to turn from their sin. Note what Paul remarks about the Corinthians, after describing all kinds of sinful people (including homosexuals): "And that is what some of you were. But you were washed, you were sanctified, you were justified in the name of the Lord Jesus Christ and by the Spirit of our God" (1 Cor. 6:11).

The abuse of visions. One other point from this section in Jude deserves brief mention before we leave it: the abuse of "visions." Jude's disparaging reference to the false teachers as "these dreamers" (v. 8) suggests that they were justifying their conduct on the basis of visions that they had received. The Bible, of course, emphasizes the value of visions; God often communicated his word to Old Testament prophets in visions, and practically the entire book of Revelation is the record of John's visions. But the Bible also recognizes that people abuse this method of revelation by making fraudulent claims to have received visions from God. There are "false prophets" as well as true prophets (see 2 Peter 2:1).

Our own day has seen a renewed interest in visions and prophecies. The Vineyard movement, in particular, has placed considerable emphasis on prophetic "words" that encourage and direct the church. Some of the spokespersons for the movement have sought to curb abuses by laying down careful and generally biblical guidelines for the exercise of the prophetic gift. But one still finds considerable abuse of the gift, as people seek to justify dubious or even sinful behavior on the basis of a vision, or try to get their own way on a contentious matter by claiming to have received direction from God.

We cannot simply dismiss visions altogether: God may still choose to communicate to his people by this means. But we must insist that any claimed visionary or prophetic message must conform to the truth of God revealed in Scripture and must be subject to scrutiny by other Christians. Paul himself insists that the messages received by Christian prophets be evaluated by other prophets (or other Christians; cf. 1 Cor. 14:29).

Jude 11–13

WOE TO THEM! They have taken the way of Cain; they have rushed for profit into Balaam's error; they have been destroyed in Korah's rebellion. ¹²These men are blemishes at your love feasts, eating with you without the slightest qualm—shepherds who feed only themselves. They are clouds without rain, blown along by the wind; autumn trees, without fruit and uprooted—twice dead. ¹³They are wild waves of the sea, foaming up their shame; wandering stars, for whom blackest darkness has been reserved forever.

Original Meaning

JUDE IS NOT yet finished with the false teachers. So concerned is he about their potential to harm his readers' walk with the Lord that he is not satisfied his strong polemic against them in verses 5–10 has done the job. He thus launches one more attack against them. Like the first one, this one also begins with three examples of notorious Old Testament sinners (v. 11). The second part of the paragraph (vv. 12–13) also follows the pattern Jude has established in that, with the word "these," he focuses attention directly on the false teachers, characterizing them in six brief and very negative descriptions.

Three Old Testament Examples (v. 11)

THERE ARE TWO main differences between this verse and verses 5–7. (1) Jude's three Old Testament examples serve to back up his "woe" pronouncement on the false teachers. The English word "woe" is a transliteration of the Greek word *ouai*, which is, in turn, the transliteration of a Hebrew word. This word was used especially by the prophets in the Old Testament to announce the pain and distress people would experience as a result of God's judgment on them. See, for instance, Isaiah 3:11: "Woe to the wicked! Disaster is upon them! They will be paid back for what their hands have done."

The "woe oracle" often included both a reference to judgment and to the reason for that judgment. In this vein, Jude mentions the judgment the false teachers will experience ("they have been destroyed") and the reason for their judgment: They "have taken the way of Cain; they have rushed for profit into Balaam's error; they [have taken the way of] Korah's rebellion."

(2) A second difference between verses 5–7 and verse 11 is that Jude does not just cite Old Testament examples, with application to come later. He directly implicates the false teachers in the sinful behavior and judgment that he describes with his Old Testament examples. Cain, Balaam, and Korah thus become "types"—people whose behavior prefigures that of their New Testament "antitypes." It is probably for this reason that all three verbs in the verse are in a tense that is usually past-referring—cf. NIV, "they have taken," "they have rushed," "they have been destroyed." Jude speaks this way because the actions of the Old Testament types were, of course, in the past. But because these people are "types," their actions are, in a sense, timeless. Thus, the use of the present tense in English may better capture the idea—cf. NRSV, "Woe to them! For they *go* the way of Cain, and *abandon* themselves to Balaam's error for the sake of gain, and *perish* in Korah's rebellion."

Jude's first example is Cain, who murdered his brother out of envy (Gen. 4:1–16; cf. 1 John 3:11). In what way does Jude think the false teachers "go the way of Cain"? He may be suggesting that as Cain murdered Abel, so the false teachers "murder" the souls of people.

In Jewish tradition, however, Cain became a classic example of an ungodly skeptic. The Jerusalem Targum, an Aramaic paraphrase of the Pentateuch, presents Cain as claiming, "There is no judgment, no judge, no future life; no reward will be given to the righteous, and no judgment will be imposed on the wicked." Jude's intention may therefore be to reinforce his accusation of the false teachers as being rejecters of authority and blasphemers (see vv. 8–10).[1] Another Jewish tradition views Cain as a corrupter of humankind; Josephus claims that "he incited to luxury and pillage all whom he met, and became their instructor in wicked practices."[2] In other words, Jude may also be pointing to the false *teaching* dimension of these ungodly people. The problem with both these latter views is that we cannot be sure which, if any, Jewish tradition Jude may have had in mind.

Balaam, the second character in Jude's list, is known in the Bible especially for his greed, an emphasis Jude picks up also by claiming that the false teachers follow the way of Balaam out of a desire for "reward" or "gain" (*misthos*; cf., for a similar emphasis, 2 Peter 2:15–16). According to the story in Numbers 22–24, Balak, king of Moab, desperate to halt a threatened Israelite invasion, tries to hire Balaam to curse Israel. Although Balaam eventually refuses to do what Balak wants, he wavers enough in his loyalty to the Lord to justify the later view of him as a man who led Israel into sin for the sake of monetary

---

1. Green, *The Second Epistle General of Peter and the General Epistle of Jude*, 172.

2. *Antiquities* 1.61 (the quotation is from *Josephus: Jewish Antiquities, Books I–IV*, trans. by H. St. J. Thackeray, LCL [Cambridge, Mass.: Harvard Univ. Press, 1957], 29). See also Philo, *The Posterity and Exile of Cain* 38–39. See esp. Bauckham, *Jude, 2 Peter*, 79, for this line of interpretation.

reward.[3] Jude may well be implying that the false teachers also are teaching what they are because they can make money by it. We know of many traveling teachers in the ancient world who taught people whatever it would pay them to teach; these false teachers may have been doing the same.

Korah's story is told in Numbers 16:1–35. He "became insolent and rose up against Moses" (vv. 1–2), leading 250 other prominent Israelites in rebellion against Moses' leadership. In response, God caused the earth to open up and swallow Korah, his followers, and their households. The text also mentions judgment by fire, as does a later commentary on the incident (Ps. 106:16–18). As early as the time of Moses, Korah had become "a warning sign" to those who might be tempted to rebel against the Lord and his appointed leaders (cf. Num. 26:9–10).

Jewish tradition followed this lead; Korah became "the classic example of the antinomian heretic."[4] Jude may therefore associate the false teachers with Korah because they too were refusing to listen to the duly appointed leaders of God's people.[5] But this may be overly specific; perhaps Jude wants to focus attention simply on the false teachers' rebellious, antinomian attitude. In any case, he almost certainly cites Korah last (out of canonical order) because of the sudden and spectacular judgment that he and his followers experienced. Such is the fate of the false teachers also, who will be "destroyed" on the Day of the Lord.[6]

Application of the Examples to the False Teachers (vv. 12–13)

IN VERSE 8, Jude made the application of his Old Testament examples clear with the phrase "in the very same way." Here he is more abrupt, probably because he has already implicated the false teachers in the sins (and judgment) of his examples. Thus he moves straight into further description without obvious connection with the examples he has cited in verse 11. Verses 12–13 contain six brief descriptions of these false teachers.

(1) "These men are blemishes at your love feasts, eating with you without the slightest qualm." The NIV "blemishes" is a controversial translation (cf. also NRSV; TEV); the word also means "(hidden) reef" (cf. NASB). The first translation finds some support from the parallel in 2 Peter 2:13, where, in a

---

3. See, in the New Testament, Rev. 2:14; for the Jewish tradition, see especially the Targum on Num. 22–24; Philo, *Moses* 1.266–68; *Migration* 114. For more detail, see the notes on 2 Peter 2:15–16.

4. Bauckham, *Jude, 2 Peter,* 83. See, e.g., the Targum; Josephus, *Antiquities* 16.1.

5. Green, *The Second Epistle General of Peter and the General Epistle of Jude,* 173.

6. The past-referring tense Jude uses here (*apolonto,* an aorist) may be "timeless," or it may be reminiscent of the Hebrew "prophetic perfect," in which a prophecy was uttered with a past-referring tense to emphasize the certainty of its completion (Bauckham, *Jude, 2 Peter,* 84).

description of false teachers similar to the one here in Jude, Peter calls the heretics "blemishes" (*spiloi*).[7] But Jude uses a different word here, so that we should probably prefer the second rendering, "reef." If so, Jude is suggesting that the false teachers, like a hidden reef that rips the bottom out of a boat, lie in wait to bring destruction on the faithful.[8] The NJB captures the metaphorical significance very well: "They are a dangerous hazard at your community meals."

"Community meals" is not a bad rendering here for *agapais*. *Agape* means, of course, "love"; but the early Christians also began to apply the word to their joyful fellowship meals. These meals usually included both the celebration of the Lord's Supper (what we might call the "vertical" dimension) and the eating of a regular meal together (the "horizontal" dimension). The false teachers, Jude implies, continued to participate in these regular community meals without any hesitation (NIV, "without the slightest qualm"; lit., "without fear"). By doing so they posed a real danger to other believers, who might be emboldened by their example to think that one could remain a Christian while following such a libertine lifestyle.

(2) "Shepherds who feed only themselves." The shepherd is the epitome of a person who selflessly watches out for others. It was therefore a natural term to apply both to the Lord (e.g., Ps. 23; cf. John 10:1–18) and to the leaders of the people of God in the Old Testament (e.g., 2 Sam. 5:2) and in the New (Acts 20:28; 1 Peter 5:2). But the false teachers were abandoning their natural responsibility to care for others, thinking only of themselves. Jude is likely alluding to Ezekiel 34:2: "Son of Man, prophesy against the shepherds of Israel; prophesy and say to them: This is what the Sovereign LORD says: Woe to the shepherds of Israel who only take care of themselves! Should not shepherds take care of the flock?'" This reference to shepherds may, of course, imply that the false teachers were leaders in the church.

(3) "They are clouds without rain, blown along by the wind." Jude's last four descriptions of the false teachers are all drawn from the natural world— and, whether intentionally or not, from each of the four regions of the earth, according to the ancients: the air (clouds), the earth (trees), the sea (waves), and the heavens (planets). "Clouds without rain" is a natural metaphor for those who do not deliver what they promise (cf. Prov. 25:14: "Like clouds and wind without rain is a man who boasts of gifts he does not give"). In a similar manner, Jude suggests, the false teachers make claims for themselves and for their teaching that they do not carry through on. Moreover, they are unstable, "blown along by the wind."

---

7. Bigg, *The Epistles of St. Peter and St. Jude*, 333; Neyrey, *2 Peter, Jude*, 74–75.

8. See, e.g., Mayor, *The Epistle of St. Jude and the Second Epistle of St. Peter*, 40–41; Kelly, *The Epistles of Peter and of Jude*, 270–71; Bauckham, *Jude, 2 Peter*, 85.

(4) "Autumn trees, without fruit and uprooted—twice dead." A tree that is still without fruit in the autumn (or "late autumn," as the Greek word suggests) has not fulfilled its purpose in being. And so "autumn trees" conveys a point similar to "waterless clouds."[9]

But why does Jude say that such trees are "uprooted—twice dead"? The equivalent terms in the Greek occur in the reverse order, with the phrase for "twice dead" coming first, and it may be best to preserve this order if we are to understand Jude's point. We should probably not assume that the language applies in any literal way to trees; Jude seems to have moved beyond his metaphor here to concentrate on the reality to which it points.

What does it mean for Jude, then, to claim that the false teachers have died, or will die, two times? Perhaps he is thinking of the false teachers' apostasy. They were once "dead" in their transgressions and sins (Eph. 2:1) but were made alive in Christ. Now, however, by rebelling against the Lord, they have slid back into the state of spiritual death (see, e.g., Heb. 6:4–8; 2 Peter 2:18–22).[10] A second possibility is that Jude refers to the false teachers' eventual judgment. The New Testament calls eschatological judgment "the second death" (Rev. 2:11; 20:6, 14; 21:8). So these false teachers, Jude may be alleging, will not only die physically; they will also die spiritually and eternally.[11] Both of these interpretations makes good sense in this context; but perhaps the second should be preferred, since Jude's readers seem well acquainted with the kind of apocalyptic writings in which condemnation is called a "second death." "Uprooted," then, completes this picture of judgment. The whole description is reminiscent of Jesus' parable about the fig tree that did not bear fruit (Luke 13:6–8).

(5) "They are wild waves of the sea, foaming up their shame" (v. 13a). Jude here is probably dependent on Isaiah 57:20: "But the wicked are like the tossing sea, which cannot rest, whose waves cast up mire and mud."[12] The word "shame" in the Greek is plural; Jude is thinking of the "shameful deeds" committed by the false teachers.

---

9. Jude may have in mind here another passage from *1 Enoch* (80:2–3; quotation is from *The Old Testament Pseudepigrapha*, vol. 1: *Apocalyptic Literature and Testaments*, ed. James H. Charlesworth [Garden City, N.Y.: Doubleday, 1983], 58):

> In respect to their days, the sinners and the winter are cut short. Their seed shall lag behind in their lands and in their fertile fields, and in all their activities upon the earth. He will turn and appear in their time, and withhold rain; and the sky shall stand still at that time. Then the vegetable shall slacken and not grow in its season, and the fruit shall not be born in its proper season.

10. Mayor, *The Epistle of St. Jude and the Second Epistle of St. Peter*, 42–43; Green, *The Second Epistle General of Peter and the General Epistle of Jude*, 175–76.

11. Kelly, *The Epistles of Peter and of Jude*, 273; Bauckham, *Jude, 2 Peter*, 88.

12. James also uses the restless sea as an image of spiritual inconstancy (James 1:6).

(6) "Wandering stars, for whom the blackest darkness has been reserved forever" (v. 13b). Ancient people believed that the heavens should display order and regularity. They therefore had difficulty in accounting for the planets, which seemed to "wander" across the night sky in no discernible pattern. It is the planets to which Jude is probably referring here (in fact, the Greek verb behind "wander" [*planao*] is the word from which we get the English "planet").[13]

But Jude may be suggesting a deeper reference. Because ancient people were offended by the planets' lack of regularity, they often attributed their movements to evil angels. *First Enoch*, the book that Jude refers to so often in this letter, gives one version of this myth:

> And I saw the seven stars (which) were like great, burning mountains. (Then) the angel said (to me), "This place is the (ultimate) end of heaven and earth: it is the prison house for the stars and the powers of heaven. And the stars which roll over upon the fire, they are the ones which have transgressed the commandments of God from the beginning of their rising because they did not arrive punctually." (18:13–15)[14]

Whether we are to see this further comparison of the false teachers to the evil angels is not clear. What is clear is that Jude has again stressed the instability of these people.

Jude concludes this paragraph on the same note that he has sounded at the end of every paragraph and sub-paragraph in this section—judgment:[15] "for whom blackest darkness has been reserved forever." "Darkness," along with "fire," is a popular biblical image for the judgment of God (see the "Bridging Contexts" section for further discussion). Jude again uses his favorite word "keep" (NIV, "reserved"), here in the negative sense of "keep under sentence until punishment" (see also v. 6).

THE LAST PHRASE of this paragraph, "for whom blackest darkness has been reserved forever," poses a problem of application. Where is this darkness that the false teachers will be in "forever"? And does this assertion square with Jude's claim that these same people will be "destroyed" (v. 11; cf. v. 5) and that the people of Sodom and

---

13. See, e.g., Kelly, *The Epistles of Peter and of Jude*, 274; Bauckham, *Jude, 2 Peter*, 89. Other commentators think that Jude may be referring to shooting stars, which fall into the darkness of the earth (Green, *The Second Epistle General of Peter and the General Epistle of Jude*, 176).

14. The quotation is from *The Old Testament Pseudepigrapha*, ed. Charlesworth, 23.

15. See v. 7b, "punishment of eternal fire"; v. 10b, "destroy them"; v. 11c, "destroyed."

Gomorrah are "an example of those who suffer the punishment of eternal fire" (v. 7)?

Jude never uses the word "hell," nor does he directly teach about it. But the language we have just noted reveals that he assumes the reality of what we call hell. He uses punishment in hell as a deterrent, to keep his readers from following the disastrous road the false teachers have taken. But how are we to interpret and apply this language? We must survey the broader biblical teaching on hell before we can answer these questions.

The word "hell" itself is the translation of the Greek word *gehenna*, which in turn is the transliteration of a Hebrew phrase that means "Valley of Hinnom." This narrow gorge just outside Jerusalem had an evil reputation. Children were burned as sacrifices there in the Old Testament period (2 Kings 23:10; Jer. 7:31; 32:35), and the prophets used it as a symbol of judgment (Jer. 19:6; cf. Isa. 31:9; 66:24). Jews in the intertestamental period therefore began using the word to describe the last judgment.[16] From this context Jesus picked up the word as a way of referring to eschatological punishment (Matt. 5:22, 29–30; 10:28; 18:9; 23:15, 33; Mark 9:43, 45, 47; Luke 12:5; cf. James 3:6). New Testament writers use other words as well to refer to this place of punishment for the wicked, such as "Hades" (Matt. 11:23; 16:18; Luke 10:15; 16:23; Acts 2:27, 31; Rev. 1:18; 6:8; 20:13, 14) and "Tartarus" (2 Peter 2:4). But they more often simply describe the punishment or use images to try to capture its nature.

The New Testament clearly teaches and everywhere assumes that after death God will punish in "hell" those who refuse to trust in Christ in this life. But evangelical Christians disagree over two matters: the nature of punishment in hell, and the duration of the punishment. We will look briefly at each issue so that we can better understand what Jude is teaching here.

(1) The most common way hell is described in the New Testament is as a fire or a place of burning. Jude uses this language in verse 8: "the punishment of eternal fire." And because this language occurs so often, many believers throughout the history of the church have thought that hell was a place where people were literally burned.[17] Even in popular parlance we hear about "hellfire," and hell is regularly depicted by artists ancient and modern as a place of fire.

But we doubt whether Jesus and the New Testament writers ever intended us to take the language in this literal fashion. For one thing, as we have seen, the word "hell" itself was associated in Jesus' day with a physical place of burning (the Valley of Hinnom). The idea of fire could, therefore, come from the image and not from the actuality. The same association with fire was

---

16. See, e.g., Joachim Jeremias, "γέεννα," *TDNT*, 1.657–58.

17. A recent defense of this view is John F. Walvoord, "The Literal View," in *Four Views of Hell*, ed. William Crockett (Grand Rapids: Zondervan, 1992), 11–28, esp. 28.

facilitated by the way in which God actually destroyed Sodom and Gomorrah—by literal fire and burning sulphur. Furthermore, "fire" is clearly used as a symbol throughout Scripture. Note, for instance, the description of God's coming in Psalm 16:7–8:

> The earth trembled and quaked,
>> and the foundations of the mountains shook;
>> they trembled because he was angry.
> Smoke rose from his nostrils;
>> consuming fire came from his mouth,
>> burning coals blazed out of it.

This does not mean, of course, that "fire" must always be an image in the Bible, but it shows that it is a natural symbol of God's wrath. Perhaps the strongest argument in favor of taking "fire" to be an image of judgment, however, is the fact that the Bible uses conflicting language about hell. In Jude, for instance, hell is presented both as a place of fire and as a place of "darkness" (vv. 8 and 13). We find the same combination of images in other biblical passages and in intertestamental Jewish passages, from which the New Testament imagery is often drawn. In the Dead Sea Scrolls, for instance, we find passages that describe hell as "the gloom of everlasting fire" and as a place of "destruction by the fire of the dark regions."[18]

Now hell cannot be *both* a place of fire and of darkness. Both "fire" and "darkness," then, as most contemporary evangelical scholars recognize, are metaphors. They are ways of trying to capture through experiences common to this world the pain and horror of hell. They plainly teach that hell is a place where people suffer agonies. But exactly what these agonies are we cannot know for sure.[19] Surely, however, the simple fact that people in hell are forever separated from the God who created them and who loves them is one of the supreme causes of torment (see 2 Thess. 1:9: "They [sinners] will be punished with everlasting destruction and shut out from the presence of the Lord and from the majesty of his power"). Nevertheless, we cannot confine the agonies of hell only to the negative experience of deprivation; the language of "fire" and "darkness," while metaphorical, points to the infliction of punishment as well.

(2) However conceived, how long will this punishment last? Here again, Christians have traditionally insisted that punishment will be eternal. They note

---

18. The quotations are from *The Rule of the Community* (1QS) 2:8 and 4:13 (quoted from *The Dead Sea Scrolls Translated: The Qumran Texts in English*, ed. Florentino García Martínez, 2d ed. [Grand Rapids: Eerdmans, 1996], 4, 7).

19. A good recent defense of this view is William V. Crockett, "The Metaphorical View," in *Four Views of Hell*, 43–76.

that, like Jude 7, the New Testament consistently claims that the punishments of hell are "eternal" (cf. also "everlasting chains" in v. 6; also Matt. 25:41; Mark 9:43, 48; Luke 16:22–24; Rev. 14:9–11). But some Christians have always questioned whether the punishment of hell is eternal, and these alternative views seem to be gaining ground among evangelicals in recent years.

The most popular of these alternatives is "annihilationism." According to this interpretation, the wicked will simply be annihilated at death or shortly after undergoing a brief period of punishment after death. The strongest argument for this view also appears in Jude: the use of the word "destroy" to refer to the destiny of the wicked (v. 10; cf. v. 5; also 1 Cor. 3:17; Phil. 3:19; 1 Thess. 5:3; 2 Thess. 1:9; 2 Peter 2:1, 3; 3:7; Heb. 10:39). Defenders of this view also argue that it is more compatible with the love and justice of God.[20]

Annihilationism certainly has points in its favor; we should not automatically exclude it as an unorthodox viewpoint. But it does not finally explain the evidence of Scripture fairly. Negatively, the language of "destruction" in the texts we have mentioned does not necessarily mean "cease to exist"; the Greek words involved can mean "cease to be what one once was." In other words, when the Bible says that the wicked are "destroyed" at the judgment, it may mean that they cease to be the kind of people they once were. Judgment involves such a transformation in circumstances as to be called a "destruction" from the standpoint of this world's perspectives.

The strongest argument in favor of the traditional view is the language of "eternity" that is applied to hell. To be sure, one must always carefully interpret such language in the Bible; it does not always mean "forever" but can sometimes mean "for a long time." But convincing evidence that "eternal" punishment means punishment "forever" comes from texts such as Matthew 25:41, where "eternal fire" is parallel to "eternal life" (Matt. 25:46). The Bible does seem to teach that the wicked will experience in hell conscious and eternal punishment.

HELL CONJURES UP in the mind images of flames and a figure in red, with tail, horns, and a pitchfork. Hell and the devil have become staples in the comedian's storehouse of standard jokes. The whole idea of hell is viewed as "medieval"—a word that connotes to most moderns ideas of intolerance, superstition, and ignorance. Surveys routinely show that most people believe in heaven but few believe in hell.

---

20. See, for a summary of these arguments, Clark H. Pinnock, "The Conditional View," in *Four Views of Hell*, 135–66 (Pinnock actually defends a variety of annihilationism, called "conditional immortality").

Christians therefore experience considerable pressure from the larger culture to dismiss the idea of hell or at least to soft-peddle it. But many, I suspect, also find in the Christian tradition itself reason to avoid the subject. They are embarrassed at what they consider extreme and insensitive references to hell by Christian evangelists. The most famous historical example is the sermon "Sinners in the Hands of an Angry God," preached by the New England pastor and theologian Jonathan Edwards in the early 1700s. Edwards sought to stimulate repentance among his hearers by picturing in great detail the torments of hell:

> The body will be full of torment as full as it can hold, and every part of it shall be full of torment. They shall be in extreme pain, every joint of 'em, every nerve shall be full of inexpressible torment. They shall be tormented even to their fingers' ends. The whole body shall be full of the wrath of God. Their hearts and their bowels and their heads, their eyes and their tongues, their hands and their feet will be filled with the fierceness of God's wrath.[21]

In our own day of bumper-sticker theology, we find Christians warning, simply, "Turn or burn!"

Now, of course, Christians can be guilty of presenting hell in an insensitive or unloving manner. But the problem, I suspect, is that many Christians simply want to avoid the subject altogether. It does not fit well into the ethos of much contemporary Christianity, with its focus on the love of God and its preoccupation with helping people to "feel good" about themselves. Yet faithfulness to the biblical message and a balanced view of God as both loving *and* holy require that we maintain and proclaim a clear doctrine of hell. And, in fact, the Lord used Edwards' preaching to stimulate a great spiritual awakening.

Jude, as we have seen, minces no words when he talks about the fate of the false teachers: They will be "destroyed" (v. 11; cf. v. 10); they will "suffer the punishment of eternal fire" (v. 7); "blackest darkness has been reserved for them" (v. 13). One frequently hears it said that Jesus referred to hell more than any other person in the Bible. This is true in the technical sense—Jesus uses the word "hell" (Greek *gehenna*) more times than any biblical author. But, as we noted above, the biblical authors normally speak about "hell" without using the word, and I question whether we really have more teaching from Jesus on hell than from other New Testament writers.

Be that as it may, Jesus certainly is not shy about using the reality of hell to motivate his listeners to obedience. And not only does Jesus refer to hell;

---

21. Quotation taken from Crockett, "The Metaphorical View," 48.

he uses imagery to describe it that is certainly as picturesque as anything we find in Jonathan Edwards' famous sermon. In Mark 9:43, for instance, Jesus encourages his followers to turn from sin, warning them about "hell, where the fire never goes out." Just a few verses later (9:48), he presents hell as the place where "their worm does not die, and the fire is not quenched."

Paul too can be quite blunt about the fate awaiting those who reject Christ and persecute his people (2 Thess. 1:6–10):

> He [God] will pay back trouble to those who trouble you and give relief to you who are troubled, and to us as well. This will happen when the Lord Jesus is revealed from heaven in blazing fire with his powerful angels. He will punish those who do not know God and do not obey the gospel of our Lord Jesus. They will be punished with everlasting destruction and shut out from the presence of the Lord and from the majesty of his power on the day he comes to be glorified in his holy people and to be marveled at among all those who have believed.

Paul's theological basis for this prediction of the punishment of the wicked is significant: "God's judgment is right" (v. 5); "God is just" (v. 6). In other words, the theological basis for hell is the holiness and justice of God. We often lose sight of God's majestic and awesome holiness in the midst of our concern to present God as loving, kind, and gracious. Keeping our balance in our view of God is a precarious matter; it is terribly easy to neglect one side of his character or the other. I think the church in our day is more often over-balanced on the side of God's love.

As theologians and psychologists have pointed out, many people project a view of their own earthly father into their view of the heavenly Father. Now earthly fathers have all kinds of personalities. But we certainly live in a time when the emphasis in fatherhood is being placed less and less on disciplining and more and more on being sensitive and caring. To put it in an extreme fashion, the image of the father portrayed in our culture is often that of a weak wimp. We cannot help but project that image into our view of God. We think of him as a sort of "grandfatherly" type who loves us, who is quite willing to forgive us—and, of course, who would never punish us. The reality of God is quite different. So holy is he that people who confronted him in the Bible fell to their knees in fear and shame. And his holiness demands that he punish sinners.

All this suggests that we should not avoid in our preaching of the gospel the "negative" side of the picture. Not only does acceptance of the good news of God in Christ mean, positively, peace with God and the promise of eternal life; rejection of that message, we must warn, means eternal punishment. True, the Bible does not make clear precisely what this punishment will be. "Fire" and "darkness," we think, are metaphors—painful and fearful earthly experiences that convey something of the torment that awaits the wicked in hell. We may even choose other images that better communicate in our day the reality and terribleness of hell. As we do so, we must ask God to preserve us from vindictiveness or from an enjoyment of the torments of the wicked. We need to preach about hell, but we should always preach about it with tears in our eyes.

Jude 14–16

❦

ENOCH, THE SEVENTH from Adam, prophesied about these men: "See, the Lord is coming with thousands upon thousands of his holy ones ¹⁵to judge everyone, and to convict all the ungodly of all the ungodly acts they have done in the ungodly way, and of all the harsh words ungodly sinners have spoken against him." ¹⁶These men are grumblers and faultfinders; they follow their own evil desires; they boast about themselves and flatter others for their own advantage.

JUDE CAPS HIS denunciation of the false teachers with a prophecy. This in itself is nothing unusual; New Testament writers often apply ancient prophecies to their own situations. But what is unusual about this prophecy is its source. Enoch is a biblical figure, but no Old Testament book contains the prophecy quoted here—or, for that matter, any prophecy of Enoch. But we do find almost these exact words in the Jewish intertestamental book, *1 Enoch*. Clearly, then, Jude takes this prophecy from *1 Enoch*. His apparently authoritative use of a book that is not part of the canon raises some obvious questions (see discussion in the "Bridging Contexts" section).

We can understand why Jude chooses to quote this particular prophecy, for it reinforces the two key points that he has made about the false teachers. (1) They are "godless" (or "ungodly," v. 4; cf. also v. 18). This word occurs three times in the prophecy (cf. v. 15) and may have been what drew Jude's attention to it in the first place. (2) The false teachers will suffer the Lord's condemnation. Enoch's prophecy, of course, foretells the coming of the Lord as judge.

As he has in the two other paragraphs within this section devoted to the false teachers (vv. 5–10, 11–13), Jude follows his reference to tradition with application. Therefore, in verse 16 we find the word "these" again used to apply the point of the prophecy to the false teachers.

Enoch was an early descendant of Adam through the line of Adam's son Seth. He appears in the Old Testament only in genealogical lists (Gen. 5:18–24; 1 Chron. 1:3), but he stands out because of the comment made about him: "Enoch walked with God; then he was no more, because God took him away" (Gen. 5:24).[1] This verse apparently means that Enoch did not die, but, like Elijah (2 Kings 2:1–13), was transported directly to heaven; this supposition is confirmed by Hebrews 11:5, which reads, "By faith Enoch was taken from this life, so that he did not experience death; he could not be found, because God had taken him away."

The combination of this extraordinary commendation from God and the almost complete silence of Scripture about him made Enoch a fascinating character to the Jews. We therefore find a number of legends about him in the intertestamental literature; at least two books of apocalyptic visions, written during this period, are attributed to him.[2] It is one of these books, *1 Enoch* (actually a compilation of several distinct literary units), that Jude quotes from.

This book was popular in Jude's day, and both he (cf. v. 6) and Peter (1 Peter 3:19–20; 2 Peter 2:4) allude to it. Because Jews often counted inclusively (that is, they included the first and the last in a series that they were counting), Enoch was considered to be "the seventh from Adam"; the genealogical list goes Adam, Seth, Enosh, Kenan, Mahalalel, Jared, Enoch (Gen. 5:1–24). Both the author of *1 Enoch* (60:8; 93:3; cf. also another intertestamental book, *Jubilees* [7:39]) and Jude probably name Enoch the "seventh" because that number symbolized perfection.

It is not clear whether Jude intends to say that "Enoch prophesied about these men also [i.e., in addition to the wicked people of his own day]" or that "Enoch also [i.e., in addition to these other texts] prophesied about these men."[3] But the NIV is probably correct to suggest the latter by simply omitting the "also" (Greek *kai*). Like other New Testament writers, Jude assumes that the prophecies find their fulfillment in Christ and the church he founded. They can therefore apply the words of the prophets to their own circumstances.

The subject of Enoch's prophecy is a common theme in Jewish apocalyptic writers: the coming of God to judge the wicked. The text Jude quotes is *1 Enoch* 1:9. In one of the latest translations of this book into English, it reads:

> Behold, he will arrive with ten million of the holy ones in order to execute judgment upon all. He will destroy the wicked ones and censure all flesh on account of everything that they have done, that which the sinners and the wicked ones committed against him.[4]

---

1. The "Enoch" mentioned in Gen. 4:17–18 as the son of Cain is a different man.

2. These books are therefore what we call pseudepigraphical, which means anonymous works ascribed to well-known historical figures.

3. For the former, see Bigg, *The Epistles of St. Peter and St. Jude*, 336; for the latter, most of the commentators, including, e.g., Kelly, *The Epistles of Peter and of Jude*, 276.

4. This translation is based on the Ethiopic language version of *1 Enoch*. The book is also extant in Greek, and fragments of it have been discovered in Aramaic and Latin. Scholars

The original prophecy that Jude is quoting probably had the word "God" or "Lord" as subject, but Jude, understanding it in light of Christ, pictures "the Lord" Jesus as the one who comes. Both the Old Testament (e.g., Dan. 7:10) and the New claim that Jesus will be accompanied at his Parousia by huge numbers of angels (cf. Matt. 25:31).

The purpose of Jesus' coming is to "judge." In this context it is clear that this judgment is the negative one of condemnation. For although it is directed against "everyone," the sequel makes it clear that the prophecy means "all the wicked." In Jude's quotation of the prophecy, he goes out of his way to stress the "ungodly" character of these people. Indeed, the use of the word three times in one clause in verse 15 creates an almost awkward reading: "to convict all the *ungodly* of all the *ungodly* acts that they have done in an *ungodly* way." We certainly do not have to guess Jude's point!

But not only are these people judged for acting in an ungodly way; they have also sinned against God in speech. Jude may be alluding to another part of *1 Enoch* at this point, perhaps 27:2: "This accursed valley is for those accursed forever; here will gather together all (those) accursed ones, those who speak with their mouth unbecoming words against the Lord and utter hard words concerning his glory." The fact that a reference to sins of speech was probably not in the original text Jude quoted suggests that the idea was an important one for Jude. Presumably he added it because the false teachers were erring especially in this way (see vv. 8 and 10).

Jude continues this focus on sins of speech in his application of the prophecy to the false teachers in verse 16. The transition from verses 14–15 to verse 16 is apparently this: Enoch prophesied about ungodly people who would be judged by the Lord; "these men" are those ungodly people. They are, Jude says, "grumblers and faultfinders." Who are they grumbling against and finding fault with? Church leaders, some say. But the biblical background of the term "grumbler" suggests that these false teachers are directing their complaints against God himself. The word used here often occurs in Old Testament passages that depict Israelites "grumbling" against God for bringing the people out of Egypt into the inhospitable desert (see, e.g., Ex. 16:7–12; 18:3; Num. 14:27–29; 17:5, 10).[5] The false teachers, perhaps, are complaining about the restrictions that God's law has placed on their "freedom" to behave as they want.

Jude's second description of the false teachers in verse 16 picks up the reference to their "ungodly acts" from the Enoch prophecy: "They follow their

---

debate about which of the versions Jude might be quoting from; most think that, whatever version he knew, he was doing his own paraphrase in Greek. See especially Bauckham, *Jude, 2 Peter*, 94–96.

5. See, e.g., Kelly, *The Epistles of Peter and of Jude*, 278; Bauckham, *Jude, 2 Peter*, 98.

own evil desires." These evil desires probably encompass both the false teachers' sexual lust and greed (see vv. 8, 10–11).[6]

According to the NIV, Jude's third accusation against the false teachers here is that "they boast about themselves" (TEV is similar). But this rendering is open to question. A more literal translation of the Greek is, "and their mouth speaks haughty [or bombastic] things." This haughty speech could, of course, have taken the form of boasting. But the context suggests the idea of arrogant speech about or even toward God.[7]

Jude's final criticism returns to the issue of the false teachers' greed, which he has briefly alluded to in verse 11. He employs here a biblical idiom that denotes partiality or favoritism.[8] We cannot be sure about the exact form this greed-motivated favoritism took. Perhaps the false teachers were currying favor with the rich while ignoring the poor. Perhaps they, like many of their ancient compatriots, were teaching only the rich because only they could pay well.[9]

JUDE'S TEACHING HERE seems to be straightforward: The Lord will return to judge ungodly people, such as the false teachers bothering his churches. But the message is complicated by the form in which he has chosen to cast it: a "prophecy" from a book that is not a part of the biblical canon. Experts in the art of interpretation use the analogy of hearing to talk about the kind of problem we face here. If, for instance, I am listening to a football game on my car radio, my ability to follow the broadcast may be severely hindered by "noise." This noise could come from the radio itself, if the station were distant or weak enough and other stations kept interfering. Or it could come from within the car, if my family persisted in conversing while I was trying to listen to the game. Noise is what keeps us from really hearing and appreciating a message.

In the same way, a person trying to "hear" a written message may also have trouble understanding it because of "noise"—those preconceptions and

---

6. See, e.g., Kelly, *The Epistles of Peter and of Jude*, 278.

7. Kelly, *The Epistles of Peter and of Jude*, 279; Bauckham, *Jude, 2 Peter*, 99. These commentators support their view by suggesting that Jude may here be alluding to *The Assumption of Moses*, where a similar idea occurs. But while Jude alludes to this book in v. 9, the reference here is not so clear.

8. The Greek, literally, means "wondering at the face." It reflects the Greek translation of a Hebrew idiom, "lifting, or having regard for, the face," that occurs in the Old Testament to refer to partiality (see Gen. 19:21; Lev. 19:15; Deut. 10:17; Prov. 24:23; Amos 5:12). James uses a similar expression (see James 2:1).

9. See Bauckham, *Jude, 2 Peter*, 99–100. He refers to Mal. 2:9.

misunderstandings that "interfere" with our ability to hear what a writer is trying to say. In Jude 14–15, most of us find it hard to appreciate Jude's straightforward message about the Lord's return because of the noise thrown up by his use of a noncanonical source. We cannot really appreciate his point—we cannot take it to heart and really believe it—because he makes it in this apparently unorthodox manner. The point, then, is that we are not going to be able to apply Jude's message until we try to clear away some of the noise his quotation creates. Thus I want to look at some of the issues and options we face as we consider Jude's quotation of *1 Enoch*.

What, specifically, is the noise that Jude's quotation of *1 Enoch* creates for us? It is the idea that Jude may be quoting as an inspired and authoritative source of doctrine a book that is not in the canon of Scripture. And it is important to note here that *1 Enoch* has never been given official canonical status by *any* religious body. It has never been in the Jewish canon, nor in the "Apocrypha" (those books accepted by the Roman Catholic church but rejected by Protestants). But doesn't Jude's use of *1 Enoch* create, then, a problem for our belief that God has inspired only those books contained between the two covers of our Bibles and that only these books are to be used as an authoritative source of doctrine? If Jude can appeal to *1 Enoch*, why can't we appeal similarly to 2 Maccabees, or Sirach, or, for that matter, C. S. Lewis's *Mere Christianity*?

These questions are not new to the modern era. Early church theologians asked the same ones. They came to three different opinions on the matter. (1) Several church fathers considered *1 Enoch* to be an inspired book based on the reference here in Jude.[10] (2) Others took the opposite tack: Because Jude quoted a noncanonical book, Jude did not belong in the canon.[11] (3) Augustine thought that Jude's reference showed that *1 Enoch* was inspired at some points, but he argued that this did not mean that the entire book was inspired.[12] As we know, it was this third view, or something like it, that the ancient church as a whole finally adopted. Jude was accepted into the New Testament canon, while *1 Enoch* was officially rejected from the Old Testament canon.[13] Can we justify this decision today? How can we explain Jude's use of *1 Enoch*?

Many commentators assume or argue that Jude's reference to *1 Enoch* shows that he thought it was an inspired book, as authoritative as, for example, Genesis and Isaiah. They point out that not only does Jude quote from

---

10. Clement of Alexandria, *Eccl. Proph.* 3; Tertullian, *De cultu fem.* 1.3; *De Idol.* 15.6; cf. *The Epistle of Barnabas* 16.5.

11. Jerome reports these doubts; cf. *De vir. ill.* 4.

12. See his *City of God* 15.23.

13. See the *Apostolic Constitutions* 6.16.3 (c. A.D. 380).

1 Enoch; he also uses the verb "prophesy" to introduce the quotation and alludes to the book elsewhere in his letter (most clearly in v. 6). But I do not think this conclusion is justified. Let me make two critical points.

(1) As I noted in the "Bridging Contexts" section on 2 Peter 3:14–18, we have solid evidence that Jews and Christians in the first century were already operating with a "closed" Old Testament canon. Jesus' appeal to Scripture, the remarkable quotation pattern throughout the New Testament (according to which only books now found in the canon are called Scripture), the lack of any evidence of dispute between Jews and the first Christians on this matter—these and other bits of evidence suggest a widely accepted and set group of authoritative writings. Jude may, of course, be different, but we should not assume that without good evidence.

(2) It is crucial to note that Jude does *not* refer to *1 Enoch* as Scripture; that is, the critical word *graphe* ("Scripture") is not used here. The cognate verb of this word, *grapho*, is used throughout the New Testament to introduce Old Testament quotations: "as it is written," and this formula is not found here either. Moreover, we find other quotations in the New Testament from sources that no one would consider canonical. Paul, for instance, quotes from the pagan philosopher Aratus in his speech to the Athenians (Acts 17:28); certainly he did not think that this writer's *Phaenomena* (from which his quotation was taken) was a canonical book. To be sure, Jude claims that Enoch "prophesied." But this word need not mean "wrote an inspired prophetic book"; it could well mean simply "uttered in this instance a prophecy." The reference, in other words, could be to the immediate passage and not to the entire book.

I conclude that Jude probably did not think that *1 Enoch* was an inspired and canonical book. We do not have sufficient evidence to lead us to believe that he differed from the apparent consensus of mainstream Jewish and early Christian opinion on this matter. But how, then, did he view this text from *1 Enoch*? His use of the word "prophesy" and the placement of the quotation—as the wrap-up to his denunciation of the false teachers— suggest that he viewed the text as having authority for his readers.

The phrase "for his readers" is important here. As J. Daryl Charles has shown, the letter of Jude seems to have been written to Christians who were "into" apocalyptic ideas and traditions. Jude may well have quoted this particular prophecy because he knew it would carry weight with his audience.[14] They regarded this book highly, and a quotation from it would be effective in motivating them to agree with him.[15]

---

14. This is called an ad hominem argument.
15. Charles, *Literary Strategy in the Epistle of Jude*, 160–61.

Clearly, Jude thought that the content of the prophecy was true or he never would have quoted it. But did he believe that the historical Enoch really uttered this prophecy? It is certainly possible; God could well have seen to it that the unknown author of *1 Enoch* included at this point in his book a genuine prophecy of Enoch. But it is also possible that Jude meant no more than that the "Enoch" of the book both he and his writers knew about uttered this prophecy.

 HAVING, I TRUST, eliminated some of the background "noise" created by Jude's use of *1 Enoch*, let us try and listen carefully to what he is saying in these verses. Two points stand out.

The Lord's coming and evangelism. The Lord is coming back to judge. Enoch, whoever we understand him to be, undoubtedly meant the Lord God, Jehovah. His prophecy echoes the many Old Testament texts that predict the coming of God at the end of history to give victory and salvation to the righteous and to condemn the unrighteous (see, e.g., Isa. 40:10; 66:15; Mic. 1:3–5; Zech. 14:5).

This coming of God at the end of history was often pictured as parallel to the coming of God on Mount Sinai, when he gave his law to Israel. Note, for instance, the similarity between the prophecy of Enoch that Jude quotes and Deuteronomy 33:2:

> The LORD came from Sinai
>> and dawned over them from Seir;
>> he shone forth from Mount Paran.
> He came with myriads of holy ones
>> from the south, from his mountain slopes.

In a move typical of the New Testament appropriation of the Old Testament, however, Jude identifies "the Lord" with Jesus. And just as God came first to redeem and constitute his people (the Exodus and Sinai) and then promised to come again to deliver and judge, so Jesus, having come to redeem and constitute his people (the cross and resurrection), is coming again to redeem and judge.

As believers, we look forward to the day of Christ's coming with eagerness and anticipation; it is the "blessed hope" that comforts us in our present afflictions and encourages us to lead a life of holiness (see Titus 2:13–15). But, as this text in Jude reminds us, Christ is also coming to judge. How should this lead us to regard the vast majority of people all around us—people who do not know Christ?

The answer is obvious, yet all too difficult really to take to heart and so to live by. We push judgment far into the future; or, worse yet, we get the idea into our heads that God will not really judge people who are living generally "good" lives. Yet the Scripture is clear: Christ will come to judge "all the ungodly" (Jude 15); and "there is no one righteous, not even one; there is no one who seeks God. All have turned away, they have together become worthless; there is no one who does good, not even one" (Rom. 3:9b–12). Apart from a relationship with Jesus Christ, all those "good" people around us are, in God's sight, "ungodly" and therefore doomed to suffer condemnation when Christ comes back.

"People need the Lord," sings Steve Green. Do we really believe it? Do we believe it enough to do something about it? To make evangelism and missions as prominent a part of our church agenda as personal wellness and the edification of believers? To give sacrificially to those who are in the front lines of gospel ministry? To share the good news of Jesus Christ with that "good" coworker or "moral" neighbor? Never should we read biblical texts about judgment at the end of history without our consciences being disturbed and moved by these questions.

The Lord's coming and self-evaluation. There is another set of questions that biblical passages about judgment should also raise before us. As believers, we should look forward to the day of Christ's coming with joy, for it brings our final deliverance from sin, temptation, and bodily weakness. But contemplation of that day should also lead to serious self-evaluation. For although we need not fear rejection and condemnation, we know our lives will be scrutinized as Christ asks what we have done with the precious blessings he has entrusted to us (see Matt. 25:31–46; 2 Cor. 5:10).

Here, then, is the second point that we should hear in Jude 14–16. Christ, Jude says, is coming to judge the "ungodly." While no believer is finally in the category of the "ungodly," we cannot help but recognize how much ungodliness still clings to us, even in our redeemed state. Jude's reminder that Christ is coming to judge ungodliness, then, should create in us not a smug satisfaction that we are not among those to be judged; it should stimulate each of us to ask about the ungodliness that is still too much a part of us.

What is "ungodliness"? The term is a broad one, encompassing any thinking or behavior that does not meet God's approval. Jude undoubtedly uses the term precisely because it is so broad. But he also focuses in verses 15b–16 on the sin of haughtiness, pride, or arrogance. The ungodly people Jude is thinking of (the false teachers) "speak against" God; they "boast of themselves," or "speak haughty things." Here is a form of ungodliness that is a plague in our day.

Many theologians, indeed, think that pride is the root of all sin. Ever since Adam, people have wanted to "be like God," and they chafe at any idea of a God whom they must worship and obey. Our society, precisely because of its great accomplishments in science, medicine, literature, and so forth, is proud and makes less and less room for God. Or, if room is made for a god, it is a god of our own creation, tailored to suit us and what we deem our needs to be. Thus we sense the need for spirituality, some vague feeling of worship—and we create the "new age" god because we are "into" nature.

I could multiply examples. But my point here is that we Christians are far from immune from the arrogant presumption of making God fit our own expectations and needs. The history of the church reveals how often Christians in every age have tended to develop a view of God that fits into their own culture. Consequently, we must ask ourselves: In what way have we tailored our view of God to fit our situation? Or, to revert to the analogy I used in the previous section, what "noise" from our culture is interfering with our ability to listen to God and to his message for us in our generation? Let me suggest two examples, one from the realm of theology and the other from the realm of practice.

(1) My theological example will, I know, be controversial. So let me say at the outset that I am not, I hope, committing the very sin I am writing against—arrogantly assuming that my own theology is correct. I want to make it clear that committed Christians can rightfully come to different opinions about the matter. I refer generally to the Arminian-Calvinist debate. I come down generally on the Calvinist side of this dispute. What I suggest here is that some people who disagree—and even violently disagree—with Calvinism can be guilty of the kind of arrogance I am talking about here. (Please, my Arminian brothers and sisters, note I am saying *"can"* be guilty of, not *"are"* guilty of, for I know many Arminians who do not make this mistake. And Calvinists can be just as guilty of this kind of arrogance.)

I once read a paper on this issue written by a student of mine, whose sole argument was that God would never choose some people and reject others because God is God of love; he simply cannot be like that. Now, if the student had carefully established from Scripture that God's love requires that he not make ultimate choices about the eternal destiny of people, I would have had no quarrel with the argument—only with the conclusion. But she did not. It was simply her "idea of God" that led her to refuse to accept any kind of Calvinist view of God's sovereignty. Never did she seriously examine her view of God on the basis of Scripture to see if it really squared with *all* the biblical data.

In discussing this issue with students and laypeople alike, I find this problem to be widespread. But don't we realize that we come perilously close in this way to standing in judgment over God—of saying, in effect, that the Calvinist view of God simply does not fit my view of God, and so it must be wrong? The Calvinist view may be right, or it might be wrong. But on this theological matter, as on any other, we must humbly listen to what Scripture teaches, willing to submit to its teachings even when they do not fit our own preconceived ideas.

(2) A current practical example of the failure of Christians to listen to God is the general tendency for us in the Western world, because of our temporal well-being and capitalist economic system, to mute God's call to his people to share their material things and "to look after orphans and widows" (James 1:27). As I write, for instance, politicians are debating welfare reform in the United States. Now committed Christians can certainly hold a wide spectrum of views on the way in which government should be involved in helping the poor. But what disturbs me as I listen to some Christians is their purely economic—or, not to mince words, materialistic—approach to the issue. For Christians, surely, the point should not be economic; it should be how the church in our day can best carry out its mandate to live out our Father's concern for the helpless in society.

The canonical question. Before we leave this section, I want to make a final comment on the significance of the canonical question that I talked about in the "Bridging Contexts" section. Perhaps the point is obvious, but it should probably be made. If Jude regards *1 Enoch* as canonical, then the whole idea of a closed canon can be called into question. The church has always insisted that only those matters clearly included in the canonical books have authority over the church and are able to instruct us about what to think and do. This has historically been a point of contention between Roman Catholics (who include the Old Testament Apocrypha in their canon) and Protestants (who do not).

But some scholars in our day are arguing that we throw out the idea of a canon altogether. And this is a far more radical step. For the point of having a canon is quite practical: It tells us what source Christians go to so that they can understand what to believe about God and what he wants his people to do. If, however, we do not have a fixed canon, then different Christians can appeal to different sets of books and come up with different versions of "Christianity."

I do not want to minimize the genuine problems involved in the historical process by which the church determined a canon of authoritative books.[16]

---

16. On this issue, see especially David G. Dunbar, "The Biblical Canon," in *Hermeneutics, Authority, and Canon*, ed. D. A. Carson and John D. Woodbridge (Grand Rapids: Zondervan, 1986), 299–360, 424–46.

But Christians believe that God superintended this process and that he himself thus stands behind the canon of Scripture we now possess. We imperil the faith itself if we give up on this issue.

Two more specific implications flow from the idea of a canon. (1) We should value these books in a way that we value no others. Christians, of course, generally agree with this principle. But in practice, and with the proliferation of Christian fiction, I find that many believers spend a relatively small proportion of their "spiritual" reading in the Scriptures themselves. What is happening is that the minds of many Christians are therefore being formed not by the Bible but by books about the Bible or books only loosely related to the biblical message. Surely we have at this point an implicit denial of the canon.

(2) We must be careful to value *all* the biblical books. Christians are always tempted to construct a "canon within a canon"—a set of books within the Bible that becomes more important than others. Martin Luther, for instance, was guilty of this. He was so enamored of Paul's teaching of justification by faith that he elevated certain letters of Paul to a central place and had a hard time with some other books (such as James) that did not seem to match Paul's message. The danger here, of course, is that we end up with an imbalanced Christianity—a view of the faith based on a narrow selection of books and passages. The antidote to this problem is to force ourselves to deal with the whole gamut of biblical revelation. In our private Bible reading, we should systematically read through all the Bible, or at least make sure we are reading representative sections. And preachers, likewise, should set up a preaching plan that exposes their congregations to the whole of God's truth, not just those books they happen to be interested in or those issues they happen to get excited about.

Jude 17–23

UT, DEAR FRIENDS, remember what the apostles of our Lord Jesus Christ foretold. [18]They said to you, "In the last times there will be scoffers who will follow their own ungodly desires." [19]These are the men who divide you, who follow mere natural instincts and do not have the Spirit.

[20]But you, dear friends, build yourselves up in your most holy faith and pray in the Holy Spirit. [21]Keep yourselves in God's love as you wait for the mercy of our Lord Jesus Christ to bring you to eternal life.

[22]Be merciful to those who doubt; [23]snatch others from the fire and save them; to others show mercy, mixed with fear—hating even the clothing stained by corrupted flesh.

JUDE IS KNOWN for his denunciation of false teachers. Because of this, many students of the Bible immediately think of this letter as bearing an essentially negative message—and one not very applicable to any Christian who is not engaged in false teaching. We can certainly understand why people have such an impression, for in verses 5–16, Jude does nothing but criticize and condemn people who are teaching wrong doctrine and leading ungodly lives.

But Jude does much more than this. We should not forget that his letter was not written to the false teachers; it was written to faithful Christians. These believers, faced with an onslaught of false teaching in their churches, needed reassurance and instruction. This Jude provides in his letter. Thus, the long central, negative section of the letter (vv. 5–16) must be seen as serving the larger purpose he talks about in verses 3–4 and 17–23.

These two passages have much in common. Both begin with the address "dear friends" (lit., "beloved," *agapetoi*). Both talk about "godless men" (cf. v. 4 with vv. 18–19). Both appeal to past teaching to make their points: The condemnation of the false teachers was "written about long ago" (v. 4); the coming of false teachers was "foretold" by the apostles (v. 17). And, just as Jude urged believers in verse 3 to contend for "the faith that was once for all entrusted to the saints," so he now exhorts believers to "build yourselves up in your most holy faith" (v. 20). By these means, Jude shows that he is now resuming the topic of the beginning of the letter: the way Christians should respond to false teaching.

Specifically, Jude tells the believers to do three things. (1) They are to remember that the apostles themselves had predicted the kind of false teaching they are now experiencing (vv. 17–19). From a human standpoint, these false teachers have "secretly slipped in" (v. 4). But God knew all along that they were coming. Thus this reminder reassures Jude's readers that God knows what is happening in their midst. He is still in control. (2) Jude's readers are to devote themselves to their own spiritual growth (vv. 20–21). They must not allow the false teachers to deflect them from their own development in the faith. (3) Jude's readers are to reach out to those affected by the false teaching (vv. 22–23). Withdrawal into their own private spirituality is not enough; Jude's readers must do what they can to reclaim these people before it is too late.

A Reminder of Apostolic Teaching (vv. 17–19)

JUDE'S ADDRESS OF his readers as "dear friends" signals a major transition in the letter, as it did also in verse 3. In the former text, this affectionate address introduced the body of the letter after the brief introduction (vv. 1–2). Here, it signals a shift from denunciation of false teachers (vv. 5–16) to exhortation of the faithful.

The construction Jude uses here is a strong one, emphasizing the contrast with what he has just been saying. The false teachers, ungodly and haughty, will be judged; "but as for *you*, beloved. . . ."[1] As Jude now turns to the faithful Christians, he begins by reminding them of something. Here we find another parallel with the earlier part of the letter, though this time not with verses 1–4 but with verse 5, where Jude "reminds" his readers of the judgment God brought on false teachers in the past. In other words, while contrasted in their address and content, verses 5–16 and verses 17–19 are parallel in "form": Both bring a reminder to Jude's readers about false teachers.[2]

When Jude asks his readers to "remember" what the apostles said, he is not just asking them to perform a mental exercise. As we noted in our comments on 2 Peter 1:12–15, "remembering" in the Bible includes the will and not just the mind. In recalling what God has done or said in the past, we are

---

1. Jude uses the nominative personal pronoun *hymeis*, usually a sign of emphasis.

2. Bauckham stresses this parallel, arguing that vv. 17–19 therefore continue the denunciation of vv. 5–16 (*Jude, 2 Peter*, 102–3). There is truth in this suggestion, as we have seen; but the contrast with what has come before stands out as even more important (see, e.g., Kelly, *The Epistles of Peter and of Jude*, 281; Neyrey, *2 Peter, Jude*, 84–85).

to take it to heart in a way that affects our thinking and behaving. Consequently, Jude wants his readers, by recalling what "the apostles of our Lord Jesus foretold," to learn how better to respond to the false teachers.

Many commentators think that the expression Jude uses here signals that the letter was written late in the first or early in the second century. They argue that "the apostles of our Lord Jesus" sounds like the description of a well-known and fixed group (or "college") of apostles and that Jude's way of speaking about their prophecy suggests that it was far in the past.[3] But neither point is clear. "The apostles" need not include all twelve apostles; Jude may simply be referring to those particular apostles who helped found the churches to whom he writes. Note how Jude personalizes their testimony in verse 18: "They said *to you*."

Moreover, their prophecy, while obviously in the past, need not have come in the far distant past. As Bauckham notes, Paul could write to his churches in almost exactly these same terms within a few years, or even months, after they were founded; see, for instance, 2 Thessalonians 2:5: "Don't you remember that when I was with you I used to tell you these things?"[4] We find nothing here that Jude, the brother of the Lord, could not have written any time during the middle or late apostolic age (c. A.D. 50–90).

In verse 18, Jude provides the "text" of the apostolic prophecy that he wants his readers to remember: "In the last times there will be scoffers who will follow their own ungodly desires." We have no prophecy from an apostle using just these words. The closest is 2 Peter 3:3: "In the last days scoffers will come, scoffing and following their own evil desire." The connection is close indeed; for instance, the Greek word in both texts for "scoffers" (*empaiktai*) occurs in only these two verses in the New Testament.

Most scholars, in keeping with their general theory about the relationship between the two letters, think that Peter is paraphrasing Jude at this point. But it is at least equally likely that dependence goes the other direction. After all, Peter is an apostle and Jude is not; it would make perfect sense for him to quote 2 Peter 3:3 as an apostolic prophecy. To be sure, Jude speaks of "apostles" in the plural. By this he plainly indicates that more than one apostle made this kind of prediction (for some other examples, see Acts 20:29–30; 1 Tim. 4:1–3; 2 Tim. 3:1–5). But there is still evidence, as we have seen, that Jude derives the wording of this prophecy from 2 Peter.

Many scholars think that Jude's use of a prophecy about "the last times" shows that he expected history to end shortly. But the New Testament

---

3. See, e.g., Kelly, *The Epistles of Peter and of Jude*, 281.
4. Bauckham, *Jude, 2 Peter*, 103.

writers regularly use this expression, or similar ones, to describe the entire period from the time of Jesus' death and resurrection onward (e.g., Acts 2:17–19; Heb. 1:2; 1 John 2:18). Once the Messiah had come, they believed, the last and climactic period of salvation history had begun. What the apostles predicted, then, was that this period of time would be marked by the periodic appearance of "scoffers."

When Peter referred to "scoffers," the context shows that he was thinking of people who scoffed at the idea of the return of Christ in glory (see 2 Peter 3:4). This eschatological skepticism never comes to the surface in Jude. The similarity between Jude 18 and 2 Peter 3:3 might suggest that Jude refers to the same kind of scoffing as does Peter. But this is not a necessary conclusion. Jude's depiction of the false teachers focuses on their licentious lifestyle and haughty attitude toward God. And the last expression in the prophecy Jude quotes, "who will follow their own ungodly desires," suggests this same idea. Probably, then, Jude portrays the false teachers as generally mocking God and his moral requirements. They are so intent on satisfying their selfish and fleshly desires that they have no place for God. By labeling their desires as "ungodly," Jude reminds us of his key accusation against them (see vv. 4, 15).[5]

Jude wraps up this brief section as he has several others (see vv. 5–10, 11–13, 14–16), by identifying the people or examples he has been talking about with "these men," the false teachers who had infiltrated his readers' churches. We again detect a note of accusation and derision in the address: *"These* men, coming to you with their grandiose claims."

Jude's first description in verse 19 of their ungodliness here is not easy to understand, because he uses a very rare Greek word (*apodiorizo*). Based on its use in Aristotle, some commentators think that the word must mean "make a (logical) distinction." They therefore think that the false teachers were erecting theoretical distinctions between two kinds of Christians. As a specific example, appeal is made to the Gnostics, who divided believers up into two categories: those who were tied to this life and could never rise above it, and those who could come into possession of true "knowledge" and so appreciate spiritual matters.[6] It may well be, of course, that the false

---

5. The Greek word "ungodly" (*asebeion*) comes last in the verse, in an emphatic position. The word is in the genitive; and the NIV, along with most modern versions, interprets it as a descriptive genitive (cf. also Green, *The Second Epistle General of Peter and the General Epistle of Jude*, 182). But it could also be subjective genitive—"desires that spring from ungodly motives" (Mayor, *The Epistle of St. Jude and the Second Epistle of St. Peter*, 47)—or the objective genitive—"desires for ungodly things" (Kelly, *The Epistles of Peter and of Jude*, 283; Bauckham, *Jude, 2 Peter*, 337).

6. See, e.g., Kelly, *The Epistles of Peter and of Jude*, 284–85.

teachers were making some such distinction. For, although full-blown Gnosticism was not yet in existence (and would not be until the second century), Gnostic-like ideas certainly were floating around in the first century.

But this may be reading more into the term than is justified. The word can also have the meaning "make separations," in the sense of "create divisions."[7] We know that one of the almost inevitable byproducts of false teaching is division within the church. There are always some who are ready to listen to anything new and different, who are ready to be swept away by whatever new wind of teaching might be blowing. Others, however, better anchored in the faith, resist. As a result, divisiveness follows (cf. NIV).

The NIV's "who follow mere natural instincts" translates a single Greek word, *psychikoi* (lit., "soulish people"). We usually think of the word "soul" in a positive spiritual sense. But Paul uses the word in a negative sense, as a contrast with "spiritual" (1 Cor. 2:14; 15:44; cf. also James 3:15). Since the "soul" is what all persons have by virtue of their physical birth, the word can connote the idea of what is "natural," in the sense of what is natural to this world. It can therefore suggest a narrow perspective or behavior that focuses solely on this world and its values. Clearly, Jude uses the word with this sense, and the NIV rendering is not therefore bad.

Just in case we may have missed the point, Jude removes all doubt by adding that these false teachers "do not have the Spirit." As possessing a "soul" is the invariable mark of a living person, so possessing the Spirit of God is the invariable mark of being a redeemed person (see Rom. 8:8–10). The language Jude uses here may be chosen as an ironic twist on the false teachers' own claims. It may have been they who were bragging about being "spiritual" (note Jude's reference to their visionary experiences in v. 8). On the contrary, Jude responds, far from being especially advanced in the things of the Spirit, they do not have the Spirit at all.

A Call to Stand Fast (vv. 20–21)

"DEAR FRIENDS" (SEE v. 17) again signals a transition as Jude now turns his attention to the believers and begins to tell them specifically what they are to do in response to the false teachers. He begins with injunctions focusing on the need to maintain their own faith. Here is the first requirement when false teaching arises: to secure one's own spiritual position. Only then is one ready to reach out and confront those who are disturbed by it (vv. 22–23).

---

7. See Bauckham, *Jude, 2 Peter*, 105.

Although the NIV does not make this entirely clear, we have in verses 20–21 four separate commands:

(1) "build yourselves up in your most holy faith";
(2) "pray in the Holy Spirit";
(3) "keep yourselves in God's love";
(4) "wait for the mercy of our Lord Jesus Christ to bring you to eternal life."

Two characteristic early Christian triads are observable here: faith, love, and hope (1, 3, and 4); and Father, Son, and Holy Spirit (3, 4, and 2).

(1) The frequent New Testament use of the imagery of "building" to describe the spiritual development of the community probably comes from the idea that the Christian church forms God's new temple (1 Cor. 3:9–15; 2 Cor. 6:16; Eph. 2:19–22; 1 Peter 2:4–10). New covenant believers no longer need a literal temple, for they themselves are now the place where God, in Christ, resides. "Build yourselves up," then, is a command that Christians together encourage one another in holding fast to the truth of Christ and in maintaining a lifestyle that reflects that truth (for a similar idea, see Col. 2:7).

As in the similar phrase in verse 3, "faith" here means what Christians believe—the doctrinal and ethical core of Christian identity. This is what the false teachers were threatening; therefore, true believers must devote themselves to the faith with renewed dedication. It is possible to translate "build yourselves up *by means of* your most holy faith."[8] But the building imagery suggests that the NIV is on the right track, taking "the most holy faith" to be the foundation on which we are to build (see REB: "you . . . must make your most sacred faith the foundation of your lives").[9]

The New Testament elsewhere puts Christ in the role of the foundation of the church (1 Cor. 3:7–17), or even "the apostles and prophets" (Eph. 2:20–22). These are not, of course, competing, but complementary images. For it is Christ who accredits apostles and prophets, who, in turn, set forth and guard the "faith once for all entrusted to the saints." Christ is the "ultimate foundation," for we rest on him alone for salvation. But the apostles and the teaching they have given are subsidiary, but necessary foundations. They reveal to us the meaning of Christ and guard against any attempt to diminish who he is or what he has done.

(2) The form of the word in the Greek text may be suggesting that the second injunction is a means by which the first can be carried out—that is,

---

8. The construction in Greek is a dative, which can have this instrumental meaning (see Bigg, *The Epistles of St. Peter and St. Jude*, 340).

9. See, e.g., Kelly, *The Epistles of Peter and of Jude*, 285–86.

by "praying in the Holy Spirit" we can build one another up in the faith.[10] Many commentators think that Jude is enjoining believers here to engage in distinctly "charismatic" praying, including, though not limited to, speaking in tongues. They suggest that this praying is a praying in which the Spirit himself supplies the words.[11] Without diminishing the importance and value of this kind of praying, I doubt whether Jude intends to be so specific. All praying that is worthy of the name will be praying that is done "in the Spirit"—that is, stimulated by, guided by, and infused by the Holy Spirit.[12] Note Ephesians 6:18a: "And pray in the Spirit on all occasions with all kinds of prayers and requests."

(3) Jude's third exhortation combines with his description of believers in verse 1 to form an interesting and instructive pairing of ideas. Christians, Jude has said, are "kept by Jesus Christ"; now he urges them to "keep yourselves in God's love." Here we find the typical two sides of the New Testament approach to the Christian life. God has done all in Christ that we need to be saved; yet we must respond to God if we are to secure our salvation. God "keeps" us; we are to "keep ourselves." Both are true, and neither can be sacrificed without missing something essential to the Christian pursuit of godliness.

Jude may be thinking as he writes these words of Jesus' command in John 15:9: "Now remain in my love." Christ loves us, unconditionally; yet we have the obligation to remain within his love for us. And this reminiscence is particularly appropriate because Jesus goes on in the next verse to note that it is by obeying his commands that we are able to remain in his love. It is precisely in this matter of obedience that the false teachers are so significantly failing to keep themselves in the love of God.

(4) Jude's last exhortation, fittingly, directs attention to the future. God's mercy is always present, but the Scriptures often associate his mercy with deliverance on the last day (see, e.g., Matt. 5:7; 2 Tim. 1:18). Here, therefore, "the mercy of our Lord Jesus Christ" is something that we are urged to "wait for." The verb translated "wait for" often occurs in such eschatological contexts. It connotes eager yet patient expectation and the kind of lifestyle that should accompany such hope for deliverance (see the use of the word in 2 Peter 3:12–14).

The connection between "eternal life" and the rest of the verse is not immediately clear. The NIV paraphrases the Greek here, taking the phrase with the word "mercy" (cf. also NRSV: "the mercy of our Lord Jesus Christ *that leads*

---

10. The verb in Greek for "pray" is a participle.

11. See Bauckham, *Jude, 2 Peter,* 113.

12. Green, *The Second Epistle General of Peter and the General Epistle of Jude,* 184.

to eternal life").[13] But the phrase can also go with the command "keep" at the beginning of the verse: "keep yourselves in God's love ... so that you may experience eternal life," though the distance of "eternal life" from the command "keep" makes this option less likely. Thus Jude is urging his readers to look beyond the disruptions created by the false teachers to that ultimate expression of Christ's mercy on the day he comes back in glory to bring his people to their eternal enjoyment of the life he provides.

A Call to Reach Out (vv. 22–23)

JUDE HAS URGED his readers to make sure that their own faith is securely established (vv. 20–21). With their own spiritual condition secure, they can now reach out to others whose position is not so certain. Thus he exhorts his readers to engage in ministry to those in the community who are being attracted, to one extent or another, by the false teachers.

But exactly what Jude is urging them to do is not clear, primarily because we are not completely certain what he wrote in verses 22–23. The manuscripts containing the letter of Jude offer a bewildering variety of different readings; at least six different forms of text exist. The difficulty of deciding which of these Jude himself wrote is indicated by the fact that four of these can be found in the text of major English translations, and a fifth commands support from some influential commentaries. We list these textual options below, dividing them into those that have two separate injunctions and those that have three:

The two-clause option

Snatch some from the fire; but on those who dispute have mercy with fear.[14]	And of some have compassion, making a difference: and others save with fear, pulling them out of the fire. (KJV)[15]	Show mercy toward those who have doubts; save them, by snatching them out of the fire. Show mercy also, mixed with fear, to others as well. (TEV; cf. also NEB)[16]

---

13. See, e.g., Kelly, *The Epistles of Peter and of Jude*, 287.

14. The translation is from Bauckham, *Jude, 2 Peter*, 108, who adopts this reading; cf. also Neyrey, *2 Peter, Jude*, 85–86. The Greek text on which this translation is based in found in the Papyrus manuscript, *p72*.

15. The text for this translation is found in some of the later uncial manuscripts, K, L, P, S.

16. The underlying text is found in the important uncial Vaticanus (B); it is supported by, e.g., Kelly, *The Epistles of Peter and of Jude*, 287–88.

The three-clause option

Be merciful to those who doubt; snatch others from the fire and save them; to others show mercy. (NIV; cf. also NRSV; NASB; REB; NJB)[17]	And convince some, who doubt; save some, by snatching them out of the fire; on some have mercy with fear. (RSV; cf. also JB)[18]

A quick glance at these options reveals a preference among recent translations for the first of the three-clause options. Note, for instance, that three of the major translations have changed from a two-clause text to this three-clause text in their latest editions (NRSV/RSV; NJB/JB; REB/NEB). I think his preference is justified. While the situation is so complicated that we cannot be sure about the original text, this text seems a bit superior to the others. We cannot enter here into the details of the arguments pro and con. But two factors tilt the scales slightly in favor of this text: It follows Jude's well-established pattern of using triads, and it seems to be the reading that best explains all the other readings.[19]

Assuming, then, that the text printed in the NIV represents what Jude originally wrote, we find that he urges the faithful believers in his audience to reach out to three different groups of people.

(1) The believers are to "be merciful to those who doubt" (v. 22). The verb translated "doubt" (the root form is *diakrino*) can also be translated "dispute," which is the meaning of the verb in Jude's only other use of it (v. 9: "the archangel Michael, when he was *disputing* with the devil").[20] But "doubt" is the more usual meaning of the word in the New Testament, and it makes better

---

17. The significant uncial Sinaiticus (א) attests this text. It is the text adopted in the two most widely used Greek New Testaments (the Nestle-Aland *Novum Testamentum Graece* [27th ed.; Stuttgart: Deutsche Bibelgesellschaft, 1993] and the United Bible Societies' *The Greek New Testament* [4th ed.; New York: United Bible Societies, 1993]). It receives solid defense in two articles: Sakae Kubo, "Jude 22–23: Two Division Form or Three?" in *New Testament Criticism: Its Significance for Exegesis. Essays in Honour of Bruce M. Metzger*, ed. E. J. Epp and Gordon D. Fee (Oxford: Clarendon, 1981), 239–53; Carroll D. Osburn, "Discourse Analysis and Jewish Apocalyptic in the Epistle of Jude," in *Linguistics and New Testament Interpretation: Essays on Discourse Analysis*, ed. David Alan Black (Nashville: Broadman, 1992), 292 (he reverses here his earlier preference for the two-clause text).

18. The textual basis for this rendering is the uncial Alexandrinus (A); cf. Green, *The Second Epistle General of Peter and the General Epistle of Jude*, 186–87.

19. For discussion of the larger issue of textual criticism in the New Testament, see "Bridging Contexts."

20. See, e.g., Mayor, *The Epistle of St. Jude and the Second Epistle of St. Peter*, 50; Bauckham, *Jude, 2 Peter*, 115. Their decision to translate "dispute" reflects to some extent, however, their choice of a different text here.

sense to think that believers are to "be merciful" to doubters than to people who are disputing. These "doubters," we can surmise, are Christians within the church who are being somewhat swayed by the false teaching. They are wavering in their commitment to the "faith once for all entrusted to the saints."

It would be easy for the faithful to shun such people or lambaste them for their doubts. But Jude wants the faithful to show mercy to them. Christians themselves have received God's unmerited mercy (see v. 2); they should display a similar mercy to people who are wavering. For mercy is far more likely than harsh rebuke to keep them within the fold of the orthodox faith.

(2) The second group to whom the faithful need to reach out are those who have gone further down the road blazed by the false teachers. In fact, they have gone so far as to be in danger of suffering eternal damnation. This is almost certainly what the word "fire" refers to here; as we have seen, fire is a standard biblical metaphor for hell (see v. 8 and the "Bridging Contexts" section on vv. 11–13). Some Christians in Jude's audience have been tempted to such a degree by the false teachers that they are teetering on the brink of hell. The faithful Christians in the community need to "snatch" them from it and save them before it is too late.

Jude's imagery probably reflects Zechariah 3:1–4:

> Then he showed me Joshua the high priest standing before the angel of the LORD, and Satan standing at his right side to accuse him. The LORD said to Satan, "The LORD rebuke you, Satan! The LORD, who has chosen Jerusalem, rebuke you! Is not this man a burning stick snatched from the fire?"
>
> Now Joshua was dressed in filthy clothes as he stood before the angel. The angel said to those who were standing before him, "Take off his filthy clothes."
>
> Then he said to Joshua, "See, I have taken away your sin, and I will put rich garments on you."

This passage plays an important role in Jude. The words "The Lord rebuke you" in verse 9, while taken originally from *The Testament/The Assumption of Moses*, clearly reflect this Zechariah text. And Jude will soon pick up the imagery of filthy clothes from this passage.

(3) Jude turns his attention to yet a third group of people: "To others show mercy, mixed with fear—hating even the clothing stained by corrupted flesh." The strength of the language at the end of the verse suggests that he is now thinking of the false teachers themselves, or at least of church members who have given their allegiance to them. The "mercy" that Jude commands here may, then, be pity and sorrow for their dreadful condition (as Luther thought). But it is more likely that the mercy is to be exhibited in

prayers for them. Even those who have abandoned themselves to the false teaching are not beyond redemption, and Jude wants believers to continue to intercede for them.

But their mercy must be tempered by "fear." "Fear" in the Bible often denotes that reverential awe with which believers should view the holy and majestic God. And this may be what Jude means here: As they show mercy on sinners, believers should fear the God who demands absolute holiness and who will judge all people on the last Day.[21] But the words that follow "with fear" suggest a different interpretation, that believers are to fear the subtle influence of the false teachers. As they "show mercy" to them, they must at the same time be cautious in their contact with them, fearing that they too might catch the contagion of false teaching.[22]

The last phrase in the verse expands, then, on this point. Jude's language is graphic. The word "stained" seems to reflect Jude's rendering of the Hebrew word for "filthy" in Zechariah 3:3 (see the text above). This word refers to human excrement. And the word for "clothing" that Jude uses here (*chiton*) refers to the garment worn closest to the body. In other words, Jude pictures the sinful teaching and practices of these people as underclothes fouled by feces.

What has caused this filthy condition? "Corrupted flesh." The Greek here has simply the word "flesh" (*sarx*). But the NIV addition of "corrupted" brings out the sense accurately enough, for Jude is using the word "flesh" here in its common New Testament (and especially Pauline) negative sense, referring to the sinful impulse. The false teachers and their disciples are following their own "natural instincts" and paying no attention to the Spirit (v. 19). They are producing teaching and behavior that is offensive to God. And, Jude is saying here, it should be equally offensive to believers. They should naturally "hate" such conduct. Even, then, as they act in mercy toward these who have fallen, praying that the Lord may bring them back, they must not overlook in any way the terrible and destructive behavior these people are engaged in.

Bridging Contexts

IF WE ARE to bring the message of Jude 17–23 into our own era, we need first, as the most basic step, to determine just what these verses are. To some readers, this may sound foolish; isn't it obvious that Jude 17–23 is just what my English Bible says it is? But it is precisely here that the problem arises. Most people know that an English translation like

---

21. Kelly, *The Epistles of Peter and of Jude*, 289; Bauckham, *Jude, 2 Peter*, 116.
22. See Green, *The Second Epistle General of Peter and the General Epistle of Jude*, 188.

the NIV is based on a Greek text. But fewer people realize that this Greek text is something that scholars have created, for we do not possess any of the "original" manuscripts of any New Testament book.

In other words, we do not have the copy of the letter that Jude actually wrote. What we have are many, many manuscripts that are copies of what he wrote. A few of these may conceivably have been copied directly from the papyrus sheet on which Jude actually wrote his letter. But almost all of these manuscripts will be further down the chain of copies—for instance, a copy of a copy of a copy of the original letter. In the case of Jude 22–23, as we have seen, the Greek New Testament manuscripts we possess offer at least six different forms of text. Which is the one Jude wrote? The question is of vital importance. For how can we apply the text unless we know what it is? What good does it do to talk about an inerrant and authoritative text if we don't even know what it is? I want to address these questions briefly in what follows.

Let me illustrate with a contemporary situation. Let us say that I am lecturing on a cold, snowy day. Let us also assume that most of my students, despite their best efforts to come and hear my words of wisdom, are not able to make it to class. Only three students, out of a class of thirty-five, actually show up—let's call them Nancy, Tom, and Richard. They naturally take notes of the lecture, and the thirty-two students who missed class need to copy these notes. Several students, among them Susan, copy their notes directly from Nancy's set. Others, however, wait until just before the final exam. One student, Aaron, copies Susan's notes. Another, Melinda, gets the notes from Sam, who copied Christy's notes, who in turn copied Richard's.

Now imagine a person doing archival research who, for some strange reason, wants to know exactly what I said in that lecture. None of the students is available to interview. All that the researcher has to go on are the thirty-five copies of my lecture, and no two of these copies are identical—not even the earliest copies of Nancy, Tom, and Richard. For students do not listen perfectly, nor do they copy notes perfectly. Mistakes of all kinds get introduced. How is the researcher to know which copy, or copies, preserves my "original" words?

Such, in essence, is the task that faces the New Testament textual critic. We possess over five thousand manuscripts of the Greek New Testament. To be sure, many of these manuscripts contain only several verses; only a few of them contain the whole New Testament. But many of them contain substantial chunks of the New Testament—for instance, the Pauline letters or the Gospels. Nor do we have the same number of manuscripts for all New Testament books. Two of the most valuable, because they are earliest, kinds of manuscripts we have are "papyri" (so-called because they are written on papyrus material) and "uncials" (which take their name from the capital Greek letters [uncials] that they are written in). The Gospel of Matthew, or portions of it, is found in eighteen papyri and seventy-six uncials; but the comparable figures for Jude are three and twelve.

What makes the textual critic's job difficult is the fact that no two manuscripts are identical. They differ from one another—sometimes only in minor ways, other times in more substantial ways. For the scribes who copied the Greek New Testament were not perfect; they made mistakes, just as the students who copied my lecture made mistakes. Some of these mistakes are easily detected. How often, for instance, have I read a student paper that ended on one page with a "the" only to begin the next page with a "the"? Obviously, the student inadvertently wrote the word twice. We find these kinds of errors in our Greek New Testament manuscripts.

But some of the mistakes are more substantial and difficult to detect. Suppose, for instance, that Nancy and Tom, as they heard me lecture on the meaning of Romans 3:25, wrote down that I claimed it referred to Jesus Christ as our "mercy seat." But Richard had it in his notes that I said it referred to Jesus Christ as our "expiation." Students copy from all three sets of notes; but, because Richard is popular and lives in the dorm on campus, more students copy from him than from Nancy and Tom together. As a result, our hypothetical researcher is faced with twenty copies of my lecture that read "expiation" and fifteen that read "mercy seat." How is he to decide which I actually taught?

He, and the New Testament textual critics like him, would pursue two basic lines of evidence. First is what we might call "external" evidence—the evidence from the thirty-five copies themselves. At first sight, he may be tempted simply to go with the majority; for, after all, it is more likely, all things being equal, that the original word will be preserved in the most manuscripts. And this, in fact, is exactly the procedure that advocates of what is called the "Majority Text" follow today in reconstructing the Greek New Testament text. Usually, though not always, this procedure results in a text that is similar to the one used for the King James Version. In Jude 22–23, for instance, we noted that the KJV has adopted a two-line form of the text. This text has more manuscripts supporting it than any of the other texts.

But modern textual critics generally agree that, in the case of the New Testament text, "all things are not equal." For the manuscripts fall into recognizable groups, based on similar readings. We call these groups "families." In the example we are using, for instance, we might find that twenty of the copies of my lecture shared certain distinctive "readings"—Richard's notes and the nineteen copied from his. In a similar way, we might detect that ten others belonged in Tom's family and five in Nancy's. The point, then, is that we do not really have thirty-five independent, equally important, records of my lecture: we have three. If a vote were to be taken, then, it would not be twenty to fifteen in favor of "expiation"; it would be two to one in favor of "mercy seat."

Most textual critics think that something like this is true for the New Testament. A large group of manuscripts reflect a type of text that is generally later and inferior to others. It would be as if Richard were a poor note-taker. That is why modern Bibles, based on the latest Greek texts, differ in the text that they print from the KJV. And that is why it is unlikely that the text of Jude 22–23 lying behind the KJV is the original one.

But there is a second line of evidence to pursue in investigating these textual issues: "internal" evidence. Here the researcher asks: What did the original author most likely write? Take my lecture again. A researcher trying to reconstruct that lecture would look carefully at the context of the disputed word, and perhaps he would conclude that that context made it more likely that I said "mercy seat" rather than "expiation." He might also check to see if I had written anything else on the subject. Perhaps he would stumble across my Romans commentary, where he would also find evidence that I would more likely have said "mercy seat" than "expiation."

The textual critic working on Jude does not, of course, have any other writings of Jude for comparison purposes. But he can look carefully at the context of Jude. Here, as we noted above, Jude's penchant for grouping what he says into threes comes into play. The textual critic may then conclude that it is more likely that Jude wrote three commands here rather than two.

The task of the New Testament textual critic is, of course, much more complicated than the analogy I am using suggests. (Suppose, for example, that Richard and Tom compared notes and came up with a composite copy.) Textual criticism is a fine art that requires a lot of training, hard work, and ultimately, sound instincts. But it is important that we understand a little of the situation so that we can have at least some idea as to why English translations of Jude 22–23 differ so radically from one another.

I want to end with a word of reassurance. Christians who learn about the kind of textual difficulties I have just described may be inclined to conclude that the New Testament text is a mess—that it has all kinds of contradictory readings and that we don't have a very good idea what the biblical authors actually wrote. This is emphatically not the case, for several reasons. (1) We have far more evidence for the text of the New Testament than for any other ancient book. Many of the plays of the great Greek dramatists, for example, have been completely lost; many others are found in only a handful of manuscripts. Comparatively, we have an abundance of evidence for every New Testament book.

(2) The vast majority of differences among the manuscripts involve spelling or grammatical differences that do not affect the meaning, or minor differences that do not materially affect the sense of the text.

(3) Virtually any defensible Greek New Testament text that we might put together would teach the same things about every important point of Christian doctrine and ethics. For example, we sometimes harp on the big differences between the text of the KJV and, let us say, the NRSV. We think of texts like the ending of Mark's Gospel (16:9–20) or the story of the woman caught in adultery (John 7:53–8:11). What is remarkable, however, is the amazing degree of similarity between the two versions. The KJV reflects about fifty manuscripts, the earliest dating from about the fifth century. The NRSV is based on over five thousand manuscripts, some of which go back to the early second century. The fact that both Bibles agree on 99 percent of the New Testament text is evidence of God's providential hand in preserving for us the text that he inspired.[23]

 VERSES 17–23 ARE the most important in the letter of Jude. It is here that Jude spells out just how he wants his readers to pursue the purpose for which he has written the letter: that they "contend for the faith once for all entrusted to the saints" (v. 3). Jude specifies three things that his readers need to do: Remember the apostolic warning about heretics (vv. 17–19); secure their own faith (vv. 20–21); and reach out to rescue people in spiritual danger (vv. 22–23). Each exhortation is as relevant today as it was two thousand years ago.

"To be forewarned is to be forearmed." This aphorism is as true in the spiritual realm as it is in warfare. Jude wants us to be ready to meet the danger of false teachers and heretics of every kind. Jesus warned of such people, calling them "ferocious wolves" dressed in sheep's clothing (Matt. 7:15). Paul warned the church at Ephesus of the same danger: "From your own number men will arise and distort the truth in order to draw away disciples after them" (Acts 20:30). John too pointed to the coming of "many antichrists" (1 John 2:18). Jude is thoroughly justified, then, to identify this warning about heretics with the apostles generally.

---

23. Readers who want to pursue New Testament textual criticism further should consult one of the standard handbooks: Bruce M. Metzger, *The Text of the New Testament: Its Transmission, Corruption, and Restoration*, 3d ed. (New York: Oxford Univ. Press, 1992); Kurt and Barbara Aland, *The Text of the New Testament: An Introduction to the Critical Editions and to the Theory and Practice of Modern Textual Criticism*, 2d ed. (Grand Rapids: Eerdmans, 1989).

And their predictions have certainly proven true. The New Testament letters themselves reveal that the truth of the gospel had hardly been proclaimed when people began twisting it to their own notions and preconceived ideas. Much of our New Testament, in fact, is a response to such challenges. And the history of the church is littered with similar examples: from the Gnostics and Montanists of the second and third centuries to the Socinians of the sixteenth to the Universalists and New-Agers of our own day.

We should not be surprised, therefore, to find in the midst of our churches today people who "deny Jesus Christ our only Sovereign and Lord" (v. 4)—either by their teaching or by their behavior, or, most often, by both. But Jude, as we have seen, focuses attention on a specific kind of false teacher: the "scoffer," the one who mocks at God and his requirements for holy living. We find such mockers in abundance outside the church in our day. I am reading just now, for instance, a book by a radical environmentalist. The book is laced with glee at the passing away of the ridiculous "Christian superstition" and the new freedom its passing brings to humankind.

But Jude is thinking of people who claim to be within the Christian church. And, sadly, we find such "scoffers" here also. Sometimes the scoffing is verbal. I think, for instance, of a "Christian" theologian who mocked in his writings at the idea that Jesus might have walked on water or multiplied loaves and fishes to feed five thousand men. But I think we more often face people who may speak quite piously about God and their faith but who mock him with their behavior. For people who consistently pursue a lifestyle marked by sin are, in effect, mocking God. They are willfully ignoring his requirements to be holy as he is holy, and they are treating lightly his threat of judgment for such behavior.

Jude wants us to be on our guard. We should not be surprised when we find people in our churches who teach or live lies. Being on our guard does not, of course, mean that we are to become critical and suspicious, probing everyone's life and immediately pouncing on anything someone says that we think is a bit off-center theologically. But neither are we to be naive, assuming that because people have made a profession of faith, attend church regularly, or are even in a position of leadership, they must be above reproach.

Consider, for instance, the direction taken by some Christian denominations in our century. Some were entirely orthodox just sixty years ago, true to "the faith once for all entrusted to the saints" and effective in evangelism and missions. But over the decades they have drifted to the point that their leaders deny many of the cardinal truths of the faith—including the need to evangelize! Yet their churches are still filled with many dedicated, orthodox Christians. I will sometimes ask these people about what their denominational leaders are teaching. Usually they don't know. If I mention some heretical idea that their seminary is propagating, they will simply not believe me. Here, I think, we have Christian people who are not taking to heart the New Testament warnings about false teachers who infiltrate the church of Jesus Christ.

In other words, without being judgmental, we must not be naive either. Part of our problem, as I have suggested elsewhere in this commentary, is that we live in an age in which truth is not very important. We are interested in whether something works; truth, even if we could find it, does not have enough "bottom-line" value for us. As Michael Green says, "We have largely lost any sense of the diabolical nature of false teaching, and have become as dulled to the distinction between truth and falsehood in ideas as we have to the distinction between right and wrong in behavior."[24]

"Contending for the faith" does not mean only fighting against heretics to preserve Christian truth. It also means fighting against our own weakness and temptation so that we can maintain our own faith. Jude knows that you can never take a person's spiritual condition for granted. Thus, before he tells his readers how to confront those affected by the false teaching, he reminds them that they must take a good look at their own condition (vv. 20–21).

Jude's exhortations to believers in these verses reflect common early Christian teaching about Christian growth. Note, for instance, the parallels with Colossians 2:6–7: "So then, just as you received Christ Jesus as Lord, continue to live in him, rooted and built up in him, strengthened in the faith as you were taught, and overflowing with thankfulness." Both Jude and Paul urge believers to look back to the origins of their Christian experience ("the faith as you were taught"/"your most holy faith"), to be "built up" in that faith, and to pray.

Three points particularly significant for current Christian experience emerge from these verses in Jude.

(1) Moving ahead in the Christian life often involves looking to the past. The growth that Jude calls for is growth in "your most holy faith"—that "faith once for all entrusted to the saints" (v. 3). The foundation must be secure before the building can go up. We can never grow *away* from our roots; we can only grow through them. In the church today, there is an increasing flirtation with what is new. We want to hear what Christianity has to say about the latest fad or issue; we want to learn new things. But in our (legitimate) eagerness to push ahead, to stretch our understanding, to make the church relevant to a new age, we must always be careful to "secure our rear," as a general would put it. Solid understanding of Christian doctrine, the

---

24. Green, *The Second Epistle General of Peter and the General Epistle of Jude*, 97.

kind of understanding that changes heart and mind—this is something we never grow away from.

(2) Jude's use of building language is, as we have seen, drawn from the metaphor of the church as the new temple. This means that Jude is urging us to be engaged in a corporate experience. We in the West have a hard time with corporate ideas. Our traditions lionize the "rugged individualist," and we inevitably tend to think of spiritual experience as a basically private matter. Protestant Christians have further stimulus to such individualist thinking. For against the Roman Catholic tendency to make the church the locus of salvation, Protestants have traditionally seen the individual as central.

In many ways, of course, this is justified: Every person must make a decision for himself or herself about Jesus Christ, and we will all have to give an account of our lives to the Lord. But spiritual experience, the Bible makes clear, is never a purely individual matter. God always works within and through a people (see, e.g., Eph. 4:1–16). "Build yourselves up," then, calls on us not just to see that our own experience with Christ is growing and strengthening, but to make sure that the church, the body of Christ as a whole, is growing and becoming stronger. And it is ultimately only by fully participating in the life of the church that we ourselves will be able to grow as we should. For none of us can mature in our faith without the encouragement, advice, and admonition of fellow believers.

I can see encouraging signs in the church today of a concern for this kind of biblical corporate experience. The day of the television preacher seems to be passing, as believers recognize that they cannot get what they need spiritually by sitting home by themselves in front of the TV set. Surely one of the most encouraging movements fostering such community is "Promise Keepers," which is getting men, who are often more private and individualistic than women, to worship, pray, and serve together.

But it is ultimately the local church in which we need to see this genuine community worked out. Here again, we see positive signs. Many believers decry the passing, over the last decade, of the Sunday night worship service and the Wednesday night prayer meeting. And there is genuine loss here. But if replaced, as they are in many churches, with small group gatherings for fellowship, prayer, and study, I am not sure that the movement is such a bad one. The New Testament local church, after all, was probably about the size of many of our small groups. Once a church grows beyond two hundred or so, the kinds of experiences that foster genuine growth—mutual accountability, for instance—become harder and harder to find. In other words, if done well, with a focus on the Word and prayer, small groups can, and should, play a major role in this "building up in the faith" that Jude talks about here.

(3) Finally, we should note Jude's command that believers "keep your-

selves in God's love." Such a command raises a question in our minds: If God's love is unconditional, why do I have to do anything to "keep" myself in it? Or, to put it another way: If I am being "kept by Jesus Christ" (or "kept by God for Jesus Christ," v. 1), why do I have to exert effort to "keep" myself in God's love?

We mentioned in passing in the "Original Meaning" section that Jude here reflects in a nutshell the typical New Testament combination of God's sovereignty and human responsibility. The tension between these two poles is resolved in several different ways at the theological level. The Arminian, for instance, insists that God's keeping power, while fully effective, is not ultimately irresistible. The believer who deliberately fails to "keep" himself or herself in God's love may fall away from that love forever. The Calvinist, on the other hand, will argue that nothing—even the believer—can thwart God's keeping power.

Rather that deal with the theological issue, I want here to focus more on the practical issue and on ground that both Calvinist and Arminian can agree on. God in his grace is exerting his power and influence daily to "keep" us, his children, in his love. The world throws at us trials and temptations without number; our own flesh is a constant drag back to the old way of life. But God provides all that we need to resist these forces and to retain our commitment to the Lord. But believers must not simply presume on this power either; we are responsible to take advantage of what he offers us. This is the point Jude makes here in verse 21.

The latter part of Jude's summary exhortations takes up the believer's responsibility for those who are wavering in their faith. As we have argued, Jude focuses on three different kinds of people. First are those who are wavering a bit in their commitment. These, Jude says, we are to show mercy toward (v. 22). Next are those who are more deeply influenced by false teaching and who are close to leaving altogether the faith they have espoused. These we are to reach out and grab, seeking to save them from the damnation that they are courting (v. 23a). Third are those who are fully committed to the false teachers' program. To these people too we are to "show mercy."

We may find in these three injunctions a helpful guideline for our own confrontation with false teachers. Although Jude commands us to "show mercy" to both the first and the third group, the context suggests that he means something different by them. The people in the first group are wavering, still not committed to the false teachers' program but not solidly rooted in the orthodox faith either. "Showing mercy" to these kind of people will probably take an active form, as we spend time with them, trying to understand the struggles they are having and at the same time urging them to recommit themselves fully to the faith as taught by the Lord and his apostles. We can identify such people as those who are young in the faith, not certain what to make of claims that Mormons or Jehovah's Witnesses are making. Or they may be people further along in the faith who are strongly tempted to get involved in sex outside the marriage relationship. As long as these people are still questioning, Jude suggests, we are not to react to them with horror or shun them but treat them with compassion.

To those who have begun seriously to flirt with false teaching, however, Jude urges a more direct approach. As his imagery makes clear, Jude considers people who have strayed into heretical ideas or who are pursuing an unbiblical lifestyle as being genuinely in danger of hell. They are poised on the brink of the abyss, and believers are to "snatch" them away from the edge before it is too late. The kind of person Jude has in mind here might be one who has just told us that she has decided to embrace "New Age" theology, or to convert to Islam, or to renounce biblical morals in favor of a sinful lifestyle. Her commitment to these false "faiths" is not yet solid; she is teetering on the brink. Our job is urgently to plead with such a person not to take this step, to rehearse the truth of the gospel, to pray earnestly that the Spirit intervene before it is too late.

We have, then, finally, the hard-core devotees of the false teaching. Yet, somewhat surprisingly, Jude says we are to "have mercy" on them also. Luther, as we noted, thought that this meant simply to pity them, for they were already lost forever. But this would be a most unusual application of the idea of "showing mercy." Probably Jude means that we are to pray for these people, though it is doubtful whether mercy here takes any more of an active form than that. For the rest of the verse, with its warning that we "fear" the teaching and "hate" the sin that they are engaged in suggests that we are to separate ourselves from them.

The New Testament regularly requires believers to pursue such a drastic course of action when they face people who claim to be Christians but who are obdurately committed to an unbiblical belief or lifestyle. Paul commanded the church at Corinth to "hand over to Satan" such a sinner (1 Cor. 5:5). John warned believers not to take false teachers into "your house"—by which he probably meant not one's private home, but the "house-church" (2 John 10–11). Such drastic action is necessary, the New Testament makes clear, both for the sake of the sinner, that he may come to realize the seriousness of his situation and repent, and for the sake of the church, so that it will not be contaminated by the false teaching and sin (cf. esp. 1 Cor. 5:5–8).

This latter point is obviously Jude's main concern. He does not want believers to become so involved in trying to rescue people committed to the false teaching that they themselves succumb to it. We must always be aware of the danger that we ourselves are in and not presume that we will be immune from the false teaching or the sin we are trying to rebuke.

An obvious practical question arises at this point: How are to determine which of these categories a particular person is in? When do we "give up" on them, sever relationships, and exclude them from our fellowship? These questions have no easy answers. But two points are helpful. (1) The decision to "excommunicate" a person should always be made by the church, or the leaders of the church, together. Paul made this clear in his advice to the Corinthian church (1 Cor. 5:1–5), and it follows, of course, the admonitions of Jesus on this same point (Matt. 18:15–17). (2) People should be excommunicated only for serious violations of biblical mandates and only when they have refused to repent of their error after repeated warnings.

Jude 24–25

🌿

TO HIM WHO is able to keep you from falling and to present you before his glorious presence without fault and with great joy—²⁵to the only God our Savior be glory, majesty, power and authority, through Jesus Christ our Lord, before all ages, now and forevermore! Amen.

MANY READERS OF the Bible are familiar with the ending of Jude's letter, although most probably do not know it comes from Jude. This doxology is frequently used by pastors as a liturgical form of dismissal, primarily because it is one of the longest and most beautiful doxologies in the New Testament. Jude expands the usual doxology "form" (see the "Bridging Contexts" section). Some of his additions may have simply been picked up from traditional phraseology, but others relate back to some important themes from the letter.

We should also note what is absent from the end of Jude: the typical matters, such as greetings and prayer requests, that close New Testament letters. The omission of these typical epistolary forms gives Jude the flavor of a sermon. Indeed, a doxology was often used in Judaism to conclude sermons, and so Jude's use of it here fits well.

All of verse 24 describes the one to whom glory is due. Jude has gone into some detail here in order to conclude his letter on a fitting note. The theme of "keeping" has been prominent in the letter. Positively, it refers to God's preservation of Christians in his love (vv. 1 and 21); negatively, to God's "securing" sinners for judgment (vv. 6 and 13). Jude now sounds the positive note one more time, although he chooses a new verb to do so: "guard" (*phylasso*; NIV translates "keep").

God's guarding has the purpose of keeping us from "falling." Jude may mean that God is seeking to keep us from sin (a form of this same word is used to denote sin in James 3:1). But more likely he means that God is working to preserve us from ruin in the final judgment.¹ The second part of Jude's description of God expands on this idea: God is able "to present you before his glorious presence without fault and with great joy."

Jude refers here again to the Day of Judgment, when all people will have to stand before God to give an account. God, Jude assures his readers, is

---

1. Kelly, *The Epistles of Peter and of Jude*, 291.

fully able to make us appear before him on that day "without fault." The word that this phrase translates (*amomos*) was originally applied to sacrifices (cf. Heb. 9:14; 1 Peter 1:19), but was then applied generally to moral purity. It is often found in this kind of eschatological context (Eph. 5:27; Col. 1:22; Rev. 14:5). On our own power, of course, we can never appear "without spot" before the Lord. But he is the "Savior" (v. 25); and through Christ, God supplies the moral purity we lack in ourselves. Therefore we can appear before him "with great joy" or "with exultation" (another word that often has an eschatological flavor; cf., e.g., 1 Peter 1:6).

People familiar with Jude's doxology from liturgical practice expect to hear at this point the words "to the only *wise* God" (the reading of the KJV). But the word "wise" should not be read here; it was probably added at some point by a scribe from the similar doxology in Romans 16:25–27. The ascription "only God" is, of course, common in Judaism; and it is therefore unlikely that Jude has specially emphasized it to counter Gnostic-inclined false teachers.[2]

The New Testament frequently calls Jesus "Savior" (fifteen times); less often is God called "Savior" (seven times outside this verse). Of course, while Jesus, through his sacrificial death, has secured salvation for us, God is the initiator of the process.

All the modern English translations add, at about this point in the sentence, a verb. There is no verb in the Greek, but, clearly, one must be supplied. Yet it is not clear that English versions are correct to supply the subjunctive verb "be," the sense then being that the doxology wishes for these attributes to be ascribed to God. It makes equally good sense to supply the verb "are," in which case the doxology is a statement about who God is rather than a call to ascribe to him the virtues named.[3] With no verb in the Greek, certainty on this matter is impossible.

The four virtues enumerated are commonly associated with God: "glory" (his weighty and majestic presence), "majesty" (his kingly status; cf. also Heb. 1:3; 8:1), "power" (his control over the world), and "authority" (his intrinsic right to rule all things). The NIV takes "through Jesus Christ our Lord" with the understood verb: It is through him that we ascribe to God these virtues. This is probably correct, although the phrase could also go with "God our Savior": God is our Savior through Jesus Christ.[4]

Jude's doxology is a fitting conclusion to his letter/sermon. He has warned the church of a serious and threatening outbreak of false teaching. He has called believers not simply to "batten down the hatches" and ride out the

---

2. Against Kelly, ibid., 291–92.
3. See Bauckham, *Jude, 2 Peter,* 119; Kelly, *The Epistles of Peter and of Jude,* 293.
4. See, e.g., Green, *The Second Epistle General of Peter and the General Epistle of Jude,* 192.

storm, but to reach out redemptively to those who are falling away. Believers can do that because their position with the Lord is secure: He has the power to preserve them intact until the Day of Judgment.

SOME UNDERSTANDING OF the background and usual form of New Testament doxologies will help us better appreciate Jude's purpose in closing his letter the way he does.

The word "doxology" comes from the Greek word *doxa*, "glory," which is usually the central virtue ascribed to God in these brief formulas. Early Christians undoubtedly picked up the doxology from their Jewish environment. Jews often used doxologies, though benedictions ("blessed be God ... ") were much more common. They sometimes used doxologies to conclude prayers and sermons. Perhaps for this reason New Testament doxologies often conclude letters or major sections of letters (e.g., Rom. 16:25–27; Eph. 3:20; Phil. 4:20; 1 Tim. 6:15–16; 1 Peter 4:11; 5:11; 2 Peter 3:18). The authors naturally felt that their sermons in letter form were appropriately concluded with a reminder of who God is.

New Testament doxologies tend to follow a common pattern, with four basic elements:

(1) The person praised (usually God);
(2) A word of praise (usually "glory" [*doxa*]; hence the name "doxology");
(3) An indication of time (usually "forever" or "forever and ever");
(4) "Amen."

These doxologies "Christianize" their content with the addition of the phrase "through Jesus Christ" (as does Jude). Jude's doxology follows this general pattern, but the author expands it, so that his doxology is one of the longest in the New Testament. The additions tailor the doxology to the point of the letter that it concludes. While it is appropriate, then, to use Jude's beautiful doxology in isolation, as an element in a worship service, we should also appreciate how its specific content functions within this letter.

WHAT CAN WE say in a few sentences about the glorious truths that we find in this doxology? And how can we say it in such a way that we do not detract from the simple beauty of this ascription of glory to God? Not for the first time, I feel as if commenting is something of an impertinence—who do I think I am to add to what Jude has already said? But let me at least try to suggest some things we need to learn from this text.

What is most important is that we be careful that these words do not become on our lips a thoughtless and even hypocritical recitation of words. Here, of course, lies the danger in using Jude's doxology in worship. We hear the words so often that they cease to have any meaning for us; they are all jumbled together in our heads ("To-him-who-is-able-to-keep-you"; "to-the-only-wise-God"). Thus, we need to pause and reflect on what these words really mean—and be prepared to live as if we meant them!

Think of the marvelous security promised to us in verse 24: God is able to preserve us so that we can stand before him on the last day spotless, forgiven, assured of an eternal "home in the heavens." Doubt and anxiety are constant companions on our earthly pilgrimage. We worry about our health, about money, about our children, about our jobs. In sober moments we perhaps become anxious about death. God does not promise to take away these worries, but he does take away from us our greatest worry: where we will spend eternity. Do we reflect this confidence in the way we live? Do we truly value heaven enough so that our earthly worries, while sometimes pressing, fade in importance in light of our eternal destiny?

Or think of the simple words "the only God." We have little trouble believing this—although many of us probably need to be more guarded about the way we talk of Father, Son, and Holy Spirit in light of this truth; we are often perilously close to "tritheism," the belief in three different gods. But do we live as if this statement is true? What idols might we be worshiping even as we recite these words? God is the only God; he demands all of our worship and obedience, and nothing must rival our affections for him.

James, using familiar biblical imagery, compares God to the bridegroom to whom we are betrothed. This is why he can accuse his readers of adultery, for by trying to remain "friends" with the world, they have not been faithful to their all-consuming allegiance to the Lord (James 4:4–5). If we claim that God is the "only God," then we must be sure that he is the only God *for us*. He will brook no rival. In other words, we must be sure that nothing, bad (illicit sex, love of money, desire for promotion or prominence) or good (our families, our ministries), becomes of higher importance than God.

Consider, finally, the implications of ascribing to God "glory, majesty, power and authority . . . before all ages, now and forevermore!" Reciting these words should create in our minds a fresh picture of the all-consuming power and wonder of our God. Perhaps only by dwelling on these words—to use the old-fashioned term, meditating—can we truly appreciate what they signify. And thus will we be drawn inevitably to worship.

Scripture Index

Subject Index

Subject Index

memory, 61, 65–67, 280–81
mockery, 166, 282
myth, 71–72, 82–83

nature, divine, 43–44, 51–53, 54–56

Old Testament in the New, 108–10

Paul, apostle, 209–12
pluralism, 97–98
power, 41
prophecy, prophets, 75–79, 163
pseudonymity, 22–24, 64–65

relationship of Jude and 2 Peter, 16–18
renewal (eschatological), 199–200, 200–202
repentance, 187–88
rhetoric, 231–33

righteousness, 35, 146

Second Coming (*parousia*), 70–75, 161, 186–89, 192–95, 196–97, 207, 219–20, 274–75
sensuality, 125–29, 135–37
servant, slave, 224–25
Sodom and Gomorrah, 104–5, 241–43, 250–51
sorites, 50–51
Spirit, 56–58

testament (genre), 23–24, 64–65
textual criticism, 289–93
tradition, 233–35
Transfiguration, 72–75, 79–80
truth, 137–39

visions, 255